Advance Praise for *Eugene Forsey, Canada's Maverick Sage*:

"I remember Eugene Forsey as a cantankerous, relentless, go-for-the-throat opponent to the Meech Lake Accord. I did not like him much, but I and most Canadians loved that he was there. His integrity, his passion, his wit, his commitment to politics, to the pursuit of justice, and to democracy are well worth celebrating. This book does just that. It also reflects our society's urgent need for engaged and rigorous public intellectuals and debaters such as Eugene Forsey was. Let's hope that it inspires other brilliant, colourful, and even bad-tempered people to speak up."
— Nathalie Des Rosiers, Executive Director, Canadian Civil Liberties Association

"Father and daughter share this unique story of intellectual independence and participation in a Canada that is far more than a supercilious European transplant. Filled with Eugene Forsey's wisdom and principles, the book makes its own contribution to building the cross-culturally respectful, responsible, and inclusive society envisioned and agreed with Aboriginal Peoples early in the eighteenth century."
— Larry McDermott, Algonquin Environmental and Human Rights Activist, Executive Director, Plenty Canada

"At a time when Canada's constitution is being widely discussed and sometimes distorted in the public mind, the wit and wisdom and clarity of thinking on constitutional matters of Eugene Forsey is most welcome. His character and courage over a long and interesting life have made Newfoundland and Labradorians proud to claim him as a native son."
— Jack Harris, MP and Former Leader of Newfoundland and Labrador NDP

"Eugene Forsey was a social democrat, an unbridled advocate for the poor, an intellectually rigorous and unfailingly diligent expert on every aspect of our parliamentary and constitutional context. Prime ministers, editors, ministers, MPs, and senators valued his insights, respected his passion, and feared his wrath. Eugene Forsey was a unique and self-propelling force in the politics of Canada, and this book is a loving but fair tribute and history of that force in all its dimensions."
— Senator Hugh Segal

Eugene Forsey in Algonquin Park, 1935. The lovelight in his eyes is for Harriet, who took the picture.

EUGENE FORSEY
Canada's Maverick Sage

Best wishes,
Helen Forsey

Helen Forsey
Foreword by Roy Romanow

DUNDURN
A J. PATRICK BOYER BOOK
TORONTO

Copyright © Helen Forsey, 2012

All rights reserved. No part of this publication may be reproduced, stored in a retrieval system, or transmitted in any form or by any means, electronic, mechanical, photocopying, recording, or otherwise (except for brief passages for purposes of review) without the prior permission of Dundurn Press. Permission to photocopy should be requested from Access Copyright.

Project Editor: Michael Carroll
Editor: Domenic Farrell
Design: Courtney Horner
Printer: Transcontinental

Library and Archives Canada Cataloguing in Publication

Forsey, Helen, 1945-
    Eugene Forsey , Canada's maverick sage / Helen Forsey ; foreword by Roy Romanow.

"A J. Patrick Boyer book".
Includes bibliographical references and index.
Issued also in electronic formats.
ISBN 978-1-926577-15-9

    1. Forsey, Eugene A. (Eugene Alfred), 1904-1991. 2. Social reformers--Canada--Biography. 3. Legislators--Canada--Biography. 4. Canada. Parliament. Senate--Biography. 5. Canada--Politics and government--20th century. I. Title.

FC601.F67F67 2012   971.06092   C2011-902875-1

1 2 3 4 5   16 15 14 13 12

We acknowledge the support of the **Canada Council for the Arts** and the **Ontario Arts Council** for our publishing program. We also acknowledge the financial support of the **Government of Canada** through the **Canada Book Fund** and **Livres Canada Books**, and the **Government of Ontario** through the **Ontario Book Publishing Tax Credit** and the **Ontario Media Development Corporation**.

Care has been taken to trace the ownership of copyright material used in this book. The author and the publisher welcome any information enabling them to rectify any references or credits in subsequent editions.

J. Kirk Howard, President

Printed and bound in Canada.
www.dundurn.com

Dundurn	Gazelle Book Services Limited	Dundurn
3 Church Street, Suite 500	White Cross Mills	2250 Military Road
Toronto, Ontario, Canada	High Town, Lancaster, England	Tonawanda, NY
M5E 1M2	LA1 4XS	U.S.A. 14150

To Roddy

*whose spirit, like his Grampa's —
loving, feisty, and brilliant —
lives on*

Contents

	Foreword by Roy Romanow	9
	Acknowledgements	13
	Preface	17
1	The Forsey Saga	23
2	Striving for Grace: An Ethical and Spiritual Framework	50
3	Standing on Guard: Watchdog for the Body Politic	75
4	Protest and Vision: Building Democratic Socialism	98
5	Trade Unions: Putting Principles to Work	124
6	Kindred and Affinities	148
7	A Reluctant Dragon: The Dilemmas of Conflict	180
8	Knowing Where We've Come From: History and Tradition	211
9	"Using Our Heads": Intellect and Education	237
10	Wit and Wisdom: The Power of Words	264
11	Serving the Common Good: The Role of Government	287

12	Navigating the Constitution: A Citizen's Roadmap	306
13	One Love: Quebec and Canada	335
14	Strong and Free: Redefining Nationalism	369
15	Partisanship and Independence	390
16	Canada and the World: A Progressive Legacy	420

| Epilogue | 432 |

Appendix: Eugene Forsey – A Brief Chronology	437
Note on Sources	441
Notes	443
Selected Bibliography	471
Index	475

Foreword

Eugene Forsey and the Power of Ideas

Eugene Forsey's life spanned most of the twentieth century and, like that century, his life was widely varied and caught up in many transformations — transformations of experience, role, public contribution, and political allegiance.

He was born in Grand Bank, on the Burin Peninsula, and had reached his mid-forties before Newfoundland, in a close vote, joined Canada's federation. From a Newfoundland outport, he became a Rhodes Scholar at Oxford. In those days, Newfoundland and the Maritime provinces were, in many ways, close to London and England. St. John's was geographically closer to London than to Canada. Many from the Atlantic region frequently visited Boston, New York, Philadelphia, and Washington. Many from the region similarly travelled to Belfast, Dublin, Paris, and Geneva before they ventured as far west as Montreal or Toronto, not to mention the rest of Canada. The people of this region worked on and around the ocean, built supporting factories and industries, and constructed ships with little connection to the financial and marketing worlds of Montreal and Toronto. It was said the Atlantic Ocean was Newfoundland's front door opening on to the world of the North Atlantic.

From a conservative background, Forsey became one of the founders of social democracy in Canada and a proponent of social reforms, joining the League for Social Reconstruction. This apparent tension also reflects his Newfoundland beginnings.

Many of the values and principles of that place concerning constitutions, government, and public policy reflected those that prevailed in England at the time. The ethos of England was still shaped by the competing views of Disraeli and Gladstone. The latter reflected classic liberalism, faith in the unseen hand of markets, and letting enterprise dictate public policy. Disraeli, on the other hand, urged an alliance between the landed aristocracy and the working class against the increasing power of the merchants and the new industrialists. He promoted the view that landed interests should use their power and privilege to protect the poor from exploitation by the market.

Conditions in Canada were very different from those in England, but Atlantic Tories still had a strong sense that it was the duty of the powerful to protect the poor from exploitation. Eugene Forsey was raised in this environment. The idea of acting for the benefit of the dispossessed has continued to prevail, extending its influence to much of Canada through his voice and the voices of Maritimers such as Robert Stanfield, Allan Blakeney, and Dalton Camp.

Clearly, Eugene Forsey was shaped by these currents of opinion, and continued to uphold them. He became a strong believer in British parliamentary government and its capacity to develop responses to human need and social deprivation. He rejected the idea that the economics of the market should be granted a free hand in determining public policy or limiting the scope of public government.

Reflecting this search for the political and social good, he moved from university lecturer at McGill to research director of the Canadian Labour Congress; from an aspiring CCF politician to a member of the Liberal Party and stout defender of Prime Minister Trudeau, committed to Trudeau's strong beliefs in a united Canada; from a prolific author and commentator to a senator and privy councillor.

As this wonderful book describes, Eugene Forsey's life reflected the rich diversity of his response to political challenges. But this diversity disguises a remarkable underlying consistency. Eugene Forsey was a constitutionalist, someone who believed that those eminent rules which govern our political processes and which by practice and by text have been in place over time must be known, respected, and followed. The alternative to ordered politics is a kind of lurching opportunism that, in time, will destroy political stability and, possibly, the political nation that is Canada. He vehemently opposed the arguments that urged independence for Quebec. He also had more immediate reasons for this opposition: his anticipation of devastating practical consequences, particularly economic consequences for ordinary Quebeckers; his outrage at the distortions of history that were being used to promote the sovereignists' options; and his concern about separation's potential impact on minorities, especially anglophones in Quebec and francophones in other provinces.

Not only was Eugene Forsey a committed constitutionalist, he was both brilliant and outspoken in defending the rules by which we are governed. Although strongly committed to progressive politics, his deepest political commitments were not to a party or program, but to constitutional order. A polity can certainly make short-sighted choices and pursue badly mistaken ideas in seeking good social arrangements; but, in time, democracy is likely to provide the necessary corrections. This is only possible, however, if the established mechanisms are maintained and kept free of manipulation. Forsey's primary loyalty, therefore, was not to faction but to values and principles — the ones that uphold constitutional order.

The strength of this belief on his part is evident in the depth of his knowledge of constitutional history and the thoroughness of his research. As constitutional scholar John Whyte has observed, "Forsey wisely recognized that at the very heart of the liberal democratic state is the system for orderly recognition of those who are to be allowed to govern and those who are allowed to succeed to power. He understood, and passionately defended, the tested restraints on the acquisition of power that make us free from oppression."

Eugene Forsey's commitment to constitutional order was often expressed through his open challenges — in speeches, books, articles, and frequent letters to the editor — to those who considered the rules of governing to be negotiable, to those who failed to understand that those rules must prevail over questionable opportunities for power and, especially, to those who cared so little about our political well-being that they did not bother to learn the lessons of constitutional history.

His pointedness and vehemence, always present and always refreshing in a society numbed by hollow political jousting, was more directed at ignorance and indifference than at political scheming. His national fame — and, I believe, his national importance — lies in his repeated insistence that Canada's constitutional rules cannot survive without memory and conviction.

Eugene Forsey's life was one of remarkable achievements and rich contributions to Canadian education, labour, social progress, and parliament. But his perfect legacy is the body of letters, comments, and articles he wrote throughout his career to constantly remind us that the enduring value of our democratic political heritage depends on our continued understanding of it and our fidelity to it.

As can be seen by his early childhood influences, so engagingly recaptured in this book, Eugene Forsey's project was, at heart, a conservative one. Like most of us, his early political outlook remained, largely, a lifelong orientation. The structures, practices, and restraints that grow up around political power reflect the goals and values that make that power not only tolerable but necessary in the modern age of liberty. Decisions of convenience and efficiency often drive us backwards into the dark and dangerous state. Canada's political society is organic and comes from specific needs and context which reflect our basic core values. When we seek to solve challenges or promote political advantage through the detachment of constitutional rules, we risk losing the state's essential and fundamental connection to legitimacy and history. Forsey's type of conservatism fosters the political conditions that allow politics and public policies that are bold, reformist, innovative and, above all, responsive to our ever changing needs.

Eugene Forsey's conservatism was central to his values and political identity but so, too, was his vision of what Canada could do for its citizens. In *Eugene Forsey, Canada's Maverick Sage*, his daughter Helen has written a beautiful book about her father, one which thoughtfully and warmly captures the essence of this great Canadian and his essential legacy.

Roy Romanow
Saskatoon, Saskatchewan

Acknowledgements

I owe a great debt of gratitude to the many people who have contributed to the making of this book.

It was my friend Jean Christie who first put the idea to me a few years after my father's death in 1991; her suggestion and her ongoing encouragement are deeply appreciated.

One of the greatest delights of this venture was interviewing people who knew my father and his work, and who offered a wealth of information, insight, and anecdote now reflected in these pages. I was privileged to talk at length with Irving Abella, Deborah Coyne, Dawn Dobson, Ed Finn, John Hastings, Michiel Horn, Dorothy Inglis, Pierre Joncas, Wendell MacLeod, the Honourable Heath Macquarrie, John Matheson, David Millar, Desmond Morton, Michael Oliver, Svend Robinson, Clyde Wells, Alan Whitehorn, and John Whyte. Many of them also provided me with valuable materials or pointed me towards other resources.

Members of my family have unstintingly shared memories and understandings. Some of the book's richest material comes from my sister Margaret Forsey, my sons Roddy Contreras and Eugene Contreras, and our cousins Jeff Bowles, Alex Hickman, and Grace Sparkes.

Others from the political and academic spheres who offered information and assistance include Michael Behiels, the Honourable Charles Caccia, Ramsay Cook, the Honourable Joyce Fairbairn, David Farr, the Honourable Royce Frith, Tony Hall, Ted Hodgetts, Roger Hutchinson, Greg Kealey, David Kwavnik, the Honourable Dan Lang, the Honourable Flora MacDonald, the Honourable Lorna Marsden, the Honourable Peter Milliken, the Honourable Lorna Milne, the Honourable Gildas Molgat, Peter Neary, Blair Neatby, James Thwaites, and Fred Vaughn. Special thanks to Donald Wright, now at the University of New Brunswick, for his encouragement, helpful suggestions, and a wonderful package of letters of recommendation written to support my father's Rhodes Scholarship more than eighty years ago.

A number of supportive groups and individuals joined in financing the research phase of this project. The Boag Foundation provided the initial seed money, followed by generous contributions from the Canadian Centre for Policy Alternatives, CR Bronfman Foundation, United Steelworkers of America, and two anonymous donors. Matching funding was granted by the Department of Canadian Heritage through its Canadian Studies Program. All this enabled me to undertake the fascinating but time-consuming archival work, interviews, and gathering of materials. In this regard I give special thanks to Tom Axworthy, Tim Brodhead, Bruce Campbell, William Fizet, David Mackenzie, Lawrence McBrearty, Glen McDougall, the Honourable Michael Meighen, the T.R. Meighen Foundation, the Honourable Hartland Molson, Rolland Péloquin, and Allen Seager.

The research itself was hugely facilitated by members of that noble guild of professionals who care for the treasures of our past in archives and libraries: Louis-G. Brillant, formerly of the Parliamentary Library; Nora Côté of the Canadian Labour Congress; Brian Murphy and his colleagues at Library and Archives Canada; Johanne Pelletier of the McGill University Archives; Bert Riggs and Mel Baker of Memorial University of Newfoundland; and Rhianna Edwards of Mount Allison University Archives. Others who helped in the project's early stages included Wendy

Acknowledgements

Robbins and Ken Puley of the CBC, John Urquhart of *Canadian Forum*, and Jamie Swift and Marg Anne Morrison of *Between the Lines*.

My heartfelt thanks to Rachel Irwin, Heather Parker, Suzanne Schaan, and Dominic Farrell, without whose kindness and quick thinking I might never have found Patrick Boyer and Blue Butterfly Books. Patrick, who knew my father and worked with him, put limitless energy and enthusiasm into preparing the book for publication, both before and after the consolidation with Dundurn. Dominic was the most patient and forgiving of editors, with a professional meticulousness worthy of my father; his help with photo licensing was much appreciated as well. I am indebted also to Kirk Howard and Michael Carroll of Dundurn, to Sonia Holiad and Jennifer Yiu of Blue Butterfly, and to everyone involved in the publication process.

The Honourable Roy Romanow honoured me by reading the text and writing the foreword, bringing to it the perspective of his own long years of service to our country. Others who read some or all of the text and offered comments are Maude Barlow, Laura Bonikowsky, Nathalie Des Rosiers, Josephine Grey, Jack Harris, Janet Hicks King, Maurice King, Penney Kome, Kate Malloy, Marie Small Face Marule, Elizabeth May, Larry McDermott, Teresa Mitchell, Bob Rae, the Honourable Hugh Segal, Daniel Tencer, and Dale Young.

Almost thirty years ago, a young journalism graduate named Chris Brown took a picture of my father at a demonstration on Parliament Hill, framed it, and gave it to me. I have had that photograph on my wall ever since, and now it is on the front jacket of this book. Unfortunately, assiduous efforts to contact Chris for permission have been unsuccessful. I am hoping he will see the book, recognize his beautiful photo, and get in touch. I also want to thank photographers Guy Nadeau and Robert Fleming for their generosity, and Anne Lauzon, Alice Nelson, and Marguerite Ritchie for their help.

Over the seventeen years since I embarked on this project, my fellow residents at Lothlorien Co-op — Janice Arthur, Peter Bunnett, Paige Cousineau, Ellen Good, John Inglis, and Linda Rush — have supported me in sickness and in health. My neighbours Sally Noseworthy and her family at my other home in Biscayan Cove, Newfoundland, kindly let me use their cabin's connection to the electrical grid, enabling me to complete urgent editing on my little laptop.

Others have helped in various ways, among them Bill Blaikie, David Blaikie, Joan Broughton, Duncan Cameron, Andréa Campbell, Susan Clarke, Parzival Copes, Graham Eglington, Martyn Estall, Judy Foote, Charles Gordon, James Greene, Ursula Hastings, Nancy Hickman, Kathryn MacDonald, Isabel Macquarrie, Edith Matheson, Chris McCreery, Frank Milligan, Sara Murphy, Janet Solberg, Michael Valpy, Danya Vered, Larry Wagg, Johannes Wheeldon, and Marie-Beth Wright.

Finally, I am eternally grateful to my sister, sons, daughter-in-law Monica Wolfe, co-grandmother Catherine Stewart, and friends Kathleen Brooks, Pam Connolly, Bruce Dodds, Celia Godkin, Marilyn Hindmarch, Anna Lenk, Ken and Joan Marisett, Dawn Martin, Jan Slakov, and Tamara Vladimirova for their kindness, patience, and practical support of all kinds. All of them have helped to make this book truly a labour of love.

Preface

"I'm getting old and infernal," my father would say with a twinkle, as he got ready to leave for his Parliament Hill office. He used his great-aunt Molly's phrase with gusto, enjoying the wordplay as much as the double-barrelled shot at himself. Since turning eighty, he found that physical tasks took him longer than they had when he was a sprightly seventy-year-old, but mentally he had not slowed down at all.

Eugene Forsey had only just begun to adopt the "old" part of the label, but "infernal" was something he had always been. Well known for the vigour of his opinions, the tenacity of his commitments, and the scathing wit with which he demolished opposing arguments, he was a thorn in the side of numerous establishments through six decades of rather public life.

When Dad took something on, he would throw himself into it with energy and emphasis. This lifetime habit got him into plenty of trouble over the years, as his controversial views and the forcefulness with which he propounded them rubbed many people the wrong way. Yet he himself failed to fit into a classic curmudgeon role, confounding such expectations with characteristic humour, humility and generosity of spirit.

Admittedly, his choice of issues could be perplexing. Even some of his friends were puzzled by his fervent advocacy of the reserve powers of the Crown, his fury over the "two nations" theory of Canada, or the vehemence with which he regularly denounced what he considered improper English.

Others could understand his passion for the issues, but had trouble with the specific positions he took. A stalwart CCFer leaping to the defence of former Tory prime minister Arthur Meighen? A founder of the Montreal Civil Liberties Union supporting the War Measures Act in 1970? An energetic proponent of an inclusive federalism opposing the Meech Lake Accord?

Each of these apparent contradictions, of course, has its own story. It wasn't that my father was unpredictable; it was just that one had to understand where he was coming from in order to understand the places where he ended up.

This book is my personal exploration of those places, and of the pathways that connect them. It is written in the belief that such an exploration holds continuing relevance for Canadians today, for many of the political and personal dilemmas my Dad faced are as current now as they were decades ago. As we grapple with those issues in their present forms, his thinking and example can inform and inspire us.

It was early in 1991 when my father passed his torch to those who would follow. He had carried it faithfully through the better part of a century — his intimate knowledge of the workings of our democracy, his vision of Canada as a better place, and his determination to always strive for the common good. At the time of his death, he must have had some sense of just how important that kind of knowledge, vision, and determination would be to those of us who remained.

He had, of course, seen the signs — too many dire indicators of worse to come. By the beginning of the 1990s, the forces he had spent his life opposing had made enormous gains, both in the public mind and in political practice. The corporate bottom line was rapidly overtaking the common good as the ultimate standard for Canadian public policy, and the human and environmental consequences of this shift were increasingly being felt. On the constitutional front, the Meech Lake battle was over, but other problems were already looming on the horizon.

Eugene Forsey, the old war-horse, was getting tired. Ever since his student days he had been fighting for what he believed in, sometimes out on the front lines, sometimes off to one side, tilting at chosen windmills. Most often, perhaps, he worked behind the scenes, "on the fringe" of public life. Now, at age eighty-six, the toll of the years was showing.

Not that this stopped him from engaging in public debate. Just a few days before his death, he sent yet another defiant polemic to the newspapers, blasting the latest constitutional proposals from the Quebec Liberal Party. But that was his final effort. On the morning of February 20, 1991, he died peacefully in his sleep.

And now Canada is left with his legacy: a legacy that, in an urgent and continuing way, is a call to action for us all. It is also a tool kit, containing a wealth of wisdom and skills, love and faith, strength and laughter — a cache of riches we can draw on for the times still to come.

"It's not everyone," a friend told me, "who gets to trace their childhood memories in the national archives!" No indeed; mine is a very special privilege, and it brings with it a special responsibility for sharing the treasures I have found.

Because my Dad was a public figure of some significance on the Canadian scene, my personal stories of him are connected to Canada's story by myriad threads. As that national story continues to unfold in the face of challenges old and new, those connections gain in importance. This book combines the public record of his life with my personal perspective, and offers the synthesis back to our country.

Eugene Forsey's "life on the fringe" made a difference while he lived, and it can continue to make a difference now. For the majority of us — ordinary Canadians who are never likely to be anywhere else but "on the fringe" — that realization is particularly important. The legacy he left us is at once both ordinary and extraordinary, and much of its relevance lies in precisely that fact.

My original motivation for embarking on this labour of love was the need to bring my father's voice into the public forum once again, to reinsert his ideas and his example into the crucial debates of our time. But in the course of my research and writing, my purpose has expanded. Beyond the responsibility for presenting his work in an accurate and accessible way, I feel a further obligation to him, as well as to the reader and to the country. I need to address without flinching not only the issues themselves, but also the gaps in my understanding of his beliefs, the doubts and differences that sometimes separated us, and the further perspectives I have developed with the passing of time and the unfolding of events.

As a result, it is not just my Dad's voice that speaks through these pages, but mine as well. I write with a daughter's love and admiration, but also, I hope, with a critic's awareness and an activist's passion. This in turn demands that I be very clear about when I am offering my own interpretations; that I acknowledge my ownership of ideas and approaches that are not necessarily his. This I solemnly undertake to do. As Eugene Forsey's daughter, I could hardly do otherwise.

Any reader looking for detachment and objectivity in these pages will thus have a fruitless search. I admit in advance to a shameless subjectivity, an intensely personal approach grounded in my own values and understandings, which overlap but are not identical with his.

This book was never intended in any case to be a standard biographical tract, an exhaustive compiling of context, documentation, and analysis. Nor have I attempted to put together a "collected works" or "selected writings." For present purposes I am neither biographer nor editor; instead, I am a traveller, journeying through the landscape of my father's legacy.

Flowing from this is the thematic structure I have chosen. The broad themes which constitute his legacy can be seen as places he dwelt in or visited, pathways he explored. He returned often to these places, deepening his understanding and expanding his knowledge of the terrain within and between them. By organizing the book around those themes, I am able to visit each of those places in turn and spend the necessary time there, without having to interrupt my stay to take off for somewhere else. I can focus and develop each theme on its own terms, avoiding the fragmentation that would be imposed by a rigidly chronological structure.

Of course, in order to conduct a coherent discussion of any of these themes, it is important to know the sequence of related events and the historical context in which they happened. To that end, I begin with a chapter sketching the main outlines of my father's life story. Together with the chronological summary in the Appendix, this should provide the reader with the necessary biographical pegs to hang the rest of the material on.

I am very fortunate that a great deal of my Dad's thinking and action is preserved in written form. He was always writing something; many of my early memories are of him banging away at his trusty old manual typewriter in the small spare bedroom he used for a study. Over the years, he churned out hundreds of newspaper and magazine articles, as well as scholarly essays and reviews, several books, and an unremitting stream of letters to the editor. In addition, he left reams of unpublished work — decades of briefs and memoranda, speeches, university lectures, convocation addresses, interviews, panel presentations, and radio and television appearances. Much of this material is still available, not only in various archival collections but also in actual use in offices and classrooms and libraries across this country. The notes and bibliography reflect the range of these sources.

Nor is it only his formal writings that survive. Even today, hundreds of individual Canadians from all parts of the country and many different walks of life still treasure their personal correspondence with Eugene Forsey, who took the time to write and answer their questions on labour or constitutional subjects, respond to their ideas and initiatives, provide exhaustive critiques of their manuscripts, or help plan strategies for action on some burning public issue.

Letters were Dad's preferred way of staying in touch with people. He avoided the telephone the way hay-fever sufferers avoid ragweed. If he wanted to invite someone to lunch, even in the same city, he would dash off a letter to them and pop it in the mail. As a result, there is a paper trail for much of his everyday life, and even some of his shortest and most mundane letters sparkle with his spirit. I repeatedly raided my treasure trove of his personal letters, spending hours entranced by the stories, thoughts, and feelings that flowed so easily from his pen.

Obviously, there is much more to my father's legacy than his writings. Many people have shared with me their memories of him as friend or family, as mentor or co-worker, as ally or adversary in academic or public debate. Their different perspectives informed and stimulated my own journey, and added immensely to the breadth and depth of my understanding.

In addition, a massive family collection of photographs and a number of audio and video tapes provided what felt almost like direct contact with him and my mother. It made me long to just sit with them again over a cup of tea and ask them all sorts of questions which now seem so obvious and important, but which I never thought to ask while they were alive.

Just to sit down and talk with him again — that was what so many of those I spoke with wished they could do. To see that twinkle in his eye, listen to those lively anecdotes, ask him about some specific point and hear him expound on it with his unfailing verve and vigour — only in memory and imagination can we do that now. But his spirit is clearly present in those memories and imaginings, and I trust it is present here in what I have written as well.

On both the personal and political levels, then, this book is a journey of discovery. I invite the reader to join me on my quest.

CHAPTER ONE

The Forsey Saga

My father's life began in Newfoundland in 1904 and ended eighty-six years later on Canada's Pacific coast. He would have appreciated the symbolism. His life, like his legacy, spans this country, and his story, like the country's, begins well before he was born.

Ancestral tales were part of my childhood — tales Dad told my sister and me of the rugged south coast of Newfoundland, the Annapolis Valley of Nova Scotia, the forested shores of Gaspé. These places and their people were woven into our identity as children by the lines traced on the family tree, and made real to us by stories passed down by word of mouth.

Thanks to that oral tradition, the personalities of many of our long-dead ancestors were vividly familiar to my father, and he in turn made them come alive for us. There was Jonathan Hickman, born prematurely at sea coming from Devonshire or Dorset in the 1740s, who ultimately lived to be a hundred years old and begat a whole clan of Newfoundlanders.

Our great-great-great-grandfather "Granfer" Symes was a sharp-tongued Grand Bank sea captain who used his quick wits to foil petty bureaucracy in the French island port of St. Pierre. Over on the mainland, our wealthy Loyalist ancestor (and I have discovered, to my dismay, slave-holder) Stephen Thorne was already in his sixties when he started a new life in Nova Scotia after the American Revolution. Some seventy years later, one of his descendents, Dad's maternal grandfather, Joseph Shaw, moved his family from the Annapolis Valley to the Gaspé, where he set up a lumber mill and founded a temperance society. In these stories the main dramatic actors were men, but they also included many remarkable women.

Dad's tales of these people were often light-hearted, but they were also fragrant with a history and an inheritance which, as a child, I had yet to understand. Even now, sifting through masses of family papers and my own memories, I continue to learn about his origins and mine, puzzle over some of the revelations, and marvel at the evidence of their continuing influence.

My father took origins seriously, not only in the historical context but also on the personal level. He attributed some of his own peculiarities to his ancestry, including what he called his "West Country English temper" and his "Ulster Irish stubbornness." Many of his pithy turns of phrase were actually verbal family heirlooms, and he always attributed his indifference to fish to a surfeit of that food in the diet of his Newfoundland ancestors. I suspect that a certain pride in eccentricity, a willingness to stand out from the crowd, ran in his blood as well.

Dad was born on May 29, 1904, in the town of Grand Bank on the Burin Peninsula in Newfoundland, which was still half a century away from becoming part of Canada. In a "biographical note" that he wrote the year before his death, he identified himself as the "son of Eugene Forsey, English Newfoundlander, and Florence Elvira Bowles, Canadian."

His father, Eugene Sr., had worked as a young man as a Methodist "probationer" on Newfoundland's isolated southwest coast. From 1893 to 1895, he tended to the spiritual welfare of the people of eight or nine tiny fishing communities scattered along a hundred kilometres of barren rocky shore. Privileged and devout, the young pastor from Grand Bank threw himself into his mission work. He travelled constantly, by skiff or on foot, from one little outport to the next, confident in his youthful strength to withstand the hardship conditions and often brutal weather. Those two years took a toll on his health, making him prone to repeated attacks of pneumonia, yet he doggedly continued on his path towards ordination, entering Mount Allison University in 1896 to pursue theology and English. It was there that he met Florence Bowles, who was studying fine arts; they graduated in 1899 and married in 1902.

By that time, although he was only in his early thirties, Eugene Sr. was having serious problems with illness. Doctors prescribed a kinder climate, and in the spring of 1903 the young couple moved to Mexico. Eugene took a desk job with the Mexican Light, Heat and Power Company, while Florence painted and wrote. When she became pregnant, her chauvinist husband sent her away to his rocky windswept homeland to have the baby. She travelled alone, by ship, from the Mexican port of Vera Cruz to Havana and then New York; from there she sailed to St. John's, where she took the coastal steamer south and westward along the rugged coast to Grand Bank. There, in the Forseys' outport home, she gave birth to her son.

Baby Eugene with his mother and all his grandparents, Grand Bank, Newfoundland, summer 1904. Clockwise from left front: George Robert Forsey, Jane Forsey, Letitia Shaw Bowles, William Cochrane Bowles, and Florence Forsey with the baby.

"My father was determined that I should be born in Newfoundland," Dad explained. "So off my mother went to Grand Bank — a place she had never so much as seen, and where she knew only one or two people she had met at Mount Allison. Fortunately, all went well there."[1]

That was the closest I ever heard him come to criticizing his dead father's patriotic and patriarchal act. Whatever opinions Florence's parents or siblings may have had on the matter, they probably never voiced any negative comment aloud. One did not speak ill of the dead, and Eugene Sr. had dropped dead of a heart attack in the train station of Mexico in November 1904, barely two weeks after Florence rejoined him there with the baby.

Shocked and grieving, the young widow had to make the long journey north once again. This time, though, she travelled not to Newfoundland but home to her own family in Ottawa. It was there, in the big Bowles house on Lisgar Street, that baby Eugene grew up, an only child surrounded by doting adults.

They called him "the baby with four mothers": Florence herself, her sisters Hazel and Sybil, and their mother Letitia Shaw Bowles. The male head of this largely female household was "Goppa," otherwise known as William Cochrane Bowles, who was the chief clerk of votes and proceedings in the House of Commons. Born in Quebec City of Irish Protestant parents, Grandfather Bowles had entered the service of the House of Assembly of the Province of Canada as a page in 1855, and retired from one of the country's highest parliamentary offices a full sixty years later.

From the time little Eugene could walk, he was taken up to "Goppa's buildings" on Parliament Hill, where in due course he was introduced to Sir Wilfrid Laurier, Arthur Meighen and dozens of other parliamentarians of the period. At home, too, the boy was immersed in a political milieu.

"Politics and gardening, and Methodist Church matters, were the main subjects of conversation in our house," he told historian David Millar in a 1970 interview. "I don't think my grandparents or their family were much interested in business or sport or anything of that sort. But politics, yes."

"The debates in the House of Commons were among the favourite indoor sports of the family," he went on. "They'd be down with 'grippe,'

Little Eugene helping "Goppa" Bowles in the garden of the big house on Lisgar Street, Ottawa, 1906.

feeling like death and destruction, and suddenly the telephone would ring and it would be my grandfather saying, 'There's a very important debate coming on in half an hour or so; if you want to hear something exciting, you'd better come.' Whereupon the entire family would pull themselves together, don ceremonial attire, and hurry up to the gallery to listen."[2]

There was another member of the family in those early days as well — a black cocker spaniel named Rex. That dog and his successors figured large in the bedtime stories that Dad used to tell my sister and me as children. We never tired of hearing about Rexie chasing the cats out of the asparagus bed in the big garden on Lisgar Street, pretending to be lame so as to garner sympathy and cookies, or learning to decipher spelled-out words like "W A L K" or "B A T H" and respond accordingly. It was Rexie's benevolent canine influence that led Dad to identify himself throughout his life as an "honourary dog."

Rex was certainly good company for his young master, who probably didn't have a great deal of companionship from other children. According to Dad's cousin the late Jeff Bowles, "Eugene didn't really fit in with the boys on the street very well. He got a start on the serious world very early in life. He was kept so busy, and he had so much to do, that he didn't have as much time to play with other boys. He was brought up to be so adult in a way; he dealt with adults a great deal. It must have made him a bit precocious, to be started that young."

Apparently so. Like his father and mother before him, Eugene was a diligent and enthusiastic student. He did well throughout his primary years at Ottawa's Normal Model School, despite being plagued as a child by "bilious attacks," which ended at age thirteen when he had his appendix out. At the Ottawa Collegiate (now Lisgar Collegiate), he consistently earned academic honours, while his extracurricular activities included acting in the school play and editing the school's yearbook and literary magazine.

All was not work and serious discussion, however; Dad remembered having a lot of fun as a child. The family never had their own cottage, but in the summers, when the Parliamentary recess gave "Goppa" Bowles some time off, Florence would take leave from her librarian job and they would go on holiday. They would travel by train to various vacation spots in Ontario, Quebec, and the Maritimes, and when Dad was eight, they spent a wonderful three weeks back in Grand Bank with his grandparents and aunts. These boyhood idylls were one source of his lifelong attachment to the land and people of Eastern Canada, particularly the Maritimes and Newfoundland; they probably also contributed to his lifelong love of trains.

By the time Eugene graduated from the Collegiate at the age of eighteen, he had developed what Jeff Bowles described as "a very strong character and will to forge ahead. He had the best memory I've heard of outside of Macauley, though he used to say that Arthur Meighen's was better. And he was a terribly hard worker, extremely hard. He did everything very fast; I think that was one reason why he accomplished so much."

In the fall of 1922, after a wonderful summer in Newfoundland, Eugene

Eugene (left) with his cousins Kenneth and Jeffrey Bowles, and his beloved dog Rex, Ottawa, circa 1920.

Forsey entered McGill University in Montreal, equipped with an insatiable intellectual curiosity and a budding reputation as a brilliant young scholar. He embarked on an honours program in economics and political science, with half-honours in English. In his frequent letters home, he shared the details of his studies. "Got 90 on my exam in Political Science. Political Economy, of which I was rather afraid, netted me 91% ... I feel very glad I chose the course I did, though I regret my Classics ... There is scarcely a single subject in any of the Faculties which I should not enjoy taking."

In another letter, he wrote, "Our English lectures continue to be fascinating, and the Shaw in me has already taken Prof. Lafleur's measure by mimicking him with, I believe, considerable success. I shall display this latest addition to my repertoire on my visit next week ..."[3] Decades later, he would entertain my sister and me with the same hilarious imitations.

It was while he was at McGill that my father's political views began to change. Up until then, he had absorbed the Conservative identity shared by his Newfoundland and Canadian families, an identity reinforced by his own personal admiration for Tory leader Arthur Meighen. But during his undergraduate years his Conservatism was subjected to a serious shaking up.

Three people in particular played a part in this. One of them was Stephen Leacock, the great humourist and head of McGill's Department of Economics and Political Science. A Tory himself, Leacock had, in Dad's words, "a marvellous gift for opening up people's minds, prodding and stirring and stimulating them, and making them realize that there was a great deal more in heaven and earth than had been dreamt of in their juvenile philosophies." Another key influence was Professor J.C. Hemmeon, a Nova Scotian radical, "a thorough-going political and economic skeptic. He had a way of just rather snickering you out of your prejudices." Finally, there was the Reverend Allworth Eardley, minister at the Methodist church Dad attended in Montreal, "a man of very fine intellect, a magnificent preacher, and politically an advanced radical." My father later credited these three men with preparing the ground for his political conversion.[4]

The shift in my father's thinking was barely perceptible at first. In 1924, he spent three weeks tutoring the sons of Vincent Massey (later to be governor general of Canada) at their country home near Port Hope, Ontario. Dad's letters from Batterwood reveal him as a young "Tory Democrat," espousing an increasingly progressive political philosophy which took working people into account and advocated social and economic reforms.[5]

The next year, while still on the executive of the student Conservative Club, he wrote an article in the *McGill Fortnightly Review*. In it, he stoutly defended Arthur Meighen's leadership of the Tories against attacks from the party's right wing, who included members of Montreal's wealthy business community. For that transgression, he was called on the carpet by the McGill administration and accused of being "a Bolshevik"!

Dad was still calling himself a Conservative when he completed his B.A., but the seeds of change had been sown. Encouraged by Professor Hemmeon, he decided to pursue what had become a lively interest in labour matters, and went to Cape Breton to research the coal mines there for his master's degree. In 1926, after completing his thesis on "Economic and Social Aspects of the Nova Scotia Coal Industry," he made another visit back to Newfoundland, then sailed for England to take up a Rhodes scholarship at Oxford's venerable Balliol College.

At Oxford, he found himself immersed in an intense intellectual atmosphere, one strongly influenced by the socialist Fabian Society and the British Labour Party. He promptly joined the Oxford University Labour Club, and continued his graduate studies under the tutelage of Christian socialist philosopher John Macmurray. Dad's three years at Oxford exposed him to some of Britain's most eminent socialist scholars, and reinforced his new political creed.

In his vacations during that time, he travelled extensively in the United Kingdom and on the Continent, accompanied by various friends and relatives, acting as travel agent, guide and interpreter for all of them. His souvenirs from those trips graced the walls and shelves of our home in Ottawa when we were growing up, and his stories of his European travels enhanced our international awareness.

He returned to Montreal in the fall of 1929, and at Stephen Leacock's invitation began teaching as a sessional lecturer in McGill's Economics and Political Science Department. He later described that position as an "academic footstool," from which he was never invited to rise during his entire time on the university's staff. But he loved McGill, and embraced teaching with characteristic enthusiasm, bringing to it many of the influences he had absorbed at Oxford.

Montreal during the Depression was fertile ground for advocates of social change. Dad's involvement was low-key at first, but he soon found himself engaged in a constant round of political and social activism: the McGill Labour Club, the Student Christian Movement (SCM), the United Church's Committee on Social and Economic Research, and the Montreal editorial group for *Canadian Forum* magazine. He attended meetings, made speeches, led discussion groups, and wrote masses of material — articles, pamphlets, and letters to the newspapers.

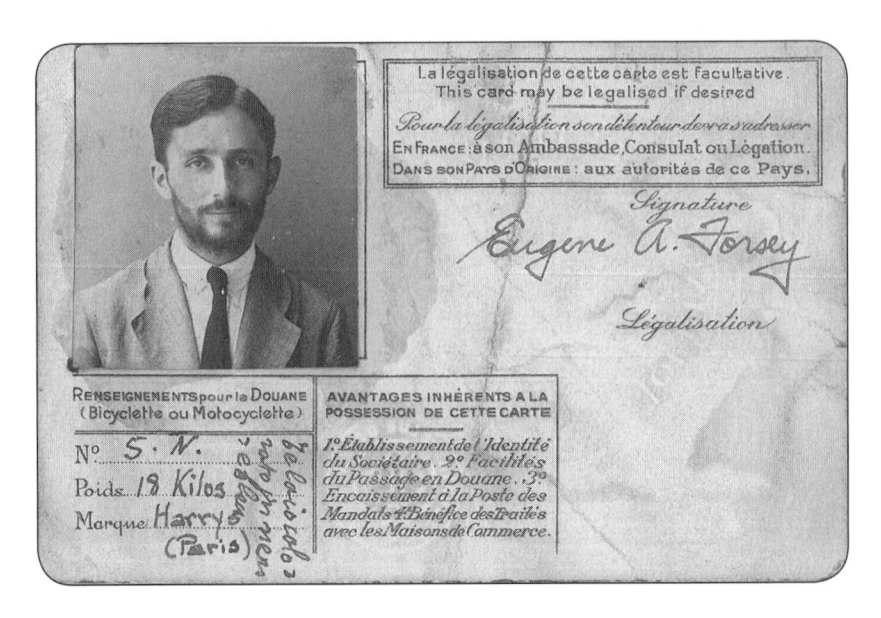

Membership card, Touring Club de France, 1931. During his three years at Oxford, Eugene did a lot of travelling, cycling, and hiking on "the Continent."

    In 1932, he helped to found the League for Social Reconstruction (LSR), and joined the local club of the new-born Co-operative Commonwealth Federation, or CCF. That summer, he travelled to the U.S.S.R., and returned energized by much of what he had seen, though he remained skeptical of communism itself. The following year, he went as a delegate to the CCF's Regina Convention, having had a small part in drafting the Manifesto with his LSR colleagues.

Meanwhile, as a junior academic at McGill, he began working towards a Ph.D. on the distribution of national income. But his teaching and other activities kept him hectically busy, and his doctoral work progressed only slowly. He also found himself embroiled in a series of disputes with the university authorities over his insistence on applying high academic standards to all his students, without favour or prejudice.

Eugene with his widowed mother, Florence Forsey, in Budapest, Hungary, 1928.

The administration wanted their young lecturer to be more flexible, particularly where the offspring of influential and wealthy citizens were concerned, and they also viewed his politics with a suspicious eye. As a result, my father's position at McGill was always shaky. In his twelve years there, he was recommended for promotion four times, and four times the recommendation was turned down. His "academic footstool" had become a fixture.

Nonetheless, on the personal level he thrived. When not occupied with activism or academic work, he spent weekends and evenings with family or friends, many of whom were active in the same progressive circles as he was. In his letters to his mother, he admitted to an occasional romantic interest, and I have noticed in them hints of mutual attractions of which he himself may not even have been fully aware. In general, though, he saw himself as "a dud with girls," and became quite philosophical about his single state.

Then, at an SCM camp in the Laurentians in May of 1935, he met Harriet Roberts, a linguist and teacher from Saint John, New Brunswick, who was working at the time for the YWCA in Montreal. Like Eugene,

Eugene and friends near Lake of the Woods, en route to Regina for the CCF's founding convention, 1933. This photo does not support his claim that he was "a dud with girls."

Harriet was intensely interested in language, culture, and religion; like him, too, she had spent time in Europe; and they shared a love for the out-of-doors. They stayed in touch, got engaged that summer at another SCM-related event in Algonquin Park, and married in November.

The photograph album they compiled over the next few years gives a taste of their early life together. There are images of my mother, younger and more care-free than I ever knew her, playing ball at a Quaker camp, knitting in the living room of their Montreal "flat," skiing in the Laurentians with the "Social Problems Club," breakfasting beside the lake at the cottage they rented in Quebec's Eastern Townships. There are snapshots of family from Newfoundland and the Maritimes, scenery from their trips to New Brunswick and the Gaspé, glimpses of old McGill: "Eugene lecturing," "Harriet at the Roddick Gates."

There is Dad's friend King Gordon, a fellow member of the LSR, his travelling companion to the U.S.S.R. and to the Regina Convention. There is his Oxford tutor, John Macmurray, toasting a hot dog over a fire

Eugene met Harriet Roberts at a Student Christian Movement camp in the Laurentians in May 1935. They took these photos of each other in Algonquin Park, where they got engaged that summer.

at a week-long SCM seminar Belleville, Ontario, in 1936, for which my parents compiled the notes. There are Grace and Violet MacInnes on the boat from the CCF Camp on BC's Gabriola Island in 1939.

The captions under the snapshots are carefully penned in my father's unmistakable hand, and many reflect his sense of fun. "Pirate at St Etienne de Bolton" shows an uncharacteristically scruffy Eugene sporting a beard. "Admiral Sir William Wink" identifies Winky, their beloved pet cat, peering intently over the gunwale of a rowboat. A formal-looking photo of Eugene and Harriet perusing a newspaper is captioned: "Receives unexpected news of belated promotion — *BC Commonwealth* headline refers to 'E. A. Forsey, McGill Economics Head.'" The date is August 1939, right in the midst of Dad's problems with McGill, two years before his contract was finally terminated.

By then, my father's commitments on the Left included an active role in the CCF as a member of the executive of the Quebec wing, and at one point as a CCF candidate for Montreal city council. He continued to work with the LSR, where he was one of the key writers and editors of their landmark opus, *Social Planning for Canada*, and with the Fellowship for a Christian Social Order, for whose 1936 book, *Towards the Christian Revolution*, he wrote two chapters on economics.

In addition, he had got deeply involved in civil liberties advocacy. As fascism gained ground in Europe, he vocally protested the Quebec establishment's sympathetic treatment of Franco and Mussolini. During the Spanish Civil War, he worked with the Aid to Spanish Democracy Committee to support the Republican cause in that country. When the Quebec government of Maurice Duplessis introduced its infamous Padlock Act in 1937, Dad and others founded the Montreal Civil Liberties Union (CLU) to spearhead the fight for citizens' rights and freedoms.

Individually as well as through the CLU and *Canadian Forum*, my father did his best to expose the "clerical fascism" that he saw as a strong and growing menace in Quebec society. In article after article, he documented the Duplessis government's increasing repression and the blatant collusion of the Catholic hierarchy.

"It seems likely," he wrote in 1937, "that we are only at the beginning of a reign of terror in which everyone who happens to incur the displeasure of Mr. Duplessis or his august Superior may expect to have his home or office ransacked and perhaps padlocked in the approved Nazi manner."[6]

As World War II approached, Dad was afraid governments at home might use the conflict as a further excuse to ride roughshod over people's civil liberties, and he did his best to prevent that from happening.

In the meantime, the McGill authorities were riding roughshod over academic freedom. In the spring of 1941, the administration finally found a way to get rid of their troublesome young lecturer. The timing was ironic. The year before, Dad's extensive work towards a Ph.D. on national income distribution had been rendered redundant by a major royal commission report, and the university had grabbed the excuse to tell him his contract would be terminated. However, he had promptly set to work on a scholarly exposition of the royal power of dissolution of Parliament — a topic of such passionate interest to him that he was able to whip it together as a doctoral thesis in less than a year. It earned him the elusive Ph.D. just in time for him to receive it at McGill's May convocation — his last as a member of the faculty.

My father's thesis included an extensive analysis and denunciation of the actions of Prime Minister Mackenzie King in the King-Byng constitutional crisis of 1926. That work put him back in touch with his old hero, former-Prime Minister Arthur Meighen — Mackenzie King's nemesis — and the connection soon grew into an extraordinary friendship. From that time until the old Tory statesman's death, Meighen was Dad's sounding board, mentor, advisor, and critic — and also a warm and wise father figure.

The thesis on dissolution did three other things as well. It established Eugene Forsey as a formidable opponent of governmental abuses of parliamentary process; it fortified the enmity between himself and Mackenzie King's Liberal Party; and it set him firmly on the path to public recognition as a constitutional expert.

Nevertheless, he was out of a job, and his professional prospects looked dim in a Canada where he had succeeded in alienating much of the academic as well as the political establishment. Fortunately, thanks to a Guggenheim Fellowship to do work at Harvard on cabinet government, he had some time to regroup. He and Harriet spent the next academic year in

Cambridge, Massachusetts, away from the rough and tumble of his time at McGill. An epoch in his life had come to an end.

The year 1942 brought major changes. On the recommendation of his CCF friends, my father was hired by the recently created Canadian Congress of Labour (CCL) as their first director of research, and he and Harriet moved to Ottawa. In November, they became parents, with the birth of my sister, Margaret. I came along three years later.

Dad immersed himself in his new job with all the zeal and commitment he had brought to his earlier academic and political work. His new responsibilities included researching a mountain of collective agreements and labour legislation, preparing briefs and speeches for near-impossible deadlines, and representing the Congress on various occasions from one end of the country to the other.

He loved his family dearly, but the enormous daily pressures of his job, his frequent travel, and his continuing political involvements gobbled up most of his time and attention, leaving Harriet with the bulk of the responsibility on the home front. Her own penchant for intellectual pursuits was one of the things that had drawn her and Dad together, but now she found herself trading the stimulating life of partner to a young activist academic for the deadening role of post-war housewife and mother. Constrained not by her husband but by practical realities as well as by the repressive "family values" of the 40s and 50s, she stayed home raising two little girls on Dad's modest salary, while still trying to maintain her own intellectual persona in the shadow of a man increasingly recognized as a star. In many ways, it was hard for them both.

But I have wonderful memories from my childhood. Often before supper, my sister and I would go out to the bus stop a block away to wait for Dad to come home from the office. As the bus pulled up, we could hear him whistling one of the "special songs" he had made up for each of us. Then, as the bus door opened, he'd appear, briefcase in hand, grinning to see us there to greet him. He used to take us for long walks in the swamp by the Rideau River where the Carleton University campus is now, showing us birds and wildflowers and animal tracks, and sharing his delight in the earth and the changing seasons. Then there were the cozy winter evenings when we'd lie in our pajamas on the rug in front of a blazing fire while he read to us from *Heidi* or *Black Beauty*, and Mum took advantage of the quiet time to write letters in the dining room.

At the same time, Dad's work was never far away. The Labour Congress was the constant backdrop to our family life. His bosses and colleagues were people like A. R. Mosher, Pat Conroy, and Silby Barrett, the wise and colourful Newfoundlander from District 26 of the United Mineworkers in Cape Breton. I don't recall ever meeting Silby, but he remains a voice of conscience for me to this day. Whenever I see someone being wooed by the rich and powerful, I can hear Dad's voice quoting him: "When dem fellers starts to slap me on de back, den I knows it's time for de workers to kick me in de pants."

Throughout his Congress years, my father was writing up a storm. In articles and letters, he addressed a whole range of labour and constitutional issues, attacking Liberal government policies and promoting the socialist project of an economy "planned from the bottom." He did as much work as he could for the CCF, running as a candidate for the Ontario legislature in 1945, and twice for Parliament a few years later. Each time, he ran in a riding where the CCF had not the slightest chance of success, and each time, accordingly, he was roundly defeated.

The "Forsey Foursome," Harriet, Eugene, Margaret, and Helen, Ottawa, 1952.

Although he now lived in Ontario, he maintained close ties with people and events in Quebec through labour and academic connections as well as the growing political movement of civil liberties and opposition to Premier Duplessis. Dad's interests in all these areas overlapped with those of a young Montreal lawyer, Pierre Elliott Trudeau, whom he first met in 1950 at the annual meeting of the Institut canadien des affaires publiques.

The 50s was a decade of both expansion and consolidation for Dad. In 1953, he went to Mysore, India, as one of the directors of a World University Service seminar. The experience reinforced his sense of global solidarity, and brought our family a new circle of international friendships, some of which continue to this day. Two years later, a convention of the International Confederation of Free Trade Unions took him to Vienna, where he once again revelled in the richness of a European milieu, altered though it was by the ravages of war. "I wish you were here," he wrote to my mother, "although you might find me too addicted to walking ... The gardens and parks are superb, with magnificent vistas. But the ruins!"

In 1956, the CCL amalgamated with its erstwhile rival, the Trades and Labour Congress. Dad had long since proven himself an asset to the labour movement, and the new Canadian Labour Congress kept him as its research director. According to the late Dawn Dobson, his new secretary at the time, he was "invaluable" — and as a consequence, terribly overworked.

Meanwhile, events were conspiring to give Eugene Forsey a higher profile in the political arena. During the infamous Pipeline Debate in Parliament in June of 1956, he again distinguished himself as a critic to be reckoned with, someone who would attack and not let go if anyone tried trifling with Canadian democracy.

This time it was Louis St. Laurent's Liberal government, and my father's public interventions on the issue may well have helped sway the electorate away from the Liberals in the 1957 election. Before that campaign began, an appreciative John Diefenbaker had offered Dad a "safe" Conservative nomination. As a loyal CCFer, Dad had turned it down. Still, when the results came in, he rejoiced in the defeat of his Liberal antagonists, who, he felt, had finally got the come-uppance they deserved.

In 1958, the new Diefenbaker government set up Canada's first independent governing body for radio and television, the Board of Broadcast Governors (BBG), the forerunner of today's Canadian

Radio-television and Telecommunications Commission (CRTC). Dad's appointment to the BBG was memorable in my young mind because it triggered the purchase of our first TV. Over the next four years, he and his colleagues worked to lay the foundation for the standards and systems that would guide the burgeoning Canadian broadcasting industry into the future. Typically, his resignation from the BBG in 1962 was over a matter of principle: the board's refusal to grant the CBC a French-language television licence in Quebec City.

Through much of the 1950s and 60s, my father took an active part in public debates on the emerging "crisis in education." As a parent and citizen, he found the so-called "progressive" approaches being promoted by American educational pundits appallingly misguided. He believed they signalled a wholesale lowering of educational standards that would have disastrous consequences for Canada's future economy and for democracy itself. His speeches and articles on the subject, peppered with phrases like "mental baby food," "fake experts," and "tomfoolery," immersed him in yet another cauldron of the hot water he was already so accustomed to.

Despite the controversies and debates, Eugene Forsey's first two decades in Ottawa were nonetheless a period of relative stability in his professional and political life. That was about to change.

When Arthur Meighen died in 1960, Dad lost the beloved friend and mentor who in many ways had replaced the father he had never known. I now believe this loss represented a much greater personal crisis for my father than I ever suspected at the time.

Almost immediately afterwards, he faced a second major loss when the CCF dissolved to form the New Democratic Party in 1961. A number of factors led to his break with the NDP at its founding convention, but the main issue for him was the party's futile effort to woo Quebec voters by adopting what amounted to a "two nations" theory of Canada. Such a policy went against Dad's most cherished beliefs and hopes for the country he loved, and he just "couldn't stomach it."

That split marked a turning point in his life. Up until then, despite various disagreements, he had been staunchly and explicitly a CCFer. Now, he had officially parted company with his political comrades of thirty years.

Although he retained strong bonds of fellowship and mutual respect with many of them, there was no denying his sense of loss.

My father never abandoned his fundamental commitment to the principles of social and economic justice that had inspired the CCF. But after 1961, the socialist aspect of his political identity began to fade from the public's view, to be gradually replaced by a more conventional perception of a constitutional *eminence grise*.

In the years that followed his break with the NDP, he turned his political energies away from partisan politics and towards the very problem that had caused him to abandon it. Canadian unity became, for him, the overarching priority. His articles and speeches were increasingly devoted to the cause of keeping Canada together. Though other issues were still important to him, he framed them within that perspective. He maintained that if the country were to break up, or if the role of the national government were drastically reduced, then even the best of plans for social or economic progress would be "just waste paper."

Whether coincidentally or not, his academic career now began to take off again. Since being forced to leave McGill twenty years before, he had continued to write learned articles for scholarly journals on constitutional and labour matters, and had done some teaching on Canadian government in the political science department of Carleton College (which became Carleton University in 1956). But it wasn't until 1962 that he was really welcomed — I cannot even say "welcomed back" — into the fold of academic respectability. In that year, the University of New Brunswick gave him his first honourary degree, the Canadian Political Science Association elected him president, and he began a year at Queen's University on a Skelton-Clark fellowship.

His time in Kingston gave him some respite from the pressures of his job with the CLC, and from tensions that had arisen at home, mainly over religion, after my sister and I hit our teens. He rented a cozy apartment near the Queen's campus, and set out to complete the book on cabinet government that he had begun at Harvard two decades earlier. But, once again, he was unable to accomplish what he hoped, for he fell ill and had to undergo surgery for kidney stones. He subsequently kept a comparative tally of his series of kidney stone operations and his growing collection of honourary degrees, and for years delighted in pointing out that the two were running neck and neck.

Back in Ottawa in 1963, his Congress employers had a new proposal for him. The CLC was to produce a comprehensive history of the Canadian labour movement to mark Canada's centennial, and they asked him to do it. He was not very keen to take on this enormous task, but there seemed to be no one else available who could do it. So he spent the next six years as the CLC's "Director of Special Projects," "buried," as he put it, "in 19th century trade union history, [in] a state of almost total ignorance of almost — not quite — everything else."[7]

The ignorance he claimed, however, was not apparent to other people. He was more in demand than ever as a speaker, panelist, and media commentator on a whole range of political events. The Ontario government named him to its Advisory Committee on Confederation, where he tirelessly advocated a mutually respectful but no-nonsense approach to the challenge of Canadian unity. Carleton University advanced him from sessional lecturer status to the more exalted rank of visiting professor. And of course he kept on writing — articles, speeches, reviews and critiques, and a constant stream of letters to individuals and to the press.

It was during this time that he got involved in the Église Unie Saint-Marc, a French-language Protestant church in Ottawa. Christianity for Dad had always been a source of renewal and strength, which he felt he sorely needed. Joining Saint-Marc's tiny, struggling congregation was also a further way for him to practise much of what he preached: his support for bilingualism; his solidarity with linguistic and religious minorities; and his belief in the essential unity of the spiritual, cultural and political realms. He remained active in Saint-Marc for the rest of his life, serving variously as steward, elder, and treasurer, and as lay minister when the regular pastor was away.

Meanwhile, my sister and I were growing up and moving out on our own, freeing our parents from the intensive day-to-day commitment that younger children and adolescents demand. Mum took advantage of this new freedom by returning to part-time supply teaching, and actually bought a car — the first our family ever had. She and Dad were also able now to do some travelling together, and they did, with trips to Newfoundland and England, where they saw old friends and pursued their common interest in the histories of their respective families.

Early in the spring of 1968, I returned from two years with Canadian University Service Overseas (CUSO) in Ecuador to find Dad enthused about the decision of his old friend Pierre Trudeau to run for leader of the federal Liberals. He was keenly aware of the irony of getting publicly involved in the leadership campaign of a party he had worked for decades to defeat, but he went ahead anyway and threw his support behind Trudeau.

"Choosing a Liberal leader," he wrote, "might seem to be no business of a rank outsider who has never voted Liberal in his life. But whoever becomes Liberal leader will promptly also become Prime Minister of Canada. So perhaps even rank outsiders have a right to say who they hope the Liberals will choose. I hope it will be Pierre Elliott Trudeau."[8]

The reason? Because "on the biggest question that faces Canada today — the question of keeping it Canada and making it the Canada of all Canadians — [Trudeau] is, I think, completely and profoundly right."[9] The issue of national unity, which had caused Dad to distance himself from his friends and allies in the NDP, was now drawing him inexorably closer to his perennial adversaries, the Liberals.

In 1969, my father turned 65 and retired from the CLC, having brought the monumental labour history manuscript up to 1902 in draft form. He continued to work on the book, preparing it for publication (a process which took another decade!) while casting about for possible academic work. The University of Waterloo offered him a one-year position as visiting professor in political science and history, which he began in September 1970. One month later, Prime Minister Trudeau appointed him to the Senate.

There he was at last — a member of Canada's Parliament, the institution he had studied, loved and fought for all his life. He had practically grown up on Parliament Hill, and now he was in his element. Despite what some of his social democrat friends still thought of the Senate, he welcomed the unique opportunity it gave him to continue his work for the common good. His appointment was a validation of much of what he had already accomplished and attempted, and at the same time a recognition of how much he still had to contribute. It was as if he had finally come home.

The new Senator Forsey dove right into his parliamentary duties, although for the rest of the academic year he had to commute between Waterloo and Ottawa. In October, in his first Senate speech, he managed to address the issues of unemployment and national unity, the responsibilities of Parliament's upper house, and the dilemmas surrounding the recently-invoked War Measures Act.[10] That maiden speech — comprehensive, genial, and provocative at the same time — foreshadowed the kind of role he would play throughout his time on the Hill.

The role of Honourable Senator embodied all of Dad's public personae at once: the economist, the social reformer, the historian, the trade unionist, the writer, the gad-fly, the civil liberties activist, the constitutionalist — along with the humourist, the gracious host, the raconteur, and the old-fashioned gentleman. In the Senate, he could be himself in a way that would have been impossible in the House of Commons. Although officially he sat as a Liberal in order to show his support for Trudeau's national unity stand, no party whip snapped at his heels demanding conformity. He actually ended up voting against the government more often than he supported it.

Dad's nine years in the Senate gave him the chance to do the kind of work he did so well: raising all sorts of issues — often highly controversial ones; highlighting their importance to ordinary people; examining them in committee; and speaking about them from a platform of established respectability. He took on everything from national unity to public purchases of modern art, from post-secondary education to the mechanisms of parliamentary democracy, from back-to-work legislation to foreign sales of Candu nuclear reactors. And he did it all in his own unique way — even, on occasion, in song!

When the Joint Committee (Senate and House of Commons) on Regulations and Other Statutory Instruments was established early in 1973, he was elected co-chair. It was a complex and demanding job which he retained until his retirement from the Senate more than six years later. From that position, he put the fear of God into various cock-sure bureaucrats, politicians, and Justice Department officials who had ignored regulations or tried to act as if they were above the law. He also sat on two special joint committees on the Constitution, faithfully carrying out his accustomed duties as official de-bunker of what he termed "constitutional fairy tales."

He was busy with other commitments as well. In 1973, he became chancellor of Trent University in Peterborough, a largely honourary position, which he nonetheless relished as a continuing link to the academic milieu. In 1974, he published a collection of his constitutional essays, entitled *Freedom and Order*. He was still working at fine-tuning the labour history opus, with its copious footnotes and index, and he continued writing and speaking on the constitution, national unity, and other social and political issues.

This period was also marked by milestones in his personal and family life. In the same year that he became a senator, he and Harriet became grandparents, with the birth of my son Rodrigo, soon followed by a second grandson, Eugene. Dad delighted in his role as "Grampa," even though he had to perform it at a distance for a few years while we were living overseas. It was during this time that my mother began to suffer from Parkinson's disease, which would gradually cripple her as the years passed. We came home from Ecuador in 1974 to find her coping with minor but advancing symptoms.

Dad was still quite robust himself, though he endured several more kidney stone attacks, each with its attendant surgery (and the corresponding honourary degree.) But Mum's deteriorating health put him under increasing stress, as did the disintegration of my marriage, which involved him in some delicate interventions on behalf of his beloved grandsons.

In May of 1979, he reached the Senate's mandatory retirement age of seventy-five. This occasioned a great foofaraw of tributes, special events, and media interviews. I caught up with him in a brief moment between two of these engagements. "I don't think I'm going to retire again," he told me. "It's too exhausting!"

Even this second retirement, though, scarcely registered as more than a minor blip on the graph of Dad's working life. He was soon ensconced in a room in the downtown law office of his friend Graham Eglington, where he continued to write and to field numerous requests for information, advice, articles, speeches, and his famous "illegal legal opinions."[11] He was consulted so often by governments, political parties, and bureaucrats, that the Senate soon gave him a small office on the Hill — something previously unheard-of for a retired senator.

Eugene and Harriet, Ottawa, 1980s.

In 1982, he resigned from the Liberal Party, tried beyond endurance by what he found to be its high-handedness and its increasingly dismal performance on many fronts. Asked in an interview what his party affiliation was now, he replied, "I should think, none. I feel myself perfectly free to applaud or criticize any of them."[12]

There was certainly no shortage of things for him to pronounce on. The 1980 Quebec referendum was quickly followed by the repatriation of the Constitution; then came the election of the Mulroney government, the resurrection of the Quebec separation debate, and, eventually, the Meech Lake proposals, which he spent three years combatting.

On the home front, Dad suffered deeply as he watched my mother's increasing pain and debility. Soon after his retirement, they moved out of the house in Ottawa's Glebe neighbourhood where my sister and I grew up, and into a nearby apartment building. For the next several years, they managed to cope fairly well, thanks to professional home nursing care for Mum, but by 1986 she was totally disabled and had to go into a chronic care hospital. This was heartbreaking for Dad, but the doctors warned him that if he tried to go on caring for her at home, he would likely succumb himself. Indeed, his own health was getting shaky, and early in 1988 he had a triple heart by-pass operation. His recovery was slow, and ten months later he had a minor relapse. He was actually in hospital again when my mother died.

It hit him very hard. In the midst of his devastation, close friends in British Columbia persuaded him to go out and stay the winter with them there, to rest, to grieve, and begin to heal.

"Now I cannot say 'we' any more," he wrote in a general letter from Victoria in March 1989. "Harriet died, November 15th last, after eighteen years of Parkinson's disease ... I realize more and more how much I owed to her, and ... how much she was the centre of my life. When I get back to Ottawa it will come home to me even more vividly, as the hour comes each day when, if we were both well enough, I'd go to the hospital to see her ... Harriet would have been 83 in January, and on November 9 we had been married 53 years."

But even now, his country called to him, and he moved beyond his grief and his physical frailty to respond. The Meech Lake Accord was threatening to decentralize the Canadian federation irreversibly and beyond recognition, and Dad threw himself into the fight against it. Once again, he found himself making speeches, going on radio and television, and appearing before legislative committees. In addition, as he told his friends, "My bad temper keeps me spluttering to the newspapers over the nonsense that so often appears in them."[13] The demise of the Accord in June of 1990 was a huge relief to him, as was the completion and publication of his reminiscences, *A Life on the Fringe*, which actually became a non-fiction best-seller.

Dad's final years brought him numerous public honours including being named a Companion of the Order of Canada and a member of the Privy Council. But the recognition that undoubtedly meant the most to him came in November 1990 when the Government of Newfoundland established a scholarship in his name.

After Christmas that year, he left Ottawa again for Victoria, with its gentle climate and the gentle care of his friends. Two months later, his valiant heart gave out at last, and he slipped away.

My father's own judgment on his life's work was not a particularly laudatory one. When asked why he had accepted the appointment to the Senate after refusing other job offers from Prime Minister Trudeau, he replied, "Because

I thought I could be some use there. And without over-praising myself, I think I was."[14] Often, though, he was despondent about his achievements. "I have accomplished nothing of any real value," he wrote in 1989. "In a variant of a phrase which has been applied to Rhodes scholars generally, I am 'an old man with a brilliant future behind him.'"[15]

But I believe the significance of Eugene Forsey's life and thought goes well beyond his own humble assessment. He had his faults, and there were gaps in his world view, but no one who knew him doubted his ability, his integrity, or the strength of his commitment to the common good. Whatever one may think of the particular positions he took, the fact that he engaged so vigorously and thoughtfully in the issues of the day sets an example for all of us as citizens of this country and the world.

CHAPTER TWO

Striving for Grace: An Ethical and Spiritual Framework

> In spite of doubts and waverings, I believe in God.... I don't know how one can get along without some belief in love and truth and beauty and goodness. They seem to me just as real as any physical facts.... I don't see how, apart from belief in God, one can find any ground for the belief in the basic equality of human beings, which, for me, lies at the root of democracy, opposition to racial discrimination, and efforts for any kind of social betterment.
> — From a 1963 letter to my mother[1]

There is not the slightest doubt in my mind that the prime motivating force behind my father's lifetime of work for justice and democracy was his religious faith. To do justice to his legacy, then, I must begin with what he saw as the foundation of everything he stood for. In doing so I will try to honour his beliefs and the faith-full living they inspired, while leaving room — as he also did — for other perspectives, including my own.

The spiritual foundation of Eugene Forsey's life was his steadfast belief in a power beyond the merely human, and the striving for right relationship which embodied that faith. Everything of importance to him rested on that foundation, from his early condemnations of capitalism to the difficult political choices he made in later years, from the delight he took in the wonders of nature to the loving guidance he gave his young grandsons.

In the process of reviewing and reflecting on his religious and ethical principles, I have found much that resonates with my own understandings, and have gained fresh insights into his. The Christian tradition he was raised in shaped the language and images he used to express his values, and they were very important to him. But as he also knew, those values extend far beyond the boundaries of any one religion, and can be found among people of all creeds and of none.

My father's upbringing combined the religious and moral values of his Methodist, Anglican, and Quaker ancestors with an intense interest in secular politics. In the home where he grew up, the practical ethics of public and private life were taken as seriously as church attendance and prayer.

In partisan terms, the Bowles and Forsey families were avowedly Conservative. But theirs was a conservatism that embraced fairness and compassion, social responsibility and citizen involvement — a far cry from the creed of "each one for himself and devil take the hindmost" that has recently become associated with that formerly honourable label. In the discussions that flowed around the dining room table at the old house on Lisgar Street, ethical considerations were a constant element.

As an undergraduate at McGill in the 1920s, Dad applied that compassionate ethic to the economic and political realities he was studying — and found them wanting. The more he learned, the more critical he became. That process was catalyzed and guided by radicals like his minister, Allworth Eardley, and his professor, J. C. Hemmeon, both of whom influenced him profoundly with their reasoned arguments about injustice and their passionate commitment to doing something about it.

Although Dad later described his youthful transformation from conservative to socialist as largely "an intellectual process of conversion,"[2] there was more to it than that. While I wouldn't presume to call it a religious experience exactly, it certainly had everything to do with an ethically based view of the world.

The time he spent in Cape Breton gathering material for his master's thesis on the coal industry there played a significant role in the shift. Historian David Millar, who conducted a series of in-depth interviews with him in 1970, sees that journey as having been "a return to roots." It reconnected my father not only to his Nova Scotian heritage but also in a sense to his native Newfoundland, with its poverty-stricken outports and its wealthy merchants who, in Millar's words, "bought and sold human lives."

I don't know to what extent Dad may have thought at the time about a class analysis or his own place within it. On the one hand, his Newfoundland family was part of the privileged merchant class, though they now earned their living, not in business, but in government service and professions — magistrate, teacher, nurse, postmistress, clergyman. The same was true of the family on his mother's side. Certainly a sense of moral responsibility, perhaps infused with a touch of *noblesse oblige*, was a strong element in his background. Moreover, he had been brought up to revere the example of his dead father, who had sacrificed his health in the service of others in the isolated fishing communities of the island's Southwest Coast.

In the mining communities of Cape Breton in 1926, the young Eugene Forsey witnessed first-hand the phenomena of institutionalized injustice, cruelty, and greed. This experience, combined with the radicalizing influences of his undergraduate years, nudged him further towards socialism. "He was finally seeing the whole regime of exploitation, exactly how it works," Millar reflected years later. "When you see that in person, well ... It set him aflame, and he stayed aflame the rest of his life."

Given the religious foundations of my father's evolving world view, it is not surprising that the socialism he adopted was closely linked to a liberating concept of Christianity. "It was very much the British Labour Party type of thing," he explained to Millar, "and a good deal of it drew its inspiration from the churches. Sometimes the people concerned had had a strong church bringing-up, like Frank Scott; sometimes they were actual ministers, like King Gordon, Gregory Vlastos. Some were people like myself, professing

Christians; some were people like Woodsworth, who I think got a great deal of the inspiration for his political and economic and social views from his religious background, but whose religious opinions I think became more and more nebulous. That was a very strong factor in the thing."[3]

A strong factor indeed, to an extent that many nowadays might find surprising. But at the time, the connection was unremarkable. Perhaps with the exception of the Communist Party, much of the early socialist movement in Canada had religious roots. Both the League for Social Reconstruction and the CCF had strong church linkages, and several of the other socialist groups Dad was involved with were explicitly Christian: the Student Christian Movement, the Fellowship for a Christian Social Order, and the Committee on Social and Economic Research of the Montreal Presbytery of the United Church. My father was only one of many progressive Christians for whom it simply made no sense to separate politics from religion. The institutions of church and state needed to be separate, of course, but at the level of thinking and action, the moral had to be linked to the political.

In Dad's view, the concept of democracy itself was grounded in religion.

"Logically and historically," he declared, "democracy is a religious conception and a religious creation. Democracy implies a belief in essential human equality. But the physical, biological, psychological facts are all against such a belief. Manifestly, human beings are not equal in physical strength, in beauty, in intellect; equality is nonsense. The only possible source for the idea of human equality is a conviction that, in spite of all the obvious inequalities, all are equal in importance ... That conviction is a religious conviction. Religiously speaking, equality is not nonsense but truth."[4]

Coming from this perspective, my father naturally had a lot to say about the role of the church in addressing the worldly concerns of the socialist and labour movements. His chapters on economics in *Towards the Christian Revolution* begin with the assertion that "the field of religion is the whole of life," and he meant it very literally.[5] For him, the intertwined realms of religion, spirituality, and ethics were not only relevant but essential to the day-to-day realities of the material world.

"The Church is concerned with the whole of life, individual and social. It cannot sign a treaty of partition leaving politics and economics to the devil ... Christian character is forged in the struggles of daily life, and most of the daily life of most people is spent in the struggle to satisfy economic wants ... Jesus did not say, 'Man does not live by bread,' he said, 'by bread *alone*' ... The Church must be concerned with the economic *because* it is concerned with the spiritual."[6]

Once those connections were acknowledged, how then, he argued, could anyone in good conscience continue to support an economic system which "forces us to spend most of our waking hours in ways which thwart and deny everything Christianity stands for"?[7]

"Capitalism has its own beatitudes," he wrote. "They are not those of the Sermon on the Mount ... Nothing could be more explicit than [Jesus'] warnings: 'Ye cannot serve God and Mammon'; 'The deceitfulness of riches and the cares of this world choke the good seed'; 'How hardly shall they that have riches enter into the Kingdom of Heaven!' We have 'spiritualized' these sayings ... but Jesus insisted on his inversion of the conventional idea, driving it home with a touch of grim humour: 'With God all things are possible' — *even* the salvation of a rich man!"[8]

However, despite his denunciation of the evils of "riches," my father refused to personalize the social and economic problems he was addressing. In fact, he thought the tendency to pin the blame on individuals could actually sabotage social change by allowing people to side-step the need for structural transformation.

> To see the problem in terms of "good" people and "bad" people is to rule out the possibility of solution. It is the qualities or defects of a system, not of individuals, which are in question. A capitalist who does not cater to money demand, regardless of "need," will cease to be a capitalist. A capitalist whose firm finds its gross income reduced must economize or make way for someone who will ... The firm is in business to pay dividends ... A humane general manager may pace the floor in anguish, night after sleepless night, but he cannot escape his fate. A flock of archangels administering our present economic system would probably produce very much the same state of affairs.[9]

These were not merely the musings of a 1930s radical. Half a century later, American activist and author Jerry Mander made an almost identical argument in his 1991 book *In the Absence of the Sacred*. In a chapter entitled "Corporations as Machines," Mander describes the "inherent rules" governing corporate behaviour. He explains how "managers are legally obliged to ignore community welfare — e.g. worker health and satisfaction, environmental concerns — if those needs interfere with profitability ... If someone attempted to revolt against these tenets, it would only result in the corporation throwing the person out, and replacing [them] with another who would act according to the rules."[10]

My father's insistence on the systemic nature of injustice, however, did not mean he absolved the individual of social responsibility. He believed that each person chooses the degree to which he or she participates in an unjust system or, alternatively, works to change it. In fact, this was the basis of his own lifelong political activism — a strong sense of personal responsibility to do his part in serving the common good.

It was his firm belief that religious and civic duty went well beyond mere pious pronouncements. In the early 1930s, he and other members pushed the United Church to adopt a series of progressive resolutions on social and economic issues. After long and bitter internal debate, the resolutions were finally adopted, but Dad was still skeptical, wondering if the church would really take the actions being called for, or fall back on general statements and platitudes.

During the Depression, when he denounced Quebec's Duplessis government, municipal authorities, and the Catholic Church hierarchy for their denial of basic freedoms, his outrage was based on moral as well as on political grounds. The same was true for his lengthy struggle against the Padlock Law and other manifestations of the "clerical fascism"[11] that ruled the province throughout that time.

His writings on these subjects were an attempt to break through the wall of ignorance and indifference that kept Quebec's troubles on the margins of public consciousness in most of the rest of the country. They consisted largely of factual reports, documenting one outrage after another for an English-language readership. One case he described was that of an unemployed French-Canadian carpenter named Lessard, who had been sentenced to two years in jail for cutting the government's padlock off the door of his own house.

"And our provincial government, which never tires of boasting of its pure and unimpeachable Catholicism, gives the Communists an object lesson in Christian charity by cutting Lessard's wife and children off relief because of the 'ideology' ascribed to the husband and father."[12]

Dad's audiences were often predominantly Christian, and he sometimes framed the social and economic problems he was addressing in religious terms, making the same links which had proved so powerful in his own political evolution. In a 1945 talk to a church-based group, he took this approach on the challenges facing the labour movement in the post-war period.

> Freedom and equality are fundamental Christian doctrines. This means that the baby in the slum is as important as the baby in the prosperous residential neighbourhood; that discrimination on account of sex, race, or creed is utterly contrary to the Christian Gospel; that "in Christ there is neither barbarian nor Scythian, Jew nor Greek, male nor female, bond nor free." It means also that these affirmations must not be left as mere affirmations, but must be translated into social reality ... such things as equal pay for equal work, the end of any discrimination against the employment of married women, the abolition of slums and sweat-shops, the provision of decent housing, decent food and clothing, decent education and adequate recreational facilities for all citizens.[13]

With or without the religious terminology, he kept coming back to essentially moral arguments. His campaigns against repressive labour legislation during his Congress years were rooted in concepts of justice and equality. When Joey Smallwood's provincial government imposed draconian anti-union legislation on Newfoundland's workers during the 1959 loggers' strike, Dad wrote a passionate piece for the *United Church Observer*: "The two Acts raise issues fundamental to the Christian, for both deny a basic freedom and a basic principle of natural justice. The basic freedom is freedom of association. The basic principle is the right to a fair hearing ... What mystifies and wounds me is not that people have attacked these acts, but that members of our own church, bred in the tradition of the Methodist

Church whose local preachers, from Christian conviction, largely built the British trade union movement, can be found to defend them."[14]

Fighting such travesties was not only my father's job, it was his passion. That same passion fueled his energy for the many other causes he took on over the years, from his defence of the rights of linguistic minorities to his growing concern for the environment and the Third World.

In 1979, he attended the annual meetings of two of Canada's largest banks to ask for an embargo on loans to South Africa, whose people were still struggling under the cruel yoke of apartheid.[15] After countering several of the arguments the banks put forward, he continued: "Oh, but surely many states are more or less repressive; surely we can't discriminate amongst them, saying 'yes' to this one and 'no' to that?' I think we can. All men are sinners, but not all are criminals, and we manage to distinguish pretty well between them for practical purposes. I think we can do that pretty well among nations too, by applying 'the commonplace quality of common sense.'"[16]

There was a similar, though less obvious, moral basis for Dad's opposition to the plethora of misguided constitutional proposals which plagued his later years. His tireless efforts on this front were motivated by his determination to maintain a workable and truly democratic system of government, in order to ensure fair treatment for all citizens and to foster a greater collective capacity for solving the problems we face.

His characteristic integration of the religious with the political came through clearly in a 1977 speech to Toronto's Empire Club on "Canada, Quebec and the Constitution": "Because this is such an important question, such a vital question, one that goes so deeply into the whole life of Canada, and in the long run, of every Canadian citizen, ... I feel it has to be dealt with in a spirit of humility, a prayerful spirit, I hope also a thoughtful spirit. I don't think a prayerful spirit excludes the use of our minds. 'Thou shalt love the Lord thy God with all thy heart and with all thy mind, and with all thy soul, and thy neighbour as thyself.'"

That was the spirit he tried to bring to all his work.

My father elaborated, in French, on his understanding of God in a sermon he preached, in French, at Ottawa's Église Saint-Marc, the small French-language United Church that was his home parish from the 1960s on.

LOVING OUR NEIGHBOUR
(From "Our Present Discontents," Acadia University, Wolfville, Nova Scotia, 1967[17])

Christian love is not witless amiability, or absolute unselfishness. "Thou shalt love the Lord thy God with all thy mind"; or, as our French Protestant Bible says, "*Tu aimeras l'Eternel ton Dieu … avec toute ta pensée,*" all thy thought. "And the second commandment is like unto it: thou shalt love thy neighbour as thyself," "*comme toi-même.*"

If, then, our love of our neighbour is to be "like unto" our love of God, it must be a love in which we use our minds, in which we think; and if we are to love our neighbours as ourselves, we must love ourselves, respect ourselves. We must will the good of our neighbour, which involves using our heads to discover what that good is.

This does not, of course, mean that we must proceed to impose on him what we think is good for him. But neither does it mean that we must incessantly, instantaneously, invariably, give him anything he happens to take it into his head to want. Nor does it mean that if he dislikes our faces, we must undergo plastic surgery. That would not be Christianity, just appeasement.

If our ethic is simply to give our neighbour everything he fancies, if his mere likes and dislikes become our rule of conduct, the only result can be the flight of reason from human affairs, the triumph of the egotistical, the grasping, the brutal; and, in the life of the community, the dictatorship of whoever can shout the loudest, or shake the biggest fist, or make the biggest nuisance of himself.

"In the beginning was the Word." The Greek word is "logos," meaning "reason." Our faith, then, is based on reason, not on magic. Obviously, it transcends human reason. But it is not an irrational faith, much less anti-rational. God is Reason.

Then there is God the Creator, who made the entire universe — infinitely great, infinitely varied, beyond our understanding or imagination — who gives us life, light, intelligence, the knowledge of good and evil, and the capacity to choose between the two.

But all that is only the prologue to the prodigious affirmation that this Creator Word is also the Word of salvation, the Word made flesh, who lived among us. God is Love.

What a majestic and moving concept! For most of the Greeks and Jews — as for many so-called intellectuals of our time — unbelievable, even ridiculous. Think about it: the Creator of the universe, who offers us his marvellous love; who comes to us, becomes one of us; who lives our life, with its joys, its sorrows, its trials, its pains, its blessings; who rejoices with us, is tempted like us and more than us; who suffers like us, with us, more than us, and for us; who gives his life for us, as the ultimate proof of his true humanity, his unity with us; who is resurrected for us, who triumphs for us, and gives us the power to triumph like him and with him.[18]

That was the God my father worshipped — a deity embodying all the values he cherished and strove for. That God was so real to him, and so essential to his very life, that when people he loved showed doubt or indifference, it troubled him profoundly.

Probably the most comprehensive and certainly the most passionately personal of Dad's writings on these matters was a twenty-seven-page letter he wrote to my mother over the winter he spent in Kingston in 1962–63. It was an attempt to bridge the gap that had been growing between them over religion. He was deeply distressed by the fact that his beloved Harriet was increasingly questioning the understandings and practices of conventional churches, while my sister and I were asserting our adolescent independence and ignoring religion almost entirely.

It's not that he was intolerant; he was actually very open to other people's differing beliefs. But with those closest to him, the differences bothered him intensely. He defined his own most fundamental values in religious terms, and he had trouble conceiving of them in any other way. I think he felt that if his wife and children did not define things in those same terms, then we had no spiritual anchor for our lives at all. That saddened and worried him, making him fear for our ability to withstand the slings and arrows that would inevitably come our way.

His long epistle from Kingston came out of months of agonized soul-searching as he tried to clarify what he did and did not believe, acknowledge what he saw as his many failings, and begin to respond to Mum's doubts and challenges.

> I believe in a God Who is our Father: good, kind, loving, wise. "For the love of God is broader than the measure of man's mind, and the heart of the Eternal is most wonderfully kind."
>
> This, however, is not the whole story; by itself, it can easily become just a sloshy "He's a good Fellow, and 'twill all come right…." God wants our love, but he also sets before us standards, and makes demands that we aim at those standards.
>
> This is where "sin" comes in. Sin is failing to hit the target, coming short of the glory of God. Sin is imperfection, which necessarily touches us all … Few have the hardihood to say they are perfect, but I dare say a good many feel that "sin" means something altogether atrocious. Of course sin can mean atrocious acts, but that's not the whole of it, or perhaps the most important part.
>
> Jesus seems to have been singularly unimpressed by the atrocious or obvious sins … What he was severe on was the shortcomings of the respectable, the "good" people, who not only felt they had committed no sins, but were proud of their "goodness" … Pride, self-righteousness, indifference to the needs of others, lack of humility, an unforgiving spirit — these were the sins he castigated, the sins that killed him, as they have killed, quickly or slowly, millions since.

These were also the kinds of "sins" Dad accused himself of in that same letter: folly, insensitivity, laziness, timidity, vanity, selfishness, and much else. He explored the questions of guilt and individual responsibility for wrong-doing, arguing that even after all other applicable explanations — physical, social, psychological, and so forth — had been taken into account, the personal responsibility still remained.

"Here again is where Christianity comes in," he wrote, "with, it seems to me, a sensible and realistic message. It doesn't say, soothingly, 'Never mind, it's all just perfectly natural; don't worry about it.' It says, '*Do* mind; even if it is all perfectly natural, it's not the *whole* of your nature; you're not just a helpless, inert victim of circumstances; you *are* guilty. But you don't need to go through life crushed by guilt. Jesus has told you, and shown you, how to get rid of it.'"

For him, this whole question of personal responsibility was a central religious issue, and one he applied relentlessly to himself.

"Our wrong-doing, or failure in right-doing, injures or breaks our relationship with God and with other people. How can we restore those relationships? I have to be sorry for my wrong-doing ('penitence'); I have to face it, admit it, be honest about it ('confession'); I have to do what I can to undo the harm I have done ('restitution'). These are the necessary conditions for restoring the right relation with God and with other people ('forgiveness'). There is no magic about it, and it isn't easy or cheap."

Dad was never one to deny his own wrong-doing; his tendency was actually in the other direction. Self-recrimination filled many of his other letters, not only to my mother, but to his dear friend Arthur Meighen and, later, to me. Mr. Meighen, bless his heart, gave a perfect answer to one of these missives: "First of all," he wrote back, "do not presume for a minute that I accept your far too modest estimate of yourself. How did you ever get seized with the hallucination that you were afflicted with laziness? Really, in my entire life I do not know of anyone so free of that infirmity. Also, I do not for a moment agree that you have mismanaged your life...."[19]

But those comforting words did not stop my father from judging himself harshly. He set very high standards for himself, and blamed himself bitterly for not meeting them. It was terribly hard for him to move beyond his deep remorse over what he considered his sins, and in my heart I understand that pain. At the same time, my mind wonders whether his particular way of interpreting Christianity may have tended to reinforce his unrealistic perfectionism, obscuring a less judgmental interpretation of his creed.

Yet, in other respects, his religion offered him great hope and support. Believing firmly that "regeneration can only come from the spirit,"[20] he sought it through the church, drawing strength, guidance, and inspiration from its fellowship and teachings.

In the early 1960s, when his neighbourhood church was undergoing changes and his family was growing more distant in religious terms, he transferred his affiliation to the francophone congregation of Église Saint-Marc. From then on, he made the struggling little church one of his major priorities, attending worship every Sunday, contributing financially, serving as both an elder and a steward, and often filling in when the regular minister was away, planning and conducting the full service in French.

In a 1965 letter to me, he tried to help me understand the support the church gave him and the responsibility he felt in return.

> I know I need all the help I can get from associating with other Christians. It is possible that I can give others some help, too, by turning up [at church], and by accepting other responsibilities. I don't think a solitary Christianity is likely to be very stable.
>
> It seems to me clear that if there were no church, the things [we] believe in and hold important would long ago have been lost in a welter of materialism on the one hand, and sheer superstition — ancient or modern, savage or learned — on the other. It is the church which has preserved the faith. But if everybody had taken a casual attitude, or a merely individualist attitude, where would there have been any church?
>
> I feel I have a responsibility to do something to keep the church going. Attending is part of that responsibility — the only part, alas, that I discharged for many years. Assuming cheerfully that other people will keep things going seems to me highly irresponsible. That is why, at Saint-Marc, I agreed to become first a "syndic" [steward],

then an "ancien" [elder], though painfully aware of my own deficiencies.

Some years later, he wrote me again on the same subject, responding to my suggestion that surely the important thing was to practise the principles espoused by the churches, whether or not one participated in their services and activities.

> I am more and more convinced that mere devotion to, and practice of, "Christian principles" isn't enough. When tragedy strikes, or even lesser trials, one needs more ...
> A large part of the population has grown up, and is growing up, religiously illiterate; and I think this has a good deal to do with many of the problems that confront us. Our society is living largely by dipping into its religious and moral capital: that is, the best and most committed people in it are, though many of them don't recognize it, drawing their principles and their inspirations from the faith that the churches, however imperfect, have preserved.

During my protracted marriage break-up — what he called my "time of great trouble" — Dad told me how the church had pulled him through the most difficult periods of his own life. "I hope you can get from religion some of the staying power it has given me," he wrote, adding, characteristically, "It is my fault, of course, if you can't"!

He also urged me to help my sons get a good foundation of religious training. "They will need all the strength they can get," he said, "to cope with the problems they already face, let alone the huge, global problems that their generation, even more than yours, will have to cope with."

My father's moral and spiritual philosophy, despite what could be seen as its limitations, was far from joyless. Aware as he was of his own failings and of the "downside" of the human condition, he was equally aware of the potential for good. If Christianity formed a framework within which he often judged himself harshly, it also nurtured his love of life and shaped his compassionate world view. His belief in the reality of "love and truth and beauty and goodness" was identical with his belief in God, and that gave him hope and comfort when he most needed it.

He was also tremendously heartened by the rise of the ecumenical movement in the 1960s. His experience of Catholic authoritarianism in Duplessis's Quebec had reinforced his old-time Methodist prejudices and left him with a rather jaundiced view of the Roman Church. But with Pope John XXIII, the Second Vatican Council, and the growth of a progressive Catholicism in Quebec and elsewhere, he saw great hope for a reinvigorated and increasingly unified Christianity.[21]

Invited to speak at an ecumenical gathering, Dad called it "a great and moving occasion, which no one, only a very few years ago, would have thought possible." He took as his text Jesus's "new commandment" to his followers: "that ye love one another."

> Loving each other does not mean simply cultivating a warm, woolly feeling about each other. It does not mean glossing over differences, or pretending they are not there, or saying they don't matter. It does not mean searching for, or even finding, a face-saving formula, a pleasantly ambiguous compromise. Our churches are not commercial corporations trying to arrange a merger, or Great Powers trying to work out a cease-fire or a balance of power or a Common Market.
>
> Loving each other ... means getting to know each other, trying to understand each other's beliefs and traditions and feelings ... We are called to seek truth and follow it. We are called to zeal, not blandness. We are called to passionate devotion, not indifference. To heed these calls, and also to love each other, does not mean ignoring each other's mistakes and shortcomings, individual and collective; it means triumphing over them.[22]

No one could have accused my father of blandness or indifference. Nor did he ignore mistakes, his own or anyone else's, though he seldom felt he had triumphed over them. In the face of those failures, he looked to the Christian church for the strength to put his precepts into practice and carry on.

THE WEDDING OF DR. ALI
(From an unpublished segment of A Life on the Fringe[23]*)*

Mr. Ali was one of the two Moslem Indian men at the 1953 World University Service Seminar. I eventually helped to get him to the University of British Columbia, where he did his Ph.D.

Dr. Ali married a French-Canadian. She, of course, wanted to be married by a priest. Dr. Ali had no objection, but he had conscientious scruples about the actual ceremony. He consulted his fiancée's priest in Montreal, and they worked out a formula that satisfied them both ("I told the father I would not say things I didn't believe.") Then the priest had to get the archbishop's approval. He couldn't, and sadly telephoned to say so.

"So," Dr. Ali said to me as we were walking up Elgin Street in Ottawa, "I wrote to the pope."

I literally reeled against the wall of the then National Gallery. "You wrote to the pope?"

"Yes, I did."

"What did you say?"

"I told him his people were interfering with other people's conscientious rights, and he ought to stop it."

"Well, I never heard anything like that in my life."

"I didn't get any reply."

"I didn't suppose you would."

"But I did get action. A few weeks later, the priest called me to say, 'Dr. Ali, it's all right about that marriage ceremony. We've had word from Rome.'"

The pope of the time was John XXIII. From all I have read of that great and holy man, and all I have heard of him from my friend Archbishop Carew, formerly a domestic prelate at the Vatican under Pope John, I am convinced that the letter actually got to the pope himself, and that it touched his warm heart and his sense of humour. At any rate, the marriage took place as Dr. Ali and the priest had planned it.

Still, he never managed to really transcend the burden of remorse he carried for not having done more. "'By their fruits ye shall know them,'" he wrote to my mother, "and my 'fruits' are microscopic." I can't agree.

In and of itself, my father's personal code of ethics was fairly commonplace: honesty, love and compassion, fairness, simplicity, sharing. What was perhaps more unusual was how very seriously he took those principles, how hard he strove to "walk the talk."

In his private life, he adhered to the canons of his Methodist upbringing, renouncing swearing, gambling, sex outside of marriage, and inebriants such as alcohol. He didn't see any of these prohibitions as particularly restrictive. To him, they simply made sense as reasonable rules to live by, fully consistent with his other beliefs and priorities.

Take alcohol, for instance.

"The number of foolish things I've done when I've been cold sober horrify me," he told an interviewer. "What I would have done had I deliberately depressed my intelligence with alcohol I can't possibly imagine. We all know we can't park our brains on the shelf; well, we can't pickle them either. Drinking is irrational and we can't afford it." Then he laughed. "You remember Gandhi? He said there were three curses in India: drink, drugs, and the British."[24]

In a guest editorial for a small publication on alcohol and drug concerns, he enumerated further reasons — very political ones — for his teetotaler stance. "I do not want to risk becoming a slave to a chemical, or part of a major public health problem. I do not want to run the risk of endangering the lives of other people ... An enormous amount of money is spent on this dangerous drug when two-thirds of the world's population never get a square meal. Huge fortunes are being made out of this destructive traffic. I do not want to contribute to the profits of an industry which is responsible for so much waste, misery, horror, tragedy."[25]

He acknowledged that being a non-drinker wasn't the choice most people made, but as he told a meeting of young people in 1962, that didn't have to be a problem. With a twinkle in his eye, he urged them not to be afraid of being in a minority. "I've been in a minority of one kind or another all my life, and had a whale of a time at it," he said. "You may be the salt of the earth, preventing the society in which you live from going rotten."[26]

On questions of money, my father was fastidious to a fault. Sorting through his things after his death, I found a classic example of that scrupulousness: a little note he had scribbled to a Senate official when he was once again working from a parliamentary office six years after he had officially "retired":

> Dear Ron, I had a message today which involved my calling Toronto. I don't think the taxpayers should be paying for any long distance calls of mine. I'll be glad to reimburse the Treasury for this one. Henceforth, I'll use the pay telephone downstairs, and pay direct. Yours, Eugene Forsey.

As a teenager, my son Roddy had an after-school job as a waiter in a restaurant. He told me what happened when he mentioned to Dad that he was considering not declaring all his tips on his income tax return. "Grampa wanted to pay me the difference," he said. "He asked me to pay all my taxes, but he didn't want me to have less money than I expected to get, so he would make up the difference. I couldn't do that, obviously. But that's the way he was; it was part of him."

Dad's insistence on honesty and responsibility went far beyond the financial realm. Through decades of involvement in the French/English debate and discord, he refused to indulge in "spin." He always made sure he never said anything in English to an English-speaking Protestant audience in Ontario that he was not prepared to repeat, in French, to a francophone Roman Catholic audience in Quebec.

Public figures who did not practise the same kind of forthrightness around difficult issues aroused his ire. In an interview with David Millar, he delivered a scathing assessment of his old nemesis Mackenzie King, highlighting the former prime minister's "bumptious self-assurance, his mendacity, his calculated ambiguities," his "capacity to denounce other people for doing exactly what he was doing himself":

> I've often said that if Mackenzie King had ever been caught robbing a bank, he would have declaimed from the housetops that he had got there just ahead of the police in order to remove the property of the shareholders and depositors from the bank to keep the police from stealing it!

GHOST-WRITING IS SIMPLY DISHONEST
(Toronto Star column, "My Biggest Beef," 1962[27])

I disapprove so thoroughly of so much in the modern world that I find it hard to say which of its numerous unpleasant features I dislike the most. I had decided to write that, and no more, when a friend pointed out to me *The Star*'s kind permission to write my "beef" myself, "or through a ghost writer," and suggested that here was a golden opportunity to say what I thought on that subject.

Ghost-writing, in my opinion, is simply dishonest. It is the very opposite of the quality of mercy: it is twice cursed: it curseth him that gives and him that takes. Any man who can't write his own articles or make his own speeches should go home, go to bed ..., and stay there until he is ready to get up and do his own work.

I have ghost-written a few speeches and articles myself. I have not balked or jibbed as often or as hard as I should [have]. I welcome this opportunity to balk and jib publicly, hoping that it will stiffen my "nerve and backbone" to refuse, in future, to be an accessory before the fact.

I shall no doubt be told that no public man can know enough about all the subjects he has to talk about or write about to be able to follow this counsel to perfection. Then let him either hold his tongue, or get himself properly briefed [and] his draft revised by people who do know. But let him write, or speak, his piece himself.

This would ... greatly reduce the number of speeches... But what a blessing that would be! Listeners would be spared a lot of shoddy frauds. Speakers would have a chance to use their brains more and their tongues less.

The public itself is to blame for much of this pestiferous business. We make intolerable demands on our leaders for speeches on every conceivable subject on every conceivable occasion. No human being could meet all these demands out of his own resources, and no human being should try to meet them by stealing from other people....

The public should stop asking for so many speeches from its leaders, [and] the leaders should take as their motto: "Have courage, my boy, to say 'no.'"

He went on to describe how, in the years between the two world wars, Mackenzie King's Liberals in Quebec engaged in repeated campaigns of divisiveness:

> They raked over and over again the embers of the conscription controversy, appealing to the worst prejudices of Quebec nationalism and lying like troopers, while King was ramping up and down the rest of the country singing psalms about national unity and high-flown moral principles. That disgusted me; it was perhaps the beginning of my contempt for Mackenzie King.[28]

"Your father's standpoint was essentially one of morality," Millar told me. "He tended to judge things by standards of duty and social responsibility. That was probably why he trusted someone like [Newfoundland mine-worker and labour leader] Silby Barrett — a simple man, not sophisticated, but by God he could tell right from wrong!"

Dad's own keen sense of right and wrong often resulted in deep frustration when he felt basic standards had been transgressed. "He was a highly moral person," Millar commented, "and of course that made him prickly. I think that's where the terrible-tempered Mr. Bang came from — the Forsey explosions."

As hundreds of letters to editors and dozens of fiery articles attest, my father exploded often in print, and the ethical element was seldom far from the surface. I suspect that even his passion for accuracy was related to the ethical concepts of "right" and "wrong" — terms which, after all, can be used in either a factual or a moral sense.

Shortly after World War II ended, General Brock Chisholm, then a top-level civil servant, made the curious public claim that the concept of right and wrong was essentially a mistake. Dad took up the issue in a letter to the *Canadian Forum*:

> … According to the reports, General Chisholm said plainly that the whole idea of right and wrong was false and disastrous. In the same speech, however, he is also reported to have exhorted his fellow psychiatrists to be absolutely "honest." I am not a psychiatrist, a philosopher,

or a religious leader, so perhaps I am out of court. But as a plain ordinary citizen, I should like to ask what becomes of honesty if there is no such thing as right or wrong? What indeed becomes of truth and falsehood, or of any values at all?[29]

Dad detested hypocrisy and greed, and he didn't hesitate to point them out when he saw them. When the Ontario Medical Association launched a major campaign in the mid-1980s demanding that the provincial government allow doctors to "extra bill" their patients, he challenged them head on.

> ... In its present campaign against the prohibition of extra billing, the OMA has dwelt repeatedly and with emphasis on the shortage of beds, the shortage of this, the shortage of that. Has it mounted a comparable campaign to end or reduce [those] shortages? Has it called on its members for extra contributions to finance such a campaign? Has it placed full-page advertisements in the newspapers for that purpose? Has it organized mass rallies on the subject? Has it threatened to withhold services unless the shortages are ended or at least reduced? If so, it has escaped my notice. But the moment it's a question of the fees of a small minority of doctors, the welkin rings, and all the resources of propaganda are deployed on a massive scale.[30]

He also had a built-in skepticism of "experts," their high opinions of themselves, and their exorbitant fees. In 1983, when a certain royal commission appointee touted himself as being "worth more than $800 a day," he commented wryly: "This is the sort of thing one usually leaves it to other people to say about one's value!"[31]

Yes, he was often hard on other people, but again, he was hardest of all on himself. "He was a compassionate man," his friend Pierre Joncas told me. "His sense of duty was perhaps at times excessive. I think sometimes he felt almost responsible for the pains of others that he could do nothing about, and then he'd get down on himself."

Eugene Forsey with his beloved grandsons Roddy (right) and Eugene Contreras at their First Communion, Ottawa, 1983.

This was especially the case in regard to his role as a father. Like many conscientious and loving parents, he measured himself against a nonexistent ideal — some mythical creature who never makes mistakes and whose children never have problems. He therefore naturally saw himself as a parental failure. Sadly, I doubt if he ever considered how the rigid gender roles of his generation, combined with the prevailing economic system, sabotaged human relationships and made such standards even more wildly unattainable than they would otherwise be.

In 1985, after a visit home during which Dad had been noticeably subdued, I got a short note from him which began: "In future, please don't tell me about anyone 'living with' someone else. It depresses me so profoundly; and that you see nothing wrong in it brings home to me once again how miserably I have failed." I think he assumed that love and commitment could not be counted on unless they were formally sanctioned in marriage — and may have been more the case in his day. He certainly believed that living together without a marriage ceremony was morally wrong. At eighty years of age, he was simply unable to change the assumptions of a lifetime.

Later on, I asked both of my sons how they saw their grandfather's attitude on these matters.

"Grampa grew up in a very Victorian household," Roddy said. "He wasn't hip at the time, let alone now. So there were some things that I wouldn't have spoken to him too much about, and he kind of avoided it too, like sex or relationships. He wasn't a Bible-thumper, he didn't tell other people that they would burn in hell because they did or didn't do x, y, or z, but he believed very strongly and quite rigidly in what I would consider traditional personal moral principles. And that's fine; I mean he was my grandfather, he wasn't a guy at school."

"He had complete faith in his own morality," Eugene told me. "He knew what he considered his morality to be, and he stuck to it under any circumstances as far as I could see. I remember his story about walking through the red-light district in Vienna and not being propositioned once. He was very proud of that!"

For Eugene, the issue of "living together" was a very personal one, but he never discussed his own choice with his grandfather.

"Grampa knew about it; he didn't say anything to me. It might have also been a question of closing his eyes to something he didn't want to see; I think he did that sometimes. But again that might have been necessary in order not to compromise himself. And I think in that way he did his utmost not to impose on other people, considering his incredibly strong views. He definitely had set views about what people should do, in his family in particular. At the same time I'm impressed by the openness he did show."

My father's religious faith was the foundation of his world view, the inspiration for his actions, and the Rock of Ages to which he clung. His deepest desire was that his loved ones should find in religion the same source of strength and guidance that he had found. One of his greatest frustrations was that, to all appearances, we did not. Yet I think now that at the most fundamental level, we were much closer than he imagined.

With all that I have been privileged to learn from friends who are Aboriginal, I am also struck by the many parallels between some of Dad's faith-based understandings and the traditional teachings of indigenous peoples in many parts of the world. The living importance of history and tradition, the spiritual essence of human affairs, the sacred nature of the material universe, the honouring of the collectivity, the preference for talking through conflicts rather than fighting, the living importance of history and tradition, the consideration for generations yet unborn, the respect for symbols and their meanings, even a wariness around writing everything down — all these are present in many traditional cultures and in my father's world view. And although Dad seemed largely unaware of it himself, I believe that resonance reflects a fundamental affinity which I share as well, as we journey together towards saner, more humane and spiritually grounded ways of living and governing ourselves.

I like John Matheson's "translation" of Dad's belief system. "Your father essentially was a socialist," he told me. "He believed that we were, as creatures of God, bound to be responsible for one another. He believed in the value and virtue of people, and he wasn't ashamed of that. There was a commitment, a faith. Eugene Forsey was a believer in goodness; I think that's what stood out."

My own spiritual understandings, of course, continue to evolve. The forms they take may be different from what Dad envisaged, but I hope that would no longer be a problem for him. I want to believe that his anxiety on our behalf has been lifted, and that he rejoices with us in the "love and truth and beauty and goodness" that he knew as God.

In the warmth of his caring, in the honesty of his doubts and questionings, in his passion for justice and his tenacious pursuit of truth, my father's gifts of the spirit continue to shine as a beacon in our lives.

CHAPTER THREE

Standing on Guard: Watchdog for the Body Politic

> There is great need for watching very carefully what takes place. No government is so good or so wise that it should be allowed to wield [its] powers without the closest possible public scrutiny.
> — Senate speech, October 27, 1970[1]

In 1973, my father, a Senator at the time, was planning to go to Chile as part of a parliamentary delegation. I was living in Ecuador with my young family, and we were looking forward to having him visit us on his way to or from Santiago. Over the summer, however, the news from Chile became increasingly disturbing: the constitutionally elected socialist government of Salvador Allende was being threatened by forces both within and outside the country.

Then, on September 11, the Chilean military under General Augusto Pinochet overthrew the elected government, bombing the presidential palace, killing President Allende, and imprisoning or "disappearing" thousands of other citizens. The bloody coup d'état shocked the world, and began a vicious right-wing reign of terror that victimized the Chilean people for years. Of course, it also put an end to the Canadian delegation's travel plans, and Dad's South American trip was put on hold.

In the aftermath of the coup, I thought a lot about President Allende and my father, and the similarities between them. Both men were born into privileged and highly political families in the first decade of the twentieth century. Both took great pride in their respective countries' long traditions of democracy, and strove over the years to ensure greater justice and prosperity for their fellow citizens. As democratic socialists, they deliberately chose constitutional means rather than revolution to bring about change, putting their faith in the rule of law and in the will and capability of the people. They devoted their political careers to the common good and to upholding the democratic mechanisms that embodied their ideals. In Allende's case, that devotion cost him his life.

Like Canadians, Chileans until then had seen themselves as citizens of a stable modern democracy — a troubled democracy, perhaps, but one whose people were collectively committed to coping with those troubles through normal constitutional means. The coup showed, tragically, how fragile even an established democracy can be.

Here in Canada, most of us still take for granted a high degree of personal and political freedom, notwithstanding the flaws in our system of government and recent trends that throw so much into question. But even in the hopeful days of the 1970s Dad knew we could never afford to be complacent. He was more aware than most Canadians of the tough historical struggles that had won us our liberties and built the constitutional structures that protect them, and he knew those gains could vanish overnight if respect for the Constitution were abandoned.

In his long years as a participant-observer in Canadian politics, he had seen our own democratic system repeatedly threatened, and attempts to improve it sabotaged, not with bombs and guns but by more subtle and persistent forces — greed, prejudice, ignorance, cynical ambition, and abuse of power. In Chile, those forces, in collusion with powerful external allies, had violently reversed decades of political evolution, turning a modern peaceful democracy into a brutal dictatorship.

Mercifully, that had not happened in Canada, but Dad understood very well that we could never afford complacency. Those same corrosive forces, left unchecked, could undermine our parliamentary structures and do away with our hard-won rights and freedoms. He saw it as his duty to expose and resist those destructive trends, wherever they appeared and whatever form they might take.

My father participated in Canadian public life so vigorously, and in so many ways, that it is hard to know where to start in describing the parts he played. The obvious career categories — academic, trade unionist, and parliamentarian — designate formal aspects of his work, but don't really convey the essence of what he did. Perhaps the best way to describe him would be as a watchdog for the body politic.

Eugene Forsey's upbringing, sharp mind, professional training, and skill with words combined with his zeal for social justice to make him one of the most effective citizen-critics and advocates of his time. His guardian role embraced not only the parliamentary and constitutional domain, but the social and economic spheres as well. Later chapters deal more fully with the specific fields of his activism, including labour, the Constitution, and national unity. To start with, however, I want to come at it from another angle, and examine three of the political functions he took on: critic and gadfly, practitioner of citizen politics, and educator on issues of government.

It is as a constitutional authority and critic that my father is most often remembered now. His knowledge of and enthusiasm about the Constitution influenced his approach to labour issues, framed and guided the stands he took as a socialist, and largely defined his public persona, especially in his last thirty years. It earned him contradictory epithets: "Tory conspirator," "Left-Wing mud-slinger and character assassin," and probably many others in between. It formed much of the basis of his friendships with Arthur Meighen and Pierre Trudeau, and served as both a bond and a source of friction with his CCF colleagues. It certainly absorbed huge amounts of his time and energy, as is evidenced by the numerous treatises he published on constitutional matters great and small, and the reams of documents and letters he left to posterity.

Some might wonder why a man like my father, with his lifelong commitment to building a better, more just society, would care so passionately about the details of the Canadian Constitution. What practical relevance did it have for a social activist and trade union official?

The answer, like many things about my Dad, is complex. But for those of us who care about his other concerns — the welfare of ordinary people, social justice, human rights, environmental sanity and cultural survival — that answer is also vitally important. For if he was right in thinking that constitutional issues matter so much, we too would do well to pay attention.

Dad understood that it was our strong democratic constitutional framework that made political and social progress in this country possible. Take that away, or allow it to be weakened, and all work towards peaceful progressive change would be put at risk. If anyone needed proof of what a country could be like without its constitution, Chile in the years of the military dictatorship after the 1973 coup provided a stark example.

This awareness underlay my father's watchdog role as he kept vigil over successive governments, Parliaments, bureaucracies, the academy, and the media. He was constantly on the lookout for signs of the kind of slow constitutional erosion he felt represented such a menace to our rights and freedoms. Long before today's global corporate interests made such massive incursions into our political process, before the evisceration of our sovereignty by US-dominated trade deals, before the curtailment of our civil liberties and human rights in the name of post-9/11 "security," before the shameful events that have brought "prorogation" into the Canadian lexicon as a dirty word — long before all of that — he was standing on guard. And he saw plenty to guard against.

It was the King-Byng affair of 1926 that got my father firmly hooked on the intricacies of the Constitution. In June of that year, the Opposition in the House of Commons had moved a motion of censure against Mackenzie King's fragile Liberal minority government, threatening to defeat it. But before the critical vote could take place, Prime Minister King took the unprecedented step of going to the governor general, Lord Byng, to ask him to dissolve Parliament and call a fresh election. Byng refused, insisting that, according to the Constitution, the elected House must have the chance to decide if it could function with an alternative government. Mackenzie King resigned and Conservative Opposition Leader Arthur Meighen became prime minister.

In the heated controversy that followed, King claimed that Byng had no right to refuse a dissolution, insisting that the Crown was, in effect, merely a rubber stamp which must grant whatever request the government might make. Meighen, on the other hand, denounced Mackenzie King's demand for a dissolution as a shameless attempt to hang on to power and avoid imminent defeat by the people's elected representatives in Parliament.

Dad was a university student at the time, and he had watched from the gallery of the House of Commons as the crisis unfolded. The confrontation and the issues it raised had a profound effect on him, and would figure largely in his later constitutional career. He was adamant that Meighen was correct, and that Byng's principled refusal to play Mackenzie King's game was not only "completely constitutional, [but] indeed essential to the preservation of parliamentary government."[2]

The inherent complexity and subtlety of the situation made it difficult for the general public to fully grasp the implications. As is the case today, this gave those in power plenty of opportunity to oversimplify and misrepresent the facts. Mackenzie King took full advantage of the confusion, making much of the alleged conflict between popular democracy — supposedly embodied in his own person — and antiquated arbitrary authority, which he identified with the governor general. King's crude and cynical appeal to the politically unsophisticated succeeded in hoodwinking enough of the electorate to put him back in office as prime minister not long afterwards.

Disappointed but fascinated, Dad kept up his watch on Parliament, first as a graduate student and then as a lecturer at McGill, writing critically about these and other constitutional matters as occasion arose. But it was not until 1943 that he made a major public impact in the constitutional field. In that year, Oxford University Press published my father's Ph.D. thesis under the title *The Royal Power of Dissolution of Parliament in the British Commonwealth*. It was a scholarly and devastating denunciation of Mackenzie King's machinations seventeen years earlier.

When the thesis appeared in print, King was again in power, having long touted himself as the democratic hero of the crisis of 1926. The book turned his protestations of injured innocence upside down. Citing constitutional chapter and verse, Dad argued that if a prime minister could shut down Parliament whenever there was a risk that the Commons might vote against the government, then parliamentary democracy itself was dead.

If Mackenzie King's narrative was accepted, he said, a government would be able to stay in power indefinitely, "spanking the electorate into submission" by an endless series of dissolutions and elections. Such an extreme situation might be unlikely, but when it happened, the only thing left that could protect the people's right to choose their own government was the reserve power of the Crown.[3]

There have been times in Canada's history when an argument about the powers of the governor general would have caused barely a ripple outside of academic circles. But when the prime minister of the day is someone who has claimed the right to stop Parliament from doing its job, the public tends to take a more lively interest. At any rate, in 1943 Dad's book on the subject produced a sensation. The Liberal editor of the *Winnipeg Free Press*, J.W. Dafoe, attacked it with a partisan diatribe, attempting to justify Mackenzie King's actions with a combination of distortions and outright falsehoods. The ensuing debate burned up the editorial pages throughout that whole summer. By the time the exchange ended, Dad's friends felt he had "left the formidable Dafoe for dead upon the field."[4]

For the first but certainly not the last time in his career, my father had taken an apparently obscure and technical constitutional issue and exposed it to the public as a matter of crucial importance for democracy. Using the pro-government press itself as a vehicle, he had demystified the King-Byng affair and shown its relevance to the freedoms ordinary people counted on. In the process, he had laid himself open to a barrage of accusations. As the Conservatives were to do sixty-five years later, Liberal partisans rushed to defend the indefensible. Determined to ignore or misrepresent what this young upstart Forsey was saying, they portrayed him as an old-fashioned monarchist stick-in-the-mud, unable to accept modern political reality. Even some of Dad's fellow socialists accepted the view of the monarchy as a regressive institution,[5] and were dismayed that he would support an appointed governor general who refused of the advice of an elected prime minister.

Of course, the real issue was whether any prime minister should be allowed to override the will of the people's elected representatives in Parliament and prevent them from performing what Dad referred to as the Commons' "most essential function" — deciding who should govern.[6] Interestingly, leading constitutional scholars today appear to agree with the Forsey view that Parliament is supreme.

My father's very public criticism of Mackenzie King's opportunistic hypocrisy naturally did not please the predominantly Liberal establishment. Nor did his defence of Arthur Meighen's role in the matter sit well with many of his CCF friends. But the widespread disapproval swayed Dad not at all. As far as he was concerned, King had flouted the constitutional safeguards of our democracy, and the only way to prevent such an outrage from being repeated was to expose the complex but unforgiving truth.

Despite the furor, or perhaps in part because of it, Dad began to be increasingly recognized as a watchdog for the interests of the citizenry when constitutional questions arose. With his detailed knowledge of the subject, he could be counted on to recognize the importance of particular constitutional clauses or conventions, and to see the dangers implicit in ignoring or defying them. And thanks to his life-long familiarity with Parliament Hill and his personal acquaintance with many MPs and officials, he knew where and how to aim his criticisms.

John Matheson, parliamentary secretary to Prime Minister Lester ("Mike") Pearson in the 1960s and later a respected Ontario judge, watched many such encounters. "I don't know of any person who approached the Constitution with such thoroughness and commitment as Eugene Forsey," Matheson said. "He had such precise knowledge on constitutional matters that he was constantly correcting other people. Somebody would say something, he'd twig to the fact that it was wrong on some important matter, and he would correct it. It was pretty devastating, you know — and pretty important. Sometimes it was quite embarrassing. I'm sure Mike Pearson was a little upset from time to time to get these rebukes in the public press."

Lester Pearson and Mackenzie King were not the only ones to feel the barbs of Dad's criticisms. From the 1940s on, no Canadian government escaped unscathed, not even that of his friend and constitutional ally Pierre Trudeau. Various provincial governments also had to face his challenges as to the legitimacy of some of their actions, particularly in regard to civil liberties and labour and minority rights, challenges he described in his memoirs, *A Life on the Fringe*.

Some of the positions my father took seemed paradoxical until he explained his reasons for taking them. He believed that in order to illuminate and defend the interests of democracy, simplistic and partisan arguments had to be dismantled, and he insisted on pursuing complicated truths even when they were inconvenient. This personal peculiarity confounded people who preferred easy labels, stereotypes, and black-and-white, "either/or" choices.

As Dad's reputation grew, governments and opposition parties, trade unions, citizens' groups, and the press increasingly sought him out for what he called his "illegal legal opinions" on issues such as jurisdictions and rights. In a 1990 speech, he reflected on these layman's forays into the domain of law. "I have been on the whole singularly lucky when the Supreme Court of Canada pronounced on the same subjects," he said. "There are a few times when I fell by the wayside; in one case I frankly think the Supreme Court of Canada was wrong."[7]

"Eugene Forsey knew what he was talking about, and you couldn't ignore him," John Matheson told me. Recalling his own time in Parliament, he went on: "We all recognized that he would address an issue in a way that was independent of partisanship. That was so valuable. He was far more of a constitutionalist than most constitutional lawyers. He became a kind of ombudsman, that's what really he was — a voice of conscience to us all. And when he said something, by God, we all had to listen."

Eventually Dad came to be regarded as a sort of constitutional oracle, consulted by those in and out of power to bestow a blessing or pronounce a curse on whatever political ventures they or their opponents were undertaking.

Sometimes the facts obliged him to uphold very unpopular positions, including positions taken by governments he despised. His second cousin Alex Hickman, former provincial attorney-general and later chief justice for Newfoundland, told me of one such instance. The province's "tie election" in 1971 had returned equal numbers of Conservatives and Liberals, along with one independent member. In the popular vote count, the Tories had won, yet Liberal Premier Joey Smallwood held onto office for four more months, despite many calls for his resignation. Alex remembered: "Eugene was called from time to time by the *St. John's Evening Telegram* and asked, were the Tories right in demanding that Smallwood resign. He gave the same opinion each time: morally the premier should resign, but constitutionally he didn't have to until he met the House and was defeated.

THE RULERS AND THE RULED
(From verses written in 1952[8])

... Respect for the Commons? Respect for the laws?
Respect for our history? A lot of old saws!
We'll give you some new ones, a [government] selection:
Such as "Who's going to stop us?" "We won the election!"
"What is done can't be changed." Once a law has been broken
By so much as one hour, the last word has been spoken;
We can break it for weeks, or for months, or for years;
If we do, it's a matter for laughter, not tears.
Laws are made not for us but for you to obey.
You must do such-and-such on a specified day.
If you don't, we shall clap you instanter in jail,
Or levy a fine upon you without fail.
Unto us the same penalties? Perish the thought!
For the citizen, yes; for the Government, not.
What is sauce for the gander's not sauce for the goose,
Except in the old, dead-and-gone British use.
For we are the rulers, and you are the ruled.
You chose us. What matter if then you were fooled?
That's just our "astuteness"; it "won the election."
That phrase triumphs always o'er every objection.
Ours by far is the best constitutional plan:
The citizen can't, but the Government can ...
Once the ballots are counted, we do as we please;
From all forms of restraint we are free as the breeze.
And the citizen's "rights" he enjoys by our favour;
This gives a "distinctive Canadian" flavour.

"There were comments coming from some of my Tory friends that obviously Eugene Forsey was in Smallwood's camp." Alex chuckled at the recollection. "I wrote your father, and sent him the clippings, and said, 'You've got to do something to save your reputation!' So he wrote me a delightful letter; I remember one phrase: 'I have devoutly prayed for the political demise of Emperor Joseph Robert Smallwood. The last thing I want to do is to keep that scoundrel in office one day longer than he should be, and he should be out now. Constitutionally, he's within his rights to stay, but he should go if he had any decency. P.S. You can send this letter to the *St. John's Evening Telegram* if you wish.'"

Happily, most of Dad's professional opinions were much more in tune with his own political and personal inclinations. But even when they were not, he insisted on looking at the facts in all their complexity. He refused to take shortcuts or allow omissions which, however tempting they might be for political reasons, could potentially undermine the integrity of parliamentary system itself.

How did he deal with the many signs that the system's integrity was already seriously deteriorating? On the whole, I think he managed to maintain his belief in Canada's political structures as a genuine embodiment of democracy — in need of improvements, certainly, but just as surely capable of incorporating them. In these days of doubt and cynicism, when the role of Parliament and the very sovereignty of national governments has been so deeply eroded, it is easy to fault him for holding on to that belief. But he was not as naïve as the criticism might imply. He was far from oblivious to the problems; indeed, he came at things from a similarly skeptical perspective. My sister, Margaret, remembers him quoting Sir Winston Churchill on the subject of democracy: "the worst system of government in the world — except for all the others." Given that conviction, he felt obliged to use his talents and privilege to try to make our Canadian version of democracy the best it could possibly be.

That commitment, of course, condemned him to an endless series of uphill battles. In 1956, for example, when Louis St. Laurent's Liberal government rammed the Trans Canada Pipeline bill through Parliament under the iron hand of Trade and Commerce Minister C.D. Howe, Dad all but despaired.

> The government tore up the rules, turned the speaker into a party hack, and made a mockery of parliamentary government, all at the behest of a few American millionaires. To Mr. St. Laurent and his colleagues ... parliamentary democracy means simply voting and getting a majority; counting heads instead of breaking

them, no question of also using them, of discussion, of debate. The very meaning of the word 'parliament,' a talking-place, is lost upon them ... With [the pipeline bill's] passage, parliamentary responsible government, for the time being, disappears.[9]

"For the time being." When he wrote those words, my father still believed that what the government had done in the pipeline debate was an anomaly, an outrage for which the Liberals would be (and were) subsequently punished at the ballot box. Till the end of his life, he continued to denounce each instance where he saw vital parliamentary traditions being overridden or procedures changed to accommodate a partisan agenda, all the while somehow maintaining his faith in the overall system.

That faith was more understandable in a time when the constitutional principles behind the rules were still widely acknowledged, when parliamentary traditions were usually respected, at least formally. Since then, however, outrageous political behaviour has increasingly become the norm, with Parliament being treated as a mere showcase, parliamentary debate as window-dressing. When governments systematically sabotage the work of multi-party committees, use orders-in-council to circumvent existing laws, appeal any court rulings that don't suit them, and implement far-reaching and controversial measures without bringing them before the House of Commons, they are demonstrating contempt not only for the people and their Parliament, but for democracy itself.

The art of parliamentary bullying has recently reached new heights. We have sadly gotten used to a minority government trying to force its will on the opposition majority, taunting the other parties by declaring virtually every bill a matter of confidence. We've seen opposition MPs, who ought to know better, fooled by a Machiavellian government and an ignorant press into believing that defeating the government on any such bill would automatically "trigger an election." We've watched helplessly as the people we elected to represent us knuckled under and played dead, abdicating their responsibility to vote according to their own stated principles and policies.

Not only does such craven behaviour allow the passage of laws that the majority of the electorate doesn't want, it also allows the government bullies to stay in power without truly having the support of the MPs we elected in good faith. And, when a prime minister succeeds in persuading the governor general to dissolve or prorogue Parliament before it can even vote confidence or otherwise, we have to wonder if parliamentary responsible government itself will survive.

My father was still part of a culture of political civility, where it was broadly understood that our constitutional system could, as he put it, "function only upon the basis of self-restraint, of fair play, of observing not merely the letter but the spirit of the rules."[10] I'm not sure to what extent he recognized the inexorable nature of that culture's continuing decline. He must have been extremely reluctant to acknowledge the devastation happening in the overall parliamentary forest as he campaigned to protect particular constitutional groves and trees.

Be that as it may, we are now faced with a most urgent challenge. If we are to stop the clear-cutting of the parliamentary landscape before we're left with a total wasteland, we need to collectively take on the role of citizen watchdog that he modelled for us.

As a young man, my father chose to study political economy because he saw it not only as a fascinating field of learning, but also a vitally important one, dealing with the mechanisms necessary for people to control their own destinies. At the same time, he recognized that the formal political arena was only one place for citizen involvement in society's decisions. Like many of his socialist colleagues, he focused much of his energy elsewhere — on trade unions, education, human rights and other aspects of social change.

All through Dad's long career in citizen politics, the academic and activist threads remained closely intertwined. His intimate familiarity with formal political structures gave him specialized tools that he was able to use in much of his activist work. The struggle against Quebec's infamous Padlock Act in the latter years of the Depression was one example. Dad and his fellow members of the Civil Liberties Union in Montreal fought the repressive 1937 law with every weapon they could muster, including a formal petition for disallowance, which asked the Dominion government to disallow, or invalidate, the provincial act.[11] Dad used his constitutional expertise to draft the complex document, researching the constitutional precedents and alternatives, and presenting it in terms of previous decisions on disallowance. Although the petition was finally rejected, it constituted a major challenge to the arbitrary power of the regime.

Taking on the Duplessis government and the rest of the Quebec establishment during those years was not for the faint of heart. One day Dad's friend Frank Scott passed on to him a warning from another very respectable Montreal lawyer. "Please tell Forsey to be very careful when crossing the street," the man urged Scott. "Please tell him to be VERY careful." Dad heeded the traffic advice, but the threat did not silence him.

In later years, he drew up three other petitions for disallowance. Two of them targetted virulent anti-labour legislation, first in Prince Edward Island in 1948 and then in Newfoundland eleven years later. In 1974, he drafted another one, this time against Quebec's Bill 22, which severely restricted English language minority rights. Each of these petitions was thoroughly grounded in law and precedent, but in each case the federal government of the day refused to challenge the provinces by invoking disallowance, even of the most appalling legislation. Still, despite the refusals, Dad felt that the petitions themselves, and the resulting public awareness, may well have contributed to the eventual demise of the offending acts.[12]

He was even less successful in the formal political arena. He ran four times for office as a CCF candidate, and lost badly each time. In later years, he would refer to these failed electoral forays as his "small, short, and inglorious political career," joking that he'd been defeated oftener and by larger majorities than any other man in Canada.

My father's lack of success on the hustings was the subject of some of the copious correspondence he exchanged with his friend and parliamentary mentor Arthur Meighen throughout the 1940s and 50s. Meighen had suffered his own share of electoral defeats and political attacks, and if anyone could understand Dad's ambivalence about it all, it was Meighen. In 1949, shortly after losing his last campaign for a seat in Parliament, Dad wrote to him:

"Though I remain convinced that I'd be a good Member, I remain equally convinced that I'm a poor candidate. I lack the common touch. I am too much the 'professor' … Worst of all, perhaps, I have very little confidence in myself, except on a very few subjects, notably the dissolution of Parliament, disallowance of provincial Acts, and a large selection of the fairy-tales that have been told about you! But this is hardly a sufficient repertoire for campaign purposes!"[13]

Nonetheless, some of the very qualities he viewed as drawbacks for campaign purposes served him — and the country — extremely well in other contexts. His professorial aspect included the thoroughness of his research, the acuity of his analysis, and his ability to expound his conclusions in compelling ways. "The real problem was to fault him," said John Matheson, "because he never made a mistake!"

That may have been overstating it, but it's true that Dad's meticulous accuracy was legendary. It was a huge asset in his Senate role as co-chair of the Joint Committee on Regulations and Other Statutory Instruments. In his memoirs, *A Life on the Fringe*, he devoted a full chapter to the exhaustive work of that committee in keeping bureaucrats and politicians on the straight and narrow.[14] The NDP's Svend Robinson, whom Dad recruited to the committee as a rookie MP, remembered him as a "parliamentary pit-bull."

"Your father could dissect a bill or a regulation in a way that was absolutely astonishing," Robinson recalled. "He had this tremendous respect for Parliament, and a very healthy dose of skepticism about the ability of bureaucrats to 'snow' politicians. That's why he saw this committee as so important, because it was a way for Parliament to actually assert its primacy."

Dad's skepticism was not limited to bureaucrats and members of the establishment; he did not hesitate to apply it to like-minded people if he thought they were wrong. In October 1970, after the Trudeau government invoked the War Measures Act against the FLQ in Quebec, almost everyone on the Left denounced it. Instead of joining the chorus of condemnation, my father publicly supported the government's decision, a stand which led predictably to accusations that he had abandoned his identity as a defender of civil liberties.[15]

This is a difficult issue for me personally. At the time of the October Crisis, I was a new mother, absorbed in my own affairs and politically ignorant to the point of irresponsibility. Without really questioning my father's position, I more or less just closed my eyes and hoped for the best. I was jolted out of this complacency some years later when I learned that several of my friends and co-workers had been among those arrested under the War Measures Act. These were people who were guilty of nothing more than being active in things like the student movement, co-op housing, or international solidarity work, where separatist sympathies were common.

Since then, my own skepticism has been augmented by my experiences of police and military overkill, notably at the Oka Peace Camp in 1990 and at the April 2001 anti-globalization protests in Quebec City.

But even now, still feeling the long-term effects of the tear gas on my health, and with fresh accounts of made-in-Canada repression surfacing almost daily, I find the accusations against my father in regard to the War Measures Act to be too facile. I know that when the FLQ kidnappings happened, he was deeply troubled by the "frightful events ... in Quebec, which have saddened us all."[16] As usual, though, he was wary of what he saw as simplistic and perilously uninformed opinions coming from critics of the government, many of whom had little knowledge of Quebec and less experience there. Meanwhile, people like his old Montreal Civil Liberties comrade Frank Scott were saying that some prompt and definitive action was necessary to avert further outrages.[17]

So Dad did what he always tried to do when faced with a complex dilemma: he assessed the situation to the best of his ability, listened to the opinions of people whose good sense, knowledge, and principles he respected, and then on that basis supported what seemed to him the best course of action possible in the circumstances. Together with Scott, Thérèse Casgrain, and Grattan O'Leary — Quebeckers and civil libertarians all — he argued that "the sensible thing to do was what the government did: use the only measure at its disposal that could be applied immediately, and then sit down to draft a piece of permanent legislation." Other options were either too slow, totally impractical, or themselves dangerous.

In fact, one of the reasons Dad and others had for supporting the government's action was itself a civil liberties argument. He pointed out that the alternative being touted by many critics — summoning Parliament and getting immediate unanimous consent for new emergency legislation to deal with the crisis — in addition to being logistically improbable, could also put at risk the very civil liberties those critics were arguing for. Choosing that course, he argued, would have introduced "the danger [of] half-baked and very dangerous legislation."

As examples, he cited two bills passed in exactly that way during or immediately after the Winnipeg General Strike of 1919 — Section 98 of the Criminal Code (against which he and other civil libertarians fought a long and ultimately successful battle in the 1930s) and an amendment to the Immigration Act providing for arbitrary deportation. "Those two pieces of legislation," he noted, "were put through in double-quick jig-time. They were two very bad pieces of legislation, and it took a long time to get rid of them. I do not think they are good precedents."

Moreover, the fact that Dad supported the invocation of the War Measures Act in 1970 did not mean he liked the way it was implemented. He warned his fellow senators at the time of the possibility of abuse. "I hope that this House will take a leading part in supplying [the necessary] scrutiny," he said, "with understanding, sobriety and good sense, but nevertheless with vigilance and concern for the liberties of the people."[18] In today's "security"-obsessed climate, we need that vigilance and concern more than ever.

My father's commitment to civil liberties and human rights came to the fore again in the late 1970s, when a Charter of Rights and Freedoms was promised as part of the repatriated Constitution. For decades, he had been pressing for something like the Charter, having seen at first hand what happened when there were no such constitutional guarantees. In a 1980 *Reader's Digest* interview, he gave a number of examples of "serious violations of fundamental human rights by Parliament and by legislatures [which] would be illegal under this Charter" — Quebec's Padlock Act, an Alberta government attempt in the 1930s to control the press, and the wartime internment of the Japanese Canadians.[19]

He cautioned, however, that such a Charter would need to be very carefully drafted. Done properly, it would be a much-needed and progressive addition to the Constitution. But without extremely competent drafting, he said, it risked turning into "a field day for cranks, a gold mine for lawyers, and a headache for judges."[20] Some would argue that this has indeed turned out to be the case.

The new Charter ran into problems before it even saw the light of day. In an eerie foretaste of accords to come, the first ministers met behind closed doors in November 1981 for final negotiations leading up to the repatriation of the Constitution. Provincial premiers insisted on inserting into the package a "notwithstanding" clause which could be used to "override" the guarantees the Charter was supposed to enshrine. Seeing their rights being traded away in return for political gains, outraged citizens across the country rose up to denounce the "notwithstanding clause" and the eleven men who had fathered it.

Dad joined the popular protest, adding the weight of his reputation and his constitutional expertise to the general public outcry. At a press conference called by a coalition of women's, Aboriginal, and disabled people's groups, he blasted the proposed "notwithstanding" amendment and called for change. "The amended Charter of Rights and Freedoms just won't do," he declared. "The provinces have shot it full of holes — great, big, gaping holes." If the amendment went through, everything from freedom of conscience to *habeas corpus*, from freedom of association to the right to equal protection of the law, would be "put at the mercy of ten provincial legislatures, which can over-ride them at will."

> "Bang" goes all the Charter's protection for fundamental freedoms and basic legal rights. "Bang" goes the ban against discrimination ... All this is bad enough. It hits everybody: men and women, native peoples and the rest of us alike. Much worse, because more blatant and glaring, is the treatment meted out to the native peoples and to women ... The Accord has poisoned the Charter.[21]

That massive public pressure campaign, led by women and Aboriginal people, succeeded in applying an antidote to the "poison." Although the notwithstanding clause was not actually withdrawn, significant limits were placed on its application, and in the years since then, attempts to "override" the Charter have become pretty much a political no-no. Like so many of the battles Dad was involved in, it was an important, if only a partial, victory.

In a 1986 interview with CBC Radio, my father reminisced about growing up in the house of his grandfather, William Cochrane Bowles, a highly respected top official in the House of Commons. "So it was at his knee," prompted the interviewer, "that you first imbibed your knowledge of and your interest in Canadian parliamentary tradition and governmental affairs?"

"Yes," Dad replied, "and he and my mother must have been superb simplifiers, because I have never had to unlearn anything they told me. I have added a good deal, of course ..."[22]

Like his mother and his grandfather, Dad too was a "superb simplifier." He had a gift for transforming often esoteric subject matter into the stuff of popular debate, demystifying complex issues and demonstrating their relevance to ordinary people. He believed that if we are to have any hope of influencing our own society for the better, we need to know how our political institutions work, what we can and cannot expect of them, and what impacts any changes to them are likely to have. Starting with his own impressive understanding of those questions, he tried to make the essential information accessible to the broader public, showing at the same time why it mattered. In John Matheson's words, Dad explained things "so simply and sensibly that he appealed to the common sense of Canadians."

These subjects, of course, aren't everybody's cup of tea. "The Constitution is often very dry material," admits political historian Alan Whitehorn. "But Eugene always gave it great life." Whitehorn recalls two lectures he invited Dad to give at Kingston's Royal Military College in the 1980s. "On both occasions he spoke to a packed hall — almost all the faculty and virtually every student we could cram in. He very much rose to the occasion, in such a historic locale and with a bilingual audience reflecting the different parts of the country. He began his talks with self-deprecating humour, then proceeded to wow both faculty and students with his knowledge, his enthusiasm, and his witty anecdotes."

My father always tried to keep his reader or listener in mind, whether he was teaching a class, speaking to a service club, whipping off a letter to the editor, or preparing a brief for a parliamentary committee. Readers of the *Canadian Forum* in the 1940s, for example, were predominantly pro-CCF, and were generally suspicious of unelected authority. In an article on the reserve powers of the Crown, Dad presented the basic themes of his Ph.D. thesis in terms those readers would appreciate. He argued persuasively that viewing the Crown as a mere a rubber stamp for the government in office would be dangerous for democracy and "perfectly suicidal for the CCF." Citing six hair-raising political scenarios to show how this "'heads I win, tails you lose' theory of the Constitution" would deliver the CCF "gagged and bound into the hands of its opponents," he succeeded in illustrating the relevance of the issue both to his partisan readers and to the public interest as a whole.[23]

Dad's political education work naturally overlapped with his roles as critic and activist. While Forsey the constitutional critic was demolishing

*Retired from the Senate, but still standing on guard, Parliament Hill, 1987.
(Courtesy Robert Fleming)*

Mackenzie King or Maurice Duplessis in the *Canadian Journal of Economics and Political Science*, Forsey the educator was going after them in the daily newspapers or mocking them in rhyming couplets. Forsey the educator also worked closely with Forsey the activist, as when his letter to the *Ottawa Journal* denouncing the Speaker's actions in the 1956 Pipeline Debate was quoted strategically in the House of Commons and almost succeeded in derailing the whole process.[24]

These efforts to raise Canadians' awareness and engage them in understanding the fundamentals of our Constitution were an essential part of his watchdog role. Over the years, he struggled continually against political ignorance, engaging in one battle after another to dispel the widespread "confusion and muddleheadedness" that he encountered among media people, academics, and politicians, as well as the general public.[25]

In today's Canada, there is a dire need for more such constitutional educator-warriors. Pervasive constitutional illiteracy was a major factor in enabling Stephen Harper's minority government to carry on with its continuing abuse of our parliamentary system, particularly flagrant in the prorogation fiascos. In 2008 — the first, and worst, of the two — most of the media allowed themselves to be dragged along when the Conservatives began accusing the opposition parties of trying to "seize power without an election." Far too many commentators simply accepted the government's blatant constitutional distortions as fact, perpetuating the myth that a defeat in the House on a confidence vote would have to mean a fresh election. Some even went so far as to describe Harper's request to prorogue Parliament as "necessary."

If the press and the public had understood the basic principles of our Constitution, the Harper government could never have got away with that shocking betrayal of parliamentary democracy — a betrayal which has already led to further abuse and is likely to haunt us for years to come. Canada is still paying the price for two decades without Eugene Forsey's voice constantly educating, reminding, and correcting us on these matters.

In the forty years before his death, though, that voice had seldom been silent. From the 1950s on, my father was in demand as a media panelist and commentator, and many Canadians got to know him through radio and television. Passion, controversy and humour carry well over the airwaves, and his lively political arguments and explanations reached audiences across the country. Particularly as the debate over Quebec separatism heated up, the broadcast networks called upon him again and again as a spokesperson for an enlightened federalism firmly based in political and constitutional realities.

Then of course there were his famous letters to the newspapers, a medium of popular discussion that has now been expanded through callback lines, internet blogs, and other interactive media. Dad half-seriously blamed his "bad temper" for his frequent forays onto the editorial pages, but in a 1974 article he made a more formal case for this means of political education and action:

> Public awareness of pollution, of the plight of the third world, and of the horrors of political persecution surely owes a good deal to letters in the press. So does public concern, and public determination to get action. So do legislation and public policy. Naturally, a good deal depends on who writes, what he writes, how he writes it, and how many people rally to his support. But a writer who knows what he is talking about, and can convey that knowledge in plain speech, can get a hearing, if what he has to say strikes the public as of real importance.[26]

Not everyone realizes the extent to which my father also pursued his vocation as educator on an interactive, individual basis, by ordinary mail. Right up to the end, he carried on a copious correspondence with a whole range of people from across the country and even beyond our borders. Friends, acquaintances, and total strangers would write him with questions and comments, or send him manuscripts or proposals to review. He always tried to reply, although sometimes in his last years he simply had to explain that his health or other pressures prevented him from responding as thoroughly as he would have liked.

After his death in 1991, my sister and I gathered up two boxfuls of his current correspondence from various surfaces in his apartment and office. He had answered some of it just before leaving on his trip to Victoria, but other piles were separated out awaiting reply. One bundle was

THE TAXPAYERS' SERVANTS[26]

On page 1 of the *Globe and Mail*, on February 2, 1982, two stories appeared in adjacent columns:

"... A federal official insisted that wage increases must be curtailed ... either by unions agreeing voluntarily to reopen contracts and take smaller wages, or by the Government's imposing wage and price controls."

"... [The] head of the new Canada Post Corporation is already getting a 'performance-based' retroactive boost in his $100,000-plus salary, even though he has been on the job only five months. The heads of nine other Crown corporations and four other top executives are also getting retroactive raises, approved last week by Cabinet, of up to 12.3 per cent ..."

The paper did not publish Eugene Forsey's response. It read:

Has the Government taken leave of its senses? Has it any conception of how the ordinary union member, asked to accept "voluntarily" those "smaller wages," will react to news of Crown corporation tycoons getting increases, and retroactive increases, of up to 12.3 per cent? Has it any conception of how any ordinary citizen will react?

To add insult to injury, [the Privy Council Office] says that "it is illegal for the government to release the salary figures" the Crown corporation heads and the other "four top executives" are getting.

What makes it illegal? Surely the Crown, the Government, as sole shareholder, can announce what it is paying the shareholder's servants? If such action really is illegal, then the law should be changed, double-quick. Don't private corporations have to reveal what their top officers get? The people of Canada are likely to agree with Mr. Bouey, Governor of the Bank of Canada, who "thinks that because he's paid by the taxpayer, the taxpayer has a right to know" what he gets, and who, accordingly, alone (so far) among the golden fourteen, has had the decency to tell us.

— Eugene Forsey

marked "Very Soon" in his shaky hand; another was labelled "Soon"; and some had no label. I still haven't been able to bring myself to throw them out.

For nine years as a senator, my father had a formal political role in keeping up the eternal vigilance which alone sustains liberty. Throughout his whole life as a citizen of this country, he proudly exercised the rights that vigilance protected. He never let the famous Canadian attributes of modesty or diffidence get in the way, and even his seriously declining health in his last years could not keep him from fearlessly denouncing whatever he saw as trickery or foolishness.

We will always need such voices, speaking out loud and clear against secrecy, injustice and error. As John Ralston Saul reminds us, "If you want to re-energize democracy, it can be done. But it is going to require the persistent stubbornness of the citizen."[28] In his life-long pursuit of the common good, Eugene Forsey was an example of that "persistent stubbornness."

CHAPTER FOUR

Protest and Vision: Building Democratic Socialism

> People will fight for a democracy which delivers the goods, which gives them a decent human life. If that means changing the economic system, then we must change the economic system. If, as a recent book contends, "Democracy Needs Socialism," then socialism we must have.
>
> — From a radio address, February 1939[1]

When my father began his career as a young lecturer at McGill in 1929, Canada was on the brink of enormous change. The stock market crash that fall and the increasing devastation of the Depression revealed an economic system out of control and wreaking havoc at home and abroad. The Dirty Thirties immersed our young nation in economic hardship and human suffering on a scale unprecedented in its history.

Throughout that turbulent decade, small groups of men and

women came together in communities across the country to protest the irrationality and injustice of this human-made disaster, and to envision a humane and workable alternative. Their alternative was socialism, and in it they saw the hope that so many had lost. Through their ideas and their actions, these socialist pioneers changed Canada dramatically. Eugene Forsey was one of them.

My father's socialism is one of the least known and least understood aspects of his legacy. However, it is far from being the least important. The same principles that guided him and his friends in their early days of socialist activism continued to inform his work throughout his life. Those shared ideals also form the foundation upon which today's movements for economic and social justice are built.

Not only are the ideals the same; so too are many of the issues. As I dug back into Dad's socialist writings, most of them dating from before I was born, I experienced a growing sense of déjà vu. Current public discourse is filled with the same issues Dad was addressing in the 1930s and 40s: the gap between rich and poor; the role of government in the economy; the power of big business; regional versus centralized authority; public versus private ownership; corporate concentration; workers' rights; social policy reform; farm incomes; civil liberties; unemployment; taxation; economic "recovery." All these questions were the subjects of intense public debate at that time, and they have become so again. Some of the specifics have changed but the themes and the powerful interests involved have not.

My father and his fellow socialists responded to the challenges of their time, and helped to transform our country. Today their words and actions are an offering towards a future that once again hangs in the balance.

> McGill, Feb. 2, 1932
> Dearest Mother,
> At last I'm making a colossal, heroic effort to catch up with arrears…. Monday was a hectic day, with great piles of work accumulated. That evening, Harper, Prof of Russian at Chicago, spoke to us on Russia. Harper is the most unintellectual-looking man you could imagine, but clever, and brilliantly well informed on his subject … Tuesday

> evening I went to the Y.M. [C.A.] to lead a group which was to discuss Socialism. They were a poor lot. About eight people, some silent, some vociferously letting loose vast swarms of bees from their bonnets, they gave me a stimulating evening nonetheless. But I question whether it was worthwhile ...
>
> Wednesday King Gordon came to dinner and stayed on afterwards to talk to Quakers about the "Christian Ethic and Social Revolution." In spite of the exciting title I found it tame stuff ... Thursday evening Church Young People's supper, speech by me on "Disarmament." A small and anaemic group, presided over by a pompous, conceited, long-winded, inveterate punster. I stirred them up a bit ... Friday night, Jennie Lee [of the British Labour Party] at the Labour Club. Good crowd and lively time ...[2]

My father's letters home from Montreal in the early 1930s give a taste of the whirl of political activity that he and his socialist friends spearheaded during those heady years. Surrounded by the appalling spectacle of Canada in the grips of the Depression, these young men and women decided it was up to them to act. They joined, or formed, a variety of study and action groups, and with the confidence and enthusiasm of youth went about the historic task they had set themselves.

> ... Friday night I go to Toronto for a week-end pow-wow with Frank [Scott], King G[ordon], [Frank] Underhill and others of the 'Forum' crowd, in hopes of founding a Socialist research and pamphleteering organization with — we hope — Woodsworth as Hon. Pres. We think we might do a good deal to strengthen his hand by supplying accurate information and trying to rouse a critical spirit among the public. I'm staying with [Jim] Macdonell of the National Trust — Massey's brother-in-law — who is much amused by the idea that he's sheltering part of a revolutionary plot![3]

That "weekend pow-wow" was the January 1932 founding meeting of the League for Social Reconstruction, and those names — Scott, Gordon, Underhill, Woodsworth, and others — are engraved forever in the history of Canada's social movements. I grew up hearing the names and must have met many of the people as a child. But I took them for granted as my parents' friends, and for years I remained completely unaware of the role these remarkable individuals played in building our country.

In a letter written immediately after that meeting, Dad reported:

> ... The Toronto trip went off well. We had a comfortable journey up in the fast train, and spent next morning and most of the next afternoon thrashing out our "basis" and "aims" and setting up a provisional organization. The discussion grew wearisome at times, and we shed in the process various possible (or impossible) adherents on both right and left: fiery Communists and chilly 19th century orthodox economists. We had quite a large and interesting and able group left, however, and I think have the chance of doing some very useful work. We've already decided the titles of our first ten or twelve pamphlets, and allotted them to our Montreal and Toronto groups ...[4]

The early years of modern Canadian socialism have been recorded and analyzed elsewhere by able historians and biographers. The LSR story, for example, has been told in Professor Michiel Horn's book *The League for Social Reconstruction: Intellectual Origins of the Democratic Left in Canada, 1930-1942*.[5] The League's own 1935 volume, *Social Planning for Canada*, much of which was penned by my father, sets out in eloquent detail its analysis and program — a program that arguably was a major influence on this country's subsequent social and political development. Other fine accounts exist of the evolution of the socialist CCF party and the struggles of the labour movement during that same period.[6] Dad's book of memoirs, *A Life on the Fringe*, adds his own perspective to the historical record, along with an array of delightful stories.

That massive body of work by others provides the broad framework for my much more personal examination of my father's role in those events and his part in the thinking that shaped them.

The socialist project that Dad and his colleagues proposed to the country in the 1930s and 1940s arose out of a reality starkly different from their idealistic vision. The ravages of the Depression were everywhere evident — massive unemployment, desperate poverty, enforced migration, shocking waste, and for many, utter hopelessness. The socialists saw their movement as crystallizing "a protest against gross inequality of income and economic power, against poverty and thwarted and repressed human lives, against waste and inefficiency, against the inhumanity and social stupidity of exploitation and war. Above all else," they said, "this protest has a right to be heard."[7]

There is not much in Dad's own writings that actually describes the plight of the farmers or the unemployed, the day-to-day misery of the poor. He was well aware of his privilege, his lack of personal experience of the desperate suffering afflicting so many. Accordingly, he turned the tools of his trade to the task of identifying and combatting what he saw as the causes of those problems.

One avenue for this kind of work was the local United Church Presbytery's Committee on Social and Economic Research, which was made up of Dad, his friend King Gordon, and J. A. Coote, all members of the Fellowship for a Christian Social Order. Despite opposition from conservative elements within the church, they persisted in delving into company reports for facts and figures from which to derive the real story — a pioneering effort in what is now called corporate research. They produced popular pamphlets explaining the intricacies of capitalist economics, and information bulletins detailing economic abuses by specific industries. They documented and vigorously denounced the exploitative pricing of basic necessities like bread, milk, and coal, and they exposed government plans that threatened to undermine civil liberties or cut back on relief for the unemployed.[8]

If Dad were a young activist economist today, he might be working with the Ecumenical Coalition for Economic Justice, or studying the effects of tax cuts for the Canadian Centre for Policy Alternatives. I can imagine him leading a workshop on restoring the social safety net, or speaking at a Council of Canadians teach-in on globalization. He would certainly be blogging, twittering, and emailing the papers to denounce a mega-merger or challenge a government plan. And he would be busily writing articles for the *CCPA Monitor* and *rabble.ca*, as he did back then for the *Canadian Forum*.

In his memoirs, he referred to his writings from that period as "nearly all ephemeral." Sadly, the themes of injustice and hypocrisy are far from "ephemeral." All these years later, many of those articles resonate with a lamentably renewed relevance. Although a few are little more than a litany of dismal statistics, he usually combined facts and critical commentary to good effect.

In 1933, when government authorities issued a call for "equality of sacrifice" by all citizens to help the country through the Depression, Dad dug up the data to see who was already sacrificing what. Not surprisingly, he found that shareholders were still raking in dividends while workers were suffering the devastating effects of rock-bottom wages and vanishing jobs. "To any humane person," he wrote, "this sort of thing is morally hideous and intolerable, made more so by [the] pretence of trading for the public good."[9] A few years later, when the government announced the beginning of economic "recovery," he had similar comments on the hypocrisy of the elites[10]:

> Unfortunately, it is now clear that the chief social-political consequence of recovery is an intense and bitter campaign of reaction. This takes [several] forms, by no means unrelated to each other: ... postponement of further social services, drastic relief cuts, stiff resistance to trade unionism, [and] ruthless disregard of civil liberties ... The attitude of ... the capitalist class seems to be: "This is our recovery, and we're not going to have organized labour muscling in on it."
> ("Recovery — For Whom?")

> ... Nor should the government be allowed to skulk out of its responsibilities on the plea of lack of funds ... It is unmistakably clear that Canadian and external capitalists did extremely well for themselves in this country last year ... The money is there, and any government which means business can get it. A good stiff *succession duty, a tax on*

undistributed profits, a levy on wealth to reduce debt charges, would enable even a Liberal government to work wonders. ("More Unemployment — Less Relief")

Mr. Dunning's budget must have warmed the hearts of his late business associates ... His new tax exemptions offer them the chance of saving from the Treasury's clutches perhaps as much as $50,000,000 ... The taxes of the poor, it will be observed, remain as they were. The one tax the Minister reduces is the tax based on ability to pay. The poor pay about two-thirds of Dominion taxes, but it is the rich who get relief ... "To him that hath shall be given." ("The Budget")[11]

Then, as now, such hypocrisy liked to wrap itself in the cloak of "objective analysis." In 1937, when a "Citizens' Research Institute" appeared on the scene with a supposedly objective report on taxation, Dad noted wryly: "[This group] announces almost in one breath that its reports are 'non-political and impartial,' and that it believes they will be welcomed by 'every man who realizes that governmental spending must be cut and taxes lowered.'"[12]

These days we hear a great deal of supposedly "objective" commentary from right-wing party hacks turned academics, and from corporate-funded think-tanks. Their claim that government "costs too much" is a perennial favourite, and one Dad countered with his own analysis. "What big business propagandists usually call 'the cost of government,'" he wrote, "is nothing of the kind. *It is the cost of services which the democratic electorate requires the government to undertake,* plus the interest on public debt ... The cry of 'overgovernment' is often an attempt to lure innocent voters into supporting candidates who will 'economize' by eliminating, not the governments, but the services."[13]

He also pointed out who would benefit if such "economizing" measures were put into effect, and who would pay. He seems to have had a crystal ball to so cogently anticipate the course governments would be taking years later: "The way would then be open to reduce the income tax and other levies on the well-to-do and throw the whole burden of public expenditure — instead of merely most of it — on the shoulders of those least able to pay."[14]

> ## OTHER EPHEMERA FROM THE *FORUM*
>
> Some time ago I had a conversation with two responsible officers of an important business organization ... I insisted that if a man did his work properly it was none of his employer's business what his opinions were or what he did with his spare time ... They were as horrified as if I had declared myself a cannibal ... They took it for granted that when an employer hires a workman he hires body, mind and soul. They would doubtless have been completely mystified if I had told them this is simply slavery and idolatry.
> ("From the Seats of the Mighty")
>
> The Lever Brothers pamphlet, "The Problem of Unemployment," ... officially endorsed by the largest body of Canadian employers [the Canadian Chamber of Commerce], explains very clearly and at some length that "full employment" does not mean full employment in the plain man's sense, but only the avoidance of "mass unemployment"; that industry cannot function effectively without a reserve of people waiting for work."
> ("Some Questions for Mr. Macdonnell")[16]

In satirical articles with titles like "Bedtime Stories for Workingmen" and "Every Man a Capitalist," he poked fun at the big business establishment. One such piece was inspired by a patronizing bit of propaganda concocted by the Canadian Chamber of Commerce in the form of an imaginary factory foreman's letter to a worker who had been attending "red" meetings. The "letter" assured the poor misguided fellow that capitalism, far from exploiting him, was entirely for his benefit, and that his own tiny bank account and life insurance policy actually made him a "capitalist" himself. Dad called it a masterpiece of Canadian fiction, which should "establish 'Foreman' as incontestably one of [our] leading short story writers."[15]

My father also contributed two chapters on economics to the book *Towards the Christian Revolution*, published in the midst of the Depression by the Fellowship for a Christian Social Order. Half a century later, he looked back on some of what he had written in that volume as "very foolish, or worse," but at the time, it reflected his determination to name and challenge the realities of a capitalist system run amok. "Capitalism," he stated, "necessarily divides society into two classes, capitalist and working class. Between the working class and those who control the means of production there exists an irreconcilable conflict ... If we deny the fact of class struggle we are indulging in sheer idealism."[17]

His explanation of surplus value similarly came straight out of Marxism: "Income from ownership is simply the product of the unpaid labour of the workers ... [the return to] owners, who simply by virtue of their ownership hold the workers to ransom.... Like class, [this] is not a theory but a fact. Exploitation is not an excrescence of capitalism. It *is* capitalism."[18]

To the modern ear, this language may sound both somewhat extreme and at the same time rather quaint. The phrasings we use today to express such ideas have evolved to reflect a growing recognition of nuances and complexities, and to address not only class, but race, gender, and other dimensions of power and powerlessness. However, the near-disappearance of explicitly socialist terminology from common parlance also points to a degree of co-optation of political discourse by the juggernaut of global capitalism. The current generalized reluctance to use even gentle and accurate words like "socialism" reflects a desire to soft-pedal radical analysis and make it more palatable and less threatening to the established order.

In any case, nowadays we use such terms as "social democracy" to refer to the ideals of Canada's early socialist pioneers. But regardless of the label, the original commitment persists: to name and protest social and economic injustice, to document and analyze its causes, and, on that informed basis, to envision and fight for a better future.

During my father's political coming of age, people around the world were watching, with hope or trepidation, the great revolutionary experiment taking place in Russia. Many young socialists, inspired by the stories they heard, dreamed of travelling there to see for themselves what was

Protest and Vision

Eugene (left) and American journalist McDermott onboard the steamer Spartak, *travelling the Volga River from Gorky to Stalingrad, 1932. His trip to the Soviet Union was inspiring, but he retained a healthy skepticism.*

happening. Dad was fortunate enough to be able to make the trip in the summer of 1932, and his hand-written epistles to his mother give a fascinating account.

"This is the country for an economist to visit just now," he enthused in a twenty-two-page letter after his first five days in Russia. "Everything humming, everyone full of ardour and 'faith' ... I can see my whole year's work re-shaping itself in the light of what I've already seen here."[19]

He went on to describe a Russian workers' clinic, "well-equipped, spotlessly clean, and in apple-pie order," and a technical institute, where "one felt the reality of the comradeship, yet the real respect for the staff." He noted the "vigorous posters announcing that alcoholism and socialism were incompatible — an excellent sentiment." His words remind me of my own 1978 visit to Cuba during the glory days of the island's revolution, when the energy and hope were likewise palpable.

Although the Russian trip did nothing to improve Dad's political or career prospects when he returned to Canada, it provided him with a wealth of material for reflection and debate. He never became a true believer, and his letters from Russia also detailed his doubts, critically dissecting the lectures they were given on various aspects of the Soviet system.[20] But when he compared what he saw there with the dismal reality of the Depression gripping Canada, he was willing to give the Russian Communists a good deal of benefit of the doubt.

Even four years later, he still felt able to write about the Soviets' approach as "the decisive answer to [the] misgivings about incentives." "Starting with a primitive economy," he wrote, "[the U.S.S.R.] has in less than two decades advanced to a leading place among the industrial nations, its standard of living is steadily rising, and it is moving towards political democracy instead of away from it."[21]

That is one of the few examples I have found in his writings where he clearly allowed wishful thinking to block out reality. His rosy view soon collapsed, however, with the widespread revelations about Stalin's purges.

Although the RCMP's security branch started a file on him after his Russian trip and maintained it into the 1960s,[22] my father was never really drawn to communism itself. I think for him the two biggest sticking points were religion and democracy. His Christianity made him skeptical of an entirely materialistic political philosophy, and his deep-rooted respect for parliamentary government would not allow him to endorse a "dictatorship of the proletariat," whatever its economic accomplishments.

So it was not a vision of a Communist utopia that my father and his colleagues developed over the next few years. Their path clearly led elsewhere, towards a "co-operative commonwealth," a vital and participatory society built on a democratic foundation of equality and sharing. The principles that inspired them were social justice, human rights, political and economic democracy, and a strong role for the state in defending the public interest. "The 'cooperative commonwealth' means neither coercion nor anarchy," Dad wrote, "but a system in which things will be done by co-operation, by free citizens and their organizations, including their governments, working together."[23]

If their goals seemed highly idealistic given the realities of the Depression, their actual proposals were very specific. Two of the best known and most comprehensive presentations of their vision were the Regina Manifesto, drafted for the CCF's founding convention in 1933, and the 1935 book already mentioned, *Social Planning for Canada*, compiled by the League for Social Reconstruction.

Dad was involved in the creation of both, and the book in particular included a great deal of his work. Its purpose was to offer to a broad readership the LSR's analysis of the status quo, and their plan for the very different Canada they envisioned. *Social Planning for Canada* detailed what social and economic justice would mean to ordinary people: full employment, fair wages and prices, progressive taxation, and basic economic security in childhood, old age, illness, or misfortune. It laid out coherent national policies for food, health, housing, "power and fuel," and transportation and communications. It presented the LSR's concept of "social planning," which would work from the bottom up, with a planning commission responsible to Parliament, and a democratic process involving citizens through their trade unions, co-operatives, farm organizations, and other groups.[24]

A key element of the LSR's radical dream was a strong role for the state — a democratic government representing the interests of all Canadians. The government would be in charge of economic planning and regulation, and would own key industries, as well as controlling banking and investment, providing a social safety net, and overseeing a just redistribution of wealth. It would also work to strengthen parliamentary democracy itself, ensuring that the planning process and its results stayed responsive to the will of the people.

Dad and his socialist friends were adamant that their policies would never mean the sacrifice of freedom or human rights. Ominous evidence emerging from Europe under fascism and from the Soviet Union under Stalin was already making all too clear the kinds of things that could happen if democracy and civil liberties were suppressed. Nor was this only a distant threat. In Canada, too, freedoms were under attack, notably in Quebec, where the link to fascism was especially evident.

The LSR group in Montreal had ample opportunity to reflect on what their socialist vision demanded, simply by observing its opposite happening around them. They worked alongside members of the Communist Party on issues of shared concern, notably the Spanish Civil War and the Padlock Act. In 1939, despite his growing wariness of Communist doctrine and practice, Dad helped persuade a divided Civil Liberties Union to publicly support nine local Communists who had been arrested under what he considered "highly objectionable" Defence of Canada Regulations.[25] For him, human rights were universal and indivisible, just as they are in the various declarations and covenants now established internationally.

People's social and economic rights were also essential: the right to an education, the right to independent trade unions and collective bargaining, and — most basic of all — the right of access to the physical necessities of life. As Dad pointed out, other rights and liberties tended to seem less important to people who were "inadequately clothed and housed and fed, or [had] to spend most of their waking hours grubbing for a bare living."[26] In the 1930s and 40s, the lives of far too many Canadians fitted that dismal description.

My father viewed all these elements of "social reconstruction" as intimately inter-connected, each leading to and requiring the others. As he told the Canadian Political Science Association in 1932:

> Political democracy without economic democracy and something like equality of income is in a very precarious condition, to say the least. Democratic control of industry without a drastic redistribution of wealth is simply impossible, and any government which tries it will soon succumb.

> But granted we must have a drastic redistribution of wealth, need that mean socialization of industry? Can't we do it by taxation and social services? No ... The only adequate and permanent policy is to get the sources of wealth into public ownership and under public control, and to use not a fraction but the whole of the proceeds for public purposes.[27]

To those who viewed Canada as a strictly "free enterprise" economy, this emphasis on state involvement was a red flag. But Dad was quick to rebut their claims to economic purity. "The business leaders who clamour for government to 'let business alone' would die of fright if any government took them at their word," he wrote in 1936. "For it is not only factory acts, workmen's compensation, old age pensions, minimum wage laws and public utility commissions which would disappear; it is also tariff protection, loans, guarantees, subsidies and half a hundred other government services and aids to business. Laissez-faire is dead."[28]

He was careful to point out that this vision "[did] not mean the socialization of any one's fountain pen or shirts or dresses or pyjamas." Socialism was concerned with ownership of the means of production, not of consumer goods. "It requires no very strenuous intellectual effort," he wrote, "to see a difference between ownership of a hat and ownership of bonds and shares. The latter necessarily involves exploitation; the former does not."[29]

For him that was the key point — to eliminate exploitation. Although over time he became less doctrinaire about the need to nationalize industry, he continued to insist on a vigorous and active role for government in that domain and in others.[30]

None of the young radicals involved in Canada's early socialist movement was under the illusion that social change would come about simply through protesting the status quo and proposing alternatives. No matter how astute the analysis or how seductive the dream, they knew they needed public opinion on their side if the necessary transformation was even to begin, let alone endure. An intellectual vanguard might push

Delegates to the CCF's Regina Convention, 1933. Eugene Forsey is third from right, front row.

The 1930s socialists saw popular educational work as the way to develop that support. "Teach the proletariat first and organize them afterwards!" — that was the message of the progressive intellectuals who led the movement. They hoped that the people, when presented with facts and reasoned arguments, would see the light and flock to embrace socialism.

In hindsight, it is easy to criticize the naïveté of this simple faith for not taking adequately into account the complexity of the factors that influence people's thinking, or recognizing how deeply entrenched are the many barriers to change. Still, anyone doing serious political work would agree that educating the citizenry is a necessary — even if hardly a sufficient — element of such work.

Education was certainly a vital concern for my father, and it was a recurring theme throughout his work. He believed that public policy had to be shaped by reason, and that education was essential for enhancing the role of reason in public discourse and decision-making.[31] Consequently, a great deal of his energy went into educational efforts to persuade Canadians that democratic socialism was the way to make this country a better place.

The written word was an obvious tool for such a purpose, and Dad knew how to use it. His writings were soon appearing widely — not only in left-wing magazines like the *Canadian Forum*, but in academic journals, labour publications, and mainstream media like *Maclean's* and

Saturday Night. But it was his letters to the editor that would become a Forsey hallmark.

While at Oxford, he had been strongly influenced by the "respected national institution" of letters to the *Times*. "In England," he explained, "infringement of the civil liberties of even an unsavoury person arouses public indignation. When I returned to Canada in 1929, the inclination to take things lying down irked me considerably. That started me writing to newspapers in defence of the unemployed and others who were having a thin time of it."[32]

His assessment of the effectiveness of those early letters to the Montreal press was modest. "My stubborn loquacity certainly contributed to my becoming more and more obnoxious to the Montreal Establishment. Just as certainly, it had no effect whatever on public events."[33]

Perhaps not directly on public events themselves (though the RCMP found them of interest). But quite possibly it did affect some readers, at least to the extent of casting doubt on the otherwise unchallenged pronouncements of the elite. Dad felt that goal was worth aiming for. In one of his old files I came across a note he had typed out for himself on the back of an unrelated document. Under the heading "Ryerson's quotation from Macauley," it reads: "No misrepresentation should be allowed to pass unrefuted. When a silly letter makes its appearance in the corner of a provincial newspaper, it will not do to say, 'What stuff!' We must remember that such statements, constantly reiterated and seldom answered, will assuredly be believed."[34]

My father's second main tool for popular education was the spoken word. This often consisted of informal exchanges at the personal level with colleagues, students, and acquaintances. Naturally there were times when his exhortations fell on deaf ears as on one occasion with Dr. Alice Wilson, his mother's pioneering colleague at the Geological Survey of Canada. Dad must have mentioned something about the historical dialectic and the inevitability of capitalism's demise. "Well," replied the eminent geologist, "of course I always tend to think of things in terms of millions of years." At that point, Dad recalled, "I gave up!"

In the 1930s and 40s, before television and the Internet, public lectures and local meetings played a much more important role than they do now, both in many people's lives and in developing the overall public discourse. Such events were frequent and widespread, and they enabled the kind of dynamic face-to-face human interaction that modern technologies strive to emulate. And although any single event might have had relatively few participants, the cumulative numbers involved were impressive.

Dad took full advantage of these opportunities. From community centres to church basements, from weekend conferences to summer camps, from modest living rooms to college auditoriums, Eugene Forsey expounded and argued and joked and persuaded and exchanged the ideas that were so essential to him and to the movement he espoused. He was often called on to make two or three speeches a week, on subjects as diverse as education in the Soviet Union, labour political action, the need for a planned economy, or the development of a third political party. But he did have his limits.

"The Westmount Women's Club want me to speak," he informed his mother in a 1934 letter. "I'm going to refuse, as I can't think of a subject 'non-partisan, non-controversial, light, but interesting' as required! Also, I'm busy ..."[35]

Like his friend Graham Spry and their fellow LSR members, Dad was an active supporter and user of public broadcasting. As early as 1934, he took part in an LSR-sponsored series of radio lectures on the local Toronto station affiliated with the Canadian Radio Broadcasting Commission, forerunner of the CBC.[36] Radio was beginning to demonstrate its huge potential for reaching beyond small groups and engaging a broad audience, and as time went on, Dad made increasing use of it.

Despite his growing public profile as a radical, he was careful to keep his political opinions out of the classroom during his tremulous stay on the McGill faculty, for reasons of both principle and pragmatism. He did, however, help out with the activities of the McGill Political Economy Club, the House of Commons Club at Royal Victoria College, and the McGill Labour Club, contributing (anonymously) to the latter's short-lived periodical, *Alarm Clock*.

Outside the university, he shared his ideas at events like the YMCA's 1933 Couchiching Summer Institute of Politics and Economics, the CCF's family camp on Gabriola Island, and the University of British Columbia's 1939 Summer School. Nor did he shrink from displaying his controversial socialist faith in the more rarified atmosphere of the "Learned Societies," as when he addressed the recently formed Canadian Political Science Association in 1932. There, he referred explicitly to "so strong a socialist as myself," and suggested people must be "prepared to turn the world upside down, to work a social revolution — not necessarily by violent means."[37]

> ## "THE ONLY PRACTICAL POLICY"[38]
>
> Pure economic individualism proved itself intolerable a century ago. Individualism mitigated by factory acts, social services, minimum wage laws and trade union action has ... conspicuously failed to provide for the vast majority of the people even security of livelihood, let alone a civilized standard of living ... In fact, in the effort to attach safety devices to our economic mechanism which would prevent it from killing or maiming most of the population, we have come near to stopping the machine altogether. In other terms, our concessions to working class discontent are killing capitalism by inches without appreciably bettering working class conditions of life.
>
> We cannot go on in this fashion, making the worst of both worlds. Still less can we go back to laissez-faire. The only practical policy is some attempt at conscious intelligent direction and social control of our economy....
>
> Ultimately, I think the possibility of a planned economy rests on our acceptance of a communist social philosophy. Note that I say a communist philosophy, not the Communist philosophy. What I mean ... is perhaps best expressed, not in the words of Marx or Lenin, but in those of a 17th century English "Leveller," Colonel Rainboro: "Really, I think the poorest he that is in England hath a life to live as the richest he." It would be hard to find a better statement of the fundamental principle of Socialism.

Dad's radical audacity on that occasion seems to have passed largely unnoticed, but such was not always the case. The following year, a speech he gave to the St. James Literary Club on the prospects for capitalism caused an uproar both at McGill and beyond. The *Montreal Star* reported that "Professor" Forsey had suggested capitalism's slogan might be "Blessed are the greedy, for they shall inherit the earth." The *Quebec Chronicle-Telegraph* the next day lamented the "spreading [of] socialist ideas among the undergraduate bodies," a trend it saw as "threatening the cause of higher education and giving alarm to parents in all parts of the country."[39]

Outraged letters poured into the principal's office from wealthy citizens and industrialists — some of them important donors to the university. Even Quebec Premier Taschereau wrote to object, enclosing the newspaper clippings. Although a handful of supporters staunchly defended Dad's right to air his political views in public, the calls for his resignation had begun.[40]

Indeed, throughout his activist years in Montreal, he was treading the knife-edge that defined the limits of academic freedom in the 1930s. His continuing refusal to cease and desist from his educational work in "political economy" — broadly defined — made him a perpetual thorn in the side of the powerful Montreal elite. The situation shifted only when he was finally forced to leave McGill in 1941.[41]

If education of the populace was regarded as a cardinal sin by the establishment of the day, direct political organizing was an even greater outrage. Here again, Eugene Forsey's name kept cropping up.

His anti-establishment ideas might not have got him into so much trouble had he not insisted on acting on them. Never one to merely theorize while others did the work, Dad took an active role in building the movement he believed in. In addition to his major commitments to the LSR and the CCF, he was deeply involved in the Student Christian Movement (SCM), the Fellowship for a Christian Social Order (FCSO), and the explicitly non-partisan Civil Liberties Union, which he helped to found in Montreal in 1937. Although not all the groups were exclusively socialist, they were all part of the struggle for social justice during the Depression and the years that followed.

And it was indeed a struggle. At every step they faced formidable opposition from the status quo. The Civil Liberties Union, for example, attempting to defend the basic freedoms of expression and assembly, found itself up against the combined might of Quebec's reactionary Catholic Church hierarchy and the Duplessis government, with disappointingly little public or political support. Even explicitly Christian organizations like the FCSO, which focused mainly on study and education rather than on direct political action, were looked at askance. Merely by virtue of their membership in such groups, people like my father risked running afoul of employers and colleagues, not only in industry and commerce but in the churches and the universities as well.

Even if there had not been such determined external opposition to the work of those progressive groups, the job of keeping them going and working to achieve their goals would still have been an enormous one. Any "civil society" organization, from a small local group to a national political party, demands a huge amount of work. Organizational maintenance can be tedious and frustrating, and much of it is of only internal or transitory importance. Moreover, as with housework, a great deal of it has to be done over and over again. When set-backs and defeats outnumber victories, and the odds seem stacked against success, it is even more difficult to carry on.

But my father believed passionately in the cause these organizations were pursuing. He saw the need for the work to be done, and knew there were only a handful of people to do it. So he shouldered his share of responsibilities, both on the front lines and behind the scenes. A 1937 letter gives a glimpse of what this meant for him.

> During all of last fall, winter and spring, I had fortnightly meetings of the National Executive of the LSR, fortnightly meetings (or more) of the provincial council of the CCF (of which I am president), two or three speeches a week, frequent meetings of the Civil Liberties Committee (of which, during most of the time, I was chairman), occasional meetings of the Spanish Aid Committee, two press statements for the CCF to help draft, two meetings of the CCF National Council to attend, a CCF pamphlet to help draft, the National Conventions of the LSR and the FCSO to attend (a dinner speech at one of them), memoranda on the "defence" estimates for nine organizations ... I did nearly all these things simply because if I hadn't, they wouldn't have got done, or not at the right time.[42]

Throughout this same period, he was also lecturing full-time at McGill, working on the dissertation for his first Ph.D. attempt, helping with the writing of the LSR's new book *Democracy Needs Socialism*, and doing regular articles for the *Forum*.

Of all these involvements, it was the CCF — the Co-operative Commonwealth Federation — that best exemplified Dad's commitment to political organizing. As a national political party with democratic means and socialist objectives, the CCF was right up his alley. In terms of the big picture, it represented a potential avenue for implementing the reforms that he and other progressive people across the country were demanding. At the personal level, the fact that it was a political party provided him with the opportunity to work with and through the British-based parliamentary system which was his lifelong passion. In the CCF, his socialist ideals joined forces with his devotion to parliamentary democracy. He became a member of the party within months of its organization, and remained so as long as it was in existence.

Of course, he was never an uncritical member. There were many internal disagreements along the way, over matters of both principle and strategy, some of which are explored in Chapter 15. But for Dad and most of his "political friends," frank discussion and debate were an integral part of the dynamics of their movement, as essential within the party as they were in Parliament and in society as a whole. The differences that arose and the criticisms he felt called upon to make in no way lessened his party loyalty.

Harriet (left) with CCF parliamentarians Angus and Grace MacInnis, Ottawa, 1941.

From the start, he was fully aware of the need for a broad-based grassroots movement to carry out the radical program that he and his comrades were proposing. "The task is immense," he stated. "The driving force must come from the mass of the people, from the uncomfortable classes. To think that we can rouse them to the necessary pitch by offering them security in their discomfort is to my mind perfectly fantastic. Just try to run an election on a slogan of that sort and see what happens."[43]

Unfortunately, the fledgling CCF fared little better than that at the polls. Dad was hopeful for the party over the long term, but he cherished no illusion that it already constituted the mass movement he knew was needed. The gap between the ideal of broad popular support and the political reality of the CCF was especially evident in Quebec, where Dad was provincial council president for several years. Many years later, he used to joke that the Quebec CCF was "a Mexican army — all generals, no privates, no non-commissioned officers, no anything."

On one occasion in the Senate, rising to speak to the mere handful of his colleagues in attendance, he commented: "One of the advantages of having been a member of the CCF for as long as there *was* a CCF, is that anything over seven people qualified as a mass meeting. I am therefore addressing, by the old CCF standard, a monster mass meeting …"[44]

It was, of course, with the CCF that my father accumulated his impressive series of defeats as a candidate for elected public office. His first campaign, in the Montreal municipal election of 1940, was an experience he thoroughly enjoyed, unsuccessful though it was. He found his three later candidacies much less enjoyable. By then, he was living in Ottawa, working with the Canadian Congress of Labour and raising a young family. In the 1945 provincial election in Ontario, both he and the party fared dismally, although the CCF had made a good showing two years earlier. He spent the next while in what he described as "almost complete political cold storage," unable to find time for very much except his heavy Congress workload and his domestic responsibilities.

"I am so completely out of everything," he wrote to Arthur Meighen in the fall of 1948, "that most of my political friends have almost forgotten my existence. Also, I suspect they feel I should be out of place in the mixture of lady-likeness and scurrility which our politics seem to have become."[45]

However, only weeks after writing that letter he was back in the fray, running in a by-election in a rock-ribbed Conservative riding against the new federal Tory leader, George Drew. His shoestring campaign was designed to appeal to people's common sense, and was neither scurrilous nor especially lady-like. But nor was it successful. Drew won handily, garnering almost four times the vote Dad got for the CCF. When the two men faced each other once more in the general election the following year, the Conservative leader won again, this time by almost double the earlier margin.

These personal electoral defeats were made much more poignant for Dad by the overall decline in the fortunes of the CCF — the party he had nurtured with his sweat and tears since its birth in the Depression years, the party he had hoped would bring to fruition his dreams of social and economic justice for Canada. Although he continued to support the CCF in every way he could through the decade of the 1950s, he became increasingly resigned to its apparent inability to attract and engage the mass of the population towards its political goals.

What motivated someone like my father to work so hard for the socialist movement? He was privileged enough to survive the Depression relatively unscathed, but he was far from untouched by the horrifying reality around him. In fact, as a Christian and as an aware human being, he was outraged. The same was true of most of his friends and colleagues. Unable to stand by as passive observers, they threw themselves into the work of transforming the existing social and economic order.

For some of a more cynical bent, that explanation may lack credibility. It relies heavily on human empathy and a sense of community — qualities that modern corporatist society likes to portray as old-fashioned and no match for self-interest. The religious element in the mix could similarly seem suspect to those who see altruism as out of date and smacking of condescension. From that perspective, the very fact of Dad's privilege raises questions. Was he motivated by guilt or a sense of *noblesse oblige*? And if so, does that diminish the practical or moral value of the work he did?

Reflecting on his commitment to the socialist cause, I cannot detect even a trace of guilt. This is perhaps surprising, given the readiness with which he accepted guilt — deserved or otherwise — in his personal life.

Politically, though, it just didn't play. His altruism was genuine: he cared about other people and identified with their suffering. His religious beliefs reinforced the natural empathy that was already there. At the same time, his sense of individual responsibility for making change was clearly related to his awareness of his own privilege.

Professor Alan Whitehorn, who has written extensively on the history of the Left in Canada, explained it this way: "Those who became radicalized by the Depression, who helped construct the LSR, were very much influenced by the Fabian socialist tradition of the Left intellectuals. One of the criticisms in recent years of the LSR was that they did have a tendency to think that the Left academics were a vanguard in the positive sense, who would provide a helping hand, not only within the working class movement, but also as state planners, social workers, administrators, once the social democrats had come to power. If you look at *Social Planning for Canada* — it was a wonderfully pioneering detailed book, but it was kind of a top down model, as was the Regina Manifesto in many ways."

My father was certainly well aware of the limitations of any "top down" tendency in the movement. In various talks and articles in the 1940s he emphasized the requirement for "planning from the bottom," and put it into specific, practical terms.[46] But he never pretended that he was himself one of the people at "the bottom."

Does this mean that his motivation was based on *noblesse oblige*? Probably to some extent. Whitehorn, for example, sees Dad as having been "very much influenced by the best qualities of Toryism — that the better educated and more affluent should provide a helping hand to the have-nots. For me, *noblesse oblige* does not have an arrogance; it has a sense of compassion. In terms of sheer talent, your dad was able to provide a helping hand to others."

Pierre Joncas, who knew Dad well from the 1960s on, agrees. He thinks my father's radicalism stemmed from "both his deep Christian convictions and his sense of *noblesse oblige*. His idea of socialism was that we owe it to our fellows. It was a question of solidarity and brotherhood, not of taxing the rich to pay off the poor to keep them quiet. There was *noblesse* in all of us, and however little we had to offer to the community, we ought to do our best to offer it. Those who had more to offer owed more to the community. It was a sense of justice."

I have no way of knowing whether Dad himself ever agonized over those questions. I know he was aware of his own privilege, but he was matter-of-fact about it. My guess is that for him, it was not something to feel badly about; rather, it gave him tools and resources to use towards the goals he espoused. The work was urgent, and he kept his nose to the grindstone and did what he thought had to be done.

Like the decade of the 1930s, the twenty-first century began with widespread protests and much talk of "vision." Fed up with the social and political deterioration of the 1980s and 1990s, and with the future so obviously on our doorstep, we were once again stretching our imaginations to try to envisage the kind of society we wanted for ourselves and our children. Much of that creative optimism has been overshadowed by events and by the urgency of the global crises now upon us. And yet it is such visioning, informed by past experience and stimulated by the dreams and actions of others, which can actually expand the boundaries of the possible.

It is amazing to me now to realize that the Left's ambitious proposals for "social reconstruction" in the 1930s and 1940s were widely seen at the time as representing very real possibilities for change — change that was perceived as either a promise or a threat, depending on one's political standpoint. Those proposals were at the core of much public debate and political maneuvering throughout those two decades, and their substance remains both compelling and controversial to this day. Thanks to the relentless efforts of the CCF, key elements of the socialist agenda, while sometimes not acknowledged as such, became central to many national and provincial election campaigns. Under the imminent threat of "socialism," the mainstream parties competed to either refute or appear to satisfy the popular demands "those damned radicals" had stirred up.

While the results for the CCF as a party were generally dismal, the results for Canada as a whole, over time, were tremendously beneficial. They included improved labour and welfare legislation, family allowances, medicare, and a broad public awareness of social justice issues — an awareness which, Canadians like to think, has in one way or another been a distinguishing feature of our society ever since.

My father's socialist vision was both very personal and very practical. He knew that political and economic theories were only as good as the results they produced on the ground. Socialism had to work in practice, to benefit ordinary people striving for a better life in an imperfect world.

In a 1970 interview, Dad called the early socialist movement "a revolt against what seemed to be crass injustice, a belief that only a pretty root-and-branch reconstruction of society would get rid of this."[47] That root-and-branch reconstruction never really happened; Canada did not even become another Scandinavia. But nor has it become — so far at least, despite disturbing trends — merely a poor northern imitation of the USA.

That we have pursued a different course is thanks in part to the vision, audacity, and hard work of early radicals like Eugene Forsey. To maintain that course, to defend the gains that have been made and build upon them, is to honour and continue their struggle.

CHAPTER FIVE

Trade Unions: Putting Principles to Work

> Unions must take an active and positive part in shaping social policy and carrying it into effect. It will not be enough for them to demand full employment, high wages, shorter hours. They will have to know how to get these things, and just how much is feasible at any given time.... Labour will have to know the answer to the employers' arguments, and be able to present a concrete, positive, feasible alternative policy. In short, its leaders will have to be industrial statesmen, and its rank and file informed citizens both of the industrial and political communities.
> — *The Canadian Unionist*, February 1945

In the spring of 1942, Eugene Forsey got a fresh chance to put his knowledge and skills to work for his socialist convictions. The door of the ivory tower had been slammed in his face, but with the job offer from the Canadian

Congress of Labour, another door had opened.

He was far from unfamiliar with labour issues. His interest in trade unions dated back to his undergraduate days and the influence of his radical professor J.C. Hemmeon, who encouraged him to do his Masters' thesis on the coal mines of Nova Scotia. Dad's intensive grassroots research in the mining communities produced a book which, in the view of historian Desmond Morton, "laid down the track" on the subject at the time.[1] On a personal level, his time in Cape Breton amounted to an immersion course in working class realities, and it instilled in him "a burning desire to be of use to workers who, in my judgement, had long been oppressed, exploited and swindled."[2]

From then on, defending workers' rights and improving the conditions of their lives was a clear imperative for my father. As an activist academic in Depression-era Montreal, he stood in solidarity with workers in many situations. He wrote articles and letters to the papers addressing unemployment and challenging the totally inadequate "relief" system. He worked with the McGill Labour Club and advocated vigorously for workers' rights through the Civil Liberties Union, the League for Social Reconstruction, and the CCF. Appalled by what fascist regimes in Europe were doing to working people, he warned against similar trends closer to home.[3] Indeed, a major provocation for his persistent opposition to the Duplessis government was its systematic repression of Quebec's working class.

But it wasn't until after he lost his university job in 1941 that he became a player in the trade union movement itself. When a research job opened up at the at the recently formed Canadian Congress of Labour (CCL) in Ottawa, his friend and former student David Lewis, then the national secretary of the CCF and later the leader of the New Democratic Party, suggested Dad for the position.

My father was in Cambridge, Massachusetts, on his Guggenheim Fellowship, working on his manuscript on cabinet government and licking his wounds from the McGill debacle, when Norman Dowd of the CCL wrote to him, outlining the proposal to establish a research department and asking if he "would be interested in work of this kind."

Dad replied by return post. "There is nothing I would like better. I think I could really be very useful to the Congress. I am very anxious to get into active work for the Labour movement, where I could use my fighting — and other — qualities to some purpose …"[4]

A few months later, he and Harriet moved back to Ottawa, where he joined the Congress staff. He spent the next twenty-seven years in a role he proudly described as that of "a trade union civil servant," putting his "fighting — and other — qualities" to use in a cause that reflected his ideals.

My father was almost the only member of the CCL staff who had not worked his way up through union ranks, and he used to jokingly call himself "the Congress's tame Ph.D." But he was warmly welcomed and quickly became part of the team. Nor was his research some ivory tower pursuit far removed from the day-to-day struggles of rank and file workers. The fledgling Canadian Congress of Labour was responding to very real and practical needs when it decided to allocate some of its scarce resources to a research department.

In that first letter to my father in Cambidge, Norman Dowd enumerated some of those needs. "The proposal," he wrote, "is [to] build up a library and compile information with regard to Labour relationships and industrial developments ... You would be called upon to assist in preparing briefs for Boards of Conciliation, the Regional or National War Labour Boards, etc., as well as preparing materials for use in wage-negotiations ..."[5]

That list turned out to be just for starters. Pat Conroy, the CCL's secretary-treasurer, briefed the new recruit on what to expect. "Your work," he explained in his broad Scottish brogue, "will be of three kinds: routine tasks, special projects, and emergencies." As Dad assumed his responsibilities, he frequently found himself obliged to squeeze the routine tasks into the scarce time left after he'd attended to the frequent "emergencies" and special projects.

Together with an assistant and a secretary, my father began gathering reference materials for the library and setting up other systems to deal with the myriad jobs that fell to the research department. They assembled and catalogued the collective agreements of all CCL-related unions, continually updating them as changes occurred. They answered a continuous stream of inquiries from member unions on specific matters, monitored employer actions and court decisions, and provided the affected unions with information to help them respond. They analyzed national and provincial government programs and labour laws, and prepared briefs and other documents presenting the workers' perspectives. They also helped develop educational materials for the Congress's member unions.

Here again, Dad's view of education as a key element in efforts towards social change came to the fore. "Unions must have the best information and expert advice they can get," he told an audience in 1949. "The general membership must understand the realities of the economic situation, at least in its main outlines. Without proper information and research, Labour will be acting in the dark, or at best in twilight. Without workers' education, there is almost certain to develop a fatal division between leadership and membership, with leadership drawing more and more authority into its own hands, yet without effective power because membership [would be] bewildered, frustrated, and in revolt."[6]

One of the research department's main tools for this educational part of its mandate was its regular bulletin, *Labour Research*. For each edition, Dad would assemble and scrutinize the available information on a particular subject, such as housing, price controls, taxation policy, unemployment insurance, automation, immigration, labour-related statistics, legislation, or the latest government budget. He would show the relevance of the issue to ordinary workers, note its impact on particular industries or regions, and explain the Congress's position or demands. He would also push for things like publicly funded health insurance, low-rent housing, or increased overseas aid, and decry government policies he believed were destructive.[7]

"Eugene Forsey was not the kind of modern economist full of quantitative methods that were in fashion even by the mid-50s," historian Desmond Morton told me. "He was, however, a man of principle, who had a lot of wisdom. He was a polymath, he knew about everything. After all, when you're the only research director, and you don't have a large staff as most of the larger unions and labour centrals do now, you have to know a great deal about a lot of things."

That was especially the case at that time, when the available technology was the communications equivalent of the Model "T." My father and his staff did all their work using manual typewriters, carbon paper, the telephone and the postal service. Photocopiers and fax machines did not yet exist, and the Internet and devices like the BlackBerry were undreamed-of. The sheer amount of time, money, and effort required in those days simply to pull information together, keep it up to date, and distribute it is almost unimaginable in today's world.

"Money Cranks"[8]

[CCL President A.R.] Mosher had a heart as big as all outdoors, but he was absolutely a push-over for money cranks. He was always expecting that somebody was going to find the economic philosopher's stone — the easy, simple, painless way out of economic difficulties. His pleasing habit was to see them on Sunday afternoon at his house and send them to me Monday morning with a request that I examine their stuff.

They were a queer lot. Every one of them had *the* final answer; he had made *the* great discovery about economics; and his scheme was *the* only scheme that would work. Quite literally, they were psychiatric cases. Perfectly harmless, and full of goodwill and earnest desire to benefit humanity, but bats in the belfry.

One polished Englishman, a retired Army officer, had a scheme he wanted to have endorsed by [leaders] in the labour movement all over the world.... He was going to go and see Gompers and Murray [of the AFL and the CIO], and the leading British trade unionist, and he was going to go and see Stalin. He was sure they would all endorse it; all he had to do was explain it to them. "I think you're somewhat optimistic, Major," I said. "From what I've heard of Stalin, he has ideas of his own, and is rather tenacious about them."

One character ... had a blue denim bag, filled with well-thumbed and extremely dirty letters from presidents and prime ministers to whom he had sent his patent funny money scheme. They read like this: "The White House. Washington. The President directs me to acknowledge receipt of your letter of February 22nd. Yours truly, So-and-so, Secretary." This poor fellow would pull these things out and say, "There you are, you see, Roosevelt endorses it, doesn't he."

"No," I'd say, "he doesn't endorse anything."

"Well, what does that letter mean?"

"It means he got your letter." Poor fellow.

In due course I didn't get any more of these cranks coming to me. They must have had some kind of secret sign that they put on my door, the way the old hoboes used to do: "This chap's no good; can't get anything out of him." Anyway, after I'd dealt with eight or ten of them, I got no more.

When Pat Conroy warned Dad that much of his work would be of the "emergency" variety, he was right. During and after the war, crises were frequent as labour fought for recognition and tried to wring concessions from employers and reluctant provincial and national governments. Canada experienced a record number of strikes in 1943, a development that saw Mackenzie King's Liberals scrambling to respond to workers' demands so as to stay ahead of the increasingly popular CCF. In February of 1944, King's government approved Order-in-Council PC 1003, which finally granted trade unions the legal status and collective bargaining rights they had been fighting so long to gain. Then, in 1945, arbitration to resolve the bitter strike at the Ford plant in Windsor resulted in the Rand Formula, the compulsory check-off of union dues for everyone in a bargaining unit.

But despite these hard-won victories, huge uphill battles still lay ahead on a multitude of fronts. Unions continued to face employer opposition and government antagonism, as well as the vagaries of a largely unregulated capitalist economy and varying degrees of internal division and member inertia. They also had to deal with widespread ignorance and anti-labour sentiment among the public at large. To change these attitudes was not only a major challenge but also strategically essential, for without broad public support, unions had little hope of making gains over the long term.

My father had accumulated considerable experience in popular education in his former role as a crusading socialist academic. Now, from his Congress office, he was running what amounted to an informal program of public relations for the trade union movement. Unlike most people in "public relations" today, however, he was no spin doctor. He simply wanted people to understand labour's perspective, consider it in its proper context, and support it based on its merits.

Always conscious of his audience, he framed labour issues for the people he was addressing, making the links with their particular interests and other important aspects of public policy. His advocacy appeared in general interest publications like *Maclean's* magazine and the *Canada Year Book* as well as (more predictably) in the pages of the *Canadian Forum*, the *Toronto CCF News*, and *The Nation*. In articles and letters to the editor, he punctured popular misconceptions and put forward pro-union arguments. His diverse audience included the readers of the *United Church Observer*,

Business Management magazine, the quarterly journal *Public Affairs*, and the *Edmonton People's Weekly*.

He hoisted the union banner in his old haunts of academia as well, at meetings of the Canadian Political Science Association, at Laval University's annual Congrès des relations industrielles, and in scholarly and professional publications. His fellow political scientists could read his analysis of collective bargaining or labour unity in *Industrial Relations* or the *Canadian Journal of Economics and Political Science*. Social service workers got his assessment of labour's post-war situation through *Canadian Welfare*, while lawyers were treated to his denunciation of the 1948 PEI Trade Union Act in the *Canadian Bar Review*.

Dad also did a great deal of public education and networking behind the scenes, in meetings, consultations, and conferences across Canada and occasionally beyond its borders. Since his numerous labour-related speeches were often extemporaneous, many of them left no written trace. Among the materials that did survive are a Labour Day message to a Toronto group on "The Real Business of Religion and Labour," a CBC tape of his address to the 1952 Couchiching Conference on unions and freedom, and a 1960 speech to the Canadian Federation of University Students on "Labour and National Development." The record even shows him participating in a panel on the future of management-labour relations at an annual meeting of the Canadian Chamber of Commerce.

The frequent inquiries the Congress received from non-union organizations and individuals were invariably channelled to the research department. My father, however busy he might be, was never one to brush someone off with a form letter. Instead, he would respond personally and in detail to each communication, tailoring it to the particular need expressed.

In his correspondence from 1944, I found a delightful example — a hand-written letter from an Anglican clergyman from Quebec's Eastern Townships expressing appreciation for "the painstaking way you have pointed out needed changes in our Quebec labour legislation." The rector hoped his church synod would formally endorse the Congress proposals. However, he thought the detailed memorandum Dad had sent might be rather too technical for the synod, in which "rural and urban members [were] unequally represented in favour of the former." He gently suggested a brief summary, based on "broad principles of social justice, [which] might appropriately be brought before such a body" for their support. Dad obliged with a concise point-form synopsis, and thanked the rector for his sympathetic reception of the proposals.[9]

It is of course impossible to say to what extent all Dad's efforts in advocacy and education actually affected public opinion. But if Canadians in 1969 showed greater understanding and sympathy towards the labour movement than they did in 1942, it is possible that he may deserve some of the credit.

"I used to *love* going to tea there at the old Congress," my sister Margaret recalled. We were talking about our childhood memories of Dad's original office; my own were pretty sketchy, hers much more vivid and complete. "I guess I was about seven. I don't remember it being a very big staff. The tea room — there was a special room; everybody went, and this Mrs. Beer made and served the tea. And also biscuits, homemade or from a very good bakery. I didn't get tea, I got milk and hot water. I remember everybody gathered round the table; they were Dad's friends, and they made a certain amount of fuss over me."

They were indeed Dad's friends. As an academic among a crowd of self-made trade unionists, he was accepted from the first, and made to feel thoroughly at home. He in turn had great admiration for the CCL officers, notably Silby Barrett, Charlie Millard, and the Congress's secretary-treasurers, Pat Conroy and Donald MacDonald, who were his immediate superiors. MacDonald in particular became a family friend, as did several other co-workers from those early years.

Margaret's enduring impression of the "old" Congress is of "a close-knit group that shared a lot of the same ideals and worked well together." After all, she says, "they were fighting for something that still needed fighting for; unions weren't necessarily a given, not as much as now. They were still sort of semi-pioneers."

One of those union pioneers was Silby Barrett, the doughty Newfoundlander from the Cape Breton coal mines who was a driving force in the United Mine Workers, the Steelworkers' Organizing Committee, and the CCL.[10] Desmond Morton calls Barrett "a natural-born genius as far as trade unionism and human affairs were concerned." Morton also sees the veteran union leader as one of my father's mentors, a "guide and inspiration" to Dad in the context of the labour movement, much the way Arthur Meighen was for him in parliamentary matters. I think that assessment is quite accurate.

Dad's treasure-trove of "Silby stories" constituted a sort of worker's Book of Proverbs — gems of down-to-earth wit and wisdom that my sister and I still quote to each other. Silby was the man who said verbal agreements "ain't wort' de paper dey're writ on"; who waged a campaign against "dem big long words as is over de 'eads of de workers"; whose mental manual of parliamentary procedure included the rule that "dere's only one God-damned fool can 'ave de floor at a time." One of Silby's favourite expressions — and Dad's — was "Leave us be h'onest."

It cannot have always been easy for my father to combine that honesty with his loyalty to the organization. Although I found very little evidence of it in his papers, the labour movement during those years was fraught with tension. Much of it came from recurring crises as powerful employers and hostile governments tried to undermine and disable the emerging trade union movement. But the larger struggle was complicated by serious internal challenges as well.

The main internal division within the Canadian Congress of Labour throughout the 1940s was between Communists and non-Communists, who were vying for leadership of CCL-affiliated unions. Secondly, there were differences between the unions that were strictly Canadian, including numerous locals directly chartered by the CCL, and a number of international unions, affiliated with the CCL in Canada and with the Congress of Industrial Organizations (CIO) in the United States. A third axis of division in the movement was between the upstart CCL, composed mainly of industrial unions, and the long-established, craft-based Trades and Labour Congress (TLC) — a rivalry that reflected the split south of the border between the CIO and the American Federation of Labour (AFL).

In light of the images I retain from Dad's recollections, as well as from my own childhood memories of the CCL as a place of warmth, solidarity, and commitment, it has been an eye-opening and somewhat disconcerting experience to review the observations of a number of modern labour historians.[11] These scholars describe a Congress plagued by internal discord and rivalries of byzantine complexity, often revolving around the very personalities Dad always spoke of in such positive terms. These documented accounts of the in-fighting, macho posturing, and questionable tactics apparently indulged in at various times by all sides, present a rather different portrait of my father's beloved Congress.

Dad's personal role, if any, in the CCL's internal struggles remains an enigma, and not only to me. As a trusted member of a small staff, he must have been well aware of what was going on, but as a "trade union civil servant" he exercised great discretion, seldom, if ever, talking about the conflicts. Someone as wise as he was would have understood that such problems were to some extent inevitable, given the political circumstances of Canadian trade unionism in the 1940s and 50s, and indeed the kind of power dynamics that tend to develop in almost any struggling organization. Nonetheless, he still had to find his own way to come to terms with the contradictions and the moral and political questions they raised.

To help me better understand Dad's position, I talked with historian Irving Abella, author of a landmark book on the CCL's trials and tribulations.[12] "Your father was the intellectual ideologue of the nationalist qua socialist labour movement in this country," Abella told me, "and a key advisor to people like Pat Conroy and A. R. Mosher. He wasn't in on day-to-day decisions, obviously, but as with everything else Eugene was involved in, he had an opinion. And more often than not they listened. I think when he wanted to be a major player, he was."

Professor Greg Kealey of the Canadian Committee on Labour History had a similar view. In fact, he saw David Lewis's action in helping Dad get the CCL research job in 1942 as directly related to the struggle between the Communist Party and the social democratic CCF. "It was pretty well open warfare for control of the Congress, and placing somebody into the only intellectual position there gave the CCF another line in." As for where Dad might have stood in regard to the skulduggery, he said, "I can't imagine he would have found it very palatable, but he obviously co-existed with it."

Abella shared with me his personal analysis of the dynamics. "Your father was staunchly anti-Communist," he said, "and blamed the Communists for a lot of things, including weakening the CCF, which he never forgave them for. As well, they were a real troublesome nettle to the success of the labour movement at a time when the future of the movement was at stake. I think that he was so committed to the labour movement, and to democracy, and to this country, and to democratic socialism, that an organization that was the enemy of all four of those things would be anathema."

He continued: "I suspect the leadership felt that if it took some temporary undemocratic manoeuvres to undermine [the Communists], then so be it, it was a small price to pay for the benefit of getting these people out of the CCL. Your father had a very fecund mind in coming up with schemes and ideas. I have no proof, but I'm sure that some of these were either generated by him or passed by him. I don't think these people at that time, who thought they were really fighting for the future of the country and of social democracy and of workers' rights, felt any hesitation at all on taking on the Communists, [though] they may have felt some twinges later on, when the Cold War was at a different phase."

Of course, Dad was far from being a typical Cold War warrior. He was familiar with communist history, theory, and practice, and he knew several communists personally. While researching his M.A. thesis in Nova Scotia in the 1920s, he had met — and admired — a number of local party members who were, as he put it later, "still enjoying the first fine careless rapture of the Revolution."[13] Though he had maintained a degree of skepticism about the Soviet system during his trip to Russia in 1932, he had been very impressed with many aspects of what he saw there. And during his Montreal years, much of his civil liberties work was done in collaboration with communists and in defence of their rights and those of other victims of the Padlock Act and Section 98 of the Criminal Code.

By the time my father started working with the CCL, however, he no longer had any sympathy with communist ideas, much less with the methods used by many in the party to gain their ends. He opposed communism for some of the same reasons he detested fascism: their disregard for democratic process; their determination to toe the party line regardless of other considerations; and their advocacy — not to mention their actual use — of violence. He had also encountered intellectual dishonesty and underhandedness in his own dealings with the party.

"A dozen years' experience of the domestic variety of Communists," he wrote to Arthur Meighen in 1946, "[has] left me with no illusions about them. They are the bitterest and most unscrupulous enemies the CCF has, and I should think I might surprise even you by what I could tell you about my personal experiences with them."[14]

A Different Kind of Communist[15]

The Communists I encountered in Cape Breton in the '20s were very decent folk, really. They were tough in their way, thorough-going Communists; they minced no words about their opponents. But they fought fair, which I don't think could always be said [of the Party] later. They were straight and they were honourable, and they didn't try tricks. Some of them had been Roman Catholics, and returned to the faith after they got disillusioned with Communism. Some eventually became ardent workers in the Antigonish Cooperative movement. I suppose the modern Communists would regard them as rather naïve.

One of the most interesting was J.B. McLachlan, the great Presbyterian elder turned Communist. A Scotsman by birth, delightful old man; a magnificent mob orator and really a splendid character. He had an extraordinary sense of humour, and a great sense of fairness, even towards people that he disagreed with very strongly.

Old McLachlan started a paper called the *Maritime Labour Herald*, and he had a wonderful piece of luck with it.... He moved and rented another house, and found in the ash-can a large deposit of papers belonging to the previous tenant — one of the company's policemen — containing all the reports on the union that had come in to the company's police department.

McLachlan was as shrewd as they come, and not a Scotsman for nothing. He published these [reports] serially in the *Maritime Labour Herald*, and of course the thing was snapped up like hot-cakes. People were named, you see. Everybody would say, "So that's what they put in about So-and-so. I wonder if I'll be in next number." Or, "By Jove, that old skunk of a policeman. I wonder if he got anything on me. I wonder if he knows about the time I did such-and-such." The sales simply soared into the stratosphere. It kept the paper going for quite a while.

It was ironic, then, that a decade later, Ontario Tory cabinet minister George Dunbar accused Dad of actually being a communist. I was in seventh grade at the time, a Cold War kid, one of the generation who were taught in school to crouch under our desks with our hands over our eyes during air raid drills because the Russians might drop an atom bomb. All I knew was that to be called a communist was bad.

I remember going to school that day feeling both confused and fiercely protective, proud yet a bit scared: my Daddy's name had been on the morning news, but not for anything good! I was afraid something awful might be about to happen. Nothing did. Dad challenged Dunbar to repeat his charge outside the Legislature, but Dunbar knew what was good for him and declined. It still annoys me that the provincial government later named an Ottawa bridge after that man.

In addition to the labour movement's internal struggles over communism, there were the longstanding frictions over the role of US-based international unions in Canada. The CCL leadership naturally wanted to maintain and strengthen its own autonomy, and ensure that the Canadian sections of the big international unions were not forced to accept policies made south of the border. However, when workers were facing powerful employers — often big American-based companies — the international unions had the size and resources to give them a huge practical advantage. So cross-border worker solidarity, as well as being important at the level of theory and idealism, was a vital element in the bread-and-butter struggles that were the labour movement's raison d'être. The CCL had to engage in a constant balancing act between its desire for national autonomy and the practical requirements of survival — its own as well as that of its member unions.

A small inkling of my father's frustration with this situation comes through in two 1945 letters he wrote to the Reverend J.R. Mutchmor, of the United Church Board of Evangelism. The Board had distributed an article on Canadian trade unions that contained an "astonishing number of inaccuracies." Mutchmor was a friend, and Dad sent him a detailed critique of the article, in particular the suggestion that the CCL was mainly made up of member unions of the American CIO.

"Nearly half the membership of the CCL is in unions which have no connection whatsoever with the CIO," he wrote. "There is a great deal of misunderstanding on this point: misunderstanding which has embarrassed this Congress." In a subsequent letter he added: "If [Dr. X.] is not aware that a favourite employer weapon against unions belonging to this Congress is to describe them all as 'CIO,' thus suggesting American control, he is about the only person in Canada not aware of it."[16]

Still, the Congress probably had to be somewhat circumspect in asserting its independence. It had to walk a fine line, trying to represent the best interests of the workers in their immediate struggles without sacrificing its own identity and independence as a Canadian organization. In these circumstances, a degree of reluctance to challenge US ascendancy was understandable. It helps explain why the CCL, and my father as one of its public figures, did relatively little to expose or denounce the dramatic increase in US control of the Canadian economy that was occurring during those years.

In any case, there is no denying the fact that the fates of the Canadian and US trade union movements were closely linked. After the AFL and the CIO joined forces in the US, the way opened for the Canadian labour centrals to do the same. In 1956, the CCL and the TLC united to create the new Canadian Labour Congress, and the era of "the old Congress" came to an end.

Throughout this time my father, gentlemanly and open by nature, found himself immersed in the tough, aggressive, conspiratorial world of 1940s and 1950s trade union politics. A fighter he was, but not that kind of fighter. I think it must have been hard for him to reconcile his own approach to things with the territorial rivalries, the Machiavellian plotting, and the dubious legitimacy of some of the manoeuvres on both sides. But I have no real way of knowing to what extent it all bothered him.

Several of his friends have speculated that he might indeed have had trouble with the direction or style of the labour movement at various times. Desmond Morton recalled that "he could be very funny about [it]." But, he suggested, the humour might have been "a way of making his frustration bearable and of avoiding any appearance of intellectual or social snobbishness which, however alien to his nature, would have instantly been suspected and would have destroyed his usefulness. People like Mosher, Barrett, Conroy, *et al.* were clever, shrewd, sometimes wise men, but their ways were not his."

The late Michael Oliver, who knew Dad from the 1950s on, told me: "I always felt that Eugene must in some ways be pretty uncomfortable working for the labour movement. There was an element of [a] real sort of toughness which was inevitably, I think, involved in trade unionism. But remember what an enormously loyal person he was. He saw himself as a civil servant with the labour movement. So I suspect that whatever feelings he had on that probably never did get down on paper. I'm not sure whether he didn't have the feelings, though."

The one place in my father's papers where I found what could be a hint of such feelings was a comment in a hand-written draft of a 1957 letter, where he refers to his role as an intellectual worker within the movement. "I think people like me, if we are trusted," he wrote, "can do a good deal to keep Labour following a reasonably sensible line. To put the unions off us might be a serious disservice to the public."[17] Some might hear arrogance in those words, but I don't. Dad was simply following Silby's maxim: "Leave us be h'onest!"

When the CCL amalgamated with the Trades and Labour Congress in 1956, my father carried on as director of research along much the same lines as before. The Canadian Labour Congress gave him a better salary and more resources to draw on, but I suspect it also meant even more work.

The late Dawn Dobson, who joined the staff at that time as his secretary, recalled the heavy workload and the hectic pace. "Everything was dumped on the research department," she told me, "because they had this clever man who headed it up, and he could do everything! He could write briefs, he could understand what people were talking about, he could synopsize, he could get to the heart of the matter right away, and then he could relay this to the people who had to talk to the press. So he was invaluable."

As a child I remember the atmosphere changing when the Congress moved to its new building on Argyle Avenue after the amalgamation. Everything was so much bigger, and somehow more formal. The old familiar office on Laurier Avenue, with the tea room where you could bring a little girl, had disappeared. As my sister acknowledges, "It had to change; that's just the way it is. But it was a lot more fun when it was still small."

Not all the fun was gone, of course. Mrs. Dobson showed me a photograph album from 1961 that some of the CLC staff had put together as a spoof. Among other things it pokes fun at Dad for his super-conscientious minimal use of expense accounts and his adamant stance as a teetotaler. "I don't know how they ever got a picture of him frowning," she said, "because I can't remember him frowning too often."

She did admit, though, that he was "very particular to work for. He could get very hyper; he was under tremendous pressures. I sometimes felt he almost carried the weight of the whole Congress on his shoulders. He also had to do a lot of travelling; he was away a great deal, you must remember that."

I do indeed, and his papers contain plenty of evidence, including a typed itinerary for the first five months of 1962, with his additions scribbled in. It lists fourteen different trips, including five of a week's duration, taking him — mainly by train — to Vancouver, the Maritimes, and Southern Ontario, as well as to Quebec City twice, to Winnipeg three times, and to Toronto on four separate occasions.[18]

Even when he stayed in Ottawa, he often worked a gruelling schedule at the office. "He was there all hours," Mrs. Dobson recalled. "In the evening, he'd come back after supper, and if it was particularly pressing, he would have a lot of things typed out." She told me about his "marathons," when he would produce a twenty- or twenty-four-page brief, hammering it out with his two-fingered typing so fast that the copy typists had a hard time keeping up. "Once he started, he just plowed straight ahead," she said. "Sometimes his fingers couldn't keep up with his mind, and you'd hear this explosion of feet rattling away on the linoleum. He'd be banging his feet up and down, out of frustration. I don't think he could get it on paper fast enough, his mind was whirling so quickly."

People weren't always pleased with what he produced, and it wasn't only employers or politicians who were sometimes put out. Veteran journalist and activist Ed Finn worked with the CLC in the Atlantic region in the early 1960s, and he relied on the research department for various kinds of information. Workers in a fluorspar mine on Newfoundland's Burin Peninsula were being devastated by an occupational disease similar to asbestosis, and Ed wrote asking how the mine's owners could be compelled to improve conditions. Dad checked it out, and replied regretfully that no adequate legislation existed, so legal action would be of no avail. Frustrated, Ed wrote again, pushing. He still remembers the letter he got back: "Dear Brother Finn, I'd like to be able to give you material to lay charges against the company. Unfortunately, I'm not here to tell you what you want to hear, I'm here to tell you what the reality is."

This insistence on realism in assessing the problems, and on practicality in seeking solutions, was characteristic of my father. He refused to patronize people by talking down to them or beating around the bush if he felt something needed saying.

"He was a very sensible man," Mrs. Dobson told me. "He wasn't pie in the sky, ever. When he was asked to endorse something such as an enormous pay raise, he would just say, 'It can't be done; it doesn't make any sense.' He was not a firebrand; he was very careful to be within the guidelines of the Congress. But he was also very wise, and he knew what would wash with the membership and what would not. His main aim was to see that working conditions and salaries were improved as much as the economy would allow. So his advice was very good, because he balanced both sides, and came out with an answer that people could live with."

I don't think Dad ever lost sight of the broader ideals and principles that had drawn him to the labour movement in the first place. Like his socialism, his trade union work was grounded in his personal and religious convictions, his view of exploitation and injustice as matters of religious urgency. The movement's goals mirrored his understanding of his faith.

"Christianity believes in freedom," he wrote. "So does Labour. Christianity believes in human equality, in brotherhood. So does Labour ... Their emphasis is different: the Church is primarily concerned with the spiritual, Labour with the economic ... But their basic aim is the same: abundant life. The Church and Labour, therefore, can be powerful allies in a common cause."[19]

One aspect of his work towards that goal involved supporting and encouraging socially progressive tendencies within the labour movement. My father and other "early intellectuals" may well have had considerable influence in this regard. Desmond Morton believes that those individuals, few as they were, were instrumental in labour's shift away from "an ethnophobic as well as an economic fear of immigration in the 1940s, even before the labour market changed to make immigration an easy sell." Dad would probably have declined the credit, but I know he did what he could to help the trade union movement take its rightful part in those broader struggles.

Democracy itself was, for him, an integral part of labour's mandate. He was convinced that the right to "a free independent trade unionism" was "one of the foundations of democracy," and he warned: "We must make our democracy concrete. The democratic state must insist that its citizens have adequate food, clothing, housing, education and leisure ... Whatever the price of democracy, we must pay it or relapse into barbarism."[20]

My father's familiarity with both these dimensions of democracy made him a particularly incisive critic. The connections were painfully evident during the war years, when the federal Liberals under Prime Minister Mackenzie King treated both Parliament and workers with disdain.[21] Dad accused the government of a wartime labour policy that was "as thoroughly and consistently anti-union as it dares to be." This was hardly surprising, he noted, given King's previous work as a "labour relations" expert for the Rockefellers and notorious anti-union employers like Bethlehem Steel in the United States.[22] Indeed, as prime minister, King helped maintain a business environment that favoured "company unions" and "employee associations" — toothless puppet organizations set up and controlled by the bosses to do their bidding while claiming to represent the workers.

Dad regarded Silby Barrett's designation of Mackenzie King as "de fadder of company unionism on dis continent," as only a slight exaggeration. "I think there were signs of company unionism before King's time," he told David Millar, "but he certainly was an extraordinarily effective foster father for it. He pushed it as long as he dared and as hard as he dared, in the Kirkland Lake strike and in others as well. Company unionism dressed up with all kinds of trimmings like 'plant committees,' but company unionism it was."[23]

By the time Mackenzie King retired in 1948, progress had been made nationally on the basic issues of union security and collective bargaining rights, but it was achieved, as Dad pointed out, only through "the persistent and long-continued pressure of the strongest kind from the unions — pressure which the government resisted just as long as it could, and to which it finally yielded just as little as it could."[24] There remained many inadequacies at the federal level, and the struggles on that front continued, but it was provincial governments that perpetrated the worst outrages against workers and their unions in the period that followed.

As legislation, policies and budgets proliferated, the Congress responded with briefs and memoranda to governments and parliamentary committees, as well as with articles, speeches, and media interviews. Most of these were probably drafted by my father. He could match any legislative expert with his detailed knowledge, and he possessed the breadth of view and the down-to-earth practicality to pull the material together and present it from a labour perspective.

In many cases, a comprehensive analysis of an existing or proposed policy was needed so that workers and the rest of the voting public could see clearly what their governments were up to. *Labour Research*, the bulletin published by Dad's department, often served as a forum for this kind of work.

For example, in a 1954 issue Dad examined the recently adopted British Columbia Labour Relations Act, detailing the sweeping powers it gave to the minister and cabinet. He showed how the act would effectively nullify union certification provisions, widen the loopholes for company unions, lead to jurisdictional disputes and severely weaken the right to strike. One provision allowed an illegal strike to become legal if the employer agreed to it in writing — an idea Dad suggested must have come from the government's "Practical Joke Department." Others, he said, amounted to "what Hitler called *Gleichschaltung*, 'coordination' of the unions — in plain English, putting them under the Government's thumb."[25]

Sometimes he was very directly involved in the actions the Congress took. In 1959, Newfoundland premier Joey Smallwood brought in draconian anti-labour legislation during the bitter loggers' strike. Dad helped bring the details of the two bills to the attention of the federal government, in the hope of getting them reserved or disallowed so as to forestall the tremendous damage they would do. When the Diefenbaker government refused to act, he penned a furious denunciation for *Canadian Forum*.

> Mr. Diefenbaker ... could have instructed the Lieutenant-Governor to reserve the bills, so that they would never have come into force ... He was asked to do it. He didn't. He could have disallowed the Acts. He has not done it. Both are flagrantly contrary to ... freedom of association and the right to a fair hearing ...
>
> The whole trade union movement in Newfoundland now lies prostrate at the feet of the provincial cabinet. But not the trade union movement alone: the basic right of freedom of association, the basic right to a fair hearing, every principle of justice.[26]

Always aware of the linkages between economic and political democracy, Dad knew that in such cases, it was all Canadians, not only workers, who were affected by the action or inaction of their governments.

For some years after the amalgamation that created the CLC, Dad kept up his relentless rhythm of work in the research department. But changes were happening in the labour movement and beyond that would shift the focus of his job, subtly at first, then in more obvious ways.

First of all, the merger resulted in an evolution of policy and leadership, bringing changes that were less aligned with his own approach. As a child I got the impression that before the two organizations joined forces, Dad had considered the Trades and Labour Congress to be pretentious and often ineffective. Some of its people, he felt, were too willing to take most of the credit for "joint" efforts in which the bulk of the work had been done by the CCL. He certainly thought the TLC was far too cozy with the Liberal government in Ottawa. Yet now they were part of a single organization.

Meanwhile, a new party was in the works that would embody a formal alliance between the labour movement — a vital constituency for social democracy — and his old "political friends" in the CCF. As part of both movements, my father had been one of the links between them for nearly two decades. "Your dad was very much committed to the labour movement getting more involved socially," historian Alan Whitehorn told me. "He had this almost unique role of Left intellectual but also key player in the trade union movement."

Ironically, it was only when the connection between organized labour and party politics was institutionalized that he ceased to act as a link. His split with the NDP in 1961, detailed in Chapter 15, both reflected and reinforced a certain distancing that was already occurring between him and some of the leaders of both the party and the labour movement.

In any event, by the fall of 1962 Dad was due for a change. He took a break from his Congress activities and accepted a one-year Skelton-Clark Fellowship at Queen's University. On returning to the Congress in 1963, he found the officers in the midst of planning a comprehensive history of the Canadian labour movement as the CLC's Centennial project. They asked him to do the job, and, reluctantly, he agreed.

From the start, he had mixed feelings about taking on this monumental task. Although history had always been one of his passions, he was not a professional historian; he had done little of that kind of work before. More importantly, his previous research work in labour, economics, and constitutional matters had always been directly linked to action — preparation for some specific follow-up aimed at tangible results. Now he was embarking on a project much farther removed from the front lines. Soon he was physically separated as well. As "Director of Special Projects" and with Mrs. Dobson as his assistant, he was given a small office in a different building in another part of downtown Ottawa.

A couple of observers have suggested that he was essentially being put out to pasture. One of them went so far as to speculate that for some of the CLC leadership, the opportunity to get Dad "out of their hair [was] a godsend." I find that overly cynical. My father's critical mind and strong moral principles may have represented a challenge to his co-workers on occasion, and there may have been a degree of coolness towards him in certain quarters after the NDP convention fiasco, but it seems to me more likely that in the decision about the labour history, practical reasons prevailed.

For one thing, as Desmond Morton pointed out, the Congress's research needs and the means of meeting them were changing with the times. The CLC leadership could see that during Dad's year at Queen's, the research department had still managed to function. As for the labour history, they knew very well that nobody would do a more thorough and dependable job of it than Eugene Forsey, and he himself could think of no one else to take it on.

Predictably, much of the work was tedious and painstaking. "It was all compiling figures," Mrs. Dobson told me, "going back and finding out when unions had been formed, and how many members there were, and did they increase or decrease, and where they were located. Eugene loved detail, but I think it became swamping. Those were really good years for him — 1963 to 69 — years when he should have been doing other kinds of work that would have been more interesting for him."

In 1969, while still deep in the labour history, Dad was asked to chair a discussion at Manitoba's Brandon University on "Student Unrest." He began by explaining to the audience that for quite some time he had been so immersed in the minutiae of the previous century's trade union

ANSWERING THE CRITICS
(From the unpublished introduction to Trade Unions in Canada: 1812–1902)

To scholars, this will be a most disappointing book. Four of them who read the manuscript were unanimous: it left undone those things which it ought to have done, and did those things which it ought not to have done. It ought to have been a totally different book by a totally different person.

As to the last, I could not agree more ... I should have told the Congress to forget the whole thing. But if I had followed that sensible and prudent course, much material might have been lost ... As it was, primary records had often disappeared, or survived only in bits and pieces. Fire, flood and fecklessness had taken their toll.

... The critics say that in some cases, the existence of a union is attested only by a mention in the newspapers. Yes, and for the simple reason that that was all I could find ... Surely I could not have been expected to warn grown-up people that newspaper reports are not always accurate?

... They complain of my descriptions of union dinners, picnics, parades, and concerts. I thought, and still think, that they give a certain colour in a work otherwise rather short of it. Our nineteenth century unions were not always engaged in battle. They had other activities, other sides; several. Class warriors may consider this beneath contempt, but I don't. Besides, I tried to give a picture of what was, not what some modern pundit might think ought to have been.

... I am told [in effect] I should have condensed by expanding, usually on a massive scale. [To do so] I should have needed far more than the years I devoted to the work, and far more knowledge than I possess. The book would either have been four times as big, or else failed to do its essential, preliminary, chronicling job. That job once done, scholars would at least have some idea of where to look for the answers to their questions.

All I would claim for this book is that I think it will give people a lot more information, more accurate, better documented and more clearly written, than they ever had before; and I think it will materially help those who want to go farther. All the rest I cheerfully leave to my youngers and betters.

movement that he was scarcely aware of current affairs. "I am a modern Rip Van Winkle," he told them, "who occasionally emerges, blinking, into the 20th century, 'among new men, strange faces, other minds … '"[27] Happily, as the record shows, Rip Van Forsey was soon fully reintegrated into the issues and events of his own time.

Despite the limitations of the process that created it, *Trade Unions in Canada: 1812–1902* should not be lightly dismissed.[28] Some have criticized it severely for its lack of critical analysis and interpretation, and Dad himself described it as "dull." But the book provides the comprehensive factual account that the author set out to provide, and it is spiced in many spots with the human interest details he always delighted in.

In Desmond Morton's view, the importance of this "voluminous, limitless history of the early Canadian labour movement" has been underrated by those who disdain the kind of detailed chronicling that Dad slaved over and prefer a broad analytical approach. "The next generation of labour historians, whom he greatly admired," Morton said, "weren't interested in institutional history, and tended behind his back to mock the work that he had done. But they couldn't do their work without his. Once again, your father pioneered in the field."

In the Acknowledgements for his own book, *Working People: An Illustrated History of the Canadian Labour Movement*, Morton pays Dad a touching tribute: "Eugene Forsey will recognize his own influence in this book, as he has influenced every serious study of Canadian labour history. His wit and scholarship remain one of Canada's national treasures."

The trade union movement was an enduring love in my father's life. The record of his later years bears this out: his references in Senate speeches to labour issues and to his own involvement in the movement; his dogged dedication as he worked through more than a decade after his retirement to get the labour history into print; the affection with which he wrote of his time with the Labour Congresses in *A Life on the Fringe*.

True, a few of his statements might sound a tad heretical. In a 1976 letter to the *Globe and Mail* on wage and price controls, he suggested that on this subject the Royal Bank of Canada and the Canadian Labour Congress were "sighing for a Never-Never Land of 'free enterprise,' … 'singing to one clear harp in divers tones.'"[29] But this kind of specific disagreement with the Congress over a particular issue in no way indicated a weakening of his pro-labour position. While he refused to ignore complexities or condone what he considered foolish, he consistently supported the interests of workers and the rights that their unions had won for them.

When someone suggested to me that Dad might have become disillusioned with modern trade unionism once labour's early struggles for recognition were over, I asked Irving Abella what he thought. "That's not my memory of him," Abella replied. "I have no suspicion at all. Certainly we talked enough for him to have at least intimated that kind of stuff. It doesn't strike me as at all like your father to have differentiated between the quality of the struggle in the 30s and in the 70s and 80s. The goals were different, and the situation, the ambience was different, but the struggle was still for dignity and a living wage and a share in power."

I agree completely: Dad never lost his labour perspective. My own favourite bit of proof is a short note I received from him in July of 1990:

> Dearest Helen,
> I am intending to get a telephone answering machine. Margaret says you have one. Where did you get it? B. got hers, I think, at Radio Shack. But that has been a fiercely anti-union crew. So I don't want to go there ... No hurry about answering this.
> Much love,
> Dad.

As to the bigger picture, I asked David Millar whether he thought my father had had a significant influence on the labour movement. He laughed. "Does the chief civil servant have an influence on the government's policies and practices?" he asked.

Mrs. Dobson summed it up more modestly. "He wasn't trying to change the world," she said, "he was just trying to get a better deal for the worker."

But that is, after all, one way of changing the world.

CHAPTER SIX

Kindred and Affinities

Royal George Hotel,
Antigonish, N.S.,
JANUARY 24, 1949

DEAREST HELEN,
THIS LETTER WILL PROBABLY START OFF ON THE SAME TRAIN WITH DADDY. BUT THE LETTER WILL KEEP RIGHT ON GOING UNTIL IT GETS TO OTTAWA AND THE POSTMAN BRINGS IT UP THE STEPS AND DROPS IT THROUGH THE DOOR.
 DADDY, UNFORTUNATELY, HAS TO STOP IN MONTREAL FOR A DAY, BEFORE HE COMES ON TO OTTAWA. OF COURSE, WHEN HE DOES COME, THE POSTMAN WON'T BRING *HIM* UP THE STEPS OR

TRY TO PUT *HIM* THROUGH THE DOOR! WHO EVER
HEARD OF SUCH A THING! DADDY'S TOO BIG!

OCEANS OF LOVE FROM
DADDY
XXXXXXXXX

This tender, playful letter, carefully printed by hand in large capitals for a three-year-old's eyes, was one of many such missives my father sent to my sister and me from his frequent trips away for the Congress when we were small. This was the Daddy we knew — a loving, simple, gentle person with a great sense of fun.

Even in his public roles, this private person almost always showed through. There was no real division between the researcher-activist-constitutional expert and the parent, neighbour, and friend. His warmth and humour, as well as his doubts and ambivalences, were never very far from the surface.

Although few of us "ordinary Canadians" are likely to become as well known as Eugene Forsey was, we have much in common with him. To borrow a phrase from his beloved Anglican *Book of Common Prayer*, we too have our own "kindred and affinities," our attachments to people and places, our passions and preoccupations, that enrich and complicate our lives. My father was no different. His personal attachments, complete with their complexities, are part of his legacy.

As I share these vignettes and reflections from his life, I hope they resonate for the reader, validating the link between the personal and the political in all our lives.

Dad always had a strong domestic streak. When my sister and I were children, he spent much of his precious spare time working around the house and our little garden. Every spring we would watch as our Daddy climbed ladders to put on the screens and awnings, taking off the big double windows that he then stored in the cellar for the season. Through the summer, he would mow the lawn with the manual lawn mower, scorning the gas-guzzling gizmos that would soon begin to shatter the quiet of the neighbourhood. With the "help" of us little girls, he and

Mum would plant and weed the garden, build and turn the compost pile, then tidy up and rake the leaves when autumn came. He would shovel his way through the snowy Ottawa winters, and then when the spring sun began to melt the piled-up snow, he'd take a boyish delight in clearing away the debris from the gutters in our street so that the water could run freely into the drains.

Dad prided himself on his shoe-polishing abilities, which shone on Sunday mornings, and on his prowess as a dish-washer, which he demonstrated every evening. My sister and I, tucked into our beds upstairs, would hear the cheery clatter of the dishes as he washed and rinsed and dried and put away. He brought to these household tasks the same meticulous perfectionism that he displayed in his professional work, and, I expect, found them much more relaxing.

I don't think he ever paid much attention to the customary divisions between men's and women's work that many of his generation insisted on. Still, neither he nor my mother was entirely immune to the sex-role expectations of the 1940s and 1950s, nor did they escape the practical limitations that those norms imposed. As a stay-at-home housewife, Mum did virtually all of the family's cooking, the bulk of the housework, and most of the child care, and she sewed many of our clothes as well. Of course, on the rare occasions when she wasn't there, Dad would happily make up a meal of canned soup or scrambled eggs and toast, somehow making these ridiculously simple suppers feel like special treats. But with the Congress keeping him at the office or travelling much of the time, it would have been hard for him and Mum to achieve even a roughly equal overall balance of household work.

Much as they loved us, being middle-aged parents of small children was clearly stressful for them both. Dad's response when his dear friend Arthur Meighen recommended a book to him when I was three is telling: "I'd like to read the book, but goodness knows when I will. My wife and I are both far from strong; our children are very strong ... I put in about three hours a day at housework and looking after the children, and about double that on Saturdays and Sundays. The amount of time used up is getting rather less, but three or four years of this have taken their toll, and now, even when I finish my share of the evening's work fairly early, I'm usually too exhausted for anything but sleep."

Kindred and Affinities

Eugene raking leaves in front of our home in Ottawa, 1958. He loved doing outdoor chores; a favourite one was clearing ice and debris off the drains in the street when the spring melt began.

Anticipating Meighen's reaction, he went on: "This tale of woe is not to enlist sympathy, for I'm far luckier than most people. My work is agreeable and interesting, I couldn't ask for nicer people to work with and for; I have a comfortable and happy home. But I have very little time, and the result is I become steadily more nearly illiterate ..."[1]

My sister and I were happily oblivious to the stress our parents were under, but now, as a mother and grandmother, I can only marvel at how much wonderful time and attention they managed to give us.

They didn't provide us with fancy toys or expensive entertainment; nor, frankly, could they have afforded them. Instead, we got heaps of fun out of very basic things. We had the neighbourhood kids as playmates, a quiet street and a back garden to play in. Dad built us a teeter-totter and a slide out of two heavy planks and a wooden saw-horse, and hung a simple wooden swing on the front verandah. He and Mum set up a tiny green pup tent for us to play in, and built a sandbox nearby that could be converted into a wading pool by judicious arrangement of a canvas tarpaulin. During summer heat waves, I remember Dad watering the garden and obligingly spraying us with the hose as we ran through in our bathing suits with screams of delight. As we got older, games of crokinole or snakes and ladders complemented jigsaw puzzles and reading aloud as indoor family pastimes.

Because of my mother's asthma and my own childhood allergies, we were not able to keep a dog or cat ourselves, much as we all would have loved to. However, other people's pets were very much a part of our lives, relationships we sustained with numerous visits, walks and treats. Animal stories were a major element in what we read, and Dad's supper-time accounts of his day would often include an encounter with a dignified feline neighbour or with a new "dog friend."

Our parents always made our bedtimes a treat, with back rubs and a story or lullaby for each of us. Sometimes when Dad was away on a trip, Mum would let us stay up "late" to listen to him on the CBC. We'd snuggle up next to the radio in the living room, bundled in a knitted afghan, listening to our Daddy's voice over the airwaves as he gave a speech or an interview in some distant place. I don't think I had the remotest notion most of the time of what he was talking about, but no matter. It still seemed almost magical, like the feeling I get now when I play a tape recording and hear his voice — so present, so alive.

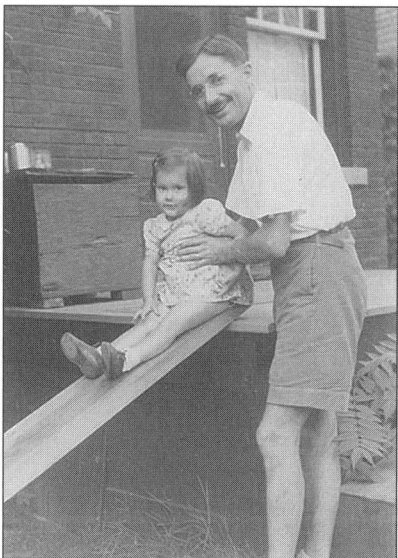

Eugene with his first-born, Margaret, in 1944, and with Helen on the homemade slide three years later.

As kids, we were never deluded into thinking there was a whole lot of money around. Dad earned only a modest salary in his early days with the Labour Congress, and he and Mum both practised a judicious frugality as a way of life. We were taught never to waste anything, never to leave lights on or water running unnecessarily, always to save and re-use items like glass jars and paper bags. At the office, Dad wrote his rough drafts of letters and documents on pieces of scrap paper, some of which are now in the Archives.

Although nobody talked in terms of "the environment" in those days, my parents' attitudes and practice of conservation anticipated that future awareness. Their habits reflected both their experience of the Depression and their personal values of balance and simplicity; they could see no sense in consuming more than they needed. Their understanding was like that of Tanzanian President Julius Nyerere: "The world has enough for everyone's need, but not for everyone's greed."

Our family had no car, and we felt no need for one. Dad rode the bus to work as a matter of course, and we all took for granted that walking or public transit was the way to get around. For outings we would catch the streetcar to the edge of town, or walk to Dow's Lake or Brighton Beach for a picnic.

On one of those occasions we saw a passerby drop a candy wrapper on the grass. Dad went and picked it up, followed the man, and handed it to him politely, saying, "I believe this is yours, sir?" The litterbug turned out to be a priest, who, suitably chagrined, apologized and promised never to litter again. The incident left me with two enduring lessons: that littering is unacceptable, and that individual non-violent direct action can be surprisingly effective!

It was great having Eugene Forsey for a father, but I'm not sure I would have wanted to be married to him, at least not at that time in history. It must have been particularly difficult for my mother, who was quite reserved, to find and keep her own balance next to this gregarious, brilliant, and controversial man. I don't think it ever occurred to Dad that that might be a problem, and even if it had, what could he have done?

Bearing her first child at the age of thirty-six, Mum took extremely seriously the job of raising two little girls — a job for which I suspect she felt quite ill-equipped. Like Dad, she was meticulous and super-conscientious, but unlike him, she seemed unable to relax and let things flow, in relation to parenting or anything else. Over time, these grew a certain emotional distance between us, a gap we only occasionally succeeded in bridging in meaningful ways. It must have grieved her deeply, especially as I'm sure she felt the contrast with how close I was to Dad.

Only years later did I realize how fettered she was by the sexist expectations that were laid on the wives and mothers of that era, and how much her own scrupulous adherence to many of those standards constrained her. Mum's self-confidence was tentative, particularly in womanly matters, and she tried very hard to do what others told her was right, whatever the cost might be to her own spontaneity and desires. And that cost was high.

My father was quite old when he told me how, early in their marriage and before they had children, Mum had wanted to pursue her Ph.D. in linguistics, the field in which she had earned her Masters degree. He told me he had encouraged her to go ahead, but he added, tellingly, "though where we'd have found the money I have no idea." I suspect that at the time he refrained from voicing his money worries to her, but she was clearly thinking along those same lines, for he said she "burst into tears," and the idea never went any further. Even all those years later, Dad was still puzzled and obviously bothered by the memory of that exchange. He didn't really grasp what had happened, or why. And it seems so sad to me now, that somehow, despite their loving

Harriet with Margaret and Helen, Ottawa, 1954. She knitted those bonnets and mittens and made many of her daughters' clothes.

relationship, the communication between them did not permit such a major issue to be talked through at the deep level where the feelings had their source.

Then there were the "other women" in Dad's life: his mother and aunt, who lived just a few blocks away from us. In some ways, this was great. Dad loved his widowed mother dearly, and it was nice for us kids to have the doting relatives close by. But Aunt Hazel was a powerful, even domineering woman — brave and intelligent, but not always very sensitive to the needs and feelings of others. Neither Nana nor Dad was very willing to stand up to her, which meant that when resistance was called for, Mum was often the only one doing the resisting. It did not make for the most harmonious relations between the two households.

These tensions, however, didn't seriously impinge on our well-being as children, or dampen my father's devotion to his home and family. His love for us was a constant in our lives and a fundamental part of his own nature. His "charity" — the same caring and concern for his fellow human beings that found expression in his politics — did indeed begin at home.

Some thirty-odd years ago, in the midst of a rather doleful conversation lamenting to me what he saw as his inadequacies as a parent, Dad suddenly brightened. "Well," he said, "at least I think I managed to provide you with a good deal of silliness."

Indeed he did. Recalling different bits of that "silliness" remains a favourite pastime for my sister and me whenever we get together. Both of us have rather low tolerance for the canned commercial drivel that nowadays too often passes for comedy, and I'm sure a big part of the reason is that we were raised on a delectable diet of whimsical Forsey humour.

Dad's sense of fun was the leaven in the bread of our everyday lives. He was quick to see the comic potential in any topic, whether mundane or momentous, and pull it out for everyone's enjoyment. Over the supper table he would treat us to amusing stories from the bus or the office, often using his ability as a mimic to make the events and people come alive. His talent for versification, which he shared with his mother and at least one of our Newfoundland relatives, provided us with additional delights.

Sometimes he was able to use humour as a way to help ease difficult situations. For instance, although he had problems dealing with Aunt Hazel's bossiness, he also had a keen appreciation of her as a strong, courageous person and a "character." By converting many of her more irritating dictums into family proverbs and quoting them lightheartedly in what were often incongruous contexts, he was able to diffuse some of the related tensions.

Young and old were drawn to his gifts of laughter and conviviality. In the words of one friend, "he bubbled." The late senator Heath Macquarrie told me about an evening in his home province of Prince Edward Island where he had "gathered together a half dozen bright genial people to meet Eugene. Although he was the only abstainer there, he was the most vivacious." Alex Hickman recalls the visits Dad made to his home in St. John's when his children were in their teens or younger. "Generally when older people came around," he told me, "particularly people that they didn't know very well, within ten minutes they would have all disappeared. But listening to Eugene they used to sit around just enthralled. They'd be there all evening."

Dad's letters, too, were often full of fun, even when they dealt with routine matters. While I was in Mexico on a student exchange, he wrote me an entire letter in rhyming couplets. Another that he sent me from Kingston in the summer of 1963 included an update on his academic work, a new stanza for an ongoing saga in nonsense verse to which he kept adding for our amusement, and a report on his new "matching ensemble" of eyeglasses and hearing aid. Of the latter, he commented: "I realize what aural delights I've been missing. With the instrument, I can hear better with my bad ear than with my good one, like the slow train to Ottawa, which now gets there faster than the fast one!"

In a missive to Margaret and me that same summer, he began by apologizing for not having written us more promptly after he and Mum returned from their trip to Europe. "The fact is that I had a large number of business and semi-business letters that had to get off by a certain date; the Liberals' antics over the budget seemed to me to necessitate a couple of bursts from me, promptly; and I've been working like a beaver on my Cabinet Government — and beavers, as perhaps you know, are notoriously poor correspondents. I dare say that the main thing for me to do is to fulfill my duties as the family's official jester …"

There followed several pages of uninterrupted fun, including some fresh nonsense verse and amusing entries from English telephone books: "Tidy, Interior Decorator, Longman and Strongi'th'arm — can't remember what they did — and Clutterham and Son, Funeral Directors and Motor Body Repairs."

The very best part of the letter, though, was an extensive addition to one of the fanciful and ridiculous family legends Dad used to invent for our enjoyment. The subject was a large plaid suitcase that he had bought in England on an earlier trip and now used on most of his travels. On this substantial piece of luggage he had bestowed a name (with an intricate history too long to explain), a gender, and a personality. In his fertile imagination, "Mrs. MacDorser" was the dignified widow of one Hector MacDorser, a deceased steamer trunk. Dad had already had "her" compose a song, to the tune of "Roaming in the Gloaming," which began: "Hector, my protector, was a handsome steamer trunk …" The reader will, I trust, forgive me for not including the full lyrics here. But for those whose interest is piqued, the sidebar contains an excerpt from that letter with copious further information about the MacDorsers.

The Tribulations of Being a Piece of Luggage
(From a 1963 letter to Margaret and me)

Mrs. MacDorser's experiences on our trip were mixed. She found the constant packing and unpacking rather nerve-wracking, and she did not like having the chalk-marks scrawled all over her, nor sticky labels pasted on her. For most of the journey, alas, she was stuffed a great deal too full, and the effect on her figure humiliated her. On the other hand, she rather enjoyed the occasions when she travelled in dignified privacy in the guard's van, up at the head of the English trains …

She was deeply moved to find herself back in England and Scotland, so full, for her, of memories of Mr. MacDorser. It made her a good deal more talkative than usual, so that we found out things we had never hitherto known about him.

She confided to your mother that Mr. MacDorser had a pet-name for her: "Pouponne"; and that, sighing over the difficulties of being a piece of luggage, he often used to say to her, "Ah, Pouponne! C'est un dur métier que le nôtre!" I am sorry to say this caused Mr. Forsey to forget himself, to the extent of calling her "Pouponne." But he did it only once: she told him, repressively, that Mr. MacDorser absolutely forbade the use of first names by an employer, let alone pet names.

We saw the shop in London where Mrs. MacDorser first met Mr. Forsey and consented to enter his employ. She did not herself visit it, as she felt it might be too emotional an experience. She had one very agitating experience as it was: as we were starting for Suffolk she saw, in the station, a younger sister, very chic. They had barely time to speak before they were whisked off in opposite directions.

In Edinburgh, it finally got home to Mr. Forsey that her sufferings from being overstuffed were becoming unendurable. So he went and bought a new suitcase: dark gray composition, plastic, etc., and labelled, in chrome lettering, "Silverline." So now Mrs. MacDorser has a butler, called "Silverline," and she finds him a great comfort. He is quiet and dignified, and efficient, and knows his place.

Mrs. MacDorser was, on the whole, glad to get back to Canada and have a little more time in one place. This constant moving about takes it out of one.

If my father endowed suitcases with personalities, it is hardly surprising that he would attribute human-type communication to animals. He regularly made us laugh by "quoting" imaginary remarks by all sorts of creatures, from the budgie bird and turtles that we had as pets to various dogs and cats of our acquaintance. Some of these flights of fancy were deliberately far-fetched, as when he had Toby, our budgie, object to humans' careless and insensitive use of terms like "detail," or ask what on earth people meant when they spoke of "getting billed" for something. Other times, it was more like simultaneous interpretation, putting into words a dog's comments on a bath or translating a cat's affectionate body language. One of his pieces of nonsense verse bore the title: "A Dog Philosopher's Reflections on Sensation," and began:

> Of all my senses, the olfactory
> I find by far most satisfactory.
> The quickness of the hand deceives the eye
> But no amount of quickness can get by
> A nose ...

Left: Eugene with "the second Rex," Ottawa, early 1930s. He regularly referred to himself as an "honourary dog." Right: Harriet with Wink, 1939. She was a "cat person" from the start, but golden-furred "Mister Wink" won Eugene's heart as well.

Besides being another expression of his gift of "silliness," I now see Dad's verbalizing on behalf of various creatures as a function of his love for animals and his winning way with them. He regularly referred to himself as an "honourary dog" — which may have been what gave him the authority to transcribe canine poetry. As well, his cross-species interpretation carried a deeper message: the recognition that other creatures have their own realities, and that those realities are worthy of respect. In this sense his light-hearted anthropomorphism fits into the same honourable tradition as E.B. White's *Charlotte's Web* and the 1990s hit movie *Babe*.

In the late 1980s, as he felt himself getting feebler, Dad drew up a list of "People to be notified in case of my death." It was a diverse roster that included seniors and young people, women and men, "new Canadians" and old, people of differing backgrounds, languages, religions and political ideas. The only thing they all had in common was that they loved my father, and he loved them.

A decade and a half later, we used that list as our starting point for invitations to a celebration in his honour held on the centennial anniversary of his birth: May 29, 2004. Although he and those of his own age were gone, the people we were able to reach led us to many others, including former Labour Congress colleagues, current and former parliamentarians, university people from across the country, friends he had met in India in 1953, staff from parliamentary or government offices, fellow members of Église Saint-Marc, people from the Ottawa neighbourhood where he and Mum lived for almost fifty years, and sons or daughters of friends from his LSR, CCF, and Congress days.

Many of his old comrades had known me as a child, but, sadly, I have little memory of them. Looking back, I wish I had paid more attention to what must have been rich and enlightening conversations on the special occasions when our parents had guests in for the evening. Although as an adult I had the good fortune to meet a few of the people — notably King Gordon and Dr. Wendell MacLeod — I never got to know most of those other remarkable individuals who meant so much to my father over the years.

Undoubtedly, his most extraordinary friendship was with former Prime Minister Arthur Meighen. Some observers have been perplexed, even distressed, by the strength of his filial devotion to that "unrevised and unrepentant" old

Tory. But I am not. From what I know of Mr. Meighen — from having met him once (a major event of my twelfth year), from all I heard about him growing up, and from my more recent fascinated perusal of the prodigious correspondence between him and Dad — I too feel affection for the man.

Thirty years my father's senior, Meighen had begun his distinguished career in Parliament when Dad was still a small boy. As a minister in Sir Robert Borden's cabinet during the First World War, Meighen had been involved in imposing conscription, which was fiercely resisted in Quebec. The fallout from that controversy haunted the rest of the Tory leader's political career and contributed heavily to the party's subsequent election defeats.

But as Dad pointed out in a moving tribute following his friend's death, Meighen could no more be stereotyped as an all-out reactionary than as a thorough-going progressive. In his two brief stints as prime minister and in his longer periods as Opposition leader and senator, Meighen had variously advocated protection for Canadian goods and industries, championed disarmament, argued for the preservation of Canadian water and forest resources, and opposed the export of hydro-electric power to the US. The record shows him as someone too aware of context, and too responsive to complexity, to be slotted into any simplistic category.[2]

My father had always been drawn to the older man's fine mind and his magnificent use of the English language. Dad deeply respected Meighen's consistent refusal over the years to compromise his integrity for the sake of mere popularity. I'm sure he particularly valued the way his old friend and mentor challenged him politically, tested his convictions, pushed him to think through his assumptions — including, by the very fact of their friendship, assumptions about labels and pigeon-holes for other human beings. And he loved Meighen's humanity — his strength and his weakness, his humour, his anger, and his loyalty. In many ways they mirrored each other.

At the World University Service Seminar in India in 1953, Dad met John Hastings, a young medical student who later went on to a distinguished career in public health. The Meighens were neighbours of the Hastings family in Toronto, and John spoke warmly to me of the bond between Dad and the veteran parliamentarian. "Really, he loved the old man," he said. "It was so apparent that he practically worshipped the ground he walked on. And I can understand it, because Meighen had a towering intellect, like your dad, and I think they were kindred spirits."

TRIBUTE TO ARTHUR MEIGHEN
(From Canadian Forum, *September 1960)*

Most of the tributes to Arthur Meighen have dwelt, and with reason, on the marvellous clarity and precision of his mind, on his amazing memory, on his superb command of English, on his unsurpassed power as a debater, on his unswerving integrity. His personal friends have borne witness to his kindness, his generosity, his loyalty, his sense of humour, his modesty and unpretentiousness, his lack of rancour or bitterness even under disappointments which might well have soured even a far less sensitive man.

But there has been one false note and one note missing.

The false note has been the alleged contrast between his unrivalled victories in Parliament and his unvaried defeats at the polls: a brilliant parliamentarian but unpopular leader. The best that can be said of this, I think, is "not proven" ... If Meighen was a failure as a party leader, then why did his opponents go on pursuing him with the bitterness and mendacity they did? Politicians don't waste powder and shot like this on a failure.

The missing note in the tributes has been the radicalism with which he terrified the rank and fashion of the Conservative party in his early years,

---

After Meighen died in 1960, Dad was haunted with regret for not having spent enough time with him in his final years. "I feel that I failed him," he wrote in *A Life on the Fringe*, "failed the friend to whom I owed so much, failed the one person above all others that I should have cherished with unceasing gratitude and delight as long as he drew breath."

I asked John about Dad's perception that he had abandoned his friend. "Oh, I never thought that in the least," he replied. "On the contrary. Your dad was leading a busy life; he was at the peak of his activity, and in demand. He lived in Ottawa, and he couldn't always be in Toronto." Then, kindly, he added, "I felt badly that I didn't see more of your dad towards the end. I think we all have these sorts of feelings."

John was one of a number of younger people for whom my father was both a friend and a mentor. "Your dad had a profound influence on me, in my formative years particularly," he told me. "I think he lifted me out and which he never quite lost. To the present generation, Meighen was pre-eminently the defender of the status quo, the last hope of the stern and unbending Tories. But when he was leader, he was the rising hope of the progressive young Conservatives....

Very few people now recall that ... he not only approved Bennett's New Deal of 1935, but piloted the bills through the Senate, and strengthened them in the process. He feared Socialism. He detested what he thought was the "Welfare State." But he was very far from being simply a doctrinaire "free enterpriser" or "reactionary"; he nationalized three railways, and he was ready to support and did support any legislation which he was convinced would really promote welfare.

He was, in short, a man too great, and too various, to be fitted into any little pigeon-hole. Those of us who felt compelled to disagree with him on many public questions may not remember "all he spoke among us"; but we shall do well to remember

"... the man who spoke:
Who never sold the truth to serve the hour,
Nor palter'd with Eternal God for power."

of what was a very comfortable, but in a way a bit of a parochial, kind of existence. He had that impact on me. The India thing started it off, and maybe it was because I connected him with that, but he had such a wide political and social interest. He had an enormous capacity for friendship, and age was not a factor. There was a twenty-five-year difference between us, and yet we became very close."

Another young student delegate at the Mysore Seminar was Manoranjna Singh (now Sivasankar). When Mano left India in the mid-1950s to study in North America, our household became her home away from home. "I spent my first Christmas on this continent with the Forsey family," she recalled recently. "I feel most blessed that I knew both Dr. and Mrs. Forsey. Both of them took good care of me." Dad even developed a warm long-distance friendship, by letter, with Mano's father in India. Although the two men never met, Dad could empathize —

prophetically perhaps — with the anxieties of having a beloved daughter so far away.

In 1987, as the national debate over Meech Lake heated up, Dad began exchanging information and strategy with Deborah Coyne, a young constitutional lawyer who had taken a strong public stand against the Accord. "The minute we got in touch with each other," Deborah told me, "it was like meeting a kindred spirit, because we had the same sort of idea about where the country was heading. I found him a wonderful correspondent, and he always exuded such warmth and integrity."

Their extensive correspondence, which she generously copied for me, shows a bond of intellect and affection that embraced not only constitutional and political matters but also their personal solicitude for each other. Among their letters is Dad's response to his young friend's invitation to drop the formality of addressing her as "Miss Coyne." He begins: "Dear Deborah, Thank you very much. The idea had faintly crossed my own mind. But my natural reverence for my youngers and betters, especially when they are learned in the law and eloquently bilingual, stayed my hand."[3]

Not all Dad's friendships began so auspiciously. The late Dawn Dobson, who worked with him at the CLC for so many years, told me about starting there as his secretary in 1956. "When I first arrived at the Congress, I quickly learned that I had been preceded by numbers of other people in the job, and they hadn't worked out very well. So I thought, 'Oh, I don't know if we'll get along at all.' Probably your father and I were both apprehensive; we were sort of like strange cats. It took about a year before he was assured that I could do the work and that I was happy in the work environment." From that time on, Mrs. Dobson was not only a trusted colleague but also a dear friend.

During his time in the Senate, Dad got to know the late Charles Caccia, the progressive environment minister in the Trudeau cabinet, whose continuing kindness was an ongoing source of comfort and pleasure. Similarly, Graham Eglington, legal counsel to the Statutory Instruments Committee and Dad's stalwart comrade in the Committee's numerous battles, was steadfastly loyal and generous, helping him out in his post-Senate years with everything from errands to office space.

The friendships my father nurtured with young and old continue to connect those who knew him in a circle of caring. Thirty years after meeting him as a young reporter working Parliament Hill in the 1970s, Taanta Gupta, now a top executive in a large media corporation, sent a note regretting that she couldn't attend our centennial "tea party." "What a delight to hear from you!" she wrote. "It brought back a rush of memories of Ottawa and times with Eugene. He was a gentleman in every sense of the word, who took pity on a lowly reporter and became her friend. He could well have been proud and chose to be humble. On May 29th, please raise a cup of tea to him for me."

Dad was one of those people for whom place is very important. There were particular spots on this earth where he felt he belonged, where his spirit was nourished and his work energized. His relationship to place was, in fact, a powerful element in shaping his identity as a Newfoundlander and as a Canadian.

His Ottawa childhood, with its frequent forays to Montreal, summers in the Maritimes, and holidays in the lake country of the Canadian Shield, formed in him enduring attachments that come through clearly in his memoirs. His affection for both Montreal and Ottawa is evident in his descriptions of the vibrant metropolis with its rich political and cultural milieu where he spent such stimulating years as a young man, and of the more sedate capital to which he returned to work for the labour movement and bring up his own children. England, too, was very dear to him as the home of his ancestors and the happy scene of his Oxford years, and there were lovely spots in the Gatineau, the Laurentians, the Eastern Townships, and Algonquin Park, where he could replenish body and soul.

But above all he loved Newfoundland — the land of his birth. Although he had left as a baby and never lived there for any length of time afterwards, he was indelibly imprinted with his Newfoundland heritage and passionately attached to that "marvelous terrible place." Indeed, in one Senate speech he described himself as "in essence simply an old-fashioned, simple, Methodist Newfoundland fisherman."[4] The love he bore his native island, and the way I seem to have inherited it, would argue strongly for the concept of ancestral memory.

> ## AN EXPATRIATE NEWFOUNDLANDER
> *(From a 1978 letter to a professor at Memorial University[5])*
>
> ... As perhaps you know, I am an expatriate Newfoundlander, fifth generation born in that country (as it then was); and the older I get, the more thoroughly Newfoundland I feel. I have said publicly, more than once, that if Newfoundlanders had had any idea that they were getting themselves into the kind of jiggery-pokery in constitutional matters that Canada is now involved in, there would have been no majority for Confederation. I often say privately that if I survive my wife, I shall go back to Newfoundland and lay my bones among my ancestors ... All persiflage aside, I share the "strong sense of country" and rising Newfoundland nationalism ...

It was not until January of 1983 that I finally accompanied him on one of his trips "home," and experienced the welcome that always greeted him there. In St. John's and Grand Bank alike, we were received with joy and celebration, as if we had just come home after being away for a while on the mainland. In a sense that was true in a way for Dad, but I had never been there before in my life. Of course, Newfoundland hospitality is legendary, but this was something more: my father belonged to Grand Bank, and because of that they welcomed me too as one of their own.

Seven decades earlier, at the age of eight, he had made his first visit back to his birthplace. He recalled being "atrociously spoiled" by his grandparents, aunts, and the rest of the extended family. Our cousin Grace Sparkes, known and loved by many Newfoundlanders as a teacher, journalist, and vigorous opponent of Premier Joey Smallwood and all his works, told me about that visit: "When I was a very little girl, I remember this little boy and his mother coming to Grand Bank and staying down at Forseys' house, which was only a hop, skip, and a jump away from where I lived. In the mornings, the family would leave their house and go by horse and carriage about three miles up Fortune Road to the place they had, called Clawbonny. There was a hay garden where they grew hay for their horses and cows, and a little summer house, and in the back they had a lovely little orchard. It was a beloved place."

Eight-year-old Eugene on the wharf at Grand Bank, 1912. He was already imprinted with his Newfoundland heritage.

All through my own childhood I had heard about Clawbonny from Dad's fond descriptions: the little farm tucked in off the rugged coast in a sheltered hollow, with its brook and waterfall and his grandfather's fruit trees, which defied the harsh climate to bear apples, plums, and cherries. He had played there as a boy, climbing the apple trees, feeding the ducks in the pond, scrambling up to the waterfall, and as a young man he had helped bring in hay from the field beyond the house. Now I saw it for myself.

The land was blanketed in snow, and it no longer belonged to the family. But Dad was so eager to take me there that we asked permission and walked in from the road. Suddenly we found ourselves out of the wind, at the edge of a snowy meadow nestled between steep wooded slopes. The old summer house was gone, but the orchard was still there, with the surrounding forest and the little brook running through. Even in winter, there was a magic to the spot. No wonder Dad had been imprinted.

Everyone we visited on that trip plied us with quantities of tea and a wonderful assortment of delicious goodies, which we could hardly refuse. As we waddled towards yet another cousin's house, Dad told me about returning to Grand Bank in the summer of 1922 and making the rounds of his many doting relatives. He had soon realized that he simply couldn't go on accepting all the food he was offered, so with waistcoat bulging and buttons threatening to pop, he would try to decline a second helping of Jigg's Dinner or a third pork cake. But the Forseys' grandson from Canada was hot news on the Grand Bank grapevine. His hosts would tell him reproachfully, "Aunt Jen said you had three of her bakeapple tarts when you were there yesterday," and he would have little choice but to partake of more.

Dad had been to Newfoundland for another visit in 1926 before sailing for Oxford, and through all the years that followed he stayed in close touch. He longed to go back, but the time and money he needed to do so were always lacking. Then, in the early 1950s, part of Newfoundland came to him. His two elderly aunts, sisters of his long-dead father, moved from Grand Bank to Ottawa to live out their final years in what had only recently ceased to be a foreign country. Mab and Blanche Forsey left behind their friends and relatives, their community, and everything familiar to them, in order to be close to their beloved nephew and his daughters. As children, we were oblivious to the sacrifice they had made; we simply enjoyed being, in our turn, "atrociously spoiled" by our Newfoundland aunties. Years later, it was their money, saved from two lifetimes of hard work, that put my sister and me through university.

The Newfoundland Loggers' Strike in 1959 finally provided my father with an opportunity to return home. He went on behalf of the Labour Congress, to support the International Woodworkers of America in its doomed struggle against the companies and their shameless ally in the premier's office. Dad's outrage at Smallwood's assault on the labour movement never abated; years later, he again denounced, from the floor of the Senate, "the failure of the Diefenbaker government to exercise [the federal power of disallowance] on that wicked, vicious, outrageous, totalitarian legislation of the late and unlamented government of Newfoundland."[6]

Alex Hickman met Dad for the first time during that 1959 visit, over lunch at another cousin's house. "He started talking about certain characters in Grand Bank who I knew when I was growing up there," Alex told me. "I didn't realize he was talking about people he'd never met, never seen, because they weren't around in Grand Bank when he was there as a young man. And he could mimic them; the accent was letter-perfect. And I said, 'How do you know about them?' 'Well,' he said, 'My aunts used to tell me about them.' You would swear that he spent all his youth growing up in Grand Bank, and most of his adult life."

When Memorial University made Dad an honourary Doctor of Letters in 1966, he travelled to St. John's with my mother to receive the degree. He began his convocation address with these words: "I was born in Newfoundland. My father's people have been here for almost two centuries, indeed some of them for more. But I have spent nearly all my life on the Mainland (even now, I always have to stop myself from saying 'Canada'), and I suppose most people would say I had lost all claim to call myself a Newfoundlander. I can only say that I have never thought of myself as anything else. And now I am welcomed home, with the academic equivalent of the fatted calf; and you have brought forth the best robe and put it on me; and no words that I can find can speak my pride and gratitude."[7]

A few weeks later, he described the rest of their trip in his letter of thanks to Memorial's President Moses Morgan. "… We had a royal reception in Grand Bank, which I had last seen in September 1926. My cousins and I were alike astonished to find how much I remembered … Harriet loved everything and everybody in Newfoundland, and her pleasure more than doubled mine, and my pride in my own country."[8]

Grace Sparkes kept me enthralled when I visited her, telling me stories about Grand Bank, the family, and the times Dad stayed with her in her St. John's home. "We would talk half the night," she said, "until I'd say, 'Eugene, you have to go. You've got a speech to do tomorrow. If you don't go to sleep you'll never get it done, you'll be too tired.' But he loved to hear stories, and he loved to tell me stories. We got to know each other very well. I felt as comfortable with him as if he were my brother."

"Coming home": Father and daughter on the road from St. John's to Grand Bank, 1983.

She told me about driving him back from some public event during one of those visits. "Afterwards, we came out in the car and looked down over St. John's, and he said, 'Now stop for a minute, Grace.' And he looked and said, 'This is where I'd like to lay my bones.' In his heart and soul, he was a Newfoundlander."

Newfoundland educator and historian Frederick Rowe, who sat in the Senate with Dad, was once asked how many senators the province had. "Although I knew that under the Constitution we were entitled to six," he said, "I embarrassed myself by naming seven. One of the seven I named, not facetiously, was Senator Forsey. While being a great Canadian, he never forgot his origins. We Newfoundlanders are very proud of the contribution he has made. We always regarded him as being, in addition to a great Canadian, a great Newfoundlander."

Others, too, saw in him characteristics which they attributed to those origins. Desmond Morton told me: "Newfoundlanders have something that is rare in Canada, and that is a gift for speech, a gift for discourse, argument. They are a peaceful people, but they love to talk, and that's something your father brought with him from the Rock."

> ## MY OWN PEOPLE
> *(From a brief address to the 1987 Grand Bank Tricentennial celebration)*
>
> Never for one moment have I forgotten that I was a Newfoundlander and a Grand Banker, or been any less intensely proud of it. My roots are here. Whenever I come back I say to myself, "I'm back in my own country and with my own people." A year ago I was saying, "I'll never get back to Newfoundland except perhaps in my coffin." Then you gave me this delightful invitation, and the effect was to rejuvenate me ... This has been a very wonderful and heart-warming experience for me. I shall be joining shortly in what I know by heart and have known all my life, the *Ode to Newfoundland*.

It was no accident that Dad's well-loved mentor in the labour movement, Silby Barrett, was a Newfoundlander. I think Dad saw in the old miner the traits of honesty, wit, courage, and tenacity — as well as that inimitable "gift for speech" — that have helped the people there survive through the generations. He surely felt he could find no finer example to emulate.

In August of 1987, my father attended Grand Bank's Tricentennial Celebration and delivered an address at the official dinner. Alex Hickman was also back in his home town for the festivities. "We spent a lot of time together," Alex told me later. "We both spoke at the dinner, and we wandered around Clawbonny ... I don't think I ever saw Eugene happier than he was on that occasion. He just revelled in the recognition he was getting from what he used to call 'my people.'"

More of that recognition was to come. In 1990, the Government of Newfoundland decided to formally express its recognition and gratitude for the contributions that Eugene Forsey, as a Newfoundlander, had made throughout his lifetime to the whole nation. They did so by establishing a scholarship in his name, for Memorial University students in the field of Canadian policy analysis or Canadian government. So it was that in November of that year, proudly accompanied by his two grandsons, Dad made what was to be his last trip home, to be honoured once again in his own country.

Alex Hickman gave me his account of the black tie dinner at Government House in St. John's that marked that occasion. "Eugene got up and said he thought he should say a few words to thank His Honour James McGrath for having him as his guest. He wouldn't trespass upon the time because it was improper to make speeches at dinner. Well, thirty minutes later he sat down, much to the disappointment of all of us." The irrepressible Newfoundlander's "gift for speech" had risen to the occasion.

"As loved our fathers, so we love; where once they stood, we stand …" The words of the old Newfoundland national anthem, beautifully done in calligraphy and framed for Dad by a friend, graced the wall of his apartment until his death, along with a Robert Pilot painting of Signal Hill and St. John's Harbour. Today, his bones lie next to my mother's on a different hillside, but part of his heart remains forever in Newfoundland.

"As a child, I remember Grampa being very warm with us, very affectionate," Roddy told me when I asked the boys for their recollections. "I always used to greet him by running and jumping up onto him. I used to climb up to where he could hold me. When he'd kiss me, his whiskers used to tickle me."

Dad loved being a grandfather, and what a joy it was to watch him in that role. Roddy and Eugene were very close to their Grampa and Grandma, even though when the boys were tiny we were overseas for three years, first in Africa and then in South America. Before we left for Ghana in 1971, my parents splurged on a Super 8 movie camera for us to take along, so we were able to send them a series of five-minute home movies and audio tapes of the boys as they grew. Mum and Dad wrote often, and also sent voice messages on tape, some of which I still have.

Both of them visited us in Ecuador, and were warmly welcomed by our extended Ecuadorian family. They quickly re-established the hugging connection with the children that thousands of miles inevitably interrupts, and got to see the beautiful Latin American country that formed the other half of their grandsons' heritage. Back home after the trip, Dad wrote to two-year-old Eugene: "Here is a letter for you from *el abuelito*, who misses you very much … I wish I could be there now to read you about '*Caperucita Roja*,' with Roddy telling me how to say the Spanish words. Are you still the fine football kicker you were when I was there?…"

"Grampa" reading to his boys, Eugene (left) and Roddy, after their return from Ecuador in 1974.

To Roddy, a year older, he wrote, "I often think of our 'trot-trots' and our 'ride-a-cock-horse to Banbury Cross'es,' and the Spanish lessons you gave me, and the stories I read to you. I hope you are enjoying the little motor cars ... Give my love to Mummy and Papi, and your aunt, uncle and cousins; and pat Bolga [the puppy] for me ..."

Dad had no problem taking feedback from a small child, as is clear in Roddy's telling of the "*Caperucita Roja*" story. "I remember Grampa reading 'Little Red Riding Hood' to me in Spanish when I was very little, and I remember chastising him for his accent. He used to try really, really hard to speak with exactly the accent I was forcing him to speak with, but he never quite ..."

Roddy had another example. "He always used to say, 'Splendid, splendid.' One time, I felt really bad, because I pointed that out to him, and he never said it again. He told me, 'You're right. That's true. I say that too much. It doesn't mean anything any more when I say it like that.' And I asked, 'Well, what does it mean?' and he explained to me what 'splendid' literally meant. I knew how he meant it when he said it, and I didn't mind, but I guess *he* minded, so he never said it again the way he used to."

Eugene recalled how their Grampa would take them up to the Parliamentary Restaurant for a meal. "That was always fun. He would bring us in and talk to senators and members of Parliament that he knew, and introduce us very proudly and say, 'These are my grandsons.' If it was somebody that spoke French, he'd say, 'Ils sont trilingues, ils parlent anglais, français et espagnol.' That was always nice — a little embarrassing, but nice."

When his grandsons were twelve and thirteen, Dad took them to Montreal by train for a day, just as he and Mum had done with Margaret and me a generation earlier. He showed them around the city's downtown, revisited the McGill campus, walked with them on Mount Royal, and took them for a ride in a calèche.

One aspect of that tour particularly impressed Roddy. "He showed us the house he used to live in with Grandma, and the trail he had run when he finished his Ph.D. thesis and handed it in, five minutes before the deadline. He had spent the entire night typing it out with his two-fingered typing, and Grandma typing it properly, and then he had had to sprint from his house to school to hand it in. I remember thinking that was really cool. Grampa was such a respected academic, and his Ph.D. thesis was a pretty heavy-duty academic work — it's still considered an authority on the reserve powers, fifty years later. And he almost handed it in late!" Such is the stuff of role models.

As the boys grew older, they would discuss many things with their Grampa — Quebec, Meech Lake, the Oka Crisis, whatever was going on. "And also personal stuff," Roddy added with a twinkle. "We didn't only stick to lofty topics. I remember being able to sit down and talk, and learn a lot every time I spoke with him. I could say, 'What do you think of this?' and he would tell me. There was never any paternalism. If he thought there was a problem with something I was saying, he'd say, 'Yes, I think there's something to that, but then there's also this … ' 'I don't remember ever being cut down. But you always had to be on your toes."

Roddy remembered his grandfather as "a very open-minded man, certainly for his time; for any time. Sure, he had prejudices; most people have. But he was, even with his prejudices, quite generous. For example, he did have the idea that some cultures were on a higher level, more evolved, but not necessarily that his own was more evolved than anybody else's. That's a prejudice, it's somewhat paternalistic, but at the same time you couldn't call it bigotry. He was from a sort of aristocratic class, an upper middle-class background. I was looking through an old scrap-book of his that he had when he was ten years old, and it's all 'British Empire, British Empire, British Empire.' What do you expect? I'd expect a lot less in terms of open-mindedness, from somebody who was so filled with that, and who really believed in it a lot too."

My own relationship with my father, while deep and loving, was at the same time far from simple. As two people of different genders and generations, we were bound to see certain things rather differently. Our major differences are explored in the next chapter. Other differences were more minor, and often amusing.

One was the slight bias Dad had against what one might loosely call "hippies." His occasional mild remarks about the "scruffiness" of some of my skiing and canoeing friends in the 1960s may just have been observations on what he viewed as eccentricity, and he certainly had a Newfoundlander's appreciation for that sterling human quality. But other comments indicated more serious disapproval. Criticizing a call for the public service to "adapt [itself] to the real conditions and the changing values of the society at large," Dad cautioned that "this could mean almost anything … It could throw the public service wide open to the standards of hippiedom."[9] That was a prospect he clearly did not relish.

So, in 1984, when this errant daughter of his moved to the country to live in a small, income-sharing co-operative, he was somewhat skeptical. I remember his careful references to the "whiskered gentlemen" among my fellow members, and his initial fears about the co-op's financial arrangements. A few months later, however, after coming to visit, he was much reassured.

"Thanks so much for a lovely visit," he wrote. "It was fine to see you so well and happy, and to see your milieu and some of your associates … I am so glad you have found 'port after stormy seas.'"

When old Forsey's not engaged in his employment (employment)
Of washing up his many pots and pans (pots and pans)
His capacity for innocent enjoyment (enjoyment)
Is much the same as any other man's ...

This fragment of silly verse, sung to the original Gilbert and Sullivan tune, was my father's light-hearted comment on his lifestyle in the early 1980s, after he had retired from the Senate. With my mother increasingly disabled by Parkinson's disease, Dad found himself taking on most of the daily household chores. He had no problem with that; he enjoyed "pottering" around their apartment, doing what needed to be done. But it distressed him deeply to be forced to watch helplessly as the disease wreaked its ravages on his beloved Harriet.

In the 1970s, when he was still in the Senate, it was not so bad: Mum had some stiffness and pain, but she could still get around and enjoy many things. When she had to have full-day nursing care (covered, fortunately, under the Congress's exemplary employee insurance plan), her home care team was headed by a skilled and dedicated Scottish nurse named Betty Collier, who became practically a member of the family and even travelled with her.

But as Mum became more and more disabled, either the illness itself or the medication began to affect her mind, making everything much harder. When she finally had to be hospitalized, an entire level of Dad's happiness came to an end, and his daily life became focused largely around his visits to her.

"I was terribly impressed," Dawn Dobson told me, "when he decided the best thing he could do for Harriet was to go to see her every day. And going to see her every day was a terrible job as far as transportation went, because he had to take three buses to get to the hospital. I used to get really worried about him making those trips, but he thought that was the best thing to do. Because they were devoted to each other, your mother and father, just devoted."

My son Eugene spoke fondly of "going with Grampa to visit Grandma, when she was sick in the hospital. It's hard to say those were pleasant memories, but I enjoyed going with Grampa and seeing the love that they both still had for each other."

Eugene and Harriet, Ottawa, 1971. Harriet was just beginning to experience the early symptoms of Parkinson's disease.

By this time, Dad was in his eighties, and his own physical health was beginning to fail. Mrs. Dobson said she was never surprised when he would phone to tell her he was in the hospital again. "He didn't get too upset; it was always as if he said, 'Well, I'm here, and they're going to take care of it. I'll be all right, and if I'm not, you'll know what happened to me.' He was very stoic about his medical problems. He really just sort of soldiered on."

Unlike his indomitable Aunt Hazel, Dad never tried to insist that "age had nothing to do with the matter." He used to joke about being "in the prime of his senility," and accepted with grace and humour the increasing limitations on what he was able to do. After one of his last speeches, when he had trouble hearing a question from the audience, he explained that he was "so infernally deaf that I'm now almost completely bilingual in a negative sense: I can't understand anything anyone says to me in either official language!"[10]

My mother's death in 1988 was a tremendous blow to his spirit. Despite the devastating effects of her long illness, he had felt her companionship as a constant support and motivation in his own life. He mourned her deeply, and never fully regained his own vitality after the loss.

But still he "soldiered on." In his 1989 Christmas letter, he recounted the multiple activities that he had undertaken through the year; then continued: "Apart from the recollections, and the controversies, what keeps me getting so little done, and so few letters answered, is the time and energy I have to spend simply looking after myself. I am now what, in Newfoundland, we call 'wonderful slow,' and have very little staying power." He followed with a list of daily tasks that will be familiar to any elderly person living alone, and ended with warm words of appreciation for the friends and family with whom, he said, he was "wonderfully blessed."

Those of his friends who lived in Ottawa helped him out in all sorts of ways. Graham Eglington took him in his car to buy groceries. Charles Caccia and his wife invited him to their cottage to relax when he was well, and brought him his mail in the hospital when he was sick. Mrs. Dobson drove him to the airport when he had to fly somewhere. When he protested, she told him, "I just do it because we're such good friends, and I've known you for such a long time, and you have always been wonderful to me, so the least I can do is drive you a few places."

My sister Margaret was his stalwart mainstay and support throughout his last years. She called him every morning to check in and chat, and lunched with him at least once a week. She was the one who gave him refuge in her apartment after the demise of Meech Lake, when the media calls to his home phone number wouldn't stop. She was the one who listened to his regrets and frustrations, his stories and memories and jokes; and who comforted and delighted him by sharing her own.

One of his most debilitating frustrations was over the diet his doctor had given him. "I guess the doctor didn't realize that this diet would be regarded in the same way as the Constitution," Margaret reflected. "These were rules, and they were all spelled out, and if they weren't spelled out adequately Dad was terrifically upset. He phoned me and said, 'It says a 'medium' cookie.

What's a medium cookie? Is it two inches in diameter? Is it one inch? They don't tell me. Then they say 'a small banana.' What's a small banana? I'm going to have to spend the rest of my life with a ruler and compass.'"

And where, meanwhile, was his younger daughter? I was off in the countryside a hundred miles away, living my own life, pursuing my own concerns, calling just once in a while, writing him only occasionally, inexplicably insensitive to the fact that he was gradually weakening and would not be around forever. In my heedlessness, I never considered the possibility that my own father might need me.

Early one evening, in the fall of 1990, I arrived at his apartment in Ottawa and found him already in bed, looking like a skeleton. I was utterly shocked. That was the first time that it penetrated my consciousness that he was actually going to die. He told me he weighed 122 pounds — the result of what my sister (and probably Dad as well) called "that blasted diet." She had been trying unsuccessfully to remedy the situation, and after that, I added my own efforts, but I think by then it was already too late.

So now, when I read in his memoirs his words of self-recrimination about Mr. Meighen's last years, I weep, not only for both of them, but for my own neglect of the father I loved. We may indeed "all have these sorts of feelings" to some extent, but even John Hastings' compassionate words cannot erase my remorse.

Happily, though, most of Dad's kindred treated him far better, and most of his affinities brought him lasting joy. And the joy and love that he brought to all our lives are a precious part of his enduring legacy.

CHAPTER SEVEN

A Reluctant Dragon: The Dilemmas of Conflict

I'm a very reluctant dragon. I suppose a long succession of defeats in nearly everything I have undertaken for the last twenty years has taken the stuffing out of me. I used to know a man who said everybody had one good fight in him. I don't know quite what or when mine was, but it appears to be over, anyhow.
— From a 1949 letter to Arthur Meighen[1]

Eugene Forsey's public reputation as a fighter was well earned. Right up until his death in 1991, anyone following political commentary or reading the letters pages in the newspapers would have been familiar with his testy combativeness and peppery wit. Despite his disavowal in the letter quoted above, he still had plenty of "stuffing" left, as his dozens of subsequent battles attest. Seldom did he turn away from challenging something he felt was unjust, muddle-headed, or pretentious.

But he was far from being simply a fractious old curmudgeon who would charge into the fray at the drop of a hat. The relish he seemed to take in fighting the good fight was matched by misgivings. A basically gentle person who cared about people as well as about issues and principles, my father had a deep ambivalence about conflict. It drained his physical and nervous energy, of which he did not have an unlimited supply, and it often tore at his soul as well, pitting his anger against the compassion and gentleness that were equally part of his nature.

As a boy, he was no scrapper. His cousin, the late Jeff Bowles, recalled that Eugene didn't get into schoolyard fights the way many other boys did. Nevertheless, he did defend himself. According to Jeff, when the other lads at Ottawa's Model School teased him, "Eugene would put his back against a wall and kick out at them. They used to call him 'Kicking Horse Forsey.'"

This boyhood reluctance to fight persisted as a subtext though all the controversies of his adult life. In a 1941 letter to his mother about the impending loss of his job at McGill, he described his dilemma: "As it is clear that if I stayed my life would be made an Inferno, I am inclined to think it is not worth while wearing myself out in a fruitless fight, which would stir up mud, some of which would stick. If I thought it would do McGill any real good, or the cause of academic freedom, I'd fight, regardless of consequences to myself. But I'm afraid the place is past praying or fighting for at this stage and on this case."[2]

Leaving McGill naturally did not transform my father's existence into a placid one. Strife seemed to follow him around, but he longed for respite. One of my enduring childhood memories is of a weary comment he made in the midst of some public controversy: "All I ever wanted was a quiet life!" It's fair to say he went about that ambition in a peculiar way.

Many of Dad's political conflicts were very public — his part in the fight against Quebec premier Duplessis and the Padlock Law, his defence of the royal power of dissolution of Parliament, his attack on the Liberal sell-out of Canadian sovereignty in the Pipeline Debate, his resignation from the new-born NDP over its "two nations" policy, his opposition to the Meech Lake Accord. Other battles, like his work with the Statutory Instruments Committee in defence of the rule of law, were waged more quietly. His private struggles — many of them also profoundly political — were known only to an intimate few.

The quandaries he faced in these situations were obviously far from unique. Well beyond the particular occasions and individuals involved, they have continuing implications for other struggles.

Public debates over well-defined opposing views were the perfect arena for Dad. He enjoyed intellectual sparring with people he respected, whatever their politics, and for him such contests were not emotionally problematic. But nor were they merely good mental exercise; he took issues seriously and would defend his point of view with spirit and elegance.

In such public confrontations, he was usually polite and considerate, a true gentleman debater. Not for nothing had he been a member of McGill's debating team (he recalled that the team usually lost) and a participant in mock parliaments. His characteristic courtesy, however, did not prevent him from being provocative. As historian Desmond Morton put it, "Eugene had a way of setting a lot of heather alight. He argued very, very hard. He could be guaranteed to stand his ground and force the other person to stand their ground. [But] he had the charm and the kind of twinkle in his eye that you knew he wasn't malevolent. Not many of us have the strength of character to go on liking people we fundamentally disagree with and whom we've quarrelled with. That's the saving grace."

"Dr. Forsey is a delightfully disagreeable man," someone commented during a CBC *Citizens' Forum* session years ago. The "delightful" part often operated even across deep political divides. A few months after the 1949 election, where he ran as a CCF candidate against the new federal Conservative leader, George Drew, Dad wrote to Drew to congratulate him on the way he had taken the Liberal government to task over a transgression of the rule of law. "I have said some hard things about you in past campaigns," he wrote, "and meant them. If I am ever a candidate again, no doubt I shall again express, with equal vigour, my disagreement with your policies. But I hope I can give credit where credit is due ... Do not bother to answer. Keep your letters for people who may vote for you!"[3] Drew did reply, with equal cordiality.

"Civility was a very important part of your father's whole way of being," Dad's friend Pierre Joncas told me. "He was a very civil as well as a civilized man. He set the example of not holding grudges; he could work with people with whom he had previously disagreed, as if nothing had happened. So long as they were civil with him, he was eager to be civil with them."

Former Newfoundland premier Clyde Wells likewise spoke appreciatively about Dad's "unfailing courtesy, the unfailing gentlemanly behaviour with which he dealt with everything."

But there were clear limits to that civility. My father did not suffer fools gladly, and his definition of "fool" was fairly broad. Although his intentions were not malicious, he was nonetheless capable of an intellectual arrogance that sometimes bordered on outright contempt. I don't think he always realized how hurtful his brilliant sarcasm might be to someone on the receiving end.

"Your dad was devastating in argument," John Hastings recalled. "He could demolish people very graciously — as he did with me as a young student — but he could also really knock the tar out of people when he chose to, people that he thoroughly disliked. And there were some that he had absolutely no use for at all; he made no bones about that."

This assessment was echoed in the tributes to him that appeared in various newspapers after his death in 1991. "Forsey was a man confident of his opinions," wrote Charles Gordon, son of Dad's old friend and socialist colleague King Gordon, "and impatient with contrary opinions, which he might describe in such words as 'eyewash, spouting from pure ignorance.'" The *Globe and Mail* noted his ability to "cut to the quick with two lines of elegant vituperation," while columnist Geoff Stevens called him "the owner of the most trenchant typewriter in the country."[4]

Professor Ted Hodgetts, who edited *The Sound of One Voice: Eugene Forsey and his Letters to the Press*, told me about serving years ago as an anonymous reviewer for a paper Dad had written on Mackenzie King for the *Canadian Journal of Economics and Political Science*. Hodgetts had suggested at the time that Forsey was perhaps not helping his own cause by using such "colourful language" in a scholarly article. The article as published was undoubtedly still colourful, however, and probably added some spice to a literary genre that sometimes tends towards the bland.

"What Eugene Forsey always stood out against," mused Desmond Morton, "was the easy solutions, the verbal gymnastics, the ways that Canadians have of being comfortable with each other by not raising issues. Canadians don't argue in public. We're not often honest, because we want to get along. Eugene thought it was more important to be honest."

"Piffle and Froth"[5]

In 1949, an admirer of Mackenzie King published two articles on the 1926 constitutional crisis. Arthur Meighen privately described them as "hum-drum piffle, hardly entitled to be called froth." Dad sent the author a detailed critique, only to receive this response:

"I should doubtless feel flattered that you would take time to write some thousands of words of academic criticism, provoked by my passing glimpses of political episodes — so much about so little. You will perhaps pardon me for refraining from returning the compliment. You make it plain from your tone of self-assurance that no answers of mine would modify your opinions ... Who am I to dare engage in an encounter with the Sir Brian Botany of the constitutional arena?... I hope you will bear up when you learn I had forgotten you had ever written a book, and it is unlikely that I should look into it for 'the facts, and the constitutional principles.' I have long avoided the controversies of constitutional hair-splitting. My articles ... merely recounted some impressions of mine on 'the Byng-King incident.'"

— C. Bowman

John Hastings agreed. "He was totally unafraid; he would say or write exactly what he believed to be the case, and that's a rare attribute. Most people trim. He wouldn't trim, and of course that's why he got kicked a few times. But isn't it interesting: by the end, that's what people admired. People recognized that he could not be corrupted."

Controversy in and of itself was not a problem for Dad. He routinely took unpopular public stands, regardless of the professional and financial consequences he risked by taking them. Even the occasional physical threat — like the warning he received during the Duplessis era to be "very careful" in Montreal traffic, and the late-night phone call and "visit" by thugs during

> My father replied:
>
> "I cannot too highly commend your prudence in refraining from any answer to the points I raised in my letter. You had made a series of statements that were demonstrably wrong. I pointed this out, giving chapter and verse... Your reply is to disclaim any intention of discussing the constitutional crisis of 1926, to proclaim your Olympian detachment from 'the controversies of constitutional hair-splitting,' and to abuse me ...
>
> "You make some play with what you call my 'self-assurance.' This is an old game: 'No case; abuse plaintiff's attorney.' Anything that could exceed the 'assurance' of your own articles on this subject, and your letter, would be hard to imagine. The Pope, speaking ex cathedra on a matter of faith and morals, could not be more confident of his own infallibility. There is just this difference between your "assurance" and mine: mine is based on facts, yours only on your own 'impressions.'
>
> "I had no reason to suppose you had ever heard of my book. It has had very limited circulation. I sympathize with your resolve not to look at it. It might shake your faith in Mackenzie King as a constitutional authority. But perhaps your convictions are beyond being shaken by anything so trivial as mere evidence ..."
>
> — Eugene Forsey

his June 1949 election campaign[6] — left him disturbed but undeterred. What did cause him anguish in conflict situations was the emotional damage and rupture of personal relationships that too often came as a result.

Searching the Eugene Forsey collection in Canada's national archives for material from the 1930s and 40s, I found a plump file documenting an internal struggle in the Fellowship for a Christian Social Order (FCSO), which both my parents were active members of. That conflict, played out in a six-month exchange of highly charged letters, drove a wedge between Dad and a number of valued friends — people he had worked closely with in building the movement. I read through the entire file with morbid fascination, reliving the whole agonizing process through his words on the brittle paper.[7]

In his initial letter, written to FCSO secretary Fred Smith in July 1940, he expressed his concerns about what he saw as the risk that the organization might be taken over by the Communist Party. He took pains to demonstrate that he was in no way a Red-baiter, citing his own extensive record of defending and cooperating with Communists, and noting that in some quarters he was still suspected of being one himself. But he was seeing signs that the Party was moving to take over the Fellowship and use it for its own purposes, and he wanted to make sure that didn't happen.

He made it very clear that his concern was non-partisan, even though he was on the Quebec CCF executive at the time. "I see no reason," he wrote, "why [the FCSO] should not include members of the CCF and members of the Communist party too ... [However,] I do not want to see the FCSO become an appendage or side-show or echo of any political party. I think it would be disastrous. The FCSO has a special job to do, from a special point of view. It cannot be tied to the tactical manoeuvres which are inevitable in any political party."

At the end of that three-page letter, he acknowledged the personal risk he was taking by writing it. "What I have said [may] deeply offend some old and valued friends, perhaps induce a doubt of the soundness of my mental powers. But after very careful consideration, I have reached the conclusion that the time has come for plain speaking, even at these risks ... I am quite prepared to discuss the matter, and to change my mind if I can be shown I am mistaken."

It took almost two months for a special FCSO committee to draft a reply, and their note was a model of brevity. It addressed none of the points my father had made; instead, it accused him of making a "quite undocumented attack." It piously exhorted him to "try to keep this a fellowship as we work towards a Christian Social Order," and closed with the hope "that this will satisfactorily dispose of this rather unfortunate little episode."

Of course it didn't. Dad responded with an eleven-page missive, taking up the committee's points (such as they were) one by one. He emphasized again that he impugned no one's motives. "I think it is both wrong and stupid," he wrote, "to question anyone's motives ... Each of us perhaps knows his own motives. God knows the motives of all of us. No one else is in a position to say anything whatever on the subject....

I was trying to indicate what I thought might be the unintended results of certain actions."

He also protested the way the FCSO officers had dealt with his concern. Some members of the executive had never even seen his original letter, hearing only second-hand interpretations of it. Moreover, the committee appeared "either to have overlooked [particular] statements or to have treated them as empty phrases."

> You were not justified in doing either. I said what I meant and meant what I said; and no one has any right to assume otherwise. In answering letters, especially when one disagrees with the writer, it always seems to me a sound rule to answer what he says, not what we think was in his mind …
>
> You say, "Let us keep this a fellowship." With all my heart. But I cannot see why a candid statement of anxiety about the consequences of certain possible actions and a request for information and reassurance should be incompatible with [that].… "Fellowship" surely does not mean a blind and unquestioning acceptance of anything the executive may see fit to do … surely [it] involves an interplay of mind with mind, not one group of minds active and another passive?

Sadly, that exchange was only the beginning. Over the following months, as Dad saw his predictions of a Communist takeover of the FCSO beginning to come true, the correspondence heated up. One of his letters, written in white-hot fury in response to an item in the Fellowship's newsletter, included the startling assertion: "I accuse no one of evil motives, not even the malicious creatures who have got the ear of the editors … and keep pouring lies and poison into it." But the contradiction was uncharacteristic.

One of his FCSO colleagues, Kingston theologian Gregory Vlastos, was deeply distressed by the widening rift, and pleaded with my father to let the matter drop. Early in 1941, when Dad was facing imminent dismissal from McGill, Vlastos wrote to him: "For God's sake, Eugene, let us work together to fight the people who are victimizing you at this very moment, and the thousands, hundreds of thousand[s of] workers and farmers and unemployed.

We can't put our heart into factional strife. We are brothers in a cause that demands every ounce of energy we can give it. Let us not spill it in civil war."

Such letters were agony for my father. His own commitment to the values that Vlastos invoked, and his personal heartache over the split, were evident in his responses and explanations throughout the lengthy dispute. Even so, he was repeatedly misunderstood or misrepresented, accused by his FCSO friends of divisiveness and unreasonableness, of Red-baiting and "political blackmail."

The correspondence finally played itself out, leaving Dad's original concerns and warnings still essentially unanswered. Events in the FCSO continued to unfold largely as he had feared, and a few years later my parents resigned their memberships in what was by then a moribund organization.[8]

Although the particular problems reflected in these letters were specific to that organization at that time, such devastating divisions are far from unique. Sadly, the story will resonate for many, particularly members of close-knit groups pursuing cherished but beleaguered goals. In the dreary business of fighting things out with friends and comrades, anguish and loneliness often seem the only recompense. The questions don't go away: when to challenge and when to concede; how to be simultaneously frank yet caring, open-minded yet firm; and — sometimes most painful of all — when to finally cut your losses and move on.

Time and again, my father experienced all those dilemmas. Time and again he gritted his teeth, made his choices, and went on. When core principles were at stake, he did not shrink from battle. But although his anger and determination might mask the depth of his struggle, those close to him knew the anguish those choices cost him.

On the home front, at least during my childhood, my father's approach to conflict was markedly different. Back then, the prospect of even a minor argument with a "lady" of the family could make him withdraw into silence like a turtle into its shell. In fact, he would sulk.

How much of this came from growing up in a house full of adults, most of them "ladies," I can't say for certain, but that was surely a factor. Through the 1940s and 50s, Dad's Aunt Hazel ran what remained of the ancestral Bowles household with all the authority and competence of a senior executive, despite being almost completely blind. The house she shared with my more tractable grandmother was only a fifteen-minute walk from ours, and Aunt Hazel did not hesitate to call on Dad for help with the smallest task. Her constant and sometimes unreasonable demands did not sit well with my mother. Dad was caught in the middle. Despite continual attempts to please both "ladies" and cope with all the resulting pressures, he never really resolved the dilemma.

A phone call from his aunt could thoroughly intimidate him. He would pick up the receiver to hear: "Eugene, the light in the corner of the drawing room has burned out. Would you come over now, dear, and change it for us?" He was seldom able to refuse. Skewered by technology upon the shaft of what he deemed a more agile intellect, his brain would simply go on strike.

He himself speculated that this dynamic might be a major source of his lifelong hatred of the telephone, which he invariably referred to as "that infernal instrument."

"My aunt is a formidably competent person on the telephone," he explained in a letter from that period. "She thinks like lightning. When she calls up and wants me to do anything, even if I have the best of reasons for saying no, she can think of an answer to each reason faster than I can bring the reason out of my mouth. I get jittery and incoherent. I have had this experience also with other people, and the only way I can cope with them is by getting cross and ticking them off. This is not something I want to do with most people; nor would it be reasonable."[9]

Hardly the image of the doughty warrior the public knew!

As he got older, though, Dad began to view his earlier domestic strategy of conflict-avoidance as cowardly and wrong-headed. The long letter he wrote to my mother from Kingston over the winter of 1962–63 expressed his bitter regret for not having confronted family differences and disagreements more directly. In an orgy of remorse, he wrote, "I never really tried to tackle a single one of the problems calmly and honestly, either with you or the girls ... Instead, I have ducked and dodged, and blamed other people, and indulged in self-pity ... I have habitually taken the path of least resistance ..."[10]

He was still voicing similar sentiments in letters to me years later, despite my protestations.

This intense awareness of what he considered his own imperfections gave him a tremendous capacity for empathy and compassion towards other people, including, on occasion, his political opponents. In 1985, when I sent him a copy of a talk I had given berating the Mulroney government, he wrote me back with his comments. He called my presentation "a magnificent philippic, with most of which I heartily agree," but urged me not to be so ready to attribute the wrongdoing to "deliberate wickedness." "I need so many allowances made for me," he explained, "that I am disposed to make considerable allowances for other people." Significantly, though, he added: "This doesn't mean not fighting them and their policies."

By that point in his life, Dad had pretty well abandoned the habit of sidestepping conflict with his nearest and dearest, and replaced it with a more characteristic willingness to risk disagreement, even if it involved a "lady" of the family. When I was the lady in question, he must often have despaired of persuading me to change my mind.

Many of the differences that arose between my father and me were relatively minor questions of degree or approach on matters where our common ground was evident. My feminism, however, opened up a more significant gap.

Sitting incognito in the audience at Memorial University during our 1983 trip to Newfoundland, I listened as Dad gave the inaugural lecture in a series on Canadian labour history. When questions were invited from the floor, I raised my hand, trembling a bit with my own audacity. "I haven't heard you mention women workers," I said politely. "Were there women involved in the trade union movement? Could you comment?"

The chair — a man — rose in consternation and began reassuring Dad that he need not answer, that the question was out of order, or some such thing. Dad motioned him back graciously. "No, no, that's fine," he said. "My daughter has every right to ask that question, and it's a good one. I'll be glad to answer it." Which, with his customary courtliness, fairness, and honesty, he proceeded to do.

It wasn't that my father didn't care about women's issues; he just didn't always notice them. When he did notice, there was seldom a problem. He was definitely pro-woman, particularly on the big, obvious issues like equality in the workplace, equal opportunities for education, and access to non-traditional occupations. And that wasn't just some theoretical position; it was something he actively encouraged and advocated for.

He and my mother consistently encouraged Margaret and me in whatever we took on — schoolwork, summer jobs, outdoor activities. Many of the things we loved to do as teenagers were hardly considered "feminine" pursuits in the 1950s and 60s, but that never bothered either of our parents. When we started rock climbing, winter camping, and wilderness canoeing, they checked out each situation and the people involved, then sent us off into the wilds. When I wanted particular work experiences, first in a veterinary clinic and then on a farm, Mum made the necessary arrangements and Dad backed her up. When I decided to study agriculture in university — a choice that some of my own peers were dubious about — my parents said, in effect, "Go for it!" They were every bit as supportive of me in my choices as they would have been of a son.

In his work, too, Dad was a non-sexist colleague and employer. I asked Dawn Dobson how he treated the women in the Congress when he directed the research department there, and she had only praise. "He was wonderful with people who worked with him, very sympathetic. He could give people a jolt, but he was never mean. And he was always very polite, tremendous manners." She gave me examples of how he had helped women staff members to advance, even if it meant losing them from the department. "He was always pushing so that they could get better jobs or have better opportunities," she said.

I spoke with Pierre Joncas about Dad's attitudes on gender. "I don't think your father ever thought men were superior to women," Pierre said. "He obviously enjoyed the company of women. If a pretty woman would enter the room, his eyes would sparkle, but it was innocent, there was nothing untoward in his manner. It was natural for him to think of them as equals. The idea that women were somehow inferior in intelligence or other abilities was just completely foreign to him; he just couldn't understand how others couldn't see how obvious it was."

In those important ways, then, Dad was refreshingly gender-blind. I expect this was largely thanks to his having grown up in a family of strong women, many of whom were in the paid work force long before that became the norm. When he was still a boy, his widowed mother had fought a tough battle for her rights as a public servant, and she subsequently became chief librarian at the Geological Survey of Canada. His three Newfoundland aunts were also self-supporting professionals: Maria, the schoolteacher with the lame leg, who taught sign language to every child in her outport school so that two deaf-mute kids would not be isolated; Blanche, who practised nursing in Mexico for nine years before and during the Mexican Revolution; and Mab, who worked as Grand Bank's postmistress and telegraph operator, linking the community with the outside world.

Dad's commendable gender-blindness, however, had its down side. The very fact that, as Pierre put it, "he couldn't understand how others couldn't see" meant that he was also blind to the presence of sexism all around him in society and, inevitably, in himself as well. For although I really never saw him treat a woman face to face as anything other than his equal, there was definitely a residual sexism that came through in other ways.

He would regularly describe women as either "pretty" or "plain-looking," whereas he rarely commented on a man's appearance. He used words like "emasculate" to mean "weaken," and phrases like "playing the parts of men" to mean acting with courage and integrity. Even in his last years, he was not above repeating some other man's virulently anti-woman comment as an amusing anecdote, and he cited with obvious relish the male put-downs that quashed feminist demands at the CCF's Regina Convention. In fact, in his gleeful recounting of Agnes MacPhail's rejection of affirmative action, he stooped to the classic patriarchal ploy of using a woman's voice to support a reactionary male viewpoint.[11]

For the most part, though, it was in sins of omission that my father's sexism showed up. His ability to deliver an entire lecture without even mentioning women was only one example. The invisibility of half the population was itself invisible to him. To his credit, once that invisibility was pointed out, he acknowledged his error and dealt fairly with the point at issue. But women, including my mother, had been pointing out such gaps for decades. If Mum could do it in the pages of the *Canadian Forum* in 1944,[12] why couldn't Dad have taken note and integrated that dimension into his thinking over the years that followed?

This stubborn inability to understand what all the feminist fuss was about reminds me of the white man I once heard complaining about the fact that Aboriginal people had begun demanding distinct collective rights. The man's perplexity was palpable. "Indians and white guys, we all used to play baseball together," he said. "The Indians were just like us. Why can't we all just be ball-players together again?"

Similarly, my father had no problem with women as long as we simply did all the normal things, behaved like the ordinary sensible people he knew us to be. But as soon as women began claiming an identity and perspective distinct from men's, and insisting on defining it in our own terms, he became puzzled, and hurt, and defensive.

I explored this blind spot further with Pierre Joncas. "Dad couldn't understand why we felt we had been discriminated against *as women*, why we therefore tried to organize around our gender," I said. "He had serious reservations about organized feminism."

Pierre mulled it over. "Perhaps …" he mused. "He *did* believe in organized labour, because labour needed …" He paused.

Exactly. Dad didn't see that women *needed* any redress, *as women*. So he trivialized and made sport of those who insisted that we did.

"This is an area where I didn't know his thinking all that well," Pierre went on. "I just observed that when he was with women he treated them as equals. But as to the remedies to the more endemic problems women faced as a group, he may not have understood them. I just don't know."

I do. Through nine years of a violent marriage, I had experienced some of those "endemic problems" myself. When I came to understand them as gender-based, Dad had trouble accepting that feminist analysis. For him, family violence was an anomaly: one of those awful things that just sometimes happen with individuals, not a common and logical consequence of patriarchal attitudes and unequal male-female relations in society.

Again, Pierre had an insightful comment: "We judge normality by what is around us. But it isn't normality we ought to be concerned about: it's health. Health and the norm are not necessarily the same thing. Your father was basically a healthy man, and he misunderstood health to be the norm. He was such a healthy person — intellectually, spiritually, emotionally — it was hard for him to understand that other people weren't so blessed. But it was not a matter of prejudice, it was a matter of inexperience, literally."

In this discussion, I am, necessarily, leaving out a great deal. Dad was by no means completely obtuse about these issues, and certainly not closed-minded. We wrote to each other about them. I sent him articles I liked; he wrote back with detailed comments and criticisms. He had some good points to make, and he listened to mine. But the situation was complicated by the fact that my ideas (not to mention my emotions) went through a difficult transition when I left my marriage. My father, and I think my mother as well, thought I was "blaming men" and condemning marriage outright. It naturally upset them to think I held such views, particularly in the context of their loving concern for my boys. They didn't understand what I actually did believe, or how those beliefs were evolving.

Lurking in the wings of these discussions between me and Dad were other touchy questions, notably gay and lesbian rights. One of the articles I sent him, for example, implied a validation of same-sex relationships. His response, though relatively mild, made it clear he did not agree. I don't think I pursued it further. In fact, this was a topic we mostly avoided with each other, each feeling, I'm sure, that to try to address it would be futile.

The boys told me about being with Dad on a social occasion when the talk turned to the United Church's ordination of gays and lesbians. "Some people there were being really nasty," Roddy said, "and Grampa was sort of approving. He would never have said things in the same way, and he may have felt a little uncomfortable that the others were being so nasty, so cruel. But he agreed with the general gist of the argument."

Eugene, too, was taken aback. "It was just a question of ignorance," he said, "and 'ignorance' and 'Eugene Forsey' are an oxymoron. But it was insulting and offensive."

I asked them why they hadn't said anything at the time. Both had similar answers: they weren't going to convince him of anything, and he wasn't going to convince them of anything, so they just didn't see the point. Having confessed to the same kind of avoidance myself, how can I blame my sons? Still, it seems strange that somehow, when we were dealing with Dad, all three of us failed to uphold the Forsey tradition of fearless defence of principle.

On the issue of reproductive choice, I fared a little better. When the name of Dr. Henry Morgentaler came up in a conversation he was having with two other men in my presence, I found the views being expressed pretty appalling. After a while, Dad's sense of fairness clicked in, and he asked me what I thought. I was outnumbered and on alien territory, but inspiration leapt to my aid. "Well," I ventured, "You know what they say: 'If men got pregnant, abortion would be a sacrament.'" The subject was quickly changed.

Going through my father's papers in his Ottawa apartment after his death, I found a thick file labelled "Helen's Troubles." It contained his correspondence with me and with my ex-husband about the breakup of our marriage, as well as letters from a few trusted friends with whom he had shared his puzzlement and worry. The contents of that file are vibrant testimony to the agonizing dilemmas he faced around personal conflict; they are also evidence of the respect, caring, and persistence he brought to his involvement in it.

Some of the thorniest recurring problems in the aftermath of my separation naturally concerned the children, then eight and seven years old. At one point, when communications between myself and my soon-to-be ex-husband had reached an all-time low, Dad stepped in as mediator. He talked and wrote to both of us, arguing with eloquence and passion for a resolution that would spare his beloved grandsons at least some of their pain. He never treated either of us with disrespect, but he did not hesitate to challenge us, even knowing it might mean further painful conflict. One of his letters to me from that time refers explicitly to his determination to take that kind of loving risk.

"Ever since your trouble came to my knowledge, I have felt that if I had taken more thought and had more courage in 1969 [the year of my marriage] I might have saved you from some of the anguish you have suffered. So, now, I am going to risk speaking when it would certainly be easier and pleasanter in the short run to say nothing." After stating his point — a difficult one indeed for me to hear — he closed with: "This is blunt, and I dare say I should have put it in terms that would be less so … I hope you will forgive me for what I may have said amiss." The letter was signed, "Your loving and anxious Dad."

These questions around men and women, sexuality and marriage, were among the deepest and most distressing things my father and I had to deal with. Indeed, one or two issues remained so painful between us that part of me wishes we had continued to avoid those particular discussions. But in most cases, the risks we took were worth it for both of us.

What I remember most clearly and hold in my heart is his unfailing caring and persistence, his acknowledgement of his own bewilderment and fallibility, his wariness of generalizations, his reminders of the need for both reason and compassion, and his willingness to hear, and then challenge, ideas of mine that he found deeply troubling. Ultimately, our difficult but loving dialogue was worth far more than either silence or capitulation on either side would have been.

How did my father choose his battles? He certainly ended up engaging in plenty of what he called "first-class rows," but he would rather not have had to. As he noted, "A first-class row for sufficient reason is tolerable, [it] may even be necessary; [but] a first-class row without sufficient reason is criminal folly."[13]

His assessment of "sufficient reason" bore no relation to the popularity of a cause or the likelihood of victory; the record shows that even his successful campaigns often started out looking pretty hopeless. Nor was he swayed, as far as I can see, by the possibility of negative repercussions on his job or income. Instead, his decisions emerged from a mix of intellectual, emotional, and practical factors that combined to enable a kind of triage.

His gut-level reaction to an issue was certainly a very strong element in the mix. He used to half-jokingly attribute his penchant for controversy to his "bad temper." My sister recalls that when asked what motivated him to write his controversial articles and letters to the editor, he answered: "I just get so angry!" But I think there was much more to it than that. I suspect he used his anger — perhaps not consciously — as a tip-off, an indicator of what needed action. Since what most often infuriated him were instances of injustice, hypocrisy, dishonesty, or "muddle-headedness," that anger often pointed him towards important battles.

Where "bad temper" did come to the fore was in clashes with people whose values or integrity he doubted. I have childhood memories of his fury over the Liberal government's cynical manipulation of the Pipeline Debate, over an American professor's ignorant pontifications about French Canada, and over the namby-pamby nonsense in some of our school texts — all matters on which he took action and had some impact. Many of his other major fights were fuelled by outrage as well, from his early battles with the McGill authorities over academic freedom to his protracted campaign against the "two nations" theory of Canada and his part in the struggle against the Meech Lake Accord.

THE VALUE OF CONTROVERSY
(From a 1957 speech on education[14])

First and foremost, face the facts. Some of them are very unpleasant. Some of them are frightening. But we shall never get anywhere if we pretend they aren't there.

Speak up, individually and collectively. If you think something right is being attacked, say so. If you think something wrong is being done, say so. Don't say, "Oh, well, who am I? Who'll listen to me? Unless I can speak through some organization, there's no use speaking at all." That is not so. I have seen, right here in Canada, cases where one man, standing almost alone, has forced even the present Government, with its huge majority, to back down. Governments, rulers, don't like rows; they will do a lot to avoid them, and even one person with a good cause can make a considerable row. There are times when rows are necessary; and when they are we should not hesitate to make them. If we can't get organizations to make them when they're necessary, we must do it ourselves.

Never be frightened by that rattling old bogey that destructive criticism is wicked. It is not. It is not enough. But it is very necessary. The prophet Jeremiah knew that: "To pluck up and to break down, and to throw down, and to destroy; … to build and to plant." The building and the planting are the ends, but you can't start building and planting till you have cleared the ground … So I make no apology for bringing out tonight my modest hammer and shovel, and trying to make my small contribution to the work.

All I have tried to do is to stir up your minds. I hope I have done that much, for that is the essential preliminary to finding any solutions. I hope also that I have been controversial, for controversy is the method by which we are governed, and the life-blood of free institutions.

Before taking up the cudgels, he would try to consider the relative importance of the issue at stake among the many priorities clamouring for his attention. At the heart of his thirty-year involvement in the national unity debate, for example, was his conviction that the social and economic advances won by the CCF and other progressive groups could only be sustained in a strong and united Canada. Similarly, the basis for his many battles in the constitutional arena was his belief that those same advances needed a solid legislative and constitutional framework to protect and further them.

Another key factor in his deciding whether or not to engage was the fit between a given issue and his own fields of expertise. Increasingly as he aged, he tried to limit his public interventions to those areas where he felt thoroughly informed and competent, and to avoid those where he believed himself ignorant and therefore of little use. Explaining why he refused an offer of the post of Indian claims commissioner in the first years of the Trudeau government, he recalled: "It would have required profound knowledge of a very large and intricate subject of which I knew nothing, and which I was too old to learn." He turned down offers from two universities to head up their social science departments for similar reasons.[15]

This cautious approach grew partly out of his years of frustration trying to undo the damage caused by people claiming to be authorities on matters that they really knew little or nothing about. Dad was determined never to fall into that trap. As well, he was genuinely humble — far too humble, I sometimes felt — about the usefulness of his "uninformed" opinions on controversial matters that fell outside his particular areas of detailed knowledge.

He also tried, with scant success, to keep his commitments from outstripping the amount of time and energy he actually had available. Even in his youth he had found this a challenge; and it became even more difficult once he had young children and a job that demanded a lot of travelling and burning of midnight oil. In those middle years, he was constantly torn between family responsibilities and various calls to battle, and later on, he sometimes wallowed in remorse for having too often chosen the public good over the private. As age took its toll on his energy, those time management dilemmas became more acute, and he began to say "no" more often.

At the time, I had little understanding of the very real limitations that kept my father on the sidelines of some important battles. As the debate over the Canada-US "Free Trade" agreement began to heat up in the second half of the 1980s, I urged him to join the fight against it. I knew that he shared many of the views of opponents of the "deal" who felt Canada was being sold down the river. I knew he regarded the Mulroney government as "a gang of pirates," not least because of their proven willingness to hand over Canadian resources and institutions to continental corporate interests. Moreover, he had spoken out in the past against the increasing economic and political control of Canada by American corporations. Yet, faced with the ominous threat of an agreement that would cement this kind of sell-out into place more or less permanently, he held back from active involvement in the fight.

I realize now that his main reason for abstaining was simply that he couldn't take on anything more at that point in his life. His energy was already severely taxed and his spirits subdued by worry over my mother's illness, and he was finding the daily tasks of housekeeping and looking after his own octogenarian body increasingly onerous. Despite his supposed "retirement," his workload was still massive — making speeches, reviewing manuscripts, giving interviews, pulling together his memoirs for publication, writing to the papers, answering correspondence, and attending various public functions. On top of all that, the fight against the Meech Lake constitutional package was gobbling up every spare minute and ounce of energy he had. But I had trouble seeing that at the time. He was my Dad, and he'd always managed to do so much. Somehow I failed to register the fact that he couldn't do even more.

The other major factor in the case of Free Trade was that it lay outside what he considered his area of expertise. He was convinced that in order to have anything worthwhile to say, he would need to do an immense amount of research and analysis about the specifics of the Canada-US Agreement — a mammoth task that he simply could not consider taking on. In vain, I tried to persuade him that he could shoot from the hip. I insisted that as a progressive and thoughtful individual, as a labour economist and political scientist, and simply as a Canadian citizen, he had valuable things to say on the subject without doing any extra research at all. But that was not my father's way. Unless he knew his ground thoroughly — and that meant thoroughly — he did not take public positions on complex issues.

This was, of course, part of what made him such an effective warrior when he did get involved. But for me at the time, these scruples of his were a source of frustration. We both shared the belief that one of the essentials of democracy is broad-based citizen involvement in issues that affect us. We both viewed with healthy skepticism any approach that gave undue weight to "expert" opinions, with all their inevitable gaps, flaws, and contradictions. Dad always insisted that reasoned discussion of public issues must admit — indeed, demanded — the intervention of non-experts, and he regularly encouraged my own propensity for speaking out, even though I was far from being an expert on anything.

Yet, when he was the non-expert himself, that principle didn't seem to apply. Again, his innate modesty played a role, together with his acute awareness of complexity, his attention to detail, and his commitment to accuracy. The Free Trade Agreement was a complex issue; it involved an immense degree of detail, and he was not an expert in the field. Above all, he simply couldn't stretch his waning strength that far. His absence from that battlefield was a major loss to Canada.

There was at least one other occasion where I felt Dad was being too conciliatory. In the fall of 1990, in the wake of the "Oka Crisis," he agreed to be a speaker or a guest at several functions sponsored by the federal government or the military. I pleaded with him not to lend the sanction of his presence to the institutions responsible for the outrages I had seen in Indian country. We were still engaged in that difficult dialogue in the months before he died.

Now, looking back, I am filled with remorse for the pressure I put on him. I assumed that he could just refuse the invitations, give a short public statement, and let the chips fall where they might. He knew, however, that some of those chips would inevitably fall back on him: more requests for interviews, explanations, justifications. Again, I was blind to the fact that at that stage of his life he simply could not handle everything that would have been involved.

In personal encounters, too, my father sometimes chose not to engage. During our trip to Newfoundland together in 1983, we stopped in for a brief visit with a distant relative, a prosperous small-town merchant. When this gentleman began expounding his right-wing views on poverty and welfare, I protested vigorously, but Dad sat with stoic patience. Back out on the snowy street, he turned to me and said, "Helen, you're like your mother. In her palmy days, she would have tried to convert the pope to Protestantism."

Here I suspect there was a bit of projection going on. After all, Eugene Forsey was famous for espousing lost causes of one sort or another. Somewhere in my growing up, I absorbed the belief that it's important to at least protest against an outrage, rather than let its perpetrators think they can carry on without even being challenged. I'm sure Dad was correct in giving my mother some of the credit, but I doubt if my determination came only from her side.

His comment probably also reflected another subtle element of his triage system: the persuasion potential on a given issue. In many of his public campaigns there was no way he could have expected to succeed in directly changing the policies or actions of those in power. But he probably did count on the sheer force and cogency of his arguments to persuade some of his fellow-citizens to change their minds, and in this he often did succeed. With individuals, on the other hand, he may have been more willing to let an issue rest if there seemed to be no hope at all of influencing or persuading the other person.

Dad tried to find gentle ways of reminding his activist daughter to keep a sense of proportion in her militancy. In my research for this book, I came across this sentence in one of his old letters: "I have a feeling sometimes that you are emphatic and belligerent not only about the big things, which you should be, but also about the small things." When I noticed the quotation in my notes some time later, I thought at first that it was directed to me. In fact, it was a letter to his friend Donald Fleming, finance minister at the time in the Diefenbaker government, addressing an apparent misunderstanding between the government and Dad's employer, the Canadian Labour Congress. Hoping Fleming would not take it amiss, he elaborated: "I have a feeling that you sometimes antagonize people unnecessarily, and lessen the forcefulness of your important statements by the forcefulness of your unimportant ones. I sometimes feel that if anyone asked you what the weather was going to be like tomorrow, you'd reply, 'The Conservative Party has always been in favour of fine weather, and I defy the honourable gentleman to produce any evidence to the contrary.' I am all for belligerence when it's needed; and it often is. But I think there are times, even in politics, for, if not the soft answer, the quiet, unemphatic answer."[16]

Admittedly, my father himself sometimes honoured this sensible advice more in the breach than in the observance. Like other mortals, he had certain buttons that could be pushed. As a result, he occasionally spent inordinate amounts of time and energy on matters that in the overall picture looked pretty trivial.

PURSUING THE MATTER
(From a 1984 letter to an Ottawa Board of Education official[17])

... Rereading your letter, I see that you wind up, "should you wish to pursue this matter further." I most certainly do wish to pursue the matter further.

In my letter, I asked for the date of the Board's next meeting, so that I could be present to register my emphatic protest against the action that had apparently been taken. If you had told me the Board had not taken [that] action, that might have settled the matter. [You] gave me [no] such assurance. Instead, you furnished me with a dissertation which was totally irrelevant to the point I had raised. I can only assume that the Board did take the action I objected to ...

I now wish to state, as plainly as I know how, *that I wish to appear before a full meeting of the Board, at the earliest possible moment, to register my protest and the reasons for it.*

It is not a matter of "clarifying my position." My position is as clear as the English language can make it. You might as well talk of "clarifying" distilled water. Your position is clear. The Board's position is apparently the same as yours; so its position is clear. My position is clear: I think you and the Board are wrong, and I want to appear before a full public meeting of the Board to place my position, and the reasons for it, before the Board.

I hope that is clear. I hope I shall hear promptly. I hope I shall not receive any more communications talking about "clarifying" anything, since there is nothing to be clarified, just something to be objected to and defended. I hope I shall get action, at last.

— Eugene Forsey

A classic example was his spat with the Ottawa Board of Education in 1984. My son Roddy, then in Grade 8, had been docked marks in math class for having written out the number "240" as "two hundred and forty." The teacher said it should be "two hundred forty." Dad went ballistic. He wrote to the school board in strong terms, demanding a meeting. After the usual bureaucratic paper-shuffle, the Board replied in what they hoped would be soothing tones. His response, excerpted in the sidebar on page 202, shows that nothing could have been less soothing.

Now, for a man about to enter his eighty-first year, a man immersed in the serious affairs of state, with an enormous workload of speeches, correspondence, and public engagements, and with a disabled wife at home, such a matter might seem of minor importance. One might think he could have let it pass. Not Dad. He persisted, and eventually got his meeting with the Board. The *Ottawa Citizen's* report on the encounter was headlined: "Forsey lectures OBE on 'proper English.'"[18]

Exactly what it was that compelled him to devote more time to how numbers were read in a classroom than to issues like Free Trade or Aboriginal rights, I'm not sure, but I do know the feeling. Call it heredity, or an identity problem, but some time ago I snapped at exactly such a bait. Fed up with repeated instances of American usage contaminating our national radio news, I made a spur-of-the-moment phone call to the CBC, and soon found myself engaged in a detailed exchange of letters on the subject with their broadcast language advisor.

Later, when I confessed to a friend that I had wasted valuable time on such a micro-issue, she brought me up short. "Did you enjoy it?" she asked. I admitted rather sheepishly that I had. "Well, then," she said, "Why not accept it as a valid form of recreation, like going for a hike?" Perhaps, for some of us, this kind of debate does function as a sort of intellectual workout, almost a sport. It gets the adrenalin flowing and exercises the mental muscles; on occasion it can even be fun. Dad, too, may have enjoyed minor skirmishes that he felt he could win, in contrast to the major struggles he so often lost. Or who knows: perhaps it was, indeed, "bad temper."

The frequent battles that were so much a part of my father's life certainly took a toll on him. Anger alone can be exhausting, and he fought each fight with such thoroughness and zeal, the sheer energy required was considerable. Had he not had ways to renew that energy, I don't think he could have kept up his fighting mettle and the fragile belief behind it that somehow, surely, it was all worthwhile.

Through decades of dissent, it was Dad's "kindred and affinities" that provided him with that vital support. Family, friends and colleagues, cherished books of poetry and prose, time spent in places he loved — all these bolstered his spirits. He drew sustenance from his religious faith and inspiration from the examples of the past, and whenever possible he lightened his load with humour. These were the sources from which he could recharge his batteries when combat left him drained and discouraged.

Two people in particular were crucial in that sustaining role. First was my mother, who shared both his intellectual bent and his devotion to principle, and whom he credited at the end of his life with having been "responsible for most of the good I have done, and none of the harm."[19] Mum was quite a private person, and politics was not the domain where she felt most at home. But she had a keen critical mind and a strong sense of justice, and she was very loyal. Not only was she his primary source of emotional support, she also served as a sounding-board and a stimulus in their continual exchange of ideas.

In the early years of their marriage, Mum was involved in my father's political work both as his partner and in her own right. Along with her other activities, she joined him in the Montreal section of the League for Social Reconstruction, compiled with him a comprehensive record of John Macmurray's 1936 seminar on politics and theology, and wrote several pieces of her own for the *Canadian Forum*. In addition, like so many wives of doctoral candidates, she typed her husband's entire thesis, contributing her comments throughout as "a most judicious critic."[20]

Later on, when the arrival of children pressed her into the mold of full-time housewife and mother, she played a less direct role in his work, but she was still very much there behind the scenes. Never blandly acquiescent, she was eminently capable of disagreeing; nor would Dad have wanted it any other way. In 1948, after the publication of one of his scathing denunciations of Mackenzie King, he confided to Arthur Meighen: "Even my wife, ordinarily my severest critic, is enthusiastic about this. She drove me on to write it; I had merely growled and grumbled at home. I can't recall any other article I ever wrote that she was more than tepid about; but she is delighted with this."[21]

There were times, as we children grew older and the issues around religion began to ferment, when Dad must have seen the family as another theatre of struggle rather than a refuge from the fray. For a few years either side of 1960, tensions ran high, and I realize now that he was probably suffering quite serious depression. But he and Mum grappled with the problems, and over time were able to re-establish their mutually supportive equilibrium.

For Harriet
September 20, 1968

… Forty years on, the hair has grayed
A little; all the rest has stayed.
Old fellow-students have filled out,
Grown well-upholstered, plump or stout,
But Mrs. Forsey has kept trim,
And still preserves her figure slim.
Nor can years wither, custom stale,
Her wit, nor does her sparkle fail.
Some pungent mot, some piercing
Phrase,
To match her penetrating gaze;
Anon, with gay and twinkling joke,
A solemn shirt-front she may poke.

The secret of what keeps her young,
Perhaps she finds in C.J. Jung
(Poetic license, this, I fear,
But else the rhyme gets out of gear!)
Her mental processes are nimble
As her deft hands with needle, thimble.
Her husband's duller intellect
Is sometimes baffled, often checked,
But even while she keeps him guessing,
She is his darling and his blessing.

For almost three-and-thirty years
She's charmed away his moods and fears,
And stiffened his backbone and muscle
For public and for private tussle,
And tried to stimulate his mind
(To easy slumber much inclined).
She's also tried to curb his rash,

Impulsive tendency to dash
Into some needless minor fight
(Like the famed, futile Spanish knight).
And though it's true she's sometimes
Failed,
At least he's never yet been jailed!

She's kept him on an even keel,
And if he's served the public weal
At times, to her belongs the credit:
Hers are the brains and heart that did it.
She's put some stuffing into him,
Yet known his ego how to trim
To size, or something near it,
Lest he'd come to be just bore and pest.
A struggle grim she's often had
To make a man of this queer lad.
But now, at last, he tribute brings,
Sadly belated; still he sings
Some praises of his modest wife,
Who's shaped the best part of his life.

His other chief pillar of support was of course his old friend Arthur Meighen. If there was one person in the world who was able to truly understand my father's political conflicts and dilemmas, it was Meighen. The former prime minister's loyal and loving patronage carried Dad through two turbulent decades of his life, and the gaping hole left by the old man's death was never really filled.

One of the strongest elements in their extraordinary friendship was their shared identity as controversial and often misunderstood public figures. Despite the thirty-year difference in their ages, both were veterans of civilian combat, lone warriors who repeatedly risked political suicide in thankless struggles over principle. That commonality cemented their bond. It mattered not one whit that they often stood on opposite sides of an issue, or that they seldom even fought in the same arena. When the opportunity did arise to take something on together, that was the icing on the cake.

Dad relished the prospect of sharing the political trenches with his beloved hero. In a 1948 letter, written in the midst of heavy work pressures and fatigue, he anticipated eventually getting back to his constitutional writing. "Also," he added, "I should be in trim to go after King's memoirs with a hatchet. I hope we can do that together!"[22]

By that time, Meighen was well into his seventies, and his health was beginning to fail. But Dad refused to give up. Three years later, immersed in the battle to keep the original Canadian word "Dominion" from being thrown out in favour of the American term "federal," he wrote to his old friend: "Perhaps we'll fight side by side at last, in this thing ... that would be the crown of many benefits you have showered on me."[23]

Among those many benefits was Meighen's constant moral support and encouragement — something that for Dad filled a very real need. To many who knew only the public Eugene Forsey, a man apparently so at ease in the spot-light of controversy, so sure of his own contentious opinions, it may come as a surprise to know that he struggled almost constantly with feelings of inadequacy and self-doubt. Not that his public persona was false or contrived; on the contrary. He knew his own intellectual capacity and had no qualms about asserting his views on what he referred to as "the very few subjects I really know something about." On other levels, though, his self-esteem was far from strong.

In a handwritten note to Meighen, dated February 24, 1950, he expressed this vulnerability, and again indicated how vital the older man's friendship and support were to him. "For some time before I wrote that book of mine [on the dissolution of Parliament] my self-confidence had been steadily undermined by a variety of people and circumstances. I haven't too much now, but most of what I have you have given back to me, and without it I should have been far less happy and useful than I am. This is something you could hardly have suspected. I think you should know it, and have some idea of how much I owe you on this count alone, quite apart from the numberless kindnesses you have done me over the years."

If my father had had more company on the public battlefields he chose, he might have suffered less from combat fatigue, and perhaps received more support from a wider range of on-lookers. Instead, the story too often ended with him fighting on, alone or nearly so, severed by a knife-edge of principle from many of his natural allies and friends. The most poignant of those stories — his split with the NDP at its founding convention — is told in detail in Chapter 15.

It's true that for such an independent and original thinker, there were certain advantages in fighting some battles on his own or in informal partnerships. But he had no ego-driven compulsion to fight alone; on the contrary, he firmly believed in collective struggle. What's more, he practised it. All through his years at the Labour Congresses, he worked happily behind the scenes in exactly such a context. Elsewhere, however, his non-partisan independence of thought and his fierce personal integrity led him to espouse causes that were often divisive. His split with the FCSO and his public condemnation to the NDP's "two nations" policy were just two of many instances where his willingness to differ made him the odd man out among his peers.

Sometimes people were grateful to him for this willingness. In *A Life on the Fringe*, he tells about a union meeting he sat in on where one member proposed a particularly militant bargaining position. Everyone else present seemed to concur, but they asked Dad what he thought. Reluctantly, since he was just an observer, he stated his contrary view. This time around the table, the rest agreed with him! After the meeting, the chair told him, "My God, Eugene, I'm glad you spoke. We all knew Bill was crazy, but none of us wanted to say so."[24]

My father could be counted on to "say so," to voice doubts or objections whenever he felt they were called for. Again and again he would speak out on delicate or controversial questions, while other people, even when they agreed with him, often stayed silent. Unfortunately, this kind of uneven division of political labour too easily becomes an established pattern, one whose unfairness is matched only by its pathetic ineffectiveness.

The Meighen correspondence contains the closest thing I've found to a complaint from Dad about this phenomenon. Sharing a letter he had received from another friend applauding his defence of the word "Dominion," he added plaintively: "I wish he'd write this kind of thing to the papers, not just to me. Lots of people speak to me on the street, or telephone me, or write to me, supporting me. Not many do anything more. If they would, there might be some chance of scaring the daylights out of the government."[25]

It comforts me to know that in his last major battle, the one over the Meech Lake Accord, he found solace and support in the company of other valiant warriors.[26] Over the three-year struggle against the Accord, he developed strong bonds of respect and commonality with many of his fellow combatants, including then Newfoundland Premier Clyde Wells. In the face of massive pressure from the political establishment to approve the flawed "deal," they were among those who refused to be silenced, insisting on speaking out and ultimately voicing the opposition of millions of Canadians.

Yet even here, Dad reached the point where he had to strike out on his own. When Prime Minister Mulroney made his final Machiavellian attempt to manipulate an agreement with the premiers before the June 1990 deadline, Wells asked Dad to be part of the Newfoundland government's delegation to the talks. As the infamous "seven-day dinner" with the first ministers dragged on, my father waited with growing apprehension in the delegation's office in the basement of Ottawa's Conference Centre. On day six, he finally concluded that Newfoundland's anti-Meech position had been eroded too far, and he passed the premier a hand-written note: "There is no point in my remaining on the delegation. I am completely in the dark, and have neither appetite nor aptitude for debates on how many angels can dance on the point of a needle, especially when there are no angels, and no needle. All these 'undertakings' to 'consider' or to 'negotiate' in a 'second round'; all the 'clarifications,' all the 'companion resolutions,' are worth precisely nothing. I am, accordingly, resigning from the delegation, and shall feel free to make any comments I see fit when the decisions are made public. I am sorry I cannot even get 'upstairs' to say all this. So there is no use my even staying [in] this office counting my toes."[27]

"It was a point in time that bothered me greatly," Wells told me five years later. "He felt that I shouldn't even make the kind of accommodation that I was prepared to make for Mr. Mulroney's proposal. And he wrote me a note to say that he felt it would be wrong for him to continue to stay as part of the team. That was one of the most difficult things that I had to accept, because I had such a very high regard for your father. It simply reflects the strength of his conviction and the strength of his principle."

Soon after the Accord's demise, Dad wrote to Wells with his postmortem reflections, and told Deborah Coyne about it. "He probably thought my letter frank to the verge of impudence," he confided. "I told him he was a good man, an honest man, a broadminded man, a conciliatory man; but that when you are dealing with pirates, snakes, liars, knaves, and

Eugene, a "reluctant dragon" indeed, leaving the "seven-day dinner" Meech Lake negotiations, where he was part of the Newfoundland delegation, June 1990.

fools, there are narrow limits to the practice of these admirable virtues ... I hope he will never allow himself to be swindled again."[28]

Like other independent thinkers before and since, my father was variously labelled an irascible eccentric, accused of being a trouble-maker, and put down for not being a "team player." Yet at the same time, many people expected him to keep on doing the hard work of controversy which they themselves were unwilling to take on. Even when he didn't volunteer on his own initiative, he would often get drafted for the front lines.

Saddled with a fighter's reputation — which he had admittedly done plenty to earn — Dad was nonetheless far from immune to the personal fallout that comes with that lonely and sometimes thankless role. His periodic pessimism and the shakiness of his self-esteem were, I think, largely due to the stress of continual controversy, the negative image it gave him in many quarters, and the political and even personal isolation he sometimes suffered as a result.

Eugene Forsey was indeed a reluctant dragon. Incapable of turning away from things he thought were wrong, he breathed fire onto a lot of burning issues. Yet he could not ignore complexities or lose sight of the human consequences of conflict. It was a gentle soul that harboured his fighting spirit, and in that mix lay both his vulnerability and his strength.

CHAPTER EIGHT

Knowing Where We've Come From: History and Tradition

> If you don't know where you've come from, it's not very likely that you'll know where you're going. I'm convinced that a knowledge of our history, and an attachment to the values that it embodies, is extraordinarily important for practical purposes.
> — CBC Radio interview, 1986[1]

My father's writings and speeches reflect the love of history and the respect for tradition that informed virtually all of his work, especially on the constitutional front. His critical analysis of contemporary realities and his dream of a better world were grounded in an understanding of what had gone before. He was aware that some of the world's most radically progressive ideas were also some of its most venerable, and he rejoiced in time-honoured traditions that reflected and strengthened the ideals he fought for.

Many elements in today's social justice movement likewise place great value on history and heritage. Aboriginal people in their ongoing struggles give central importance to traditional teachings, ancestral places, and the customs of millennia. Annual celebrations such as Labour Day, Black History Month, and International Women's Day pay tribute to the vital role played by past struggles in the progress that has been made. The horrors of slavery, pogroms, and the Holocaust are memorialized in the hope of preventing their recurrence; that is why Holocaust denial is prosecuted as a hate crime. Many oppressed groups are pushing the dominant society to acknowledge its own history, its own legacy of rights and wrongs, in order to be able to join with integrity in the building of a better future.

The gifts we receive from the past include much more than just what we call "history." Every culture's inheritance is a rich tapestry made up also of language, religious beliefs, means of livelihood and enjoyment, local customs, artistic expression, and more. In my father's case, that tapestry was woven largely with words. Not only did oral and written language serve him as a vehicle for expression and communication in the here and now, it also linked him with people and events of years gone by, giving access to a vast storehouse of ideas and images from other decades and centuries. In turn, he saw the language of the present day as a living heritage to be cherished, defended, and passed on to future generations.

Dad's traditionalism was seldom limiting or restrictive; it did not keep him mired in reactionary attitudes. In the main, it nourished his commitment to necessary social change. Far from treating the past as a rule-book to be unthinkingly followed, he viewed it as an irreplaceable source of learning, pleasure, and identity, and — as often as not — a fount of inspiration.

"Prove all things; hold fast that which is good." St. Paul's injunction to the Thessalonians was a guiding principle in Dad's life, which he often cited.[2] The proving of all things is a theme of the next chapter; holding fast what is good is the substance of this one.

My father clearly drew comfort from the deep historical roots of the radicalism he had adopted. In one of his early speeches, I came across a moving quotation — originally from an English "Leveller" of the seventeenth century — that epitomized the principle of equality between rich and poor.[3] The allusion sent me scurrying to our old *Encyclopaedia Britannica*, where I found the "Levellers" described as an important English political party in the mid-1600s. Linked to the "Agitators"(!), they called for such radical reforms as equality before the law, the abolition of trading monopolies, and parliamentary supremacy over the king — generations before later groups with similarly egalitarian ideals were labelled "socialist."[4] It is humbling to have to admit that I hadn't known anything about them before doing the research for this book.

It's not that I wasn't brought up to respect the past. My sister and I absorbed a good deal about our heritage from our parents through the stories they told or read to us, the things they did with us, and the simple family traditions that linked daily life with times gone by.

The "Forsey foursome" used to gather at the piano to sing, or sit around the fire for reading aloud. We savoured Mum's New Brunswick fish chowder, gobbled up Nana's scones and preserves, and learned to make our great-aunt Hannah's hard gingerbread with bacon drippings and molasses. Sunday dinner and other special occasions brought out the heirloom china and linens. When visitors came, Mum would remove the plastic coverings from the antique furniture in the living room and allow her little girls to sit there like grown-up ladies.

In summer, we would make bouquets of fragrant white blossoms from the rose bushes Mum had brought from her great-grandmother's old garden in Saint John. When autumn turned the woods to red and gold, we would collect maple leaves and press them between sheets of wax paper for cards or decorations. Every Christmas Eve, we hauled dusty boxes of fragile old ornaments up from the cellar and made chains with popcorn and paper to adorn a balsam fir, which we always kept for the traditional twelve days.

Dad didn't have much in the way of holidays when we were small, but we spent several summers with Mum in the Maritimes, where we played with our cousins and got to know some of the places that had shaped our own and our country's history.

On two occasions, our parents took us on a weekend pilgrimage to their former haunts in Montreal. We travelled by train and stayed in the lovely old Laurentian Hotel. I remember walking around Dominion Square, looking up at the Sun Life Building — a "skyscraper" in those days

— and then going for a drive up Mount Royal in a horse-drawn calèche. On later visits to that beautiful city, I found memories around every corner, redolent of the years my parents spent there when they were young.

At home in Ottawa, we would take the bus up to the hallowed precincts of Parliament Hill, where Mum or Dad would point out the statues of historic figures and tell us about them. We'd ride the elevator up the Peace Tower, past the great carillon bells, and look out over the parapets at the confluence of rivers with their great rafts of logs, and the two cities spreading beyond. Once Dad took us inside the Parliamentary Library, where we were awed by its towering walls of books and the great iron doors which, back in 1916, had blocked the fire that destroyed the rest of the building.

During royal visits, we would join the throngs that lined the Driveway along the Rideau Canal, to wave our little Union Jacks and take snapshots, which we proudly mounted in our photo albums. In the lead-up to the young Queen Elizabeth's coronation in 1953, Mum made us matching skirts from material printed with crowns and orbs and sceptres, and we spent happy hours putting together an elaborate cardboard cut-out model of the coronation procession, complete with golden coach and snow-white horses.

Family weekend in Montreal, Eugene and Harriet taking their girls up Mount Royal by calèche, 1950.

Many were the family picnics we enjoyed at the Dominion Experimental Farm or on the shores of the Ottawa River at Britannia Beach and Rockcliffe — places Dad had loved as a child. He took us to the railway yards to watch the shunting steam engines, and to the old Victoria Museum nearby — now the Museum of Nature, but in those days an eclectic and, to a child, fascinating mix of dinosaur bones, old fur trader costumes, and rocks from the Canadian Shield. Then he would show us his own small collection of rocks and fossils, and encourage us to search for fossils ourselves in the riverbank shale. He also had a stash of old coins and postage stamps that he shared with us, explaining where they came from — Newfoundland, his parents' time in Mexico, or his own travels in Europe during his student days.

All these things, I realize now, were providing us with a basis for integrating into our young lives our personal and collective inheritance. Through osmosis, we were absorbing elements of our identity, growing strong roots to anchor and nourish us so that we might flourish.

Our parents rarely made these lessons explicit, though they did occasionally remind us that much of what we enjoyed in our own early years had been built by past labours and won by past struggles. Perhaps they should have insisted more on those connections, for at the time I was largely oblivious. It took me decades to grasp an understanding of history as a source of collective identity and an ongoing record of human striving towards a better society.

That kind of awareness may have skipped a generation in my case, but it emerged again in my sons, both of whom took an active interest in history and made it part of their studies at McGill. "Grampa was definitely the guy to talk to about that stuff," Roddy recalled. "He was living history."

Dad lived up to that designation. "I can remember a great many people who go a long, long way back in our history," he told David Millar in 1970. "I remember one man who was elected to Parliament in 1867, half a dozen who were elected in 1874, and a good dozen who were elected in 1878. This has been rather useful to me sometimes when I've been talking to classes in Canadian government. I'm able to set somebody right by saying, 'Oh no, you've got his name wrong. I knew him.' And they look at me as if I had suddenly walked down the plank from Noah's Ark!"[5]

"SIR JOHN A. AND THE YOUNG FELLOW"[6]

When Bruce Hutchison wrote his biography of Mackenzie King in the early 1950s, he included this imaginative reflection on King and Sir John A. Macdonald seventy-odd years earlier.

"Old Tomorrow, neck-deep in the congenial conspiracies and huge constructive labours of Ottawa and often deep in liquor; the commonplace and unknown youth in Berlin [now Kitchener, Ontario] — there was a chancy combination of circumstances worth pause and pondering. Some commonplace youth in an unknown corner of Canada today, would be worth pondering also if we could identify him."

Dad wrote:

John A Macdonald, at sixty-three,
Had climbed to the very top of the tree.
William Lyon Mackenzie King
At four years old, didn't mean a thing.
Macdonald stood at the foot of the throne,
King was a small boy, completely unknown.

My father was renowned for his ability to cite historical chapter and verse to support his arguments on social, economic, and constitutional questions. Former Newfoundland Premier Clyde Wells called him "an absolute walking encyclopedia of Canada's constitutional and governmental history." With perhaps a touch of hyperbole, he added: "I don't know that there was a single event in Canada's 125 years that he wasn't able to draw on to support a position or an idea that he was putting forward."

It's one thing to be a walking encyclopedia, another to make that knowledge relevant to vital questions in the here and now. Dad tried, with considerable success, to do both. He had an uncanny ability to pull obscure elements out of the historical and literary record and relate them to current realities.

> Macdonald was often deep in rum,
> King still sucking his little pink thumb.
> Macdonald neck-deep in constructive labours,
> King at play with his juvenile neighbours.
> John A Macdonald, who'd founded a nation,
> King, who'd not tasted a single ovation.
> There's a contrast worth pause and pondering,
> Combination to set you wondering!
> But here's another, still more exciting,
> Conjured by magic of Bruce's writing:
> Somewhere today, betwixt ocean and ocean
> (Where it may be, we haven't a notion),
> King's youthful heir, unidentified,
> Waits, all unknowing, for Fortune's tide,
> Never suspecting a destiny sinister
> 'S planning already to make him Prime Minister.
> If we could find him, here, there or yonder,
> He too would be a fit subject to ponder.
> But as we can't, we must leave him unsung,
> For a later Muse theme for the harp and the tongue."

In a 1990 speech on the possibility of Quebec separation, he raised the question of "*le grand nord*," the huge expanse of Cree and Inuit land formerly known as the District of Ungava, and explained why an independent Quebec's potential claim to the territory might be tenuous.

> [Ungava] was given to Quebec in 1912 by the Quebec Boundary Extension Act, as a province of Canada, and at a time when there was not one single French Canadian living in the whole territory.
>
> Now you may say, "That's an extreme statement, what warrant has he for that?" I had, years ago, repeatedly made

speeches in which I had said, "I don't think there were ten French Canadians in the whole territory." And then I thought, "My boy, you'd better be careful. Somebody may look up the figures, and show you that there were twenty or twenty-five." So I went to the census of 1911, and all I could find on national or ethnic origin were figures for the whole of the Territories. No good. Then I remembered what Professor Jim Mallory said about Sir Robert Borden: "Sir Robert Borden, who never left anything to chance." I said, "That's it. I remember Borden well; that's right."

So I went to Hansard and looked up the proceedings on the Bill. There, sure enough, was Borden. And I could just hear the old man saying it: "Mr Chairman, it occurred to me that it might be of advantage to have some figures on the national or ethnic origin of the inhabitants of this territory. I have therefore applied to the Department of the Census, and they have furnished me with the following figures: Indians 663, Eskimos 543, Halfbreeds 46, English 8, Scots 2." Period. Not one French Canadian in the whole territory. If you doubt me, go and look at Hansard for 1912, page 6161, and you will find precisely the figures I've given you.[7]

Of course, the impact of history goes well beyond such detailed specifics. The question of relations between French and British in what is now Canada is a case in point. Dad maintained — along with Sir George-Étienne Cartier and Sir Wilfrid Laurier — that after the battle of the Plains of Abraham, the French and British populations actually sustained and preserved each other, mutually protecting their emerging societies from being absorbed by the United States.

> If the French-Canadians had revolted in 1776, or 1812, or backed the English-Canadian Annexation Movement in 1849, there would probably be no British Canada.
>
> But without the British tradition, and the British alliance, there would certainly be no French Canada.

Eugene with his mother, Florence Forsey, Parliament Hill, 1942. Nana herself had practically grown up on "the Hill," where her father, William Cochrane Bowles, was a high official.

Where did French Canada get its democratic institutions? From France? From the rocks, the woods, the streams, the soil, or some other such "purely" Canadian source?

No. From Britain. Without those British institutions, could French Canada have preserved its language, its

> schools, the special position of its church in Quebec? Could it have preserved them as a state or states of the American union? If Canada had not been British, there would have been no French-Canadians or Acadians, just some millions of American citizens of French origin.
>
> Each of our two great parent traditions is an essential part of the Canadian tradition. Together, they have preserved our national existence. Alone, neither can survive. Together they must still preserve our national existence. That was the vision of Macdonald and Cartier. It is not obsolete. It shines with the same light now as it did nearly a century ago, indeed brighter and stronger.[8]

The past forms part of our collective psyche, and it can have a profound effect on our attitudes and actions. For Dad, our non-revolutionary history was one of the defining elements of our heritage as Canadians. Our early leaders, he pointed out, chose a peaceful, cooperative, incremental process of self-determination as the path to nationhood. That choice was neither imposed nor reactionary, and generations later it continues to shape who we are as a country.

In a speech to the United Empire Loyalists' Association, he stressed this theme.

> Our Loyalist ancestors were not a collection of old mossbacks who didn't believe in popular liberty. They were every bit as much devoted to popular or constitutional government as the revolutionaries were; in fact, rather more so. That was really the essential point they were making: that any changes necessary could be made by peaceful, constitutional, legal means ... They were devoted to certain principles which are at the basis of our national life now — or should be. They believed in constitutional monarchy. They were devoted to the principle of representative government [and] to the rule of law ...
>
> So I think it's time for people like ourselves, who believe in the basic principles which our various ancestors stood

for, to assert ourselves. We ought to be in the forefront of the battle to maintain [those] essential principles."[9]

Despite my father's strong historical bent, the urgency of some of the contemporary issues he was involved in made him wary of burying himself too deeply in the past. At times during his work on *Trade Unions in Canada: 1812–1902*, I know he questioned the value of what he was doing. He had to remind himself that past events can resonate with remarkable force in the present. As he noted in the introduction to that magnum opus: "What does emerge, unmistakably and most surprisingly, is the persistence of problems, of attitudes towards them, of methods of dealing with them, of arguments about them ... One might have expected to find the accounts of unions in the last century of almost purely antiquarian interest: 'old, forgotten, far-off things, and battles long ago.' On the contrary, what one finds is, over and over again, startlingly contemporary. Change a few names, dates and figures, and the tale might have come from yesterday's newspaper."[10]

This often remarkable relevance of history to current reality was the reason behind my father's passion for keeping the record straight. False statements posing as historical fact roused him to incandescent fury. In the introductory notes to his 1974 collection of essays, *Freedom and Order*, he addressed the perennial need for "intellectual slum clearance" in the field of constitutional history. "The whole subject is one on which ignorance, confusion and muddle-headedness abound and persist, even among people who ought to know better ... The general public have too often been 'hungry sheep' who have looked to the learned and not been fed, or, worse, fed soap bubbles or sawdust."[11]

Throughout his long career, he spent an enormous amount of energy digging out the "bubbles and sawdust" wherever he found them, and replacing them with incontrovertible historical evidence. His diligence, though, was not always appreciated.

"In one learned work I once had to review," he told McMaster graduates in 1984, "I found twenty-six errors of fact on a single page; in another, fifty-nine in a single chapter. What is worse, when I pointed this out, academic personages, more than once, just smiled and said, 'Well, you have very strong opinions,' or 'Of course, there are two sides to every question.' But if an author says the Senate threw out the Natural Products Marketing Bill in 1934, and the Senate *Hansard*, p. 698, shows the royal assent, what on earth have my opinions — strong, weak or middling — got to do with it?"[12]

Some might question the need in today's world for such meticulousness in portraying the details of long-ago events. Even if the misinformation is being used to advance dubious arguments, many would just shrug and leave the wrangling to academics. But Dad saw beyond that, to where crucial current issues hung in the balance. "This is not just pedantry or nit-picking," he insisted. "Much public discussion of great public questions has been bedevilled and envenomed by fairy-tales spun from an intricate tangle of un-facts."[13]

In his 1967 George Nowlan Lectures at Acadia University, he listed "seven devils of pseudo-history" that Quebec separatists and their sympathizers were already invoking in the national unity debate.

> Why do I make such a song about these errors, learned or vulgar? Why do I call them "devils"? First, they cloud the real issues and befuddle people's minds. Second, they have given many of the English-speaking "intelligentsia" a guilt complex ... which makes it impossible for them to see straight, and induces in them a compulsive urge to try to make the rest of us see crooked ... Third, you cannot build a house on the foundation of bad dreams or sick fantasies. These errors envenom the discussion of difficult, delicate, and complex problems on whose solution the very life of this country may depend.

Noting the tendency among some well-meaning anglophones to accept at face value whatever supposedly historical accusations Quebec sovereigntists came up with, he went on: "Confessing one's own real sins, and trying to make amends, is good. Confessing other people's imaginary sins, and trying to get them to make a burnt offering of their country for misdeeds they never committed, is well-meaning, but dangerous ... The undoubted sincerity of the purveyors of all this dangerous nonsense makes it not one whit less nonsensical and only more dangerous."[14]

Time and again, my father's commitment to reconciliation and reform in contemporary Canada led him to take on the often thankless task of reviewing and correcting the historical record. If clarity, wisdom, and decency were to prevail in addressing the great issues of the day, he was convinced that the starting point had to be a reality-based understanding of the past.

Nor was he alone in emphasizing the need to keep the historical context clearly visible in such debates. In *Reflections of a Siamese Twin*, philosopher John Ralston Saul writes at length about the "mythology of the victim" that too often gets substituted for reality when "practical memory" is eliminated. Saul describes the 1995 Quebec referendum as taking place "in an atmosphere devoid of a real past or present … Our future was debated and decided as if we had no past. No experience. Therefore no reality."[15]

When that kind of knowledge vacuum is filled by false versions of past events, the resulting distortions can be used to push particular political agendas. Posing as history, the distortions bestow on those partisan efforts an aura of authority and respectability that they don't deserve. Dad felt a moral obligation to refute the "un-facts" in order to restore honesty and reason as the basis for public discourse.

One of the false claims he repeatedly had to confront was the notion that the Fathers of Confederation had designed Canada to be highly decentralized. During the national debate over the Meech Lake Accord in the late 1980s, former Liberal cabinet minister Eric Kierans weighed in on the pro-Meech side. The Accord, Kierans declared, was "the closest we have come to following the original intent and meaning of the British North America Act since Confederation itself. It reflects more accurately the view of what the original Fathers of Confederation thought they were agreeing to … They never intended that the provinces should become as dependent as they, in fact, became."

In a cutting response, Dad cited twenty-three clauses of the BNA Act and verbatim quotations from Sir John A Macdonald, and concluded: "Mr. Kierans, plainly, has never read, or has completely forgotten, the British North America Act. He has never read, or has completely forgotten, the Confederation Debates."[16]

Indeed, all the original documentation emphatically contradicted Kierans's hypothesis of an early plan for a highly decentralized Canada with powerful provinces calling the shots. Yet even today, this particular piece of pseudo-history continues to be propounded, whether through ignorance or cynicism, as a basic constitutional principle. It is still frequently used to bolster the claims of the "province-worshippers" and intensify the centrifugal forces that weaken Canada as a nation.

A related historical travesty has been the frequent portrayal of the Fathers of Confederation, French- and English-speaking, as "merely a lot of mixed-up kids with a dreadful sense of colonial inferiority" who didn't really know what they were doing.[17] Having read all the texts of the negotiations leading up to 1867, Dad knew that image to be completely false. He honoured these early architects of our country as creative and clear-headed reformers with a vision of a great new nation evolving from its diverse origins to embody a shared ideal of the public good.

Here again there are parallels with the work of John Ralston Saul, who likewise underlines the Fathers' commitment to a creative vision of democracy and fairness evolving from what had gone before. "None of the key players [in Confederation] were small-'c' conservatives," writes Saul. "They had an original and long-term idea of their undertaking ... closely linked to ideas of social equality."[18] Although he and Dad differ in some of their interpretations and emphasis, both of them stress how original and forward-looking the Fathers of Confederation were, and how relevant their basic approach remains.

"Your dad had an unusually strong sense of tradition and its place in society," John Hastings told me. "His views were an interesting mix of progressive, even radically progressive thinking, and a real sense of tradition. He knew the history of how things had emerged and developed, and the intricacy of the relationships; he could talk about the development of freedoms. It was a very central thing."

Just how central was evident in my father's long campaign to keep the word "Dominion" as the official designation for our country. From the 1940s onwards, Liberal governments had been using every means at their disposal to quietly eliminate the use of the term, ignoring the fact that the word had been deliberately chosen by the Fathers of Confederation to reflect the power and dignity they envisioned for their new country.

With Arthur Meighen cheering him on, Dad shone a floodlight on the government's "sneak-thief attempts to get rid of 'Dominion,'" and proceeded to fight tooth and nail to keep it. He brought to the battle all the erudite historical knowledge and furious will at his command, and did so, he noted in 1989, "not wholly in vain. Most people will probably be surprised to learn that 'Dominion' is still the legal title for this country."[19]

The original draft of his memoirs included a chapter entitled "Trying to Stop the Theft of Canada's History," which detailed the whole story. That chapter didn't make it into the published version of the book, but its thirty pages make for lively reading, as do the letters he exchanged with Meighen throughout that period.

"The Liberals, not content with controlling the present, are now trying to control the past by systematically falsifying our history," he complained in one of those letters.

Meighen responded in kind: "It is nothing better than childish to call on the whole country to cast away a designation of which we have all been proud." And again: "No country ever became great by the defamation of its traditions and the soiling of its past."[20]

For both men, the issue was far more profound than it appeared on the surface. They saw the persistent attempts to remove the word "Dominion" as "creeping republicanism," with significant and controversial changes being smuggled in behind people's backs in order to pave the way for the pro-American agenda of Prime Minister Mackenzie King and his continentalist successors. "The spirit behind this business," Dad warned at the time, "will vitiate our whole national life if it is not checked now."[21]

History has proven that warning sadly prophetic. Without ever admitting what they were doing, the Liberal governments of the 1940s and 50s were already working towards the further integration of our country with its monolithic neighbour to the south. By engineering the virtual disappearance of a unique Canadian term grounded in our history and our identity as a nation, they helped set the stage for passive public acceptance of the continentalism we now see embodied in NAFTA, the "Security and Prosperity Partnership," and other forms of "harmonization" between Canada and the US.

The Trudeau government used similarly underhanded tactics to pass its 1982 legislation changing the name of our national holiday from "Dominion Day" to the singularly unimaginative "Canada Day." Dad appeared before the Senate committee reviewing the bill, in a futile attempt to get it stopped, or at least critically examined.

"The whole thing is [based on] an extraordinary collection of fairy tales," he said. "Not less extraordinary is the number and quality of the people who have accepted them as gospel and been ready, on this flimsy basis, to forego what ought to be one of our proudest — and most purely Canadian — words and the tradition it enshrines."[22]

The relentless undermining of the term "Dominion" over the years is part and parcel of the colonial mentality that has guided our increasing subjugation to the United States ever since it began. Our country has been sold down the river piece by piece, from the St. Laurent government's imposition of the American-controlled TransCanada Pipeline in 1956 to Jean Chrétien's sell-out in the North American Free Trade Agreement nearly four decades later.

Canada's acceptance of "free trade" with the United States in 1988 was itself a blatant example of ignoring the lessons of the past. Although for reasons outlined elsewhere my father was not active in that fight, David Orchard and others took up the historical cudgels in a valiant campaign to stop the fateful "deal." They documented our country's repeated rejections of continentalism in the "free trade" elections of 1891 and 1911 and at intervals since. Even Mackenzie King, the Rockefeller protegé who pushed so hard for Canadians to follow "the American road," had not dared to risk incurring the wrath of the people by agreeing to a 1948 US proposal for a customs union; the arguments against it were too strong.[23]

It took years of forgetting that history before Brian Mulroney's southward-looking government managed to impose the Canada-US Free Trade Agreement on an unwilling people. Even then, it only went through because the massive anti-free trade vote was fatally split by narrow partisanship, and, as Dad told Tom Earle in 1989, the "first-past-the-post" electoral system allowed the continentalist minority to come up the middle and win.[24]

In that crucial election, the free traders' battle cry was, in effect, "Forget the past!" Avid to usher in their glorious "free trade" future, they fabricated the myth that Canadians had previously been too timid and reticent to engage with the world. Their vaunted trade deal, they claimed, would show us to be "a strong and confident people [who can] embark on new ventures without fear of losing their identity."[25] These days, as similar "new ventures" beckon, we need to remember how dearly we are still paying for that one.

There are some who take a condescending attitude towards my father's attachment to the past, tending to see it as mere nostalgia — quaint, romantic, even endearing in a way, but hopelessly out-of-date and irrelevant. Ted Hodgetts, at the conclusion of his book of Dad's letters to the editor, wondered rhetorically: "How will we remember Forsey's responses to all these forces [of change]? Will it be as a twentieth-century King Canute: a lone figure relying doggedly on due process and what he liked to call common sense … to settle differences and preserve the established order in seemly fashion?"[26]

But that's unfair. Dad never unthinkingly defended "the established order"; quite the contrary. As he told a young audience in 1966: "I am not suggesting that we should become magpies jealously guarding collections of ancient junk, or keepers of old curiosity shops. But neither should we be carried away by the cult of the merely new, any more than of the merely old."[27]

What he did object to was the kind of knee-jerk response that automatically favoured anything new. He deplored the insistence that every proposal for government support or private funding must be "new" or "innovative."

"A Senator once complained to me that none of the witnesses before [a] Senate Committee had produced a single new idea for dealing with unemployment. He nearly fell off his perch when I replied that what mattered was not whether the ideas were new, but whether they were sensible!"[28]

Nowadays, with the cult of the new perhaps stronger than ever, the unthinking demand for novelty above all else has condemned many good and proven programs to death by a thousand cuts.

It's true that there was more than a hint of nostalgia in my father's relationship with the past. Long before he reached the status of "senior citizen," he looked back with tenderness to earlier times, sometimes lamenting that he had been born fifty years too late. He mourned the loss of slower, simpler ways of life and the values they represented, eying with downright dismay some of what threatened to replace them. At one point he even wrote: "I disapprove so thoroughly of so much in the modern world that I find it hard to say which of its numerous unpleasant features I dislike the most."[29] And that was almost five decades ago.

Eugene in 1983, in the graveyard in Grand Bank where his father and grandfather are buried.

Nostalgia, though, is not to be despised unless it becomes paralyzing or obsessive. With Dad, by and large, it was the opposite: his love of the past energized and inspired him. It provided him with an emotional and intellectual anchor, with enduring values, with points of reference as the world and the country changed. Combined with his critical abilities and rigorous logic, his respect for the history he knew so well made him a thoughtful and extremely well-informed contributor to public debate on a whole range of important issues. Whether we agree or disagree with him in any given case, we ignore such input at our peril.

His understanding of Canada's history and traditions is, of course, open to other criticisms. He deeply loved this northern land, with its fields and mountains, lakes and forests stretching from sea to sea to sea. But like most public figures of his generation, he approached the discussion of Canadian identity from a mainly European standpoint, interpreting our heritage almost entirely within the terms and framework of the dominant settler cultures.

"Canada is not just a land mass, floating in empty space," he insisted. "It is a community of human beings, rooted in time and history. A Canadian is the inheritor of at least two great traditions, the French and the British, which are constantly being enriched by the contributions of the native peoples and of the newer immigrants."[30]

This rather circumscribed focus on our evolution since European contact was the basis for Dad's reluctance over the years to endorse various suggestions for a distinctive Canadian flag. Long after Parliament adopted the red and white maple leaf banner in 1965, he still could not resist referring to it as "not even multi-cultural or agricultural, [but] silvicultural."[31] Although he did not take a very active part in the flag debate, he did join with others in May 1964 to sign an open letter to Prime Minister Pearson, asking that the maple leaf proposal be reconsidered in favour of "a new design which asserts our history."

"The very essence of this country's history," they wrote, "and the reason for our national distinctiveness, has been the long and often turbulent marriage of French and English heritages ... The creative tension between the two founding peoples has been a guarantee to other racial groups of *their* continued identity, in contrast to the American concept of the melting pot. These are the positive facts of our history; they give Canada its sinews. The nation is strong enough to face its own past proudly, and to assert it ... We believe that a distinctive Canadian flag should reflect this."[32]

Pre-Cambrian Rock, and the Magnetic Pole
(From a speech at Queen's University, circa 1978[33])

Some twenty-five years ago, a certain politician said we must have a "distinctive Canadian flag," from which the Union Jack must disappear. But he stopped there. So I made game of him in some nonsense verses which ended with this:

There's just one little gap in the speech that he made,
Which must sure be the reason the thing's been delayed.
He said what to take out, but not what to put in.
Perhaps he's in doubt about where to begin.
So some pointers to guide him may not come amiss,
Some helpful suggestions. To start with, how's this?
The whole thing must be native, must reek of our soil,
But there must be no hint of the pioneer's toil;
For the pioneer brings in a touch of the past,
Of history, of Europe, and that is the last
Thing we want in our purely "Canadian" flag.
Like the crosses and fleur-de-lis, 'twould be a drag
On our national pride, and a blot on our 'scutcheon.
Surely all must agree this objection there's much in.
Well then, what shall it be? Is the answer not clear?
It must have the two things which have always been here:
Pre-Cambrian rock, and the Magnetic Pole.
These are fit to express the "Canadian" soul!
There's naught "foreign" in these; neither British nor French;
And neither emits a historical stench.
A Pre-Cambrian culture that's truly our own,
A Pre-Cambrian culture that's bare to the bone!
And the Magnetic Pole perfect symbol would be
Of the boast of our song, "the true North strong and free."
For these let our daughters and sons "stand on guard"!
Let these be the theme of some national bard!
These inspire a "distinctive Canadian" muse!
And death to the traitors who homage refuse!

Dad himself seldom used the phrase "two founding peoples," but in his speeches and writings he continually paid homage to Canada's "two great traditions" — the British and the French. He made his view clear in a 1962 speech: "There are those who, in the name of a 'pure' Canadianism, would have us renounce the French tradition, or the British, or both. But to do so would be to renounce Canada itself. For Canada without these two basic traditions would not be Canada at all."[34]

In the constitutional and legal context in which my father did much of his work, this makes a good deal of sense. The formal establishment of Canada as a nation was indeed the work of far-seeing leaders whose cultural and political heritage came from Britain and France. The Fathers of Confederation naturally — and, it can be argued, wisely — drew on what they saw as the best and most applicable aspects of their dual heritage in designing the structure for the new country.

The concepts of liberty, equality, and fraternity articulated by the French were reflected in parts of the BNA Act, particularly the language provisions and the protection of the Napoleonic Code as the civil law in Quebec. The principles and structure of our constitutional monarchy came to us from Britain, where the parliamentary system of "responsible government" was continuing to evolve from centuries of popular struggle.

Most Canadians today are ignorant of the fascinating history of those early democracy movements on the other side of the Atlantic. I am not alone in not having known who the Levellers were. But the more we learn, the less we can credit the notion that our British heritage is one of oppression. Indeed, as Dad was constantly pointing out, it was those long-ago struggles in Britain that gave us our basic rights and freedoms, as well as the essential safeguards, such as the independence of the judiciary, which continue to underlie the law in this country.[35]

The dangers of ignoring or dismissing those inherited constitutional principles are extensively documented in my father's constitutional writings. One example was his denunciation of the 1949 action of a Liberal cabinet minister in suppressing a report he was legally bound to release.

> The Minister broke not one law, but two, the Combines Act, and another, far more essential, far more venerable, the very bulwark of our liberties, the very foundation

of our institutions ... Three centuries ago, the English people beheaded one king and drove another into exile to establish the principle that Government is subject to the law, not above it.

To be sure, it was the Cabinet, not the Crown itself, which thus trampled on the Constitution and overthrew the rule of law. But as [Canadian parliamentarian Edward] Blake said in 1873, "It makes no difference to a free people whether their rights are invaded by the Crown or by the Cabinet. What is material is that they shall not be invaded at all."[36]

Our legal system itself has evolved from its twin European roots — the French model of civil law in Quebec, English Common Law in the rest of the country, and Canadian criminal law, which, like our constitution, has grown from its British origins. "We have adapted, modified, added to, subtracted from" the criminal law, Dad explained, "to meet our own distinctive needs. But [it] is also still basically British, notably in its fundamental assumption that an accused is presumed innocent until proved guilty." (Unable to resist the chance for some fun, he went on to tell a story "which exemplified the contrary assumption": "A certain Quebec judge in times gone by, when an accused pleaded 'not guilty,' would look down over his glasses, shake his head sadly, and say: 'If you were not guilty, you would not be here.'"[37])

However, when the discussion is extended beyond the legal and constitutional realm, Dad's emphasis on the British and the French as founders of Canada becomes inadequate. Even in constitutional terms, it neglects the debt we surely owe to the Haudenosaunee (Six Nations) Confederacy for their ideas on federalism. But a much bigger problem with the heavy French/British focus is that it renders invisible the role that Aboriginal people played in our country's evolution — a role so far-reaching that Canada is well described as essentially "a Métis civilization."[38]

These days, there is growing appreciation of the myriad ways in which the Aboriginal peoples of northern North America shaped economic, social, and political life in this land from the time of contact onwards. The other side of that coin is, of course, the enormous weight of injustices that colonialism imposed on those original inhabitants, to whom the colonizers owed their

"THE CANADIAN TRADITION"
(From a 1962 speech at the University of New Brunswick[39])

The Canadian tradition is, of course, much more than just French or British. We have modified what we have taken from France and Britain, even the languages, the law, the political institutions. We have borrowed liberally from other countries, [and] have developed some traditions that are distinctively our own.

But the French and British traditions remain basic. The French and English languages, French civil law and English common law, enjoy a status granted to no others. Our parliamentary institutions — essentially British, though modified and adapted to our needs and circumstances — are the indispensable framework for our whole national life.

We used sometimes to be told that we should get rid of the French tradition, anglicize the French-Canadians and the Acadians. Luckily, we hear less and less of this. More and more, the French fact in Canada is accepted, with growing understanding and appreciation, as part of our national inheritance. But we still hear, with distressing frequency, exhortations to get rid of the British tradition. We are told that we have outgrown it, that it is "foreign," that it's time we developed something "purely Canadian."

But the British tradition in Canada is not "foreign"; it is just as Canadian as the French. Curiously enough, the "pure" Canadians never call the French tradition "foreign," never say we've outgrown it, never call on us to get rid of it, [telling] us we can't be truly Canadian until we do.

The fact is that to talk of "developing something purely Canadian" which will be neither British nor French is literally nonsense. It is like the mid-western American college which posted a notice: "The following are the traditions of this college. They will go into force at four o'clock this afternoon."

very survival. A view of Canadian history that tends to whitewash the story of European settlement and claim exclusive credit for the founding of our country is unacceptable, however unintentional the offence.

There are other problems as well with the "two traditions" description of our national heritage. Even fifty years ago, when Dad was writing about our French and British roots, those were not the only settler cultures demanding recognition. Canada was changing, and not just in the ways his socialist generation had envisaged. Besides the First Nations, Métis, and Inuit, a multitude of other ethnicities had already made major contributions to building this country, and their numbers and importance in Canadian society were increasing rapidly. If that society was constantly being portrayed as essentially French and British, where did the Chinese and the Somalis, the Ukranians and the Pakistanis, the Jews and the Jamaicans, fit in?

My father would never have wanted to offend or exclude anyone. He was sincerely open to the increasing diversity of our population, and his awareness, like that of many other Canadians, expanded during the 1970s and 80s. In the same 1978 speech in which he extolled the British and French traditions, he also made clear the breadth of his ideal. "The 'total Canadian,'" he said, "would be multicultural. The nearer any of us get to that, the more totally Canadian we shall be."

Moreover, he insisted that all of us, regardless of our origins, can proudly claim the traditions that Canada has made its own. "Are these [British traditions] only for those of British blood? No. They are every bit as much the heritage of the rest. The fact that they did not spring straight from the Canadian Shield, or the waters of the Saguenay or the Mackenzie, does not make them 'foreign' or un-Canadian. They are bone of our bone for all of us."[40]

The same applies to all the other aspects of this country's natural and human heritage — in the many diverse traditions of which, Dad affirmed, "*by virtue of being a Canadian*, I can claim some share."[41] The multicultural Canada my father believed in belongs to all of us, and whatever our culture or history, our roots make us not less, but more, ourselves.

"Don't Discard Past, Forsey Warns," ran a headline in the *Peterborough Examiner* in May 1971 after Dad gave a speech to the local Canadian Club. In it, he declared that it was "absurd to think Canada could achieve Canadianism by denying the past"; that discarding our heritage would leave the country "rootless and fruitless, floating in empty space."[42]

Since then, there have been many signs that Canadians have failed to heed that warning. A 1997 study by the Dominion Institute, which polled historical knowledge among our country's youth, highlighted an abysmal lack of knowledge of key aspects of our heritage. Ongoing public discussions of things like Aboriginal rights, the status of linguistic minorities, and provincial versus federal powers, are too often based on myths or historical distortions — the "fairy tales" that Dad used to rail against. Gross abuses of democratic process by those in power are now being met with apathy or even approval, thanks to the vast ignorance of our parliamentary heritage that prevails at practically every level. It seems that our own history has been rendered all but irrelevant in the popular mind.

Ignoring the heritage of yesterday cripples responsible citizenship today. Canada's ongoing struggles over unity and identity, the continuing handover of our economy to global corporatism, the inexorable yielding of democracy to political cynicism and corruption, are all testimony to the weakness that comes, at least in part, from neglecting our roots. And as my father noted, "It is a poor gardener who destroys the roots of his plants."[43]

Canada today provides plenty of evidence of the harsh and lasting consequences that follow when policymakers ignore history or spurn tradition. Many First Nations remain impoverished and exploited largely because governments and corporations continue to stand in the way of historic Aboriginal rights to land and resources. Prairie farmers have been struggling to stave off economic disaster since the early 1980s when the Crow's Nest Pass Agreement on grain shipping rates, established "in perpetuity" in 1897, was abolished in order to placate the big railway companies. The demise of the cod fishery off Newfoundland came about largely because governments ignored the warnings from people who had been fishing for generations, and allowed corporations to discard traditional harvesting methods in favour of new — and destructive — industrial fishing technologies. None of these injustices could have been perpetrated in a context of genuine respect for the past.

But despite such betrayals, our society is also showing some hopeful signs. Among the general public, an increasing wariness of "the merely new" is evident in the popular resistance to genetically modified foods and to some of the hi-tech "advances" being promoted in nanotechnology, pharmaceuticals, and other fields. More Canadians are reviving the tried and true practices of organic farming and gardening, and turning to "old-fashioned" energy choices such as wind power and conservation.

First Nations, Inuit, and Métis people have re-invigorated many of their traditional practices, and have been winning land claims and court compensations for historical wrongs committed against them. They have also been pointing out to the rest of us the importance of understanding our own history. The 1997 report of the Royal Commission on Aboriginal Peoples noted the lack of familiarity of non-Native Canadians with vital aspects of our heritage, and exhorted us to start paying attention to the past which has shaped our collective present.

That was very much the position my father took. As he reminded us a year before he died:

"For the preservation of our heritage, there is only one real safeguard: that the Canadian people should know their history; know it, understand it, remember it, and keep on watch against ignoramuses and spinners of fantasies. In Sir Winston Churchill's words, 'We cannot say, "The past is past," without endangering the future.'"[44]

CHAPTER NINE

"Using Our Heads":
Intellect and Education

Let us use our heads. Use them, that is, not simply as things to balance hats on, or to count in an election or public opinion poll, but use them for thinking. The results may not be all we could wish; the machinery is not always first-class, and even when it is it can make mistakes. But ... we are likely to make rather less of a hash of things if we do use our heads than if we don't.
— From a convocation address to McGill University, May 1966[1]

My father began one of the last speeches of his life with a disclaimer. "I am not an intellectual," he stated, "far from it. And sometimes when I contemplate some of those so described, I am rather thankful that I don't feel I deserve the title."[2]

His protestation was light-hearted, but I think he was also quite serious. On the one hand, like the musical amateur who refuses the exalted title of "musician," I suspect he felt the word "intellectual" properly denoted a rare and special status that neither he nor most other mortals could really lay claim to. At the same time, he was put off by the pretensions — often combined with actual incompetence — of many people who had no such qualms about touting themselves as both learned and brilliant.

Regardless of the label, Dad loved the realm of the intellect and excelled in it. Gifted with a fine mind, he used it as a tool to move through mazes of complexity, break barriers of bafflegab, and foil, where he could, the machinations of vested interests.

The seriousness with which he treated learning and logic was evident early on, and it manifested itself throughout his life. His upbringing, and his years at McGill and Oxford, laid the foundation for a long career of fearless insistence on "using our heads" for the common good.

As a bookish youngster at school, Eugene Forsey regularly carried off top scholastic honours. Nor was his learning confined to the classroom. An entry he wrote for the Ottawa Collegiate Institute's yearbook would seem ridiculous to anyone observing Parliament today, but in 1921 it made some sense: "Perhaps we students too often fail to realize the priceless advantage which we have over our fellows in other cities in the presence here of Canada's legislators, the greatest among her sons, from coast to coast. Perhaps too, our loving teachers, in mistaken zeal, inflict upon us too much homework for us to go to the galleries of Parliament and improve our minds."

When he arrived at McGill in 1922, he found in academia a garden where he blossomed. His first letters home are filled with enthusiasm, even wonder. "How full life is of entrancing things to think of, to talk about, to see, to hear, to read, to do," he exclaimed. He described his professors, their courses, and the intellectual challenges they presented. "I am at present engaged in trying to fathom [Adam Smith's] ideas on Free Trade," he wrote. "I am going to take another swat at him tomorrow with the assistance of a note-book and pencil, and shall try to clarify his ideas and my own — which latter are probably the more in need of it."[3]

Eugene studying in his "digs" at Oxford, 1926, surrounded by the books and newspapers that were so much a part of his life. The uncropped original snapshot shows a McGill pennant on the wall.

Later, when Dad became a teacher himself, his love of learning and his fascination with his subject matter conveyed themselves to his students. His knowledge and enthusiasm helped to make him both a popular and effective lecturer. His success with his students was not matched, however, by respect or recognition from the McGill authorities who, preferring their instructors compliant and conventional, repeatedly attempted to muzzle him or get rid of him altogether.

The materials in the McGill Archives from the 1930s show clearly that Dad's socialist politics were a major part of the problem he posed for the higher-ups. They also show another large factor: his repeated refusal to fudge the marks of students who failed his courses.

His stubborn determination to uphold academic standards by failing unqualified students was a perennial irritant to the administration, who were anxious to stay on the good side of parents and benefactors, and repeatedly tried to override his judgment. Even some of his academic colleagues thought he should give at least some of his failing students a break. "'Such nice people,' I was told; 'worked so hard'; 'parents so poor' (or, in one case, if I am not mistaken, so rich!)."[4]

According to the documentation, however, even students he had "ploughed" made no complaints about his teaching. Despite the obstacles and objections put in his way, he managed to have his contract renewed each year, though repeated recommendations by the head of his department for promotion were turned down. In 1939, as pressure mounted for his dismissal, he met with the dean of arts about his status.

> Dr. Hendel made it clear that he was not discussing my teaching work, on which, indeed, he was careful to report some very commendatory comments ... His chief ground for refusing promotion seemed to be that he was not satisfied that I showed "good judgment" in my activities ...
>
> [He] said that I was known as a "pleader" rather than a "scholar." I refrained from saying that even if the statement was true (I had given evidence to the contrary), the difference between me and a good many of my colleagues, including some recently promoted, was that they were not known as anything. Nor did I say that the terms were apt to be question-begging, nor point to the numerous examples of eminent scholars who were pleaders par excellence ... The implication seems to be that one must not, even outside the classroom, take sides on a public question. This ... is a novel and most dangerous doctrine, from which I wholly dissent and by which I decline to be bound.[5]

Professor Michiel Horn, in his book *Academic Freedom in Canada*, highlights the cases of my father and his LSR colleague Leonard Marsh, both eventually expelled from McGill for "test[ing] the limits of academic free speech by stating unpopular views on matters of public interest." Horn concludes that in the long run, "expelling Marsh and Forsey may have damaged McGill more than it did either of the two men themselves."[6]

At the time, however, such a result was far from evident. Dad's final months at his alma mater were painful, as is clear from the letters he wrote to his mother during that time. In one of them he recounted the university's most recent attempt to create some excuse for firing him. "The whole episode shows about as well as anything could the degradation of intellectual standards around this place," he wrote. "It is simply impossible for me to stay on here one minute longer than I have to keep the wolf from the door. There is not the slightest chance of my getting a promotion here, if I accumulate a whole pile of degrees and live to be as old as Methuselah."

A few weeks later he wrote: "It may interest you to know some of the students are starting a petition for my retention, and one colleague … has written a very strong letter of protest to [Principal] James. I fear it was a very rash act, and he may suffer for it. If I had known ahead of time, I should have dissuaded him, for it can do me no good now. But I think it was a noble gesture. Harry Barker, under-janitor, says, 'They'll be sorry, sir, when they've let a good man go. I know what the students say.'"[7]

McGill's students did lose their controversial teacher, but others eventually gained him back at Carleton, Waterloo, and various other universities. My sister and I still sometimes hear from former students who remember fondly his passion for his subject and his rigorous attention to facts and logic. One described his teaching style as ranging "from straight lecture to the Socratic method to scintillating repartee and imitations."

The late Professor Michael Oliver called him "an extremely attractive lecturer," and stressed "how warm and how appealing to students he was." Desmond Morton agreed, recalling how Dad "enchanted" a group of students at Toronto's Erindale College when he conducted a seminar there in the mid-1970s.

The teachers he most admired were those who stirred up people's minds and obliged them to think for themselves. That was what he tried to do himself, not only in his teaching but in everything he did, and the results are there to be seen.

"Prove all things; hold fast that which is good." That maxim guided my father through decades of work in the social, economic and political domains.

To "prove all things," of course, requires evidence. "It is one of my 19th century eccentricities," Dad told the Couchiching Conference in 1965, "that I still believe you need evidence for things. I am totally unimpressed by the mere say-so of Professor X or Dr. Y, no matter how eminent he may be. Mere opinions, on matters of fact, are like the idle wind, which I respect not."[8]

His characteristic insistence on evidence and accuracy was already clear while he was still an undergraduate. In 1925, he wrote to the *McGill Daily* in response to a piece on the rights and grievances of the Maritime provinces, with which he expressed "strong sympathy." However, he said: "An argument is known by the company it keeps, and when supported by palpable absurdities, it merely throws discredit on the cause it is meant to serve. I am sorry that [the author] has weakened a thoroughly sound case by vague, inaccurate and loose statements."[9]

He took a further three columns to dissect and correct those statements, demonstrating his early tendency to provide too much evidence rather than too little. He would present the reader with reams of detail to wade through, often stopping short of actually stating his own conclusions. He was probably trying for a rigorous objectivity, but as a style of argument, it was more exhausting than effective.

Before long, though, he began to include more of his own analysis and opinion. His 1932 speech to the Canadian Political Science Association demonstrated that shift. After outlining his proposition for a planned economy, but before detailing his rationale, he told his audience: "It is not so much what opinions one holds as why one holds them, that matters. That I think planning incompatible with capitalism is probably neither particularly interesting nor particularly important. The reasons *why* I think so may, however, provide a basis for discussion by people better qualified to give an impartial judgement."[10]

By that time, my father's characteristic meticulousness had given him a reputation as a detail fanatic. Talking with Professor Oliver about the early days of the CCF, I mentioned Dad's modest claim that his contribution to the drafting of the Regina Manifesto had been only "some very minor comments, possibly suggesting that a sentence might be broken here or a comma put in there."[11]

"Yes," Oliver replied, "but you know, even in those days, nobody dared publish anything without showing it to Eugene. Otherwise they'd be sure to get, if they were lucky, a personal letter with all the corrections. If they were unlucky, it could appear anywhere."

For my father's friend Pierre Joncas, what stood out was "the power of Eugene's intellect, the logic of his arguments, the persuasiveness of the facts he would marshal in support of those arguments. He didn't want people to yield to *him*, he wanted them to yield to the evidence, to the facts, not because it pleased him, but because that's where the facts led."

I think that's true. In one of his convocation addresses, Dad urged the graduates: "First, get your facts straight. Never let your theories, wishes or prejudices — your pre-judgements — blind you or deflect you. Getting the facts is not always easy. Even when it is easy, some people blithely utter, even commit to print, statements which are demonstrably un-fact, and make them the basis of conclusions."[12]

Facts, though, were only the starting point. To work with the facts, he insisted on the "the application of what Sir Robert Borden — too optimistically, I fear — called 'the commonplace quality of common sense.'"[13]

In a Senate speech dealing with the report of a parliamentary committee, he began his remarks: "I think on the whole it is a sensible report. If that seems faint praise — a tepid adjective — let me assure honourable senators that, from me, it is not. The number of people who are highly intelligent and highly educated but who have, it seems to me, no common sense, is staggering. For me the word 'sensible' is one of the most laudatory adjectives I could employ."[14]

"Sensible" in turn meant something that could actually work in practice, something that at least fell within the realm of possibility. Often, when he indicted some high-sounding idea as "nonsense," it was because it was impossible to implement.

One example was the plan for a "Guaranteed Employment Act" included in the proposed program for the New Democratic Party — the new party that was to succeed the CCF in 1961. When my father saw the draft, he was appalled. He pointed out that no democratic government could possibly guarantee every adult citizen a job, and it would be political suicide to promise to do so.[15] The fact that it was his friends and political allies putting forth this foolishness in no way deterred him. "Error is still error, folly is still folly, nonsense is still nonsense," he said, whoever it came from, and wherever it was located on the political spectrum.

The practical impossibility of implementation was also one of Dad's main problems with the "sovereignty-association" concept put forward by

Quebec nationalists, and to various well-meaning proposals for blanket bilingualism throughout Canada, regardless of the numbers of French- or English-speaking people living in the area.[16] Similarly, he considered most of the post-1982 suggestions for Senate reform to be totally impracticable, since the opposition they were sure to arouse in various regions would prevent them from getting the provincial approvals now required under the repatriated Constitution.[17]

Besides impracticability, Dad cautioned against three "booby traps" to watch out for when trying to assess whether a given plan or proposal met the criterion of "sensible." The first was vagueness and ambiguity, whether accidental or deliberate. This was one of his major objections to the Meech Lake Accord. "The defenders of the Accord," he commented, "sometimes come close to suggesting that ambiguity is a virtue in constitutions; the more ambiguities the merrier." He disagreed.[18]

A second and related pitfall was the temptation to embrace "general principles" without doing due diligence as to their real implications. In his 1967 George Nowlan lectures, Dad warned against agreeing to broad conceptual proposals before being "quite sure what practical consequences they involve."

"It is altogether too easy," he said, "to fall into the trap of accepting some innocent-looking general principle, only to find that, worked out to its logical conclusion, it will deprive us of our shirts, trousers, shoes and socks, leaving us with only our underclothes and our neckties."[19]

Finally, he cautioned against being seduced into supporting some scheme by the argument that it was less extreme than some of the alternatives. "Let us ask of any proposal, not, 'Is it more, or less, crazy than some other?' but 'Is it sensible?'"[20]

Despite his emphasis on facts and common sense as essential to any discussion, he recognized the importance of other elements. I remember him exclaiming in frustration over accusations that he was being "too emotional" about the Quebec/Canada debate. "Of course I'm emotional about it," he protested. "It's my country we're talking about!" He also bridled at the suggestion that Canada had "outgrown" its connections to Britain and France.

"Is [something] outgrown, 'not adult,' simply because it is not intellectually tidy, not deducible by relentless Cartesian logic from some grand general principle? It is at least arguable, in the light of modern psychology, that it is over-intellectualism which is outgrown, less than adult. Should we try to outgrow judgement, common sense, our whole emotional nature? Emotions, the non-intellectual, are not necessarily unreasonable."[21]

Indeed, without the emotions that fuelled and guided my father in his many campaigns, his endeavours would have been largely sterile. They would likely have gone largely unnoticed as well, for it was the passion with which he criticized a proposal or defended a cause that touched people's hearts as well as their minds, and moved them to action.

Given the value Dad attached to "using our heads," it is not surprising that he had strong ideas about education. He was an enthusiastic supporter, both of the kind of popular education already mentioned in the context of trade unions and political movements, and of the formal public education system, from grade school through university.

Mind you, he had enormous respect for people who had acquired their learning informally. Some of the people whose intelligence and integrity he most admired, like the CCL's Silby Barrett and CCF MP Angus MacInnes, had had relatively little schooling. Nonetheless, he believed that good public education was "a human necessity and also a political necessity," key to building and broadening the ability of citizens to participate effectively in their society.

"Merely registering your preferences without discussion is not genuine democracy. Reasoned discussion ... is necessary; and if you are going to have reasoned, informed, useful discussion, then you must have people who have some conception, however limited their knowledge ... of the values involved, some civilized conception of what discussion means. To provide this is one of the functions of education."[22]

Not the only function, obviously. Dad recognized the importance of educating people to fill a modern economy's need for scientific and technical know-how, and job-market training. But he made it clear that the role of education in a democracy was far more fundamental than that. "A democratic state must see to it that its citizens have the opportunity to be really men and women, not mere drudges or cogs in a machine. That means education — compulsory free education for all children up to high school leaving age, and equal opportunity for all who are intellectually capable of it, to secure a higher education regardless of their economic position. It means also extensive and continuous adult education work.[23]

Speaking to a national seminar of university students in 1960, he stressed the need for quality in the education provided at all levels. "Labour wants education with backbone — real education, with some intellectual content; not this namby-pamby, niminy-piminy stuff that is handed out to such a large extent in schools now."[24]

He knew whereof he spoke, for he followed my sister's and my schooling closely. The 1950s was a period of a lively public debate over the "crisis of quality" in Canadian education. In 1953, Professor Hilda Neatby of the University of Saskatchewan had published her book *So Little for the Mind*, eloquently documenting many of the same criticisms that my father had begun voicing. The book produced a tremendous uproar, provoking savage denunciations by the various educational "experts" whose doctrines she questioned.

Dad leapt to Neatby's aid with impassioned articles, letters, and speeches. He joined her in denouncing public school curricula that they both saw as insultingly over-simplified and often error-laden. He railed against the patronizing absurdity of an arithmetic text entitled *Growing Up with Number*, and the "irrelevant goo-gooism" of some of the responses to their criticisms.

At a 1957 conference on education, he expounded on what he saw as a crisis in the field, beginning with the economic constraints. Characteristically, he noted that the total amount of money Canadians spent each year on alcohol and tobacco was significantly larger than all public and private educational expenditures combined.

> You don't have to be a continuing Methodist like me to feel that we ought to be able to spend at least as much of our national income on education as on those two narcotics ... But there are things wrong with our education that all the money in the world will not put right ... [There is] a crisis of standards, of aims.
>
> We need to ask what we are trying to do in our educational system. The stock answer is that we are trying to educate everybody. Are we? We are trying to give everybody a certain length of time in buildings called schools. But are we really trying to educate them, train their minds, or [are we] simply trying to keep them off the streets? Are some of our high schools becoming largely adolescent play-pens?

"EDUCATIONAL TOM-FOOLERY"
(From a 1957 speech[25])

Children need something they can get their teeth into, something solid, something to build mental bone and muscle. The teachers are doing their best. But look at the text-books they are sometimes saddled with!

My children, in grades 6, 7 and 8, were obliged to use two spellers which had to be seen to be believed. These books were based on an actual count of words used by pupils in a school or schools in an American town. The grade 6 one had, by actual count, over sixty words of three letters — words like "hop," "mop," "bug," "jug." [The children] were also warned of some particularly tough words, "demon words," of which two were "I" and "am."

Now I simply refuse to believe that an average child of ten or eleven still has to learn how to spell "mop" or "hop," or that [they] will find "I" or "am" really tough. This same book actually went out of its way to tell the children that the word "heir" occurred so seldom that it "wasn't a spelling word"!

The American educational pundits who produced this tom-foolery talk at great length about "rich experiences" and the joys of acquiring "dictionary skills." What average child of ten or eleven is going to get any experience but a yawn out of learning "bug" and "jug," and being told not to learn "heir"?

And the second speller is just as bad. It includes, for example, a few observations on what it calls the CNR's "helpers." Apparently the authors felt that to introduce twelve-or thirteen-year-olds to the word "subsidiaries" would be too "rich" an "experience." Or perhaps the children in What-not, Ohio, or wherever it was, didn't use "subsidiaries."

The same book lets itself go with a whoop on "democracy," notably on the limitations on the powers of our provincial Legislatures. Unfortunately, the Canadian "revisers" just blithely substituted "provincial" for "state" in the original American text. So along with the spelling rubbish, our children get a nice little parcel of misinformation about our history and government.

Our educational rulers complain that many of our children are "bored" in school, that they "lack motivation." Who wouldn't, fed on this kind of gruel?

Practically every child now gets into high school, automatically, by age alone. An astonishing number get promoted, year after year, by age alone. A surprising number of duds get through high school and even into university. The universities lament incessantly that they get hordes of students who can't write decent English and have never had a proper grounding in elementary mathematics and science ...[26]

Responding to the claim that lower standards were just the price we had to pay for democratizing education, Dad put forward his own interpretation of the universality principle: "I'd give every child every scrap of real education he could take. But when he'd had it, I'd chuck him out of school and let him earn his keep ... [This] might, probably would, create employment and welfare problems. Very well. Let us deal with them as such, by employment and welfare policies, through employment and welfare agencies. Let's stop trying to make educational institutions do an employment and welfare job, for which they are not fitted, and allow them to concentrate on doing their own, educational job ... I don't think it's fair ... [or] democratic to do anything else."[27]

Like Neatby, Dad was critical of many aspects of the "progressive education" approach being promoted largely by American "experts." "Some of the newer educational theories and practices have been excellent for the dull child [and] the very young child. [But] the real casualties of the system are the average children, [who] are the majority. What the people who now run the schools seem to forget is that most children are not dull, and that all normal children grow up. So these gentry go on feeding normal, growing ten- and eleven- and twelve- and thirteen-year-olds on mental baby-foods."[28]

As recipients of some of that mental baby-food, my sister and I were nonetheless fortunate enough to be well nourished. We received plenty of hearty supplements at home, and we were also blessed with several excellent teachers whose skills and attention helped to compensate for the inadequacies of the system itself.

My childhood memories of Dad's ongoing campaigns on the educational front are somewhat vague. I suspect I found it slightly disconcerting; after all, other kids' parents didn't go into orbit over a spelling text. To the extent that the whole thing registered at all in my youthful consciousness, it probably did so mainly as just another of my father's idiosyncrasies, which, depending on circumstances, would puzzle, embarrass, or move me to pride.

Besides making speeches and writing articles, Dad took his protests directly to the educational authorities. In one of his letters to his comrade-in-arms Hilda Neatby relating the latest outrages from his daughters' schools, he enclosed a missive he had just written to the local board of education, and promised a copy of the "blast to the Minister" he was about to send. He concluded: "I wish to goodness I had the time and strength to run for the School Board myself and stir things up. But I haven't ... I breathe a prayer that you will not 'falter or fail' in your efforts to knock some sense into the thing in this country."[29]

I asked the late veteran educator Winton Roberts what he thought about the controversy over the American-style "progressive" education that Dad was so opposed to. Roberts had been education director for the Chateauguay School Board near Montreal in the 1950s, and had also taught at McGill's Faculty of Education. He responded by pointing out that during the post-war baby boom, class sizes often reached forty-five pupils, which, according to him, made it next to impossible to provide the kind of education he believed Neatby and Forsey were calling for.

This was, however, something Dad had taken into consideration.

> We are told that classes are too large, so that teachers can't do their best work. Why are they too large? Partly because we don't provide enough money, but partly also because we don't chuck the duds out.
>
> The parents wouldn't stand for it? If so, isn't it about time the rulers of the schools summoned up enough spunk to tell the parents some home truths? They are always prating about being the leaders of the community; let them do some leading. Parents may have more common sense than they think.[30]

According to Roberts, Neatby's book did spark changes, but probably not the ones she intended. Her criticisms of the status quo in the public system, he said, gave a tremendous boost to the movement towards private schools, as fed-up parents who could afford the fees flocked to seek those costly alternatives. Roberts drew a parallel with the more recent promotion of private and "charter" schools, and the corresponding undermining of the public school system.

Such an outcome, I'm certain, never occurred to Dad, who was strongly against privatizing education or other essential public services. His support for the public system was rock-solid, and his entire critique was framed in those terms. When he saw that system being undermined by what he considered nonsense and incompetence, closed-mindedness, and arrogance, he denounced those things and demanded changes. For him, it was simply a question of the public education system cleaning up its act, applying common sense to the problems, and reinstating real respect for everyone involved — children, parents, and teachers.

My father's reverence for the cerebral had its down side. He was no snob in the social sense, but when it came to intelligence, I'm afraid it was a different story. Compared with other forms of snobbery, his intellectual version was relatively benign, since it seldom affected the person in question — unless, of course, they went around claiming to be the latest Einstein or some kind of infallible authority. Within the family circle, though, Dad would sometimes allow himself comments he would never have made publicly.

From the supper tables of my childhood I recall the vivid expressions he would use about people of whose mental capacity he had a low opinion. "Brains that would rattle in a peanut" was one; "not well furnished in the upper storey" was a Grand Bank expression for the same thing. Even some of his writings include phrases like "amiable mugs" or "minds open at both ends, with the gales of heaven blowing through." Under this kind of influence, I remember growing up with a vague sense that being stupid was almost worse than being bad.

For a few years at the Canadian Congress of Labour, Dad suffered a series of very inadequate secretaries. One of them possessed a B.A., and he made his little girls giggle when he said it must stand for "Brains Absent." Another was an "honours" graduate from a high school of commerce. "She was a most amiable girl," he recalled later. "I wish I had half as nice a disposition. But she was one of the most utterly incompetent employees

"PECUNIARY DEGREES"

(Published anonymously in Canadian Forum, September 1936[31])

Several recent events suggest that our rulers ... may seek a revival of the honorary degree racket. If bankers cannot be peers or textile magnates baronets, if newspaper owners and coal merchants can look no higher than the Senate, even the humblest millionaire who ever failed his high school entrance can still aspire to an LL.D.

To protest against this is futile. After all, universities must live, especially in a period of "recovery," and capitalism must be served. But can we not at least vary the drab monotony of the honorary degree, fit it to its recipients with a little more appropriateness, perhaps even raise the whole thing to a level approaching common honesty? In other words, why not a series of pecuniary degrees?

For some, the obviously fitting thing would be the D.E., Doctor of Exploitation. This might be given in three forms: D.E. (Ag.), D.E. (Cons.), D.E. (Op), according to the particular class — farmers, consumers or workers — which had been the main subject of the great man's efforts. Similarly the D.L., Doctor of Lobbying, might indicate in brackets the special proficiency of the recipient.

Then there could be the D.I.D., Doctor of Interlocking Directorates, e.g. "D.I.D. with great distinction in the manufacture of underwear." D.T.E, Doctor of Tax Evasion, might be varied: D.T.E. (Income) or D.T.E. (Succession).

There might be times when a university wished merely to record its gratitude for value received, without specifying the precise field in which the eminent personage had won his triumph. There might be people — bootleggers, for instance — to whom such a reference would be embarrassing. For such cases, there should be a general purpose pecuniary degree, the C.O.D.

I ever had."[32] When at last the very capable — and "amiable" — Dawn Dobson joined the research department as his new secretary, his relief and gratitude were manifest, and his lamentations about office incompetence became a thing of the past.

My father's intellectual snobbery was totally unrelated to a person's level of formal education. In fact, I think the more education a person had, and the more exalted their official position, the more rigorously critical Dad tended to be in his assessment of their abilities. "The mere fact that somebody is a Deputy Minister or a Professor of Education or a Director of Curricula does not impress me," he said. "He may be all right, or he may not. By his fruits, not his title, I shall know him." [33]

His skeptical attitude towards advanced academic degrees and imposing titles may have been formed initially by his encounters with both during his embattled years at McGill. A letter to his mother from that time referred ironically to the "magic letters Ph.D.," while another noted that although one of his potential thesis examiners knew "virtually nothing" of the subject at hand, the man did possess those "blessed letters."[34]

Subsequent experience did little to dispel his misgivings about the actual competence of many supposedly learned individuals. I must have been nine or ten when he got into a lengthy exchange with an American professor who was writing a book on French Canada. At home we listened to Dad's exasperated accounts of Professor X's repeated factual errors and his obstinate unwillingness to accept corrections. I remember asking what seemed to me to be a key question: Was Professor X a nice man? Rather petulantly, Dad replied, "Oh, I suppose he's *nice* enough ..." He was at a loss to explain to a puzzled youngster why "niceness" wasn't the point in this context.

Ineptitude among academics or others revered as "authorities" never ceased to aggravate him. Mental slowness on its own he could tolerate, but combined with pretentions it triggered his eloquent contempt. It was the source of the grim relish with which he would quote his composer friend Healey Willan, who used to refer to "the intelligentsia though-God-knows-why-they're-called-so."

"It is staggering the number of so-called 'authorities' who solemnly purvey as fact statements for which there is no evidence whatsoever, and which are often even demonstrably contrary to the evidence. What is worse, even learned audiences often admire the Emperor's new robes, and are visibly distressed or tolerantly amused when that eccentric character Forsey points out that His Majesty is in fact stark naked."[35]

When the *Ottawa Citizen*, in November of 1954, published a critic's "savage denunciation" of Hilda Neatby's book on the school system, Dad was provoked to respond.

> Like the professional "educators," Mr. G. is perfectly willing to accept criticism of "progressive" education. But so far it has defied the wit of man to produce any specific criticism which they will accept, or even tolerate. It's always a case of, "Father, may I go in for a swim?" "Yes, my darling daughter, but don't go near the water."
>
> Mr. G. is particularly scornful of Dr. Neatby because she ventures to criticize even though she admits she is not an "expert." For him, apparently, the schools are the experts,' and the fullness thereof ...[36]

My father's wariness of "experts" was linked to his insistence on the democratic right of every citizen to take an active part in defining society's problems, setting priorities, and seeking solutions. In his view, it was an abdication of civic responsibility to leave everything to specialists, whether competent or otherwise, and he took his own responsibility very seriously. At the start of his speech to the education conference, he laid out his credentials: "I am a citizen, concerned with the future of this country and the quality of its future citizens. I am a parent, with two children in school. I am a taxpayer, helping to pay for the whole thing. If we believe in democracy, then every one of us has a perfect right to say what *we* think should be done by *our* schools and universities with *our* money to train *our* children and shape the future of *our* country ... Democracy means the rule of the people, not of any experts whatsoever. In a democracy, the experts are our servants, not our masters."[37]

Of course, he recognized the limitations on general knowledge imposed by a complex and fast-changing society. As he told the 1960 seminar of university students: "All of us are now in the position where our knowledge is bound to be extremely limited, because there is so much that no single human being can touch more than a tiny percentage of it."[38]

But he had always maintained that we should not shy away from involvement in public issues just because of the inevitable incompleteness of our knowledge. In a 1945 talk about the responsibility of religious institutions to address social issues, he said: "The Church should not take refuge in delays or evasions, on the plea that it must wait till it has all the facts. It will never have all the facts. But it should take reasonable care to see that it knows what it's talking about."[39]

The obligation to know what you're talking about was all the more serious for anyone claiming expertise in a given field. Rampant incompetence among constitutional "authorities" inspired some of my father's most scathing commentaries, but his censure also extended to other domains, notably education. In a review of the Neatby book he roundly chastised certain educational specialists for their "ignorance, arrogance, blandly unconscious totalitarianism, and almost unbelievable incapacity to write plain English."[40]

Cautionary words about "experts" were likewise part of his 1957 speech on education.

> I am not saying that we should pay no attention to the experts. On the contrary, [we should] listen carefully and respectfully to everything they say, on the subjects on which they are experts, and provided they really are experts.
>
> How can you tell? I have no infallible test. But I think there is one that will weed out most of the fakes. If [English-speaking experts] can't say what they have to say in clear, grammatical English, then almost certainly they have nothing to say that is worth saying.
>
> There is another test which I think will help us to distinguish the real expert from the fake: Is he humble? Is he willing to listen to other opinions than his own and his friends'? Is he willing to admit that he may possibly be wrong? Or does he think he knows it all? Does he "welcome criticism, provided it's constructive"? That last is an almost certain mark of the humbug; for almost invariably "constructive criticism" turns out to be something "whose margin fades forever and forever as we move."[41]

In view of the emphatic self-assurance — some might even say arrogance — with which my father was wont to state facts and defend his own views, did he really meet his own criterion of humility? Although he never claimed to be an expert himself, except on some areas of the Constitution, he took controversial positions on many things, and stood by them unless or until he was persuaded otherwise. Together with his insistence on factual evidence, this tenaciousness gave him a certain reputation for rigidity.

That didn't necessarily bother him. "Some people appear to think that flexibility is one of the cardinal virtues," he said, "that it is an absolute. These people, I think, might well propose that our national animal should be the jelly-fish. ... On this matter of rigidity or flexibility, the value of either of these two attitudes depends on what you are being rigid or flexible about."[42]

Of course, he acknowledged that rigidity, like flexibility, could be overdone. Indulging in a bit of hyperbole to make his point, he recalled a former colleague, "a very strong character, [with] very firm moral principles. With him, even the smallest decision was a matter of profound moral conviction. Even if it was only which hat or necktie he was going to wear, he had a feeling that he had done this for cosmic reasons, and that he could, as an honest and upright man, have made no other decision. Which meant that he could be on occasion pretty inflexible. If you haven't got quite such far-reaching and profound moral convictions as that, there are moments when you can say, 'Oh well, after all, why make a song and dance about it?'"[43]

Still, he himself was sometimes seen as unbending, even by people who liked and admired him. "There was nothing you could mention that Eugene didn't have an opinion on," Alex Hickman declared, "and whatever that opinion was, it was not subject to change."

Dad did change his mind, however — more than once, and not only on minor matters. Most obvious are the shifts in his political party affiliations discussed in Chapter 15. Other questions on which he reversed his position included our involvement in World War II, the advisability of abolishing the Senate, and Canada's chances for survival if Quebec were to separate.

On the first of these, he wrote a contrite letter to Arthur Meighen a few years after the war had ended.

> I am sorry to say I must disabuse your mind of another idea. I did agree with the CCF stand in 1939 [to limit Canada's war participation to economic assistance]. I think now I was just wrong and stupid. At that time, I was still taking too many of my opinions, uncritically, from "the intelligentsia" — but even that is overstating it; I ought not to blame any of my stupidity on anyone else. The only prominent CCF member I can recall who was then absolutely right was Angus MacInnis. As in every

other case where I have differed from him, he was right and I was wrong. His strong common sense was worth all the education in the world.[44]

When my father was appointed to the Senate in 1970, his old CCF friend and CLC colleague Stanley Knowles, MP, ribbed him about having formerly advocated abolition of that august chamber. Actually, Dad had changed his mind on that matter many years before, when he realized that "if the existing Senate were abolished, we'd have to create another to take its place." Federations across the Western world, he pointed out, demand representation of their constituent units, and the Canadian provinces would never agree to relinquish the regional representation our own upper house was designed to provide.[45]

As for Canada's prospects if Quebec were to separate, he addressed the question in his lectures at Acadia University in 1967. "Could Canada without Quebec survive? I used to say, 'Probably not.' I have changed my mind. I do not think our succession state need collapse, or fall into the maw of the United States. It would still have plenty of reason to exist."[46]

It is not uncommon for outspoken people to be accused of rigidity. Pierre Trudeau, too, was often seen as unduly rigid. But Dad told a different story. Some years before entering politics, Trudeau had asked him to comment on a draft of a paper he had written. Dad pointed out one incorrect statement, and explained the problem with it. I remember him telling someone about Trudeau's reply, which delighted him. "'I didn't know this. I was wrong. I must change it.' Just like that. You didn't get any of this throat-clearing and shuffling of feet and 'Oh well, I'm really right anyway' from Pierre Trudeau. No. 'I was wrong. I must change it.' And change it he did."

Dad saw this kind of flexibility and openness — the willingness to admit to uncertainty, ignorance, or error — as a crucially important quality for any human being, expert or otherwise, public figure or ordinary citizen. Once, when I was waxing dogmatic about something, he quoted to me Oliver Cromwell's famous plea to the Church of Scotland: "I beseech you, in the bowels of Christ, think it possible you may be mistaken!"

"We should be willing to confess ignorance," he told McMaster University graduates in 1984. "And it should be a genuine confession of ignorance, not the kind that begins with, 'I know nothing of this subject,' followed by a 'but'; for example: 'I know nothing about the Canadian Constitution, but the Legislature of Ontario can charter a bank.'"[47]

Once again it came down to common sense and good judgment, always tempered by humility.

In his preface to *A Life on the Fringe*, Dad mentioned a Ph.D. thesis about himself that he had never seen. He noted with amusement a remark the doctoral candidate had made: "He said his supervisor and colleagues could not make out what made me tick: too many glaring contradictions in what I had said and done. I doubt if this book will give them any clues."[48]

Dad's comment was unfortunately prophetic. As it turned out, the 1987 thesis was rife with errors of fact, misquotations, and sloppy reasoning. Worse, it betrayed an astonishing inability to understand the essentials of my father's thinking, much less the fundamental values and approaches that tied his apparent "contradictions" into a consistent whole. A sorry example of exactly the kind of "intellectual" endeavour Dad worked so hard to counteract, the dissertation managed to pass muster by no fewer than five academic reviewers. For this effort, the author received his doctorate — a fact that says more about ignorance and irresponsibility in parts of academia than even Dad might have been ready to believe.

Just as incredibly, this appalling opus was published as a book seventeen years later by the press of a second university. By that time, a great deal of additional and highly relevant material was available, notably all the writing my father had done in the final years of his life. Those writings, in particular his memoirs, *A Life on the Fringe*, represented an authoritative voice on numerous subjects that the thesis had simply got wrong. But there was no evidence that either the author or the publisher of the book had even noticed that material, let alone taken any of it into account. Indeed, barring a few shifts in word order and the rearranging of several sentences starting with "but," the text was identical with the original (badly) written dissertation. The book provided no update (even though the thesis — inexplicably — had covered very little about its subject after the 1960s); there were no content revisions whatsoever, and almost the entire collection of original errors (including many of the typos) was still intact.[49]

That this monument to incompetence was the product, first of a university faculty and then of a university press, shows that the criticisms Dad was making years ago of our system of higher education remain alarmingly relevant.

> [One] thing that's wrong, is that university people produce, or praise, or both, so much shoddy work ... Of course, there is much magnificent work coming out of our universities. But there is also some shocking, and inexcusable, shoddy stuff ... A great many books by Canadian professors are peppered with elementary errors of fact; mistakes that I should not have supposed any educated Canadian would make, let alone people who are supposed to be scholars. I know everybody, even the most careful and painstaking scholar, makes occasional mistakes, even in major works. What I'm talking about is not occasional mistakes but whole pyramids of them ... Yet not one review [of one such work] in any of our learned journals so much as mentioned a single error ... The general tone was such that if God had written the book, he would have blushed.[50]

Dad attributed these inadequacies largely to the fact that the universities not only allowed unqualified people to graduate and even teach, but that they also "let in too many people who are incapable, or ill prepared, or both."[51] As he knew so well from his experience at McGill, this was nothing new, and the intervening years had done nothing to change his assessment of the problem.

"The right to a university education is not like the right to vote," he told York University graduates in 1972. "It belongs only to those who are capable of profiting by it. Letting in the others, and worse, letting them out with degrees, is a prize example of what Bernard Shaw called 'soft, cruel hearts.' It is cruel to the victims, cruel to the real students, cruel to the teachers, and cruel to society. It is also fraudulent."

What, then, should the universities be doing? In his view, they needed to work to prepare their graduates to use their intellectual abilities to grapple with the enormous challenges of the modern world. Once again, that meant that university people had to learn to "be both radical and conservative; [to] practice what I call St. Paul's Christian skepticism: 'Prove all things; hold fast that which is good.'"[52]

At Mount Allison University in New Brunswick, Dad outlined in more specific terms what he saw as the central task of institutions of higher learning:

> Universities ... must lay the foundations not only for advanced study and research ... but also for the training of a genuinely educated and responsible citizenry. We need, more and more urgently, not only great scientists, great doctors, great lawyers, great philosophers and theologians, great engineers, great scholars in the various disciplines, but also a whole host of ordinary people who have developed such not-so-ordinary qualities as respect for facts, a sense of relevance, and plain speech ... If democracy is to be a using of our heads instead of just a counting of them, we must have citizens with these qualities, and lots of them.[53]

Dad had a special fondness for the smaller universities like Mount Allison, his parents' alma mater, and Trent University in Peterborough, Ontario, where he served as chancellor for several years in the 1970s.

"Teaching is often best carried out in the smaller institutions," he told the Mount Allison graduating class. "One of the most frightening aspects of contemporary society is its sheer bigness, and the depersonalizaton that inevitably brings with it. And nowhere is this more fraught with peril than in education. We cannot hope wholly to escape bigness, but we can mitigate it. We can preserve at least some islands, some oases, where the individual person is not dwarfed by the institution. In education we not only can preserve these islands, we must."

Speaking in 1966 at what was then still a "small university," Memorial in Newfoundland, he came back to the importance of language. "An English-language university should give the student a capacity to speak and write plain English, should teach him to value and respect one of the great languages of the world, and to use it accordingly. Graduates should be able to say what they have to say grammatically, intelligibly, and with some regard for the dictionary meaning of words. If the learned can be made to put what they have to say into plain English, some of the fancy nonsense which plagues us will become nonsense so plain and unmistakable that its power to lead us astray will be gone."[54]

His own decision years before as an undergraduate — to pursue combined honours in both English and political economy — not only reflected his twin passions, but also helped him hone the skills he would use throughout his life to shape his analysis and present his arguments. If Eugene Forsey exemplified the effectiveness of such studies, it is little wonder that some reactionary politicians today are reluctant to support general arts education.

It has long been clear, however, that our colleges and universities are allied in myriad ways with the vested interests of the establishment. The risks inherent in this situation are exacerbated by an ever-increasing assortment of well-financed efforts by corporate and government elites to use post-secondary institutions for their own purposes. In his 1972 address at York University, my father acknowledged the problem.

> To a large extent ... training [is] slanted to serve the interests of those who control our society; in *any* society it is bound to be more or less so. If the training were taken out of the hands of the universities, the situation would be worse. There would be even less chance of professional people being really educated, aware of something beyond their own specialty, critical of themselves, their job and their society.
>
> We are already producing far too many technically qualified specialists who have little or no notion of the social framework in which they work: medical syndicalists who think the health services should be controlled by the doctors; public officials who know little law and less history ... Some of the culprits have the outward and visible signs of being highly educated. I prefer the description of a plain-spoken friend of mine: 'They have frequented educational institutions.'[55]

THE UNIVERSITY IN A TROUBLING WORLD
(From a 1972 convocation address[56])

It is not the function of the university either to preserve, or to change, the existing order — economic, political, theological, philosophical, academic or other. Individual professors or students have a perfect right to the strongest opinions on all these matters, and to work for the triumph of their opinions. But a university, by its very nature, cannot even have opinions, except on the conditions of its own integrity, its freedom to do its essential task, which no other institution can perform ...

The business of the university [is] the critical study of our society, and other societies. From that critical study, action — reforming or conserving or both at once, revolutionary or counter-revolutionary — may well issue. But the university is not the instrument for such action.

The university's business is the mind: thought, not action; the preservation of the heritage of knowledge; the enlargement of that heritage; the pursuit of truth; the teaching of the methods of that pursuit, including such elementary things as respect for facts, sense of relevance (rare and precious), plain speech (equally precious, and getting rarer).

Don't our universities do military research? Yes, some. I wish they didn't. There is danger of their being sucked into the military-industrial complex, which would be betrayal and death. As long as we live in an international jungle, our universities go in peril of that. Getting us out of the jungle is not their function; but neither is getting us farther into it.

Are our universities on the side of the exploiters, the manipulators, the oppressors? To some extent, certainly. But Canadian universities are much less so controlled than they were a generation ago: "I could a tale unfold" on that subject.

Every university ought to be constantly alert to guard the freedom it has, constantly working and fighting to widen it, to be something more than just a reflection of the society in which it lives. That is your true revolutionary function. If you neglect that, we shall get not a better society but a worse.

And yet, despite the caveats, Dad continued to believe in the promise and potential of higher education. In his later years as he became more and more concerned about the sheer magnitude of global problems, he tried to convey something of that persistent, glimmering hope to university graduates. Speaking in 1984 to the McMaster graduating class, he said:

> I hope I can say something you will find useful, perhaps even heartening. But I don't find it easy.
>
> When I graduated almost sixty years ago, there were problems. There always are, there always have been. But they didn't seem insoluble. On the whole, we could say: "God's in his heaven, All's right with the world."
>
> You face a world darkened by hideous threats: environmental catastrophe, massive famine, nuclear war, terrorism ... What used to [be called] "the eternal verities" are more and more called in question, mocked, denied. The economy is out of joint, and the economists seem to offer only wildly conflicting ideas of how to set it right. You know far more than we did sixty years ago, and you have, to help you, a technology beyond our wildest dreams, which may bring problems beyond our worst nightmares ...
>
> Have I, then, "naught for your comfort"? Not quite. Reason remains, under God, our best hope; and university graduates are — or ought to be, in general — the best custodians of that hope, the best bearers of the light it can bring.[57]

In 1966, Dad's old alma mater, McGill, awarded its troublesome former lecturer an LL.D. and asked him to give the convocation address. He began: "I can't help feeling some satisfaction, not untinged with amusement, in the contrast between McGill's opinion of me now, as expressed in Dean Cohen's citation, and its opinion thirty-odd years ago, when I had it on the authority of the then Principal that I was one of the University's two leading headaches. Perhaps I've improved; perhaps McGill has changed;

Two doctorates from McGill: same university, two very different occasions. In 1941, as one of McGill's "leading headaches," Eugene received his Ph.D. just after being fired from his lecturer position. Twenty-five years later the university invited him back to receive an LL.D. and give the convocation address. (Courtesy Montreal Gazette)

perhaps I deserved the reproaches of those days as little as the kind words of these. Or perhaps it is simply Time, 'Annihilating all that's made/To a green thought in a green shade.'"

He concluded with these words: "If anything I've said ... has in any degree stirred up anyone's mind, I am well content; for I remain convinced that using our minds is, under God, the best hope we have."[58]

CHAPTER TEN

Wit and Wisdom: The Power of Words

> The pressure was there [to drop the term "Dominion"]. Why not give in? After all, each change was relatively "minor," "mere words." What, after all, are words? Just one of the things that distinguishes man from the beasts ...
> — From an unpublished chapter of the memoirs[1]

Words. They were the vital medium in which my father lived and breathed. His passion for language was part and parcel of his zest for life, and it sparkled through all he said and wrote. It flavoured and enhanced his public crusades, and even motivated some of them.

Admirers and critics alike acknowledged his "twinkling wit," his "usually sulphurous letters," the "cool, rhetorical style which marks a man who knows that he is right." "Words," wrote one interviewer, "are Senator Forsey's hobby. Blessed with a keen intelligence and an ear for languages, he collects, blends, respects and savours words with the meticulous care of a true connoisseur."[2]

Dad's attachment to words went much deeper than just the pleasure he took in them. He firmly believed there was a close connection between the ability to speak and write in good, plain language, and the ability to think straight. Again and again he pointed out the importance of clear and concise communication, the need to avoid vagueness and ambiguity. For him, words were links between thought and action — precision instruments that, used with integrity, could accurately describe reality, help pinpoint what was wrong, and open the way toward solutions.

His fondness for words and books started early. The "Baby Book" my grandmother kept of his first years is filled with anecdotes of his learning to talk, including an early command: "Book, book — get, get!" These infantile literary leanings were strongly encouraged by the adoring adults who made up his immediate family, and for whom reading and conversation were as much a part of life as eating and sleeping. It is small wonder that words, both spoken and written, were among little Eugene's favourite playthings, and later his chosen tools.

Nor was it only English words that he learned. His Quebec-born grandfather Bowles was fluent in French; his mother knew Spanish and some German; and one of his Newfoundland aunts still lived in Mexico. He quickly absorbed the attitude that learning languages was not only natural but also fun. Each language was an open door, beckoning him to engage with different people, different cultures, and even — through Latin and Greek — with historical eras long gone by.

An anecdote from his high school days illustrates where his youthful values lay. One of his teachers at the Ottawa Collegiate simply could not handle a class, and the result was often chaos. Sixty years later Dad confessed: "I myself once raced round and round the classroom under his impotent eye, in pursuit of a classmate who had seized my copy of Tennyson's poems."[3]

As a young man travelling in Europe, my father delighted in practising his German and French, and even picked up a smattering of Italian. In one of his letters home, he gleefully recounted how a Russian lady at the League of Nations in Geneva had mistaken him for a Spaniard while conversing with him in French. Not long after, two French girls had remarked on his *"leger accent espagnol."* His explanation: "Occult influence of baptism in Mexico City!"[4]

His zest for languages was one of his best cards in his courtship of my linguist mother, and it remained a constant in our family life. At the Forsey supper table, dictionaries or encyclopaedias often made their appearance beside the dishes as Mum and Dad checked the origins or precise meanings of words that came up. My parents also encouraged my sister and me to explore different languages, investing in sets of "Linguaphone" lessons for us and supporting our participation in cross-cultural exchanges during our student years. A generation later, they had the satisfaction of seeing their two grandsons grow up fluently trilingual.

Dad's own fluency in French was amply demonstrated in speeches, articles, and letters, as well as in the more than twenty French-language services he conducted at his beloved Église Saint-Marc in his later years. Complimented by someone on his use of the French subjunctive, he replied, "You use the subjunctive a terrible lot in addressing the Deity."

His 1962 presidential speech to the Canadian Political Science Association was delivered in an eloquent bilingual flow. "I confess I was tempted to try doing the whole thing in French," he explained. "For one thing, the idea of springing an entire speech in French on a predominantly English-speaking audience appealed to my sense of fun. But I have become rather tired of elderly gentlemen indulging in undergraduate pranks, and my humane instincts revolted at the thought of the sufferings of the French language, and of the audience of both languages. So I decided that I should conform to the great Canadian tradition of compromise, and speak partly in one language and partly in the other."[5]

As his remarks about "the sufferings of the language" make clear, Dad felt that his command of French was not always what he would have wished. Even though he was sometimes mistaken for a francophone, he remained modest: "If I'm on my day I can get away with it," he told an interviewer, "but I can just as easily make the most appalling boners."[6]

Nevertheless, his aptitude in the language was strong. Among the French-language letters in Dad's correspondence files was one that surprised me with its warmth. It was from one of his most adamant sparring partners in the Quebec sovereignty debate, professor Jacques-Yvan Morin, and it contained a gracious compliment on his French. "*Cher Monsieur et ami*," it began. "*Votre bonne letter* ... (Your kind letter and the confirmation of the date of our upcoming debate arrived at the same time …) *Je vous remercie des sentiments que vous exprimez si bien dans la langue de Racine* … (I thank you for the sentiments you express so well in the language of Racine …)"[7]

English, though, always remained my father's first linguistic love. He revelled in the richness and versatility of the language of his ancestors, from the ancient phrasings of the King James Bible to the contemporary wordsmithing of Dorothy Sayers, from the pronouncements of Queen Victoria or Sir John A. Macdonald to the satirical delights of Gilbert and Sullivan, from Shakespeare's timeless verse to the twentieth-century storytelling of Agatha Christie.

What he read flowed into what he wrote, giving his work a literary flavour that was often humorous or ironic. In his original memoirs manuscript, the "Literary Allusions" appendix was prefaced with these words: "The reader will have observed that I seem unable to avoid introducing into my discussions quotations and paraphrases from literary classics — in which I am obviously, and happily, steeped. I offer the following list of sources …"

His writing style was richly seasoned — here a metaphor, there a proverb or an apt quotation with a twist of his own. Leafing through his book of constitutional essays, *Freedom and Order*, I quickly came up with a dozen examples. The phrases themselves sounded familiar, but I needed the *Oxford Dictionary of Quotations* to identify the sources. Two were from Milton, two from the Bible, one from Chaucer, one from the Anglican *Book of Common Prayer*, and the rest from different eighteenth- and nineteenth-century writers whose names, Dad would be appalled to discover, I did not even know. Nor am I alone among his readers in sometimes having assumed that some ringing phrase was a Forsey original, only to find out later that it came from Tennyson or Browning.

Literature and language were also a strong thread in my father's bond with his mentor and soul mate, Arthur Meighen. From the beginning, he had been captivated by the Tory leader's marvellous use of the English tongue. Later, as the friendship between the two men grew, the passion they shared for the language permeated their prolific correspondence. One of Dad's most treasured gifts was a 33 1/3 rpm recording Meighen sent him in 1954 of his magnificent tribute to "The Greatest Englishman in History," William Shakespeare.

Coming from a highly literate family and strongly influenced by Newfoundland's oral tradition, my father was himself a great story-teller, as readers of his memoirs will know. John Hastings thought the flair for narrative and anecdote must have been a family trait. "There must have been a long history of very sharp and witty people," he said. "That doesn't just spring out of nowhere."

Wherever it may have come from, Dad's recall of detail, his irrepressible sense of humour, and his skill as a mimic could bring to life the personalities of the past and make the events he told about unforgettable. For journalist Charles Taylor, "[Forsey's voice served] as an impeccable instrument for his anecdotes, running a gamut of accents and emotions, seldom faltering amid the torrent of perfectly crafted stories ... I was struck by his impish wit and [the] suppressed mirth [that] came to modify his severity." Sandra Gwyn called him "the thinking man's Rich Little," while another interviewer compared him to a juggler: "He tosses words, quotations and anecdotes into the air, keeping them aloft with a sense of humour and split-second recall, moustache twitching and black eyes snapping ..."[8]

Sprinkled throughout his conversations and writings were spontaneous quotations from what he fondly referred to as his "funny books," notably Somerville and Ross's *Adventures of an Irish R.M.* (Registered Magistrate), Ian Hay's *Happy-Go-Lucky*, and the novels of P.G. Wodehouse. Wodehouse especially became an enduring family favourite. His ridiculous stories of antics and intrigue in English upper-class society provided the perfect counterpoint to the serious matters that occupied most of my father's attention.

One of Dad's great delights was to retrieve a piece of Wodehouse frivolity from his prodigious memory and recycle it. In the middle of formal speech or a lunchtime conversation, he was as likely as not to come out with some hilarious gem from that irreverent master of the adjective and the simile. Even today, Wodehouse characters like the Duke of Dunstable, Galahad ("Gally") Threepwood, Lady Constance Keeble or Lord Emsworth's "pig man" George Cyril Wellbeloved, figure frequently in my conversations with my sister, who has inherited Dad's ability to quote them precisely and at length.

Wodehouse invented amusing names for people and places; Dad collected them from real life. He used to bring the telephone book to the supper table and regale us with the odd names he found in it. Whenever an opportunity arose, he would add to his mental store of such items, and pull them out later on to insert into conversation or even written form. No matter what serious matters were occupying his attention, he managed to find time for this kind of fun. Even in the midst of the battle over the Padlock Act in 1938, he apparently could not resist taking time out to write a short piece for the *Canadian Forum*, entitled "What's In A Name?"

"Few people in search of amusement would think of seeking it in the pages of investment manuals or directories of directors. Yet they might go farther and fare worse. Comic masterpieces they will not find, but incredibly apt names of company directors and officials they will. And if they broaden the field to include roadside advertisements, the daily newspaper, and chance acquaintances, they will soon be astonished at the richness of the treasure that lies all about us."

From just such sources he went on to extract a list that included "Yapp and Howell, vinegars"; "Turner, Parker and Weaver, auto supplies"; "Mr. Quiett, author of 'Principles of Publicity'"; "Lawless and Ida Sledge, C.I.O. organizers"; "Messrs Sharp and Fox, authors of 'Business Ethics: Studies in Fair Competition'"; "Swims Brothers, fish"; "Burns Brothers, coal"; "Grimes, cleaner"; "Dunnington Grubb, Landscape Architect"; and "Mr. Hailstone, curate of the Church of England." He went on to note: "Recent Dominion and provincial elections have provided us with candidates so delightfully named as Mr. Stork of Gull Lake; Mr. Scarlett, Communist; Mr. Reason, Independent Liberal; Mr. Virtue, Reconstructionist; Mr. Ghostley, Social Credit. Let the investment manuals beat that if they can!"[9]

Once, on his return from a Congress-related event in Halifax, he recounted with glee how a colleague named Jones had accidentally forgotten a pair of trousers in a hotel room when packing to come home. Remembering a sonnet by William Wordsworth that began: "Jones!" Dad produced a parody:

> Jones! Till at last you came to claim your pants
> In Halifax, that morning ere we left,
> I feared that you might find yourself bereft
> At the plane's door, while chilly winds from Hants
> Played round your legs....

CAPITALIST PROPAGANDA POTPOURRI[10]

Note to Stanley Knowles, CCF MP: "These are doggerel versions (with occasional comments) of speeches by [CPR President J.R.] Beatty, [W. McL.] Clark (secretary of the Canadian Chamber of Commerce at the time) and A.O. Dawson, which my wife and I concocted and which I thought might amuse you. In many cases their quite astonishing badness is the fault of the speakers rather than the versifiers, for the doggerel is usually almost verbatim from the speeches! I wish I had the clippings. I can't even recall the dates, now (Feb. 1937, about). If you had the parallel passages, you'd be astonished. (Signed) E.A.F."

I am not a trained economist myself,
But because I have attained to power and pelf,
I can take my economics from the pages of the comics,
And what I say puts all else upon the shelf.

It's my courage and my enterprise and vision,
My capacity to make a quick decision,
It's my energy and thrift which with these combined to lift
Me to topmost place. What cause here for derision?

It is good old-fashioned honesty, hard work,
That the world needs, not this tendency to shirk
I observe among the Red unemployed who lie abed
Take their ease upon relief, a curious quirk!

He used to play with words while riding the bus to work or waiting for an appointment. I've seen the backs of envelopes covered with lists of words he scribbled searching for the right rhyme for one of his "nonsense verses." My boys told me about playing Scrabble with their Grampa: "He had such a great vocabulary, but he had no sense of the way the game was scored. He'd have a great time arranging his letters to come up with all sorts of words, but he never won. It was so funny. He just didn't pay any

> There are too many Rhodes scholars in the land.
> They've become (alas for Rhodes!) a desperate band
> Who suggest more food and clothing (the idea fills me with loathing)
> For the masses whose cupidity they've fanned.
> If they'll take a job in office, bank or mill,
> I'm prepared to guarantee that they soon will
> Learn that workers are secure, that of jobs they're always sure,
> With pay ample to meet every daily bill.
>
> Where is poverty? Canadians enjoy
> Air and sunshine, drains, paved streets for girl and boy;
> Fire escapes and quarantine in each hamlet may be seen,
> And most cities many garbage men employ.
> What I want to know is, Shall we subsidize
> All the misfits that our system now supplies?
> Give amenities and doles which destroy immortal souls,
> Filching from them self-respect, life's highest prize?
>
> No. The spiritual riches shall be theirs,
> Not our filthy lucre, interest, bonds and shares.
> These in well-concealed reserves we shall keep for our preserves.
> Thus we free the poor from sordid, earthly cares.

attention to the value of the letters or the spaces that would have doubled or tripled his score."

Sometimes he indulged in bilingual word play. When Russell Bell, his former assistant in the research department left the Congress to work for the Economic Council of Canada, Dad composed a verse that he recited at the farewell party. After a lively and fanciful rendering of the shocked dismay of the entire staff on hearing the news of Bell's departure, he went on:

Psychologists and such may say,
"Too much emotion you display.
Your attitude is too possessive
Your lamentations are excessive
We understand your grief and pain,
But your loss is the nation's gain."
Little they've plumbed our depth of grief!
The saddest part's beyond belief.
Not for ourselves alone the knell:
The world has heard the last of Bell.
In our bilingual state, by gosh,
Henceforth he'll be "Monsieur LaCloche"!

Given all this, a comment by my father's old friend Charles Caccia is hardly surprising: "People remember Eugene," he said, "as much, if not more, for language and laughter as they do for his fights, integrity and political positions." Yet any distinction between the political and the linguistic aspects of his legacy is somewhat artificial. For Dad, the two were seldom far apart, and he often used both literary allusions and humour to achieve political ends.

One instance among many was the fight against Section 98 of Canada's Criminal Code, introduced in 1919 during the Winnipeg General Strike, which made it illegal to sell or circulate anything that taught, advocated, or defended the use of force to bring about governmental or economic change. Dad of course opposed such sweeping limits on freedom of expression. In a *Canadian Forum* article, he had fun showing how the Bible, Milton, and even the *History of England* used in Ontario's high schools might all "fall victim to the new censorship."[11] He and his fellow civil libertarians managed to get the section abolished in 1936.

In politics as in other realms, my father insisted on calling a spade a spade. His socialist writings in particular provide some startling examples, notably in the form of explicitly Marxist language. In this, however, he was far from alone. Especially during the Depression, words like "capitalist" and "working class" were routinely used simply as practical tools for getting a grip on reality. And by no means only by people on the Left. Business interests themselves, on the defensive against the perceived threat of radical change, tried to appropriate socialist terms so as to strip them of their real meanings and render them useless.

Dad's own use of such terminology was not merely a question of contemporary usage or personal style. Words and symbols, he knew, could be far more powerful than they might appear. He understood intuitively that putting names to things can help people develop their own analysis and build a basis for action. As he explained at the start of the section he wrote for *Towards the Christian Revolution*: "The first step towards changing society is to understand the existing society ... We must start from the world as it really is, try to find out what basic forces are in operation, and then work in and with and through them to a new world which is *possible*."[12] In the pages that followed, he tried to promote that understanding by using the most accurate words he knew to provide the factual basis of his argument for change.

This recognition of the link between words and political action is echoed in the grassroots popular education techniques pioneered by the Brazilian educator Paolo Freire in the 1960s — techniques that have been applied since then in many other parts of the world with remarkable results. Experience with this innovative approach demonstrates that when oppressed people learn to name the elements of their powerlessness, they gain not only literacy skills but a vital tool for resistance and transformation. Similarly, numerous feminist theorists and activists have shown that when we finally call women's oppression by its name, the naming itself becomes an empowering force in the ongoing struggle against patriarchal injustices.[13]

The extraordinary power of naming is, of course, a two-edged sword. The term "spin" was not current in my father's time, but the phenomenon certainly was. Then, as now, those with vested interests were constantly trying to put innocuous labels on outrageous policies and actions. If they could make the label stick, they found it that much easier to manipulate public opinion, minimize criticism, and forestall any reasoned examination of the issues.

Such sleazy tactics roused Dad to eloquent indignation. When a professor speculated during the Depression that certain "taxpayers were inclined to be 'unduly pessimistic when making their returns,'" he responded in verse:

> ## "Oratorical Flights and Verbal Parachutes"
> *(From a 1970 interview[14])*
>
> Another thing I couldn't stand about Mackenzie King was his abominable misuse of the English language. I always knew which parts of his speeches ... had been written by somebody else, because the parts he had done himself wouldn't parse; no kind of grammatical construction.... On his loftiest oratorical flights he always took along a verbal parachute so that he could bail out if need be. This was, I think, the explanation of the extraordinary contortions that he indulged in, the clouds of ambiguity. He always was able on some subsequent occasion, if accused of having said "A," to point out that in parenthesis number 83, in the 15th line or 14th page of a particular sentence, he had carefully inserted such-and-such a qualification.
>
> The perfect example of his style was a sentence in his letter of resignation to Lord Byng in 1926. I once stopped three ardent Liberals in rhapsodies on Mackenzie King's literary style, simply by quoting this sentence — it stopped them like a bullet:
>
>> Your Excellency will recall that in our recent conversations relative to a dissolution, I have on each occasion suggested,

> When a millionaire does not declare the whole of what he earns,
> Some call it "tax evasion," and their wrath against him burns.
> But a kindlier phrase the man himself from Prof. Woytinsky learns:
> It's "unduly pessimistic when making his returns."[15]

My father denounced spin whenever he saw it, and the *Canadian Forum* was often his vehicle. He used its pages to dismember a corporate pamphlet claiming that "full employment" meant only "the avoidance of mass unemployment;" the Canadian Chamber of Commerce's dismissal of social security as "shotgun charity"; Mackenzie King's "fervent professions of

> as I have again urged this morning, that, having regard to the possible very serious consequences of a refusal of the advice of your First Minister to dissolve Parliament, you should, before definitely deciding on this step, cable the Secretary of State for the Dominions, asking the British Government, from whom you have come to Canada under instructions, what, in the opinion of the Secretary of State for the Dominions, your course should be, in the event of your being presented by the Prime Minister with an Order in Council having reference to a dissolution.
>
> You see, there's a beautiful verbal parachute. When he was accused later of having told Byng he should get orders from Downing Street: "Oh, oh, oh, no, I, I never, ehh, I never suggested anything of the sort. I, I merely suggested that he should, ehh, get, ehh, the advice of a, a very eminent and respected British political figure, the Secretary of State for the Dominions ..." But what he left out was "asking the British government, from whom you have come to Canada under instructions, what your course should be." This was absolutely classic Mackenzie King pidgin English. No, my literary sense was always offended by his performances.

devotion to ... the supremacy of Parliament;" and the fraudulent labelling of the American-controlled TransCanada Pipeline as "all-Canadian" by its continentalist government promoters.[16]

Certain other words and phrases might not exactly qualify as spin, but they seemed to hold a similarly irresistible appeal for the naïve or indifferent. One example was what Dad referred to as "the magic word 'moderate.'"

"Over and over again," he fumed, "I have been told that Mr. X's hair-raising proposal is 'moderate' because it is rather less hair-raising than Mr. Y's ... Well, the man who asks me to jump out of a third-storey window can, I suppose, be described as 'moderate' by comparison with one who wants me to jump from the seventh storey; but in either case I shall be dead. Let us expunge from our vocabulary ... this misleading and irrelevant word."[17]

Dad never ceased to be astonished and dismayed by the fact that so many people routinely fell for such verbal obfuscation. His lifelong contempt for Mackenzie King was deepened by the fact that the longtime Liberal leader managed to maintain his power and popularity largely through his bumbling and deceitful use of words. Once again, language was inextricably linked to the political and ethical fundamentals it either expressed or confounded.

It was not only the direct social and political implications of such linguistic travesties that offended my father, appalling though those often were. It was also the intellectual dishonesty, the hypocrisy, and the total disrespect for language that they embodied.

"Respect for the word — to employ it with scrupulous care and an incorruptible heart-felt love of truth — is essential if there is to be any growth in a society," wrote the late Dag Hammarskjöld, long-time U.N. secretary general and Nobel Peace Prize winner. "To misuse the word is to show contempt ... It undermines the bridges and poisons the wells."[18]

Dad's similar horror of language abuse was closely linked to his insistence that issues needed to be thought through and debated on the basis of reason and evidence. As noted in the last chapter, he was convinced that our use of words is fundamental to the way we use our heads. He fought hard on many fronts to expose and reverse the damage done when words were used sloppily, or, worse, "twisted by knaves to make a trap for fools."

A prime example of the latter, touched on earlier, was the on-again-off-again effort, begun by Liberal governments in the 1940s, to remove the word "Dominion" from Canada's official documents and from popular use. Dad called the offensive "a long campaign of bad law, bad history, bad logic, untruths, prevarications, self-contradictions, cringing, crawling, wriggling, squirming and sheer nonsense, against which I battled for years."[19]

Challenged to justify their actions, government people offered a whole series of feeble excuses. They maintained that the word "Dominion" implied inferiority, that the British had imposed it on Canada during the negotiations that resulted in the BNA Act of 1867, that it was a "humiliating" designation for an independent country. Dad pointed out

"DOMINION" – OUR CANADIAN WORD[20]

In October, 1982, the Senate Committee on Legal and Constitutional Affairs held hearings on Bill C-201, to replace "Dominion Day" with the designation "Canada Day." My father appeared as a witness, though to no avail.[21]

"Dominion," as a legal and constitutional term, is perhaps the most purely Canadian word in the dictionary.

… We are told that there is no French translation. That is not surprising, since "Dominion" is an old French word which English borrowed and preserved…. In fact, there is an official, well-established translation: "Puissance." … [Moreover,] as early as 1917 it seems to have been officially decided that no translation was necessary; that Canadian official French can simply re-borrow "Dominion" from English …

Modern Canadian official French has had no hesitation about borrowing, recently, purely English words like "leader." Why should there be any objection to re-borrowing the old French word "Dominion," sanctioned by more than a century of official usage?

The Fathers of Confederation set out to make a nation. Incidentally, they distinguished carefully, in both languages, between "nationality" — the English, French, Scotch and Irish "nationalities" — and "nation" — the one nation, the "seule et grande puissance" — which was to be. They did not set out to make a league of semi-independent states, or a "community of communities." They believed, accordingly, in the primacy of the nation over its parts. They gave the central Parliament the residual power in legislation, in a deliberate rejection of the American system. "Dominion" was the outward and visible symbol of this primacy of the nation over its parts. Canada was to be "one Dominion … divided into four provinces."

Is this a moment to weaken that symbol of "one Canada"? To give aid and comfort to forces which would crib, cabin and confine a national Government and Parliament already far more limited than the Fathers of Confederation intended them to be, and beset by problems — Canada-wide, continent-wide, world-wide — which even the strongest provinces would be utterly unable to cope with?

that, on the contrary, the term was coined by the Fathers of Confederation precisely as a proud and unique title for the "great new nation" they were founding. Moreover, he said, "Canada has grown since 1867, and the word 'Dominion' has grown with it." As for the supposed humiliation, he was adamant. "'Dominion' is *our* word, perhaps the only distinctive word we have contributed to political terminology ... The French version of the British North America Act translates 'Dominion' as 'Puissance.' Is it humiliating to be called a Power?"[22]

The anti-Dominion forces responded with the claim that the word might not be understood by foreigners. Dad reiterated his accusations of "shaky history [and] shaky constitutional theory," and went on, with bitter irony: "But let that pass. The real point is that though 'Dominion' doesn't really 'imply inferiority,' we must 'sacrifice' it because some 'foreigners' think it does. Similarly, I must change my name because some people can't spell it. What true Canadian, faced with a choice between preserving our historic traditions and sacrificing them to the ignorance (real or imagined) of 'foreigners,' could hesitate for a moment?"[23]

Some critics have poured scorn on this "cockamamie crusade over a couple of words." Even Dad's old friend Frank Scott once dismissed his advocacy of the term "Dominion" as a "fondness for ancient words."[24] But much more was at stake than a mere quibble over semantics. As noted in Chapter 8, my father was convinced that the true purpose of the anti-"Dominion" campaign was to bring Canada closer the United States by undermining our constitutional system of responsible government and alienating us from our roots.

John Ralston Saul has a somewhat different but complementary understanding of the importance of the Canadian word "Dominion" and the sad significance of its decline. He too notes that it was originally introduced to represent the power, "puissance," which the new Canadian nation would exercise from sea to sea. But Saul also emphasizes another important aspect of the term's biblical origins: its association, particularly in Psalm 72, with concepts of "egalitarianism, inclusion and justice," of "responsibility to ensure the welfare of the people." He laments that by the 1950s, "the term had been slowly devalued by those who did not have the self-confidence to embrace the full Confederation process ... The colonial elite destroyed the word."[25]

While the government was engaged in surreptitiously making Dominion disappear, it was also attempting to introduce parallel changes to the *Canada Year Book*, likewise without notice or public discussion. Dad reflected caustically on that effort:

> The 1954 edition changed "House of Commons" and "Parliamentary Representation" to "Federal Government Legislature." This, of course, was quite in tune with the prevailing attitude in the highest circles, that Parliament is the property of the Government.
>
> It is perhaps surprising that some official spokesman did not pop up to explain that "Ministry" and "House of Commons" were "errors that have crept into official usage." It is also perhaps equally surprising that those dear and convenient "foreigners" weren't trotted out again. After all, "House of Commons" doesn't mean much to a Frenchman; ..."Parliament" doesn't mean

Eugene as part of a television panel, probably in the late 1950s. The media already recognized him as an articulate and provocative spokesperson on a wide range of public issues.

much to an American or a Russian. Why not call it "Congress" or "Supreme Soviet"? And surely foreigners would understand us better if we called our provinces "states"? Of course the whole performance should offend our national pride.[26]

There were, and perhaps still are, some who would condemn my father for his persistent use of the word "national" to refer to our country. The "two nations" theory of Canada, popularized in the 1960s, took advantage of the all-too-common willingness to disregard facts and evidence, and applied a bilingual version of what Dad called "Humpty-Dumptyism. 'When I use a word,' said Humpty Dumpty, 'it means just what I choose it to mean.'"[27] Lewis Carroll aside, Dad objected to people in the real world trying to "revise the dictionary to remould the meaning of words nearer to their hearts' desire."[28] When they did that, he insisted, it resulted in misunderstanding or worse. "I don't think we have any right to play ducks and drakes with the dictionary, English or French, in this fashion," he said. "Neither language is anyone's personal property, and people who treat either as if it were usually trip over their feet before they are done."[29]

In speeches and articles, he put the word "nation" under a bilingual microscope. He explained that in both French and English, the word has two distinct meanings — one sociological, the other political. In addition, he underlined the distinction between "French Canada," which embraces Canadians of French origin and speech from coast to coast to coast, and "Quebec," a province where large numbers of non-francophones also live. Speaking at the University of Western Ontario in 1966, he examined how then-Quebec premier Daniel Johnson had contrived in Humpty-Dumpty fashion to blur both distinctions in a presentation addressed to the Dominion-provincial conference that year.

"On page 2," Dad noted, "the [French-Canadian] 'nation' is 'sociological.' On page 3, hey! presto! it is 'juridical and political' ... The 'sociological nation' is whisked off the stage, and a 'juridical and political nation' whisked on in its place ... This [nation] is to be 'juridically and politically recognized' by, 'among other means,' a 'new constitution,' which ... 'will give Quebec all the powers necessary to safeguard the Quebec identity.' French Canada disappears up one of M. Johnson's sleeves, and Quebec pops out of the other."[30]

Subsequent events have shown that this kind of verbal manipulation does indeed "undermine the bridges and poison the wells." Words like "nation" continue to play a crucial and often less than honourable role in the ongoing tug-of-war over Quebec sovereignty. In November of 2006, when Stephen Harper introduced a motion in the House of Commons declaring Quebec "a nation within Canada," very few people seemed to understand the potential implications of this cynical manipulation of a few "mere words."[31] We would do well to pay attention to the warnings of word-loving people like Hammarskjöld, Saul, and Forsey if we want to preserve our collective ability to understand our reality and defend our values.

"Guard well our English speech," my father exhorted his fellow anglophones, "as the French Canadians are guarding their French."[32] As a determined language activist, he practised what he preached.

At every opportunity, he berated those who strayed from the path of what the Quakers call "plain speech." He took on "the fussifiers — professors and officials [who] simply will not use plain words or plain phrases if they can find fussy ones. They think they are being correct and elegant [when] actually they are just being prissy and pompous and tiresome."[33] He challenged writers and politicians who were "imperfectly acquainted with the dictionary," never mind basic grammar, and warned against bad translations that imposed foreign constructions onto the English language. He sounded the alarm about a "linguistic epidemic" spreading north from the United States, which threatened the meaning of words like "fulsome" or "dissemble," the past tense of verbs like "fit" and "lie," and the very survival of the subjunctive mood.[34]

He was particularly impatient with some of the verbiage emanating from the ivory tower. "I'm afraid that we too often put professors under pressure merely to spill ink onto paper," he told a Memorial University graduating class, "and then judge them as the farmer judged the cakes at the Irish country fair: 'That's a fine, weighty cake! We'll give that one the prize!' What makes it worse is that much of the academic poundage is dreary stuff; elephantine, Germanized English; much ado about very little; two grains of wheat hid in many bushels of chaff."[35]

Not long ago I came across an example of the kind of verbal carelessness that used to drive him to distraction. Under the heading "Federation" in the 1997 edition of an official publication I found the statement: *"The Canadian government is a federation ... "*[36] How a "government" could be a "federation" was not explained. A country can be one, of course, and its system of government can then be described as federal. But to describe a government as "a federation" betrays a gap in logic and a heedlessness of language that my father would have deplored.

Not surprisingly, Dad was very much a language traditionalist. This was especially so in regard to religious liturgy. An official patron of the Anglican Prayer Book Society, he was dismayed by the changes incorporated into that church's *Book of Alternate Service*, as well as by the modern translations of the Bible that have replaced the King James version in many places of worship. I think he was dubious from the start about the claims of sexism, exclusion, and historical or linguistic inaccuracies that the new editions were attempting to address, but in any case, he objected strongly to the way those problems were dealt with. He lamented the elimination of so much of the "unparalleled beauty, dignity, and reverence" of the older texts, the loss of the poetic cadence of the passages, and the disappearance of the rich legacy of familiar wordings that so often adorned his own work.

He also had problems with modern efforts to replace sexist language with non-sexist alternatives in secular discourse. I would like to be able to report that he acknowledged the problems and supported a common search for language-sensitive solutions, but in reality he tended, at least early on, to resort to disparagement and ridicule. However, his later writings show his attitude shifting over time. Grudgingly at first, then more naturally, he modified some of his own English usage to get rid of the structural sexism. He never got to the point of saying "chair" or "chairperson" instead of "chairman," but in his final years he was habitually using "men and women," "him and her" instead of the old false generics.

Among my father's archival papers are files entitled "English Usage and Errors: Correspondence"; "Language, Use of: Clippings, Notes, Articles"; three more that he designated: "Corrections to Other Writers' Work"; and another — a fat one — labelled simply "Errors." Much of the material comes from the mass of papers and documents that arrived on his desk for comment. He spent endless hours going over them, checking and correcting both factual content and language. Some of that work he enjoyed, as is clear from the cordial letters he wrote to several of the authors. But a lot of the rest of it had him pulling his hair out.

"I have had to read dozens of manuscripts and books by [university] graduates and professors, [who] can't speak or write plain English," he lamented. "[Many] are so badly written that I would have been thrown out of public school if I had perpetrated such stuff: plural subjects and singular verbs; sentences without any verb at all; words used without any regard for their dictionary meaning; obscure disquisitions starting nowhere and getting nowhere; malapropisms; mixed metaphors; horrible fussifications; abominable translations from the simple into the unintelligible; sheer fog."[37]

"He was such a good editor," recalled his long-time Congress secretary Dawn Dobson, "that many people sent their manuscripts to him for vetting, and were surprised when they got back a list of 52 or 65 footnotes! Someone from the Department of Labour said to me, 'Where else could you get anything edited so wonderfully well, and for no charge?'"

Dad's adopted role as editor, however, did not necessarily make him sympathetic to editors as a class. In fact, his insistence on clear and expressive language was a frequent source of friction between him and the editorial staff of various publications. Many of these people were, in his opinion, "ignorant of good plain English words and phrases, tone-deaf to the cadence of English prose," and possessed of "a fixed desire to blunt, flatten, dehydrate." He wondered "what [they'd] have done with Chaucer's 'Tell forth thy tale, and spare it not at all!' I dare say [they] would have transformed it into: 'Recount your narrative, and utilize whatever resources you believe to be necessary.'"[38]

I have several of the letters he wrote protesting the editorial ravages inflicted on articles he had submitted for publication, and spelling out his view of an editor's job: "It is an editor's function to correct actual mistakes of fact, spelling, grammar; actual misuse of words; to draw attention to ambiguities and obscurities; to suggest changes which will get rid of these; to suggest cuts, or expansions of certain points; always, to make or suggest the *minimum* of changes, *not* the *maximum*. It is not his or her function to put a writer's text through the mincing machine; or to substitute for what a writer is trying to say a little thing of his or her own invention, what he or she thinks the writer *ought* to have said."[39]

"ADVICE FOR EDITORS"
(From a 1986 letter to the chief editor of a major publishing entity[40])

Some editors and sub-editors seem to think that they are endowed with an infallibility more than papal. They are not, and their principals should tell them so before they begin their work. They should have written instructions along these lines:

1. You are entitled to correct mistakes in punctuation, spelling, grammar, names, dates, without reference to the author. (Even here, they should be warned to be cautious. Even some people who are supposed to be educated are often imperfectly acquainted with the dictionary and over-confident about names and dates ...)

2. You are not entitled to add, or insert, material of your own or anyone else's, without the author's permission. To do so is plagiarism in reverse.

3. You are not entitled to change word order, or the order of paragraphs, without the author's permission. Changing word order can take the stuffing out of a statement, or destroy its cadence, casting a pall of banality.

4. You are not entitled to delete anything (except under 1, above) without the author's permission.

Any editor has a perfect right to reject any article, but he has no right whatever to print an amended version with the name of the original author, without that author's consent. In other words, any editor, when he gets an article, has a perfect right to say: "This won't do. The old boy has lost his marbles (or, it's too stuffy, or too pompous, or too flippant, or too obscure, or too full of jargon, or too long-winded, or too summary). This rubbish goes direct to the waste-basket. Our Mr. (Miss, Ms., Mrs.) can do a much better job." But in that case, Mr. (Miss, Ms., Mrs.) X or Y should get credit for his (her) superior scholarship or literary gifts, not have his (her) light hidden under someone else's bushel.

This trusty old manual typewriter was once described as "the most trenchant typewriter in the country." After Eugene Forsey's death in February 1991, cartoonist Fred Sebastian depicted it with a note inserted into the carrier: "Dear Editors: You're on your own. E.F."

Years of misplaced editorial attempts to "correct and improve" his English wore out my father's tolerance. A scathing missive to one unfortunate offender stated, in part: "Your text is really an insult.... I particularly object to your pomposifying my style: replacing short Saxon words by long Latin ones. Anyone who knows my style, reading what you have written, would recognize at once that it was not my work at all ... Upon what meat do you editors feed, that you are grown so great?"[41]

In 1979, when he was in the final throes of revising his labour history book for the University of Toronto Press, the chief editor there asked him if he would consider writing his memoirs. In a hand-written reply, Dad thanked him for his "most generous and flattering suggestion," but declined. "I'd once again be put on the rack and under the thumbscrew by some editor who disliked plain, idiomatic English, had a horror of fun, and was determined to make me dignified. No thanks! not while I retain possession of a moderate proportion of my wits ..."[42]

Ten years later, though, he decided to take the risk after all. The happy result, *A Life on the Fringe*, is written in plain, idiomatic English, is full of fun, and is dignified only in spots.

"How Eugene Forsey could write," said Jeffrey Simpson in the *Globe and Mail* after Dad's death in February 1991. "His pen was as sharp as his mind. His prose was clean and cutting, sprinkled with literary allusions, turns of phrase, puns, quotations (he once clobbered me with an extensive quotation from Goethe, in German); in short, the whole panoply of literary tools."[43]

All who knew my father, and many who did not, remember his way with words, his "gift of speech," the wisdom behind his wit. Given his love of "plain English," perhaps the tribute he would like best was one from columnist Charles Lynch in February 1991. "Wherever he's gone," said Lynch, "I wish he'd write."[44]

CHAPTER ELEVEN

Serving the Common Good: The Role of Government

Governments in democracies are elected by the passengers to steer the ship of the nation. They are expected to hold it on course, to arrange for a prosperous voyage, and to be prepared to be thrown overboard if they fail in either duty. This reflects the original sense of the word "government," as its roots in both Greek and Latin mean "to steer."
— From the introduction to *How Canadians Govern Themselves*[1]

There's a line in a Newfoundland folk song that reflects my father's view of the proper order of things aboard Canada's ship of state. It says: "The captain's below making tea for the crew." Likewise government, the captains are there to serve the passengers and crew. The fundamental duty of every government is to pursue the public interest, and every government, whatever its stripe, is ultimately responsible to the people.

Eugene Forsey spent his life sailing Canada's political waters, with a master seaman's knowledge of governmental navigation and the law of the constitutional sea. Today, his understanding of the role and purpose of government provides an important basis for public discourse at a time in our history when many people treat "government" as almost a dirty word.

The principle that the state exists to serve the people is part of a longstanding Canadian tradition in which governments play a wide-ranging and creative role in our collective life. This view stands in sharp contrast to the notion — prevalent in the United States and increasingly being pushed on Canadians — that the less "government" there is, the better.

Dad had no use for that approach. His definition of political economy was "the management of the public household, the community" and for him the ideal society was a "co-operative commonwealth," with all sectors working together for the common good.[2] The business of government was to implement those concepts — a mandate as challenging as it was broad.

In the introduction to *How Canadians Govern Themselves*, my father elaborated on the multitude of ways in which our everyday lives are affected by government policies and activities. His list of examples could be rather intimidating, but given the needs of a complex modern society, it makes sense.

> We cannot work, eat or drink, buy or sell or own anything, go to a hockey match or watch TV without feeling the effects of government. We cannot marry or educate our children, cannot be sick, born or buried without the hand of government somewhere intervening. Government ... sets the conditions that affect farms and industries; manages or mismanages the life and growth of cities, [and] is held responsible for social problems, pollution and sick environments.[3]

The idea of government as an active and positive force is far from new in Canada. It was well established from early in our history as a country, and was accepted and implemented by parties of differing views. In a more comprehensive and radical form, it was a key element in the vision that Dad and his colleagues in the CCF and the League for Social Reconstruction put forward in the 1930s,[4] and was a basic assumption underlying the demands of the trade union movement in the years that followed.

In his work with the Labour Congresses, Dad hammered away at the need for comprehensive economic planning and strong government programs in areas like social security. Through speeches, articles, and the *Labour Research* bulletin, he shared information and analysis that would help workers and other citizens press effectively for positive change. It was, in fact, this kind of cumulative citizen pressure that forced governments to improve the old age pension, unemployment insurance and welfare systems, and eventually to create programs such as low-rental housing, disability benefits, and public health care.[5]

My father's job gave him plenty of opportunity not only to watch government at work, but also to observe the range of public attitudes towards it. He took issue with some of the negative views of the state that prevailed in many quarters during the Cold War era. "I must strongly dissent from the assumption that the extension of state action necessarily limits freedom," he declared. "It can, but it doesn't have to. The big state has developed largely as a defence of the freedom of the common people against big business. Much of the big state's action is designed to give the common people economic freedom — freedom from fear — without which the other freedoms will not mean very much to large masses of our citizens."[6]

Speaking to a young audience in 1960, he was even more direct. "I find sometimes a tendency for people to think that if a public authority spends money it is a terrible thing, but if it is spent by some private body, then that is magnificent. [They think] that taxes are an unmitigated evil; that public activity of any kind is something to be cut down to the smallest possible proportion; that private enterprise is always good and public enterprise is always bad. These seem to me extraordinarily silly and irrational attitudes, which may be disastrous for us."[7]

Before Saskatchewan's medicare concept finally became a national program, Dad spoke at a meeting of the medical profession to push for a comprehensive national health plan. After outlining the crying need for such a plan, he addressed the arguments that were being used against it. One was that medicare would be "socialistic."

My answer to that is, "Oh! Fudge!" So are public sewage and garbage disposal, public water supply, public highways, the public post office, public education. The only sensible question to ask about any of them is not, "Is it socialistic?" or "Is it free enterprise?" but, "Will it do the job, and do it better than any alternative plan?"

Let's not be frightened, either way, by labels. Labour isn't frightened ... We want to preserve, and indeed increase, personal freedom. But we are not afraid of asking our governments, which we choose and can control, to provide for us services which no one else can.[8]

The kind of government activity my father believed in was, and still is, anathema to right-wing ideologues. They take the line that governments should exist only to maintain an army, a diplomatic corps, and a currency, all of which should be geared to serving corporate interests. In some circumstances, they would require a few other functions, such as providing public funds to bail out those same private corporations when their capitalist house of cards shows signs of collapse. But the vision they put forward is all about "free enterprise," with the state standing on the sidelines applauding the "invisible hand" at work.

One need not be a socialist to recognize the truth of what Dad and his LSR colleagues wrote about this in *Social Planning for Canada*:

> Canadian business men are fond of demanding that governments should "let business alone." [But] ... while it would be delightful [for them] to get rid of workmen's compensation, factory acts, minimum wage laws and so forth, it would be anything but agreeable to be deprived of tariff protection, bounties, interest-free loans [and] guarantees of bonds and bank loans ... or to be asked to repay the enormous gifts from public treasuries to private concerns. Any serious attempt to carry out such a program would throw the whole economy into chaos.
>
> In practice, of course, our business leaders put a good deal of government interference water into their laissez-

faire wine. Nowhere more freely than in Canada have business groups insisted on governmental aid in finding and keeping markets, in transporting goods to these markets, in financing business expansion.[9]

These days, we could add many more examples to the list of government initiatives that serve private interests at public expense — "contracting out" and "public-private partnerships," tax breaks for domestic and foreign mining companies, "Team Canada" tours by public officials to promote business interests overseas, not to mention the billions in bail-outs handed over to industry when the cracks in the system begin to show.

Nonetheless, the disingenuous appeal for "less government" has again become a rallying cry for the right wing in Canada. A massive deception being perpetrated upon a weary people — ironically by governments themselves — in a multi-facetted campaign to favour corporate interests by denigrating government in the public mind.

The 2009 *Canada Year Book*, put out these days on a business-oriented "cost recovery" basis by Statistics Canada, is one example of how this false minimalist approach is being promoted. Its twelve-page "Government" section is buried somewhere in the middle of the book and consists almost entirely of charts and tables showing public revenues and expenditures. The introductory paragraph neatly disposes of its subject: "The three levels of government provide Canadians with services that cannot easily be offered by private companies," it says. "The federal government is responsible for national defence and international diplomacy, the provinces and territories ensure that Canadians have access to health care and education, and local governments keep our streets clean and our communities safe."[10]

There you have "government" in a nutshell — or so the public officials who authorized this insulting portrayal would have us think. My father would have been quick to denounce it as a hoax, and to point us to the real role government plays in our society — not as an occasional reluctant substitute for "private companies," but as a vital economic and social force for the public good.

Government involvement in the economy takes three main forms: regulation and control of business and industry; service and aid to private enterprise; and government ownership and operation of commercial or industrial entities. The authors of *Social Planning for Canada* pointed out that these functions sometimes overlap. "For instance," they said, "an official grading of farm produce is both a service to the farmer and a regulation of his business. Similarly, government ownership and operation of canals is a service to shippers and ship owners, and many boards and commissions render technical service at the same time as they are exercising regulatory powers."[11]

For my father, fair and sensible regulation was a necessary part of every government's mandate to protect the public interest. As a Labour Congress employee, he was constantly pushing for effective government regulation in labour matters as well as in social and economic areas like transportation, energy, housing, health, and immigration. During his time on the Board of Broadcast Governors, he did his part to strengthen and implement a regulatory regime for Canadian radio and television. Later, in the Senate, he took on the complex and painstaking job of co-chairing the Joint Committee on Regulations and Other Statutory Instruments, whose mandate was to help ensure accountability and the rule of law by keeping a close eye on regulations and on how they were implemented.

Although regulation is an integral part of the mix of public and private that has always characterized Canadian society, it is also highly controversial. Regulations frequently raise the ire of business executives, urban developers, property rights proponents, and a host of others who view private interests as paramount. Unfortunately, numerous examples of ill-conceived or badly implemented regulations have added fuel to the fire, tending to give the whole concept of regulation a bad name in many circles. The forces decrying "government" have wasted no time latching onto the issue as an easy vote-getter.

Dad was as critical as anyone of bad regulations, and he saw plenty of them, particularly in his work with the Statutory Instruments Committee. But he was equally clear on the need for good ones. Nor could his position be dismissed as a remnant of socialistic thinking from bygone days. Referring in the Senate to his own upbringing as a Conservative, he reminded his colleagues that there was "an old Conservative tradition, both in this country and in Great Britain, that the state should intervene whenever sufficient cause is shown for doing so."[12]

"Sufficient cause" might be social, economic, or environmental — this last a dimension my father addressed with increasing urgency in his later years. In his convocation address at Carleton University in 1976, he foresaw a need for "massive government regulation, planning, and in some cases, spending" to reduce pollution and save the environment.[13] He had the same message for a meeting of Liberals that same year: "Pollution, in its myriad forms, threatens simply to destroy life on this planet," he told them, "and here the case for 'free enterprise' and 'the free market' is about as weak as anything can be. Here, governments must intervene, massively and decisively, or we shall all disappear."[14]

In 1983, shortly after my father quit the Liberals, he received a questionnaire from the Conservative Party, listing various Conservative policy priorities, one of which was to eliminate "unnecessary" federal regulation. Dad responded: "This sounds a good deal like the Cowboy in the White House — de-regulation for de-regulation's sake, privatization for privatization's sake. *What* regulation is 'unnecessary'? If I agreed to this point, I might find myself a (very minor) party to a gigantic business ramp, Exploiters Unlimited."[15]

And yet today the pressure for deregulation remains unrelenting in almost every sphere, the unsurprising exception being that of "security," where regulation is enjoying an unprecedented heyday ever since the 2001 World Trade Center attacks. In other areas, though, it is either being watered down or left to the tender mercies of industry "self-regulation." This often involves imported systems with trendy labels like "HACCP," now in widespread use in the mega-food industry. Officially, the acronym stands for "Hazard Analysis Critical Control Points," but it has been described by those who have seen it in operation as "Have A Cup of Coffee and Pray."

The legitimate purposes of regulation — fairness, protection of the public and the planet — can also be subverted by governments themselves through rules designed to benefit vested interests or serve other nefarious ends. Such legislation typically enables ministers or bureaucrats to achieve administrative short-cuts or allow politically powerful interests to circumvent an inconvenient law, legalizing what would otherwise be illegal.

This was one of the many problems my father saw with Quebec's Bill 22 language law. "One of [its] most objectionable features," he said, "[is] the enormous scope left to administrative discretion. I went through and counted 17 different places — and they were on matters of substantial importance — where it says, 'the Minister shall make regulations ... or some administrative authority shall decide. Power is placed in the hands of public servants, officials, functionaries ... The degree [and] the kind of administrative discretion provided for is dangerously wide."[16]

Dad's vocal opposition to this kind of thing often put him at odds with powerful elements within government, particularly in cases where implementation of an existing statute was administratively complicated. He was unimpressed by attempts by officials to justify breaking or bending the law in such cases. "The bureaucracy, and to some extent sometimes their political masters, seem to think that the administrative convenience of the executive government is a basic principle of our Constitution," he told an audience in 1978. "Whereas it isn't a principle of our Constitution at all but an idea often subversive of our Constitution."[17]

Whether such legislative finagling involves wide-open ministerial discretion, "self-regulation" by industry, or off-loading responsibilities to compromised bodies like the Canadian Food Inspection Agency, the usual pretexts are "efficiency" and "competitiveness." These two buzzwords are much beloved by business-oriented governments and in industries like oil, agri-business, and pharmaceuticals, where giant corporations constantly clamour for speedy approvals and the loosening of applicable restrictions.

Too often, efficiency and competitiveness are invoked for the benefit of those corporations — the bureaucracy's so-called "clients" — regardless of the consequences for anyone else.[18] Once these concepts are accepted as primary, they can be used to justify drafting an act in such a way as to leave important details to be defined under its regulations, as the Quebec government did with Bill 22. Key provisions can then be put in place or changed by the cabinet acting alone through an Order-in-Council, without Parliament's involvement.

One of many current examples involves toxic mine wastes. Under the federal Fisheries Act, it is illegal to dump toxic material into fish-bearing waters. However, in 2002 the government amended the Act's Metal Mining Effluent Regulation (MMER) to allow the minister to reclassify lakes or other freshwater bodies as "tailings impoundment areas," thereby enabling the industry to sidestep the prohibition. A number of pristine lakes have since been handed over to mining companies for them to poison at will, and more are threatened.[19] The arrangement is certainly "efficient" for the companies; rather less so for the lakes and the fish.

Interestingly, John Ralston Saul suggests that efficiency and democracy are to some extent incompatible. "The rise of democracy," he says, "is tied closely to the idea that the citizen should slow down the leaders; slow down their efficiency ... Democracy isn't about decisiveness; it is about consideration. It is intended to be inefficient."[20] This resonates with Dad's insistence that democracy means using our heads, not just counting them; that "government by discussion" is the essence of the parliamentary system; that diligent committee work and the Senate's function of "sober second thought" are essential to responsible government.

Views like these have gone out of fashion in many quarters. Bureaucratic restructuring, "regulatory reviews," trade deals, and cross-border "harmonization" have knocked the teeth out of some legislation and prevented other regulatory measures from seeing the light of day. There have been constant attempts at both the federal and provincial levels to phase out or privatize publicly run regulatory mechanisms and related services like the Canadian Grain Commission, independent government laboratories, and experimental farms. Government funding for monitoring and enforcement is also often neglected, while public concerns about the resulting loss of accountability and democratic control are largely ignored.

I asked former NDP MP Svend Robinson, who sat on the Statutory Instruments Committee under Dad's co-chairmanship, how Dad reacted to signs of this trend. "He was appalled by all that," Robinson told me. "This turning things over holus-bolus to the corporate sector and abandoning any kind of public accountability was just complete anathema to him."

Despite huge problems in sectors like food safety and transportation, government regulation continues to be weakened or replaced by corporate "self-monitoring" and toothless "voluntary initiatives." Global corporations and powerful trading partners continue to pressure us to let the fox guard the chicken coop. But for the sake of both present and future, we need to reclaim our understanding of the proper regulatory function of government and renew our support for it.

One of the distinguishing characteristics of Canadian society that my father always emphasized was its flexible mix of public and private endeavour in an overall context of freedom. "'Free enterprise' is not the same thing as a free society," he pointed out. "Nor is 'the free market.' They may serve the free society, but they are not the same thing. They are means, not ends ... That is why we live in a mixed economy, not a 'free enterprise' or 'free market' economy."[21]

In this regard, Canada is very different from the United States, where what Dad called the "doctrinaire notion of the primacy of private enterprise"[22] is so widely embraced (although there, too, government and business are closely linked.) The sensible way to decide about public or private enterprise, he believed, was to ask in each case: "Can such-and-such an industry be safely left to private exploitation, with or without public regulation? Or is it safe only in the hands of a public authority? Can this other industry be better run by private enterprise or public?"[23]

This pragmatism, he noted, was also part of a long, non-partisan, and very Canadian tradition. "It was not socialist zeal, or abstract theories on public ownership that led Whitney and Beck to set up Ontario Hydro, or Borden and Meighen to nationalize three railroads, or R. B. Bennett to establish the CRBC (the predecessor of the CBC), or Mackenzie King to make the Bank of Canada wholly publicly owned, or C.D. Howe to create Trans-Canada Air Lines, or Borden to advocate nationalization of the telephone industry. It was solid, practical reasons."[24]

As the League for Social Reconstruction had pointed out back in the 1930s, those practical reasons often had at least as much to do with providing benefits and advantages for Canadian capitalists as with serving the public interest.[25] But the point still stands: in Canada, pragmatism has regularly trumped ideology on questions of public versus private.

My father's pride in our matter-of-fact acceptance of the public ownership option was disturbed, however, by signs that this sensible Canadian approach was being eroded. One such sign was a section in a 1971 report of the Senate Finance Committee that recommended "a constant search for governmental activities ripe to be handed over to the private sector." Dad objected to the Committee's "sweeping, *a priori* theoretical pronouncements" on a subject that was not even germane to the substance of the report.

"[This] is rather alarming to those of us who feel it is very valuable and useful, indeed necessary, for the Government to carry on enterprises [that are] not necessarily [just] public services which have to be performed

> ## "'RIPE' FOR THE PRIVATE SECTOR"
> *(From a 1971 Senate speech[26])*
>
> The thing that worries me is this remark about governmental activities being "ripe to be handed over to the private sector." That phrase "governmental activities" in itself takes in a pretty wide sweep. If it is intended to refer to social services or social security, I can scarcely credit my senses …
>
> If it is intended to refer to business enterprises carried on by the government, again I find myself uneasy. It seems to suggest that enterprises which are sickly, or at all events puny infants, should be nourished with tender loving care by the Government until they show signs of being not merely able to stand on their own feet, but able to bring in substantial profits to private enterprise.
>
> [This] seems to suggest that all the duds, all the deficit-producing enterprises, should be left to the Government. But the minute there is any sign of revenue coming out of it — oh, horror, shades of Karl Marx, red ruin and revolution! — we must immediately hand these things over to private enterprise …
>
> It is unfortunate that this very sweeping statement, and this extraordinary adjective "ripe," should be in here. There they are: fruits, first of all, green and small and hardly worth looking at. Then as they ripen, swell out and become rosy, attractive and juicy — then private enterprise comes along.
>
> For the life of me, I cannot see why this general principle should be adopted. It savours of the American dogmatism on economic subjects which is one of our most noxious importations from the United States."

regardless of how costly [or] unprofitable they are, but [also] services which can actually bring in revenue to the government of Canada or of the province, or for that matter to municipal governments."[27]

For Dad, the trend towards privatization or dismemberment of Crown corporations and other public institutions and services placed ideology above common sense. He argued that if the reasons an institution was established in the first place still existed, to jettison it would be foolish.[28] Today, the same logic would apply to government laboratories and research stations, the Canadian Wheat Board, and the CBC, all of which, having served the public good for decades, have either been disabled in whole or in part, or are increasingly threatened with extinction.

He was, of course, a strong advocate for the CBC and its public, non-commercial status. During a Senate debate on broadcasting, one senator contended that Canada's public broadcaster ran a "deficit." Dad responded: "I do not think there is a deficit. There is a grant made out of public funds … to the CBC as a public service. It was never set up to be a paying commercial proposition; that was not the intention at all. Just as you do not expect the National Gallery to show a commercial profit, you cannot expect the CBC to. That is not what it is there for. … I believe the CBC, with all its faults — and it has some, like any other organization — has been a major factor in preserving the two distinctive Canadian cultures which we possess … We must maintain the CBC, and strengthen it."[29]

His skepticism about the supposed superiority of private for-profit enterprise in radio and television had been reinforced by his experience on the regulatory Board of Broadcast Governors between 1958 and 1962. As he explained in the same Senate speech, those four years of close contact with private broadcasters had left him with "a very poor opinion of them."

> Over and over again we got the impression that when these people spoke — often in purple passages — about their devotion to the public interest and their desire to promote Canadian programming and Canadian talent, it was very much what the Irish call "big offers and small blows" — a lot of talk, but very little action. In general, the impression left on me was that the theme song of private broadcasters could very well have been taken from that Gilbert and Sullivan opera, "The Pirates of Penzance":
>
> "Oh! I am a pirate king. Yes, I am a pirate king;
> And it is, it is a glorious thing to be a pirate king."
>
> To get rid of the CBC and turn our broadcasting over to this collection of gentlemen fills me with horror.[30]

Transportation was another sector of the mixed economy where my father urged a strong role for government. He was convinced that it was not an option to leave the whole transportation sector in private hands. In a country as large and sparsely populated as ours, the movement of people and goods could not be expected to always turn a profit, particularly in more remote areas. Since adequate transportation was obviously essential for the public good, he believed it was a matter for government to address.

The Canadian Constitution itself, Dad pointed out, reflects the recognition of this reality. In order for each of the four Atlantic provinces and British Columbia to agree to join Confederation, there had to be detailed provisions for railway and ferry linkages, and these were written right into the terms of union. "[Without] this essential factor of transportation in our Constitution," he said, "you would simply not have the Maritime provinces, or Newfoundland, or British Columbia ... It is a matter of fundamental national importance, a fundamental undertaking that was given to the peoples of these provinces when they came into the union ... There is some ground for thinking that [these provisions] have been treated in a rather lighthearted and cavalier fashion sometimes since ... This is not the way in which a solemn undertaking given by a great nation to its constituent parts should be treated."[31]

Throughout his Senate term and the years that followed, Dad staunchly supported government ownership and maintenance of Air Canada, CN and VIA Rail as vital public services. One of the main things that led him to leave the Liberal Party in the early 1980s was what he considered the shabby mishandling of "the VIA Rail business" by the Trudeau government.

"Cutting out all those trains without any proper hearings — it was a complete violation of the whole spirit of the Transport Act," he told Tom Earle in 1985. "It should have been done with some chance for the people concerned to make their case. That was all provided for in the act, but they just went beyond it. That riled me."[32]

The dismantling and privatization of Canada's transportation and energy sectors have continued since my father's death, under both Conservative and Liberal governments. Petro-Canada, for example, went to the private sector in 1991, CN Rail in 1995. Current proposals at various levels to try to combat budget deficits by continuing to sell off federal or provincial Crown assets — some of them, like Atomic Energy of Canada Limited, of strategic importance and delicacy — would rile him even more.

"A SLICK WAY TO SKIN THE PUBLIC"
(From a 1980 article[33])

"Privatization." I was introduced to this hideous word, and foolish and destructive idea, about a year ago [by] a high civil servant. He embarked on a nonstop oration on "privatization," its wonders and its glories.

The torrent of words left me a little uncertain about some of the details. I do know that education was to become a matter of a contract between parent and teacher. Like most other public services, it would be contracted out. By the time he had finished, he had left the public sector little, if anything, beyond defence, taxation, and the punishment of crime. He may not have left even those.

The orator gave me to understand that all this was the latest thing, intellectually ... Unfortunately, the fad has been taken up by both the British and Canadian Conservative parties. In Canada its most blatant, and lunatic, manifestation has been the proposal to dismantle Petro-Canada, handing over to private enterprise all its activities that make a profit and keeping for the taxpayers all the rest — at any rate until they made a profit.

There may be a particular case for handing over a particular public enterprise to the private sector. or a particular private enterprise to the public sector. But each case should be judged on its merits, not on the basis of some high-blown general notion or academic catchword. Only solid, practical reasons, not anti-socialist zeal or abstract theories of "free enterprise" (which often means unbridled monopoly or oligopoly) should govern public policy on what ought to be nationalized (or provincialized, or municipalized) or "privatized."

"Neo-conservatism," of which "privatization" is the first instalment, looks to me like just a fancy name for the biggest international romp ever mounted by the rich for skinning the poor. It is just a slick, highfalutin synonym for something very far from "neo" and much closer to the very old "Every man for himself, and devil take the hindmost."

"Privatization" and the "neo-conservatism" from which it springs should be consigned to the rubbish heap where they belong, before they rob and enslave us.

Given the wide range of functions involved in good government, how is the sharing of those responsibilities worked out within the complex framework of a federation? In Canada, the Constitution specifies certain provincial and federal powers, but within that framework there is often flexibility, and the balance and mechanisms for implementing it continue to evolve.

My father believed that jurisdictional issues between Canada and the provinces should be decided based on what would best serve the public good in every part of the country. As detailed in the next chapter, this, for him, most often meant that the central government should be in charge.

Foremost among his "solid, practical reasons" for taking this position was the need for what he called "a real country," a national presence strong enough to preserve and build on what Canadians had already achieved in the way of shared prosperity, social programs, and regional equality.

"Only a real country, with a powerful national Government and Parliament, can have any hope of controlling inflation and restoring full employment," he said. "Only a real country can maintain the unemployment insurance, the old age [and] disability pensions, the family allowances and child tax credits, the medicare, which we now enjoy. Only a real country can give the people of the poorer provinces anything like modern educational and social services."[34]

Dad was uneasy about the considerable shift of power away from the central government that had taken place in the years since Confederation. It struck him as a dangerous illusion to suppose that transferring even more powers to the provincial level would be beneficial. At a 1964 conference, he outlined the problems he saw with a number of such suggestions:

> I am afraid some of [these] proposals could destroy or fatally weaken the federal power to stimulate economic growth and integral job creation, to control inflation, and to keep in order our international accounts ... [They] may lead to economic distortions well beyond those necessary to preserve historical collectivities and help disadvantaged provinces or regions. They might impoverish the population of the country and of all provinces ... At the least, there would too often be a

useless, even wasteful duplication; a formidable pile-up of paper; a multiplication of committees, an almost endless series of delays, rampant paralysis of the conduct of highly important public business.[35]

Another major concern was the huge and growing challenge of maintaining some control over our own economy in a globalized world. "If we are going to do anything in the way of promoting Canadian economic independence," he declared, "we are going to need a strong central government, at least as strong as the central government we have now … We are going to need that primarily for two reasons: first, to prevent the 'have-not' provinces from opening their gates as wide as the sky to external investment; and second, to compensate those provinces for development they might have had [without] the measures considered necessary to promote the national interest.[36]

Up against the enormous power of global corporations, he said, a fragmented collection of smaller governments operating from the provincial level would be especially vulnerable. "To deal with [the corporations] effectively, we [will] have to have international controls," he said. "This leads us on to a vast uncharted sea. We certainly cannot have international controls of multi-national corporations unless we have effective national states to take part in creating those controls. The problem of creating such controls from a series of fragments of existing nations simply compounds the enormous difficulties which already confront us in any attempt of this sort."[37]

Those fears are more relevant than ever nowadays, with the World Trade Organization and a plethora of trade and investment agreements infringing on practically every aspect of our lives. If Canadians across the country are to have any hope of controlling or even influencing our livelihoods, our environment, and our collective destiny now and in the future, we need a national voice that is able and willing to make itself heard in global forums on our behalf.

Dad's commitment to equality and fairness for all citizens was a further reason why he was reluctant to see any further provincialization of powers. As a proud fifth generation Newfoundlander, and part Nova Scotian, he was particularly aware of the risks of requiring smaller provincial governments to take on what were essentially national responsibilities: dealing with macroeconomic problems; shouldering the costs of health care and social programs to meet national standards; providing support for culture and heritage.

Downloading more federal responsibilities to the provincial level, he predicted, would widen the gaps between richer and poorer provinces, and weaken the broader Canadian identity. Assigning cultural matters exclusively to the provincial domain, for example, would not only mean abandoning the concept of Canadian culture as such, it would also be both impractical and unfair.

"The bland assumption that all the provinces are able to go in for this sort of thing," he wrote in 1979, "flies in the face of reality. The big, rich provinces can do it, [but] with what consequences? The small, poor ones cannot; at any rate without massive help from that central government which [these] recommendations would enfeeble."[38]

Behind these concerns lay factual evidence gathered over years of observing Canada's economic and political realities. According to historian Alan Whitehorn, "Your dad had a vision, like many in the CCF, that the only way we were going to survive as a society and provide a helping hand was with a strong presence of the federal government. The old CCFers were quite skeptical of decentralization of power to the provinces. They had seen in the 1930s a number of provinces on the verge of bankruptcy, and the magnitude of the problems was beyond the scope of provincial boundaries. So if there was a solution, it would have to be at the level of the government of Canada, if not at a higher level."

For Dad and many of his contemporaries, Whitehorn said, "the federal government was probably a more benevolent force, not only for redistributing the wealth in Canada, but as a force for democracy. Too often in the past provincial governments had had a parochial authoritarian culture — the Union Nationale government in Quebec, Social Credit in Alberta. The most famous example is of course the Padlock Law in Quebec, [which] inspired your Dad and others to challenge the unconstitutional approach of a number of provincial governments." In other words, it was not abstract political theory that made those social democrats wary of decentralization; it was their own concrete experience.

The years did nothing to shake my father's conviction that if large chunks of national jurisdiction were to be handed over to the provinces, Canada would risk becoming nothing more than a collection of semi-independent minor states with little power or influence, at home or in an increasingly inter-dependent world. He warned that if this trend continued, the central government and Parliament would be reduced to "merely marginal conveniences, to do for the glorious and immortal Provinces the odd jobs they could not somehow do for themselves."[39]

Over the past few decades, under an increasingly decentralized system, various provincial governments have indeed used their growing power to wage war on federal involvement in areas like labour, health care and the environment. In too many cases, enforceable national standards aimed at ensuring equality among citizens, whatever region they happened to live in, have fallen by the wayside, despite their constitutional legitimacy and their practical benefits. As a result, we have suffered from an inter-provincial race to the bottom as provinces compete with each other to curry favour with the private sector and attract big-time corporate investment.

One example of this fragmentation was the dismantling, in the mid-1990s, of the Canada Assistance Plan (CAP). The CAP used to require provincial programs to meet national standards for federally funded social programs. It was replaced with the much looser Canada Health and Social Transfer (CHST), giving not only Quebec but all the provinces essentially free rein to do with the federal money as they wish.

Dad had pointed out some years earlier the dangers of abandoning enforceable national standards set by an act of Parliament in order to substitute vague phrases like "compatibility with national objectives."

"What does 'compatible' mean?" he asked. "It may mean simply not flying smack in the face of what the [federal] government has said. You might have the situation between a province and the government of Canada [with] the government of Canada saying 'Well, yes, all right, you've got a token program, you're doing something about child care, it doesn't fly in the face of our policy, so all right, you get the money.'"

When national standards give way to such broad generalities, the stage is set for a deteriorating patchwork of policies and programs that weaken the system as a whole and aggravate disparities between provinces. The vision of equality for Canadians from coast to coast to coast gets blurrier, and the ability of our national government to do anything about it effectively disappears.

The two decades since my father's death have seen a serious diminishment of the role of government in Canada, in terms of both perception and reality.

With the notable exception of whatever the powerful choose to define as "security matters," there has been a relentless push to reduce the ability of governments to develop pro-active policies, implement regulations, build effective programs or own and control economic entities.

Many of the government functions that Dad fought so hard to win, and then to defend — policies and programs like universal medicare, unemployment insurance, affordable housing — have been picked away at, starved of funds, or stripped of effective authority. Almost all political parties now promote tax cuts in their election platforms, feeding the resentful ignorance that defines all taxes as infringements on personal liberty, rather than as payment for public services and investments in the common good. And far too often, governments at all levels have put their authority and their resources at the service of global corporations and our own privileged elite. This is ultimately a betrayal of their oath of office — their responsibility to act in the best interests of the people as symbolized by the Crown.

As Canadians come to realize the consequences of what has been happening, we have the option of changing course. Although the government detractors, the "free enterprise" cheerleaders, and the "province-worshippers" have indeed managed to undermine much of what we know as Canada, they have not to date succeeded in entrenching their destruction in the supreme law of the land. Constitutionally, Canadians have not shut the door to an eventual reversal of these disintegrative trends.

We need not go on maligning government as evil. We need not continue the downward slide of deregulation, privatization, and provincial power grabs. My father set an example, never ceasing to demand that governments fulfill their true role as the servants of the people, and implement our traditional shared values of equity and compassion.

However battered and bruised our political structures may be, we still possess the essential framework for responsible government — a Constitution that allows us, if we so choose, to take back our country and restore the vital role of government in our lives.

CHAPTER TWELVE

Navigating the Constitution: A Citizen's Roadmap

> A Canadian Constitution should be a working plan for the peace, order and good government of the Canadian community.... The most important thing about it is not that it should be pretty, or incorporate the latest thing from Paris or Moscow or Westminster or Brasilia, but that it should work, and work for Canada.
> — "Our Present Discontents," Acadia University, 1968[1]

Not for nothing did people refer to Eugene Forsey as Canada's leading constitutional authority. The Constitution was my father's vocation, his perennial passion, the field of his most detailed and extensive expertise. His fascination with it spanned his years in academia, his work with the labour movement, his sojourn in the Senate, and his "un-retired" retirement. It was, in fact, his lifelong hobby — surely as complex and consuming a hobby as anyone could wish for.

Our country's Constitution is complex and sophisticated, evolving as it has over hundreds of years. Its proper implementation by citizens and politicians therefore requires detailed knowledge of its intricacies, and full respect for its principles. My father had both, and he put them to use in defence of democracy and social justice.

The role of constitutional watchdog is needed more than ever in these days of prime ministerial prerogative, disdain for Parliament, and staged election threats. Yet the knowledge necessary for that role is seriously lacking. Canada is suffering an epidemic of constitutional ignorance and misrepresentation, not only amongst the general public, but also among many of the academics, media people, and politicians who ought to be implementing and defending the democracy our Constitution embodies.

Given this national knowledge deficit and the dangers it represents, it is more important than ever to draw on the vast store of written and recorded constitutional material that my father left behind. Much of it continues to be publicly available, and it makes informative and often entertaining reading, but a comprehensive review would fill volumes. My purpose here is both more modest and more urgent: to set out the main tenets of Eugene Forsey's constitutionalism in clear terms that speak to Canadians today, so as to put that resource once again at the service of the common good.

In order to grasp the essence of my father's constitutional expertise and put it to work, we need to acknowledge how his fundamental assumptions apply to political systems. These prior convictions show up again and again in various forms throughout his writings, and they represent the unshakable foundation for the specific positions he took.

First of all, at the risk of repeating myself, I must highlight his insistence that government exists to serve the common good. "His whole thrust," John Matheson recalled, "was that through the agency and exigencies of government, we were going to live better together as human beings. We were going to make peace, we were going to distribute wealth more equitably, we were going to play fair in our system with everybody." Dad knew, of course, that governments often fail to live up to this ideal, but it nonetheless remained for him their only raison d'être.

Second, he believed that structure is necessary for a free and equal society. Where structure is lacking, there are no safeguards against abuse, and the door is open for what he termed "the dictatorship of whoever can shout the loudest or shake the biggest fist."[2] It is not accidental that he entitled his 1974 book of constitutional essays *Freedom and Order*. "Democracy is not just a matter of majority vote" he wrote. "It is self-rule *within a constitutional structure which makes it possible*. Destroy the structure and the self-rule is gone."[3]

Next, a political framework must be functional. My father's approach was eminently practical. "A constitution should be a working plan for governing a community," he said, "and the emphasis is on 'working.' ... Let us ask of any proposal, 'Will it work? Is it the proposal which will best serve the purpose? Will it do good, or harm; and if it is likely to do both, will it do more good than harm, or less?'"[4]

The fourth key element here is his conviction that facts matter, words have meanings, and reason is essential. As already noted, Dad was appalled by the historical inaccuracies, verbal juggling, and sloppy thinking that littered the constitutional landscape. In his view, relying on "pseudo-history," magic phrases or vague generalizations served only to "cloud the real issues and befuddle people's minds," making sensible and balanced discussion impossible.[5]

Finally, the spirit of our Constitution is vital to any application of its specific rules and conventions. Decency and fair play, honesty, moderation, responsibility, and respect for the principles and the symbols representing those ideals — these, for Dad, were the elements that gave our Constitution its life and strength, its ability to serve the interests of the people. Without that spirit, he said, "our whole system crumbles into ruins."[6]

My father was also a constitutional nationalist. He valued the uniqueness of the Canadian Constitution, its roots in the British parliamentary tradition, its respect for our two official languages, its ability to evolve as our country evolved. He saw it as a key element of the Canadian identity.

"Anyone who compares our Constitution with any other," he declared, "will soon discover that, constitutionally at least, we unmistakably have an identity; our Constitution differs markedly from any other, as it should, since it is intended to govern us, not some other people. I cannot for the life of me see how we can enhance our identity by trying to make ourselves look more like somebody else."[7]

These, then, were the philosophical underpinnings of his approach, the table on which he laid out his constitutional roadmap. That roadmap can help Canadians navigate the highways and byways of our system of government, identify its major contours, and locate its landmarks as we continue our political journey through its terrain.

My father's own constitutional writings are actually more like a road atlas than a regular map. The dedicated traveller wants all the information — a large-scale depiction of every back road, every stream or beaver pond, every nook and cranny in every area they may be passing through. Each page of the atlas therefore shows in detail a segment of the whole, and a locator map at the front shows how they all fit together. Similarly, most of Dad's constitutional essays, articles, and letters deal in depth with some particular political circumstance or event, some specific aspect of the larger system. In what follows, I have tried to sketch out a sort of locator map for his constitutional atlas.

Five fundamental features emerge clearly from that massive body of work as the basis of the Canadian Constitution: the primacy of Parliament, responsible cabinet government, the role of the Crown, the rule of law, and our unique federal structure.

The Primacy of Parliament

The keystone of our form of democracy is Parliament — the House of Commons and the Senate at the national level, (the legislatures provincially), and the monarch.[8]

Dad called Parliament "the very Ark of the Covenant of the Canadian tradition."[9] It is indeed the nation's ultimate authority, second only to the electorate that it represents. The primacy of Parliament over the executive government was a people's victory won in England through generations of struggle, and it is entrenched at the heart of our Constitution. The April 2010 ruling by House of Commons Speaker Peter Milliken recognized and reaffirmed this principle in the face of an attempt by Prime Minister Stephen Harper's government to withhold information Parliament had requested. The Speaker, with hundreds of years of history to back him up, ruled that the government must do Parliament's bidding, whether it wants to or not.

It is also Parliament, not the government in power, that actually makes the laws that rule us. A government can propose a bill, but it is the MPs and senators or the members of the provincial legislatures who decide whether or not it will become law. Those people are our democratic representatives, and it is their majority votes that finally determine the political decisions that are made.

But the functions of Parliament involve much more than simply voting. "Parliament is not just a voting place," Dad wrote. "It is also, pre-eminently, essentially, a talking place, a *parlement* ... Parliamentary government is not just a matter of counting heads instead of breaking them. It is also a matter of using them. It is government by discussion, not just by majority vote."[10]

Perhaps surprisingly, that description has often been most clearly true of the Senate. Based on his own observation and experience, Dad staunchly defended the upper house as a chamber of "sober second thought," where legislation is thoroughly reviewed and often made more effective and humane.[11] Noting as well its largely non-partisan investigative role, and the practical limits on its powers, he affirmed its "value as a protector of the public's right to be heard, [and] its indispensability for the proper working of our parliamentary system of government."[12]

The ideal of "government by discussion" is far from new. "Talking until all agree" is a time-honoured tradition for the people of many Aboriginal cultures, reflecting a basic philosophy that is vital to participatory democracy. Dad likewise believed that many heads are better than few, and that the questioning and explaining, the shaping and reshaping, the give and take involved in honest discussion eventually result in far better decisions than simple yes-or-no voting.

To what extent are Canadians truly "governed by discussion" these days? Viewers of Question Period in the House of Commons or even actual debates on the parliamentary television channel may feel they are watching little more than schoolyard skirmishes, or at best a choreographed spectacle. There may be some sort of discussion going on, but not much in the way of government.

WHY KEEP THE SENATE?
(From a 1974 article[13])

Every federation, old and new, has an upper house, and precisely because it is a federation. The states, provinces or regions which make it up insist on being represented as such in the federal legislature. The smaller and less populous ones are always afraid that a legislature based solely on "rep by pop" will overlook or override their interests. They want protection against the passing of legislation that would injure them.

The Senate as now constituted does much good, and is politically too weak to do any serious harm. What good?

First, detailed revision of legislation, with an opportunity for all interested parties to have a full hearing. The Senate has an immense reservoir of legal and administrative talent and experience, and its committees do this legal and revisory work efficiently, thoroughly and cheaply.

Second, investigation of public problems. Senate committees come much cheaper than royal commissions, and their reports very often lead to changes in government policy and legislation, fairly promptly.

Third — if rarely — emergency protection of the people against some gross violation of liberties, or legislative proposals which would threaten the very existence of the nation, or bills to which a substantial proportion of the population is, manifestly, furiously opposed. In the last 40 years the Senate has, to my knowledge, never thrown out a bill, and only once insisted on an amendment — when it felt that the measure gave a minister unwarranted arbitrary powers....

Most of the proposed reforms of the Senate I have seen would give it more power to make a nuisance of itself, which is not what it should be. A Senate appointed by provincial governments would give those governments their own private monkey-wrenches to dislocate the national political machinery. The Senate was not intended to represent provincial governments, [but] ... to represent provincial and regional interests in national legislation and policy.

As noted in Chapter 3, my father, too, lamented the decline he saw in the standards of parliamentary debate since he had first sat in the Gallery as a boy, rivetted by the many "superb speakers" expounding their arguments. He acknowledged that in modern times, what goes on in the House of Commons has been restricted and impoverished, due not only to the complexity of the issues and the huge masses of legislation to be considered, but also to the changes in — and abuses of — parliamentary procedure over the years.

In addition, globalization and related forces are shifting the locus of power from the political to the corporate realm, further weakening the effectiveness of our democratic structures. Global economic pressures are cited to excuse government inaction on climate change; the threat of challenges under NAFTA or the WTO discourages legislative progress on the environment and social programs; and a revolving door between government offices and corporate board rooms almost makes lobbying itself redundant.

Nonetheless, our federal and provincial parliaments do continue to discuss all new laws, government budgets, and many other matters of public interest. The people we elect to represent us do this constantly, both in committees and in the legislative body as a whole, shaping, revising, and on occasion even blocking proposed legislation. This legislative work constitutes one of the two central functions of Parliament in Canada's constitutional democracy.

Responsible Cabinet Government

Parliament's other essential function is to determine who will actually do the governing. In our system, the executive — the prime minister or premier and the other cabinet ministers who form the government — is a creature of the elected legislature. They must depend on the people's elected representatives to stay in power, for they can be thrown out of office by a parliamentary vote of censure or non-confidence in the House of Commons.

This means that decisions on who will govern are made not just in a general election every four years or so but on an ongoing basis, whenever Parliament is in session. If a majority of MPs don't like what the existing government wants to do, they can force its resignation and open the way for an alternative. This powerful accountability mechanism is what makes every cabinet literally "responsible" to Parliament, and through Parliament to the electors.

When properly understood and adhered to, this aspect of the system ensures "real responsibility" in the political sphere.[14] When it is ignored or subverted, however, democracy itself disappears. As my father put it: "A system in which Parliament exists, debates, votes, only at the pleasure of a jack-in-office, is a snare and a delusion."[15]

This direct cabinet responsibility constitutes one of the most important differences between our way of governing and that of the United States. In his popular handbook, *How Canadians Govern Themselves*, my father called the American system "neither responsible nor responsive.... Parliamentary-cabinet government, by contrast, is both." He explained that in the US and other republics, the president and the Congress are elected separately, for fixed terms, and they stay in office until their respective terms are over, even if the executive and legislative branches are seriously at odds.

"In the United States, president and Congress can be locked in fruitless combat for years on end. In Canada, the government and the House of Commons cannot be at odds for more than a few weeks at a time. If they differ on any matter of importance, then, promptly, there is either a new government or a new House of Commons."[16]

The first of those alternatives — a new government with the same elected Parliament — has been too often neglected, with huge consequences for the country. Eighty-odd years ago, Mackenzie King created his own twisted version of the events of the constitutional crisis of 1926 to bamboozle a disconcerted electorate into returning him to power.[17] Ever since, the mistaken notion that a prime minister always has the inalienable right to get Parliament dissolved and call an election has persisted in many quarters, based on a perilously misguided interpretation of "democracy." Dad's eloquent and comprehensive arguments against that notion, most notably his Ph.D. thesis on dissolution, may well have prevented the total loss of the constitutional principles involved, but the danger remains.

Canadians were forcibly reminded of the forms that danger can take after the new Conservative Party formed a minority government in 2006. In his first term in office, Stephen Harper developed a strategy of declaring every government bill a matter of confidence, effectively enabling him to bend an irresolute and divided Parliament to his will. Like Mackenzie King before him, he exploited the myth that if a government was defeated in the House on a matter of confidence, it automatically meant a fresh election, with all its attendant hassle, public expense, and perceived risk to the opposition parties. Harper got away with this game because too few people understood or were willing to implement the basic principles of responsible government.

"In a Parliament which is recently elected," my father wrote, "if one government cannot carry on with the existing House, and an alternative government is possible, and there is no great new issue of public policy, then the government which cannot carry on should resign and make way for one that can ... Politicians have no right to inflict on us the conspicuous waste of a series of general elections just because we elect a Parliament that does not suit them. It is our Parliament, not theirs. They are our servants, not our masters."[18]

If the governing party has a majority in the House of Commons, the power of MPs to hold the government responsible is vastly reduced in practical terms. MPs on the government side rarely defy party discipline and break ranks, particularly when their dissenting votes might tip the balance and lead to defeat. But with a minority government, the balance of power is held by MPs who are from neither the government nor the official Opposition. These members can choose to either keep the government in office or force a change, simply by throwing their support behind one side or the other. That possibility can exercise a strong persuasive influence on policy decisions — a dynamic Dad appreciated.

"When a government knows it may be hanged in a fortnight," he said, adapting a phrase from Dr. Johnson, "the knowledge may broaden its mind wonderfully. Having to get support from outside its own party may not only help a government to do good and sensible things, but also prevent it from doing bad and foolish things. This is just as important, and may even be more so. A government with a clear majority may go lickety-split in the wrong direction. A government without a clear majority is more likely to stop, look and listen."[19]

"Minority government," he went on, could "confer on us some incidental benefits not to be despised. It could restore some of the lost power of the House of Commons and of individual members. We might once again have real debates, speeches which changed votes, government by discussion."[20]

Minority Government – 'Problem' or Promise?[21]

Minority government can be not a "problem" but an opportunity, not a threat but a promise ... We may have to learn to live with [it]. It may have certain inconveniences. It will certainly be nerve-wracking at times. But it may turn out to give us quite tolerable or even very good legislation and administration ... If we use our brains we can survive any amount of minority government, even thrive on it ...

[A] popular Canadian notion about minority government is that it is necessarily bad — incompetent, weak, indecisive, if not worse — [and] that it cannot last. This is false ... The official theory has seemed to be that elections are held to give some party a clear majority, and that if one election does not do it, there must be another at the earliest possible moment. The electors have just done their sum wrong and must be made to do it over again until they get it right ... Are we to go on spanking them by a series of general elections, once every ten months or so, till they pass?

Most people presumably vote for the party they think best in the hope that it will get a clear majority to carry out the policies they favour. But no one except a clairvoyant can tell beforehand whether any party will get a clear majority ... The supporters of all parties may persist, election after election, in voting for the party they think best. They may refuse to be bullied into voting for anyone else ... If that means minority government, then the politicians will just have to lump it. It is our Parliament, not theirs.

Minority government may bring home to us that what is constitutional depends ultimately on what is reasonable, on the application of what Sir Robert Borden (too optimistically, I fear) called "the commonplace quality of common sense." Behind the precedents, behind the dicta of authorities, lies reality. As long as any one party has a clear majority, we can get along fairly well on clichés, rules of thumb, the wooden application of time-honoured phrases. When no party has a clear majority ... we have to look at the realities the phrases were intended to explain. We have to use our minds, rendering "the debt of our reason we owe unto God."

While he acknowledged the gap in this regard between the ideal and the contemporary reality, he also affirmed the potential of responsible cabinet government to truly represent the will of the people and act in the public interest. All his efforts were aimed at making sure that potential was maximized.

The Role of the Crown

"Responsible government means not only responsibility to Parliament, or to the electorate," my father wrote, "but also responsibility for the interests of the nation as a whole." Those interests are represented by the Crown, "the … embodiment of the interests of the whole people" — not a particular group or interest or party.[22]

This principle was the foundation of Dad's lifelong attachment to the monarchy — an attachment that, I confess, puzzled and even mildly irritated me for years. Why, with his radical views on so many things, would he cling so tenaciously to some quaint relic of a feudal age? Why, as a progressive Canadian nationalist, would he remain so obstinately loyal to a British institution, especially one that seemed to symbolize not only arbitrary political authority but social and economic hierarchy as well?

As usual, though, when I delved further into this apparent contradiction in his thinking, it began to dissolve before my eyes. It wasn't that he liked everything about the monarchy. Even back in the 1930s, he publicly agreed with his friend Frank Underhill's condemnation of the "irrational mystical attitude" of some people towards the Crown.[23] I'm sure he would also have been glad to see major reductions in royal wealth and complete elimination of the hanky-panky now so often associated with the Royal Family. But none of that was essential to the monarchy itself, and he was never one to throw out the baby with the bathwater.

Again, for him the essence of the monarchy was its impartial representation of the common interests of the citizenry as a whole, as opposed to the power and partisan interests of any particular government or political party. In that context, the trappings that make the monarchy such an easy target for criticism — feudal custom, aristocracy, wealth, and trans-Atlantic geography — were all irrelevant.

The role of the Crown as the ultimate representation of the Canadian people is the basis of the oath of loyalty to the monarch that has long been required of anyone becoming a Canadian citizen, accepting elected office, or taking a job in the civil service or the military. It represents the fact that citizens and public servants owe their allegiance, not to the particular government that happens to be in office, but to the common good of the whole nation as symbolized by the Crown.

The distinction is a crucially important one. As the Supreme Court made clear in 1985, the loyalty owed is to the Crown, not to the political party in power at any one time. This has far-reaching implications for cases where, for example, a soldier disobeys an order to commit a war crime, or a public servant "blows the whistle" to prevent serious harm to the public.[24]

On the practical level, the most direct role of the monarch or governor general in the democratic process is in safeguarding the process itself, ensuring that the protections built into our Constitution are brought into play whenever they are needed.

"It [is] *our* business ... to govern ourselves," my father wrote. [It's] the Queen's business to see that our power to govern ourselves is preserved, and that her servants, *our* servants, do not become our masters."[25]

In his Ph.D. thesis, "The Royal Power of Dissolution of Parliament in the British Commonwealth," and in his long crusade against the "rubber stamp theory" of the Crown, he drew on case after case to show the necessity of retaining these "reserve powers" to protect democracy. The governor general must be able and willing to ensure that the elected Parliament is allowed to do its job. In certain exceptional cases, that may involve refusing the advice of the ministry in power if that advice runs counter to the constitutional principles of responsible government.

Lord Byng's refusal of Prime Minister Mackenzie King's request for a dissolution in 1926 was one instance of this. Indeed, Dad described the PM's request as "utterly unprecedented and subversive of Parliamentary government."

"Parliament showed signs of deciding against him," my father wrote, "so he tried to prevent it from deciding at all. It was tantamount to allowing a prisoner to discharge the jury by which he was being tried ... If the Governor General had granted the request, he would have become an accomplice in a flagrant act of contempt for Parliament."[26]

THE GOVERNOR GENERAL AS DEFENDER OF DEMOCRACY
(From an unpublished paper, August 1984[27])

If no party gets a clear majority in [a] general election ... the incumbent Prime Minister can resign; the Governor General then asks the Leader of the Opposition to form a government. [Or], even if [he] has fewer seats than the official Opposition, he can meet the new House of Commons. If it supports him, he remains in office. If it defeats him, he resigns, and the Governor General sends for the Leader of the Opposition....

Any intervention by the Governor General would be grossly improper. It is not the business of the Governor General to decide who should form the Government. It is the business of the newly elected House of Commons.

[However], if the incumbent Government attempts to carry on for an extended period without meeting the new House, financing the country's business by means of Governor General's special warrants, then at some point Her Excellency would have the duty to insist that Parliament should be summoned; [and] to refuse to sign any more special warrants till it was summoned. She would have to say:

"Prime Minister, responsible cabinet government means government by a cabinet with a majority in the House of Commons. No one knows whether you have such a majority. The only way to find out is by summoning Parliament and letting it vote.... It is not for me to decide who shall form the Government; it is for the House of Commons. I cannot allow you to prevent the House of Commons from performing its most essential function. That would be to subvert the Constitution...."

The Governor General's action is our only protection against a gross violation of the very essence of our Constitution. The courts could do absolutely nothing. In law, the Government could stay in office for a very long time. True, it would have to summon Parliament within twelve months, ... but it could then prorogue [or] dissolve it and repeat the performance a year later ... The only protection against such conduct is the reserve power of the Crown ... to refuse such prorogation or dissolution, and, if necessary, to dismiss the Government which advised such prorogation or dissolution.

It was eighty-two years before Canadians were subjected to another such flagrant and subversive act by a prime minister — and this time, shamefully, it succeeded. In December 2008, Stephen Harper managed to persuade the governor general to prorogue the recently elected Parliament before it could pronounce judgment on his government. Dad would have led the denunciation of this travesty, echoing what he wrote in 1967:

> Ministers are not the people's masters but the Queen's servants, bound to let Parliament meet, bound to let it vote, bound to abide by its verdict unless there are substantial reasons of public policy for appealing to the electorate.
>
> But if a Prime Minister tries to turn Parliamentary responsible government into unparliamentary irresponsible government, only the Crown can stop him. Only the Crown can keep government responsible to the Parliament and Parliament to the people; only the Crown can prevent the Prime Minister, prime servant, from degenerating into a prime despot, the whole process into an elaborate farce, swindling the public at the public expense, with the public helpless to protect itself.[28]

My father was acutely aware of the sensitivity and complexity of the Crown's role in ensuring that the principles of cabinet responsibility were upheld. As "the indispensable centre of the whole parliamentary democratic order, the guardian of the Constitution, ultimately the sole protection of the people,"[29] the Crown had to remain strictly neutral in political terms. That is why he insisted that the governor general and lieutenant governors stay permanently aloof from partisan politics; for only by remaining impartial could they hope to fill such a delicate and important role.[30]

Given his understanding of the monarchy and its historical evolution in this country, Dad rejected its portrayal by some as a foreign relic of colonial times. For him, the title "Queen of Canada" was an accurate designation for an institution that was anything but foreign, one that "stands for a Canadianism which, while utterly loyal to Canada, looks beyond Canada. It reminds us that nationalism is not enough." As "Queen of a world-wide Commonwealth," he said, the sovereign also represents the rights and interests of people across the globe — an important element for anyone with a healthy wariness of narrow chauvinism.[31]

Dad's stubborn monarchism, then, was much more than an attachment to tradition, much more than just a question of not fixing what ain't broke. It expressed his wholly rational commitment to preserving both the democratic values and the practical advantages of the Canadian Constitution, in which the monarchy plays a quiet but vital part.

The Rule of Law

Another fundamental element of our political system is the principle that everyone in our society is subject to the law, which is created by the citizens through their elected representatives and impartially implemented by an independent justice system. The rule of law, together with the principle of judicial independence, plays a key role in thwarting the abuse of power. "No one, no matter how important or powerful, is above the law," my father wrote.[32] No government, company, group, or individual can impose their will on the courts; all must abide by a judge's decision whether they like it or not.

"Freedom depends on law. But law which can be set aside whenever the Cabinet sees fit, for as long as it sees fit, without Parliament or the people hearing a word about it, is not law at all. It is a shadow. It leaves the citizen utterly defenceless. Such liberties as he still appears to have are no longer rights, just favours of the Government in office ... Where no law is safe, no citizen is safe."[33]

If this assertion seems rather sweeping and theoretical, it is worth looking at what it means in practical terms. Take for example anti-pollution laws. If a government were allowed to exempt whomever they wished from rules and regulations enacted by Parliament and applied to everyone else, those rules and regulations would be worthless. The government and its friends would be above the law, free to wreak whatever havoc they pleased on the environment and the citizenry without facing any consequences.

And that happens. Despite the common belief that Canada's laws are generally followed in official circles, there are numerous exceptions, large and small, deliberate or otherwise. Dad devoted an entire chapter of *A*

Life on the Fringe to the uphill battles he and his colleagues on the Joint Committee on Regulations and Other Statutory Instruments had to fight against attempts by the government or the bureaucracy to bypass legislated requirements and ignore the rule of law.

Moreover, as noted in the previous chapter, some legislation seems actually designed to be subversive of its own purported intent. Canadians would be appalled to realize how many laws explicitly allow for exemptions, notably under their regulations, which do not always undergo parliamentary scrutiny. When such legislation is used to favour vested interests at the expense of the common good, the rule of law itself comes into question.

Bad laws, which may be unfair or worse, present a profound dilemma for citizens who may find themselves unable, for reasons of conscience, to obey, but who also respect the importance of maintaining the rule of law in a free society. In our flawed democracy, the usual advice about writing letters, signing petitions, and voting in elections may not be an adequate response in an urgent or dangerous situation.

It is in these situations that people may choose non-violent civil disobedience. When I joined with others on several such occasions to defy the law and risk arrest, my father never tried to dissuade me; indeed he was quite supportive. He himself, however, chose to fight for change mainly on the formal political and legal fronts, exercising eternal vigilance in the effort to maintain the rule of law as a bulwark of justice.

A Distinctive Federal Structure

Canada was founded in 1867 as a federal state with four provinces and two official languages. Today it has a vast land mass divided into ten provinces and three territories, with a population representing a multiplicity of cultures and origins.

My father's understanding of Canadian federalism, and of the shifting balance among its various elements, was based on both historical and contemporary realities. His description of the challenge that confronted the founders of our nation still rings remarkably true. "The Fathers of Confederation were faced with the task of bringing together small, sparsely populated communities, scattered over immense distances and divided by deep divergences of economic interest, language, religion, law and education. To all these problems, they could find only one answer: federalism."[34]

Right from the start, these innovative statesmen were determined that the new country should be "'one people and one government,' ... '*un people nouveau et puissant*,' ... 'a new nation, a new nationality,'" not a league of states or of sovereign or semi-independent provinces.[35] Each of the four provinces that joined to form Canada in 1867 had its own interests, but each was also cognizant of the interests of the whole. Confederation was worked out among them as a practical and forward-looking agreement to create a single nation, "*une grande et puissante nation*."[36] The record shows that it was never a question of a "pact" between two "founding peoples," or an agreement between English and French to co-operate for certain purposes—suggestions Dad decried as "fairy-tales."[37]

The Fathers established a federalism shaped to fit Canada's particular needs, to avoid the pitfalls and mistakes of the war-torn American republic they saw to the south, and to ensure "peace, welfare, and good government." (That was, in fact, the original phrase; the British Colonial office substituted "peace, order, and good government" in the wording of the BNA Act.)[38] They put in place a strong central government, charged with ensuring the well-being of the country as a whole, and provincial governments that were to be responsible for more local concerns. Special provisions guaranteed Quebec's retention of its own system of civil law, and the official use of French as well as English for both the Province of Quebec and the Dominion.

The British North America Act (the BNA Act, now the Constitution Act, 1867) deliberately gave the Dominion government broad powers, embracing all matters — foreseeable or otherwise — that were not specifically assigned to the provinces.[39] Since then, federal jurisdiction has been chipped away at, particularly in the years when interpretation was in the hands of the Judicial Committee of the British Privy Council, before Canada's Supreme Court assumed its full powers.

Dad referred to the members of the Judicial Committee as "the wicked Stepfathers of Confederation," and charged them with having "greatly weakened many of the central powers and in many respects turned our Constitution inside out and upside down."[40] But despite their rulings and other more recent attempts to amend the Constitution itself in that same direction, the federal government continues to retain many powers, and in some areas shares jurisdiction with the provinces.

My father supported the strong powers originally given to the central government in the BNA Act, including the constitutional mechanisms by which it could "disallow" or "reserve" provincial legislation that went against the country's interest. Although these mechanisms remain in the Constitution today, they have not been exercised in many years, and in practical terms they may even be defunct. Governments in Ottawa have been extremely reluctant to risk angering a powerful province by disallowing a law its legislature has passed, even in cases of the most outrageous Acts.[41]

In general, Dad was a pragmatist in regard to the division of powers. He believed jurisdiction should be divided or shared "on a functional basis, a basis of which can best do the job."[42] But for reasons explored in more detail elsewhere, he was wary of the indiscriminate broadening of provincial jurisdiction at the expense of the national government. "Our country," he noted, is "already the most decentralized federation in the world, with the possible exception of Switzerland. How much farther can we go without making Canada a political Cheshire cat, of which, you may remember, nothing remained but the smile?"[43]

It is not only the elements listed above — what might be termed our Constitution's basic content and principles — that make it uniquely suited to Canada as a modern evolving nation. There is another dimension to it that my father saw as one of its outstanding virtues: an inherent flexibility that enables it to adapt to changing realities. This is why he called it "one of the constitutional masterpieces of all time … marvellously framed to provide for the new, the unexpected, the unforeseen and unforeseeable."[44]

On a map, much vital information is conveyed through cartographical conventions such as contour lines and symbols, rather than being described in words. Similarly, Canada's Constitution consists of much more than its written documents — the Constitution Acts of 1867 and 1982, plus the more than twenty other acts or orders that are legally recognized as part of it.[45] Its unwritten elements — custom, practice and constitutional "convention" — play a key role, giving our system much of its flexibility and helping to make it user-friendly.

Dad stressed the fact that unlike the American Constitution, where every detail is spelled out, our own contains a number of gaps or "silences."

"Much of the working Constitution ... and not the least important part, is not written down at all. It is pure 'convention,' that is, habits, practices, usages, customs, which have grown out of repeatedly successful ways of dealing with particular problems, and which can be changed or abandoned when they cease to work satisfactorily, without any change at all in the law."[46]

Suggestions that all the gaps should be filled in drew his condemnation. He maintained that not only would any attempt to spell it all out be a labour of Sisyphus, it would effectively freeze the organic evolutionary process inherent in our present system and prevent further needed adaptations. If everything were formally codified in the written Constitution, then any change, however simple and appropriate, would require a lengthy and complex amendment process, and might well never happen at all.[47]

"Most of those 'silences,'" he said, "far from being defects in the BNA Act, are among its greatest glories. They leave us room to breathe, to move, to develop, to improvise, to innovate, to meet new situations by ... the exercise of common sense."[48]

Again, in constitutional matters as in other things, his emphasis was on using our heads. For him, common sense was the basis on which all constitutional conventions ultimately rest.

His respect for the flexibility built into our Constitution in this way was an important factor in the strong views he held on constitutional change. In order to meet changing needs or deal with new developments, he pointed to a whole range of existing options for adaptation and rebalancing, options that are regularly used as situations arise and our system evolves.

"Special needs ... can be met by administrative delegation, [as] in agricultural marketing and highway transportation, by concurrent legislation, as in family allowances, [and] by agreements between the Dominion and one or more provinces under which each government and legislature undertakes to use its powers in a specific way."[49]

As he explained to the Canadian Bar Association, "The advantage of such arrangements, as against constitutional change, is that they can be fairly easily and quickly changed if they do not work well."

"The BNA Act was never meant to be, nor should it be, exhaustive,"

Eugene signing copies of his popular handbook, How Canadians Govern Themselves, *at the annual meeting of the Human Rights Institute, Ottawa, 1986. (Courtesy Marguerite Ritchie and the Human Rights Institute, Ottawa)*

he reminded the lawyers. "It was meant to be, and is, just the skeletal framework of the Constitution. The people who want to get rid of the 'silences' would transform it from a skeleton into a straitjacket."[50]

It's not that my father was necessarily opposed to constitutional change. In fact, he pushed for it himself on several occasions over the years, notably with regard to the need for Dominion jurisdiction over unemployment insurance and certain other labour matters, and for a bill of rights to safeguard civil liberties. But his proposals were always geared to correcting specific problems, not to revamping the entire Constitution in order to suit some vaguely defined ideal. In his view, constitutional change could be justified only in the clear absence of an adequate alternative, and even then undertaken only with the greatest care.

"Let us never forget," he wrote, "that, because a constitution is what it is, changing it by formal amendment is an immensely serious business.... We are dealing not with abstractions but with lives: the lives of Canadians now living, and of Canadians yet unborn. It is therefore, in sober truth, like marriage in the Anglican *Prayer Book*: 'Not by any to be taken in hand unadvisedly, lightly, or wantonly, but reverently, discreetly, advisedly, soberly, and in the fear of God.'"[51]

This caution is what lay behind his formidable record of objections to the many schemes for constitutional change that kept cropping up during the last decades of his life. The Eugene Forsey papers include brief after brief, speech after speech, assessing and criticizing these efforts, among them various proposals put forward by Quebec academics and politicians during the 1960s, the 1972 Report of the Special Joint Committee on the Constitution, the 1978 Constitutional Amendment Bill, the 1979 Report of the Pepin-Robarts Task Force on National Unity, the Ryan proposals, the patriation package of 1981 and 82, and of course, the infamous Meech Lake Accord.

Perhaps it was a premonition of things to come that spurred him to say, as early as 1967: "Our Constitution is not a toy for politicians or professors to play with, or a canvas on which they can plaster constitutional surrealism or modern abstracts or pop art. The constitutional draftsman is an architect, not a painter."[52]

And the required architectural task was one of renovation, not of designing a whole new building. "The Fathers [of Confederation] wrought well," he wrote in 1962, "and laid our foundations deep and strong. But the building is still unfinished, and parts of it have suffered some damage through the years. It does not need a bombing squad or a wrecking crew. But it does need alterations, repairs, additions, the expansion of certain rooms; and all of us have to be made to feel at home in it."[53]

Although some of those renovations have since been carried out, our country is still regularly faced with the question of what further changes need to be made and how that should be done. Suggestions abound, and if Dad were here today he would still be responding in his inimitable style to each proposal, each new idea.

First he would check the proposal out for accuracy, to debunk any "fairy tales" it might be based on. He used to say that he was going to devote his declining years "to compiling a book of Canadian constitutional fairy tales, and it would have to be loose-leaf, because scarcely a day passes without some fresh addition."[54] To base discussions about constitutional change on false premises, he said, was both wrong and self-defeating.[55]

Next, he would run the idea through a series of tests for clarity, common sense, and practicality. Were there ambiguities that might lead to problems? What about implementation: would the plan work in practice? Exactly how would it deal with particular issues, specific scenarios? What would it lead to, what would be its logical outcome, what spin-off effects would naturally follow?

"Somebody has got to say, 'Look, what will work? What will not work, and why?' If you are deciding what you are going to do with the future of the country, it's no use vapouring off in the stratosphere somewhere. You've got to get down to brass tacks."[56]

He would look especially closely at how the new arrangement would affect the common good. What would the impact be on ordinary people, on workers, minorities, Aboriginal people, the poor, the unemployed, the people in the outlying regions of the country? What would it really turn out to mean in terms of things like health and social programs, the environment, regional disparities, civil liberties, people's control over their own lives, and how they govern themselves?

And would the proposed change and the method for accomplishing it be legal and democratic? Would it respect the rule of law, the primacy of Parliament, and the other pillars of our system of responsible government? Or might it undermine them? Might it weaken or conflict with citizens' existing rights?

In these and all other respects, he would insist that any amendment be properly drafted, with great care taken to prevent ambiguity and to ensure that it would not inadvertently create more problems than it would solve.

Finally, he would query the actual need for the change, and its political feasibility. Could the same purpose be accomplished in some simpler and better way, without a formal constitutional amendment? And could the change as proposed ever actually get through the necessary amending process? If not, then, he would ask, why spend the time and energy on it?

These were the criteria he used in responding to proposals for Senate reform. He pointed out that any change involving a constitutional amendment would require the approval of seven provinces with half the population, and given the differing provincial interests, it would have as much chance of being passed as he had of being named Archbishop of Canterbury![57] On the other hand, many useful reforms could be made without touching the Constitution.

"The present system of appointment leaves a good deal to be desired," he said. "We are short of opposition people and representatives of labour. I would like to see a guaranteed minimum number of opposition senators. And I agree with the [suggestion] that half the senators should be appointed by the central government from lists submitted by the provinces … This process would give us a much wider range of opinion than we have now, because you would have [provincial] governments of different political stripes. It would give us representation of various interests. experiences, and walks of life."[58]

My father's cautious approach to constitutional change grew out of his understanding of the Constitution itself and of the multitude of issues it embraced. That same understanding made him skeptical about recurring proposals for a Constituent Assembly coupled with a plebiscite or referendum to usher in a "new Constitution."

For one thing, he was adamant that we did not need "a new Constitution." Our old one, he said, "revised, improved, amended," would continue to serve us well.[59] Indeed, when we consider the constitutional mayhem that has plagued so many other countries — various Latin American republics that have gone through twenty or more "new" constitutions since the 1800s, modern-day African and Asian nations still struggling with the sorry legacy of colonialism, even the United States with its cumbersome and problematic electoral process — it seems clear that we could have done much worse.

Dad also had serious doubts as to whether a "Constituent Assembly" would be an appropriate or practical instrument for creating constitutional change. Because of the complexity of the task, just coming up with workable constitutional revisions for electors to vote on would require extensive experience and knowledge, as well as "political skills of the highest order."[60]

"A Constituent Assembly would probably produce not one draft constitution but a dozen. And if the drafts were submitted to the people, only by a miracle could the bewildered electors return a majority for any one of them. A Constituent Assembly is a recipe for chaos."[61]

Moreover, like John Ralston Saul, he was wary of plebiscites and referenda.[62] He felt they tended to be perilously simplistic — "superficially ultra-'democratic' device[s]" that "need very careful watching." Historically, they had often proved to be divisive, exacerbating differences rather than resolving them.[63] Still, in his last years he came out strongly in favour of the

Australian system for constitutional amendments, where the final stage of the process is a binding national referendum.[64]

He also saw possible value in such a vote in certain other special cases. "I think there's a good deal to be said for Mr. Patrick Boyer's bill for referenda on questions of major importance," he told Tom Earle in 1989. "For instance, if we'd had a referendum on the free trade question, that would have been defeated; the bulk of the people of the country didn't want it … You don't want a referendum on every bill that comes up, but … I think you could have adoption of binding referenda in certain cases."[65]

The more I read of Dad's work on the subject of constitutional change, the more I understand his caution as the logical consequence of his knowledge and experience. He wanted the very best for Canada, and he believed our present Constitution already provided a large measure of that. He was unwilling to see its vision, its values, or the flexible and well-tested practical mechanisms for governance that it embodied, put at risk through poorly-thought-out proposals, even those inspired by well-meaning reformist zeal.

However, he never denied the possibility of constitutional improvements, never retreated into a knee-jerk defence of the status quo. In fact, in a 1979 article he questioned whether anyone at all took such a position. "Does anyone argue that we should simply preserve the existing Constitution at the point it has now reached, that there should be no changes? Are there any 'stand-patters' in this debate? If so, on their demise, they should be stuffed and put in the national museum, which, by charging admission, could soon pay off the national debt."[66]

Eugene Forsey was no "stand-patter." He put a huge amount of time and energy into constructive criticism of proposed constitutional reforms, while actively encouraging the kinds of change he saw as worthwhile. Those who knew him would expect nothing less.

Despite his openness to sensible, well-thought-out constitutional change, my father has often been called a constitutional conservative. In the original sense of the word, this is accurate: as already noted, he believed in conserving things of value from the past, and he did not seek out change for its own sake. He was convinced that our present Constitution gave us "the most delicate, the most flexible, the most efficient form of government that the world has yet found, and the one most responsive to the public will."[67] It followed that such a system was well worth conserving, and any failures were likely to be due to it being honoured more in the breach than in the observance.

It is far from correct to assume, however, that Dad's constitutional conservatism represented some kind of contradiction with his views on social and economic issues. As the preceding pages show, his constitutionalism complemented and supported his commitment to the labour movement, human rights, and social justice. In both his theoretical work and his political practice, he used his constitutional expertise to defend ordinary citizens, minorities, and "have-nots," and to try to strengthen the national fabric so as to maximize the rights, freedoms and potentials of all Canadians.

This consistency with his progressive ideals doesn't mean that his work in the domain of the Constitution is beyond criticism. From my own present vantage point, I can see some gaps and "silences" in his constitutional writings, or at least some aspects he might have paid more attention to.

Largely missing from what he wrote is an examination of the deficiencies of our "first-past-the-post" electoral system, and the potential advantages of alternatives like proportional representation. The few references I did find, however, show his critical awareness of the distortions that result from the present system, and a generally favourable attitude towards alternatives.

For example, in a 1977 article he noted the dissatisfaction many people feel with our present system. "This dissatisfaction [is] increased by the way our electoral system works. In each constituency, whoever gets the largest number of votes gets the seats, though his vote may be much less than half the total. The result is that very few governments ever get a majority of the total popular vote."[68]

A case in point, as he told Tom Earle, was the Canada-US Free Trade Agreement, which was instituted against the will of the people. "Thanks to the first-past-the-post system in elections, the government, represent[ing] a minority of the electorate, came through with a large majority in the House of Commons," which then passed the agreement into law.[69] Such a situation, he said, "could of course be remedied by proportional representation. But try and get it! The minor parties which would gain by it can't get the majority to bring it in. The major parties which would lose by it, won't bring it in."[70]

In a discussion of Senate reform, he commented to the same effect. "A Senate elected by proportional representation could say to the Commons,

'We represent the people *better* than you do! No noise from the cheap seats, if you please!' [But] with proportional representation it's a case of '*Si jeunesse savait, si vieillesse pouvait.*' Those who want it have no power to get it; those who have the power don't want it."[71]

His assumption that we would likely never manage to switch to a different electoral system was probably the reason why he never really went into the pros and cons of proportional representation, preferential ballots, or a single transferable vote. Nor did he examine the various examples of alternative systems in use elsewhere, or explore their implications for federalism and democracy.

Yet even as I raise the issue, I can almost hear him urging us to do as he always did, to ask the questions that he would have asked. How do the various alternative proposals stand up in terms of practicality, logical consequences, legality, need, feasibility, impact on people and regions? Now that he's gone, we have to do our own homework on these things, "using our heads" as well as the tools he left us.

At the immediate practical level of parliamentary conventions and procedures, my father's primary concern was always to preserve democracy. During the 1956 Pipeline Debate, he protested with all his might — and with some effect — against the St. Laurent government's authoritarian use of the closure rule to limit debate, which constituted an abuse of power and a departure from accepted parliamentary practice at the time.[72] But as the years passed and the use of closure became commonplace, he seems to have come to accept it as a *fait accompli*, perhaps even a necessary evil in view of the complexity and sheer volume of legislation required to govern in modern times. He did note that in the British Parliament, it is the Speaker, not the government, who decides whether and when to apply closure — something that keeps a more effective check on its potential abuse.[73]

He lamented the way closure and other changes to the rules have effectively stripped the opposition parties of the power they used to wield even when the government had a majority.

> Till 1913, it was possible for an Opposition in the House of Commons to force a government to go to the people in a general election. There were no time limits on speeches. There was no closure. There was no time allocation for

the successive stages of a bill. So an Opposition could, by obstruction, by filibustering, preserve the right of the people to decide on a new issue of crucial importance.

It was a formidable power ... to be exercised only on rare occasions, on issues of first-class magnitude to which there was strong and widespread opposition across the country. But it is a power the Opposition in the Commons has now lost. The last vestige disappeared with the adoption of the new rule that prohibits the long bell-ringing the Conservatives used so effectively against the Trudeau government.

Now, therefore, if there is a great new issue of public policy on which the electors have not been consulted, only the Senate can protect their right to be consulted. Only the Senate can force a general election, as it did on Free Trade. Then, of course, it accepts the verdict of the electors."[74]

If the official Opposition in the House of Commons is now rendered relatively powerless whenever a government has a majority, individual MPs have even less clout. Whatever side of the House they are on, their hands are effectively tied by the unwritten obligation to vote the party line, an obligation vigorously enforced by top-down leaders and their parliamentary "whips." This rigid party discipline undermines the primacy of Parliament by severely limiting the extent to which our elected representatives can truly represent us and hold governments accountable.

My father's writings on responsible government contain some discussion of this issue, but not a great deal. It's not that he was unaware of the problem. He even took a rather morbid pleasure in quoting the song from Gilbert and Sullivan's *Iolanthe*:

> When in that House MPs divide,
> If they've a brain and cerebellum too,
> They've got to leave that brain outside,
> And vote just as their leaders tell 'em to.

"That is somewhat of an exaggeration," he told an interviewer, "but it's not too far from the British and Canadian system of government."[75]

He noted, however, that while this was true of the House of Commons, the Senate was relatively free of rigid partisanship, particularly in its committee work. It was a freedom that he practised himself throughout his nine years in the upper house, and he thought it should be expanded.

"A reform many of us are rather keen on," he said, "is that on appointment, every senator should sever completely his ties with any political party, at least for senatorial purposes. Once we are in here, we should regard ourselves as Independents. There should be no party whips, and on every bill we should vote exactly as we see fit, not on the basis of what the whip tells us. That is what I have done all along. No whip has ever come near me; if he did he would get a flea in his ear, I can tell you!"[76]

Dad would clearly have liked to see more such flexibility in "the other place" as well. In his presentation to the Special Committee on Reform of the House of Commons in January 1985, he called for a slackening of party discipline in the Commons to give back-bench MPs more clout, although he cautioned against attempting this through formal changes to the Constitution. He also noted that in the early days of our own Parliament, as in the current British system, non-essential government bills were often voted down without the government feeling obliged to resign or ask for a dissolution.[77] This is a particularly important point to note if we hope for a measure of parliamentary co-operation and stability in times of minority government.

My father clearly felt some discomfort with the increasingly marginal role of elected members, but the problems go even deeper. For one thing, ever since the days of the Trudeau government, there has been a growing concentration of power in the person and office of the prime minister, a trend exacerbated by the influence of American-style presidential politics on our public life and the corresponding cult of "The Leader" in political parties.

I'm not sure to what extent Dad acknowledged this gradual but relentless shift of real power into the hands of the prime minister and cabinet and away from Parliament. However, one of the many things he objected to in the Meech Lake Accord was the huge power it would have given to the prime minister and the premiers through the entrenchment of first ministers' conferences, running the risk of reducing Parliament and the legislatures "to not much more than echoes" in certain respects.[78]

At an even more fundamental level, one might view as naïve my father's apparent faith in the potential for governments, under our Constitution, to act independently for the good of the people in the face of globalized power and wealth. This naïveté is most apparent in some of his writings from the 1930s and 1940s, when he was still putting much of his hope into the idea of "planning from the bottom." As the years passed, events obliged him to acknowledge major limitations on the power even of national governments to carry through the kind of comprehensive planning he and his socialist comrades had once envisioned.

Still, I don't think he ever deluded himself into believing that a good system of government could protect us from all harm. Rather, I think he saw our Constitution as a necessary though not sufficient bulwark against political abuse, a proven and flexible framework that can continue to provide the best possible options for us as citizens to reclaim the power that is rightfully ours — if only we will recognize those options and use them.

In order to do that, we must insist on the primacy of the constitutional principles that Dad explained with such eloquence and defended so fiercely. Those enduring principles underlie and form the basis for all the precedents, all the conventions, all the rules. Every bit of our Constitution — all the written and unwritten pieces that comprise its intricate whole — make sense only if intelligently understood and applied according to those principles.

It is a mistake to argue, as some supposed "constitutional experts" insist on doing, that because a particular prime minister or governor general made a particular decision in a particular situation, therefore the same decision must be made in any similar situation forever after. The "precedent" may or may not have been well grounded in the applicable constitutional principles, and if it was not, it should not be used to justify further aberrations. Fundamental principle and common sense must take priority over precedent.

In the midst of one of his many battles to defend our constitutional heritage, my father wrote to Mr. Meighen: "All hope of social or economic or any other kind of reform disappears if we surrender that most incomparable instrument."[79] His long years of constitutional work were rooted in that same conviction: that unless we keep and strengthen the democratic means by which we govern ourselves, none of what we value and strive for is safe.

The constitutional roadmap he left us can help guide us on our way.

Chapter Thirteen

One Love: Quebec and Canada

I have spent most of my life in or on the edge of Quebec. I have Quebec ancestors. I lived in Montreal for sixteen years. I thought I was going to spend the rest of my life there, and looked forward to doing so. But I say losing Quebec is not the worst thing that could happen. Losing Canada is the worst thing that could happen.
— From a 1990 speech to the Union Club, Victoria[1]

In the last three decades of his life, Eugene Forsey's most widely known political stand was on the question of Canadian unity. In some respects, his adamant federalism was even more fraught with contention than his early socialism had been. Some of his political friends and allies could not understand why this staunch supporter of progressive causes would actively oppose Quebec independence and allow that one issue to sometimes overshadow other important priorities.

But my father's commitment to keeping the country together sprang from his passionate attachment to both Quebec and Canada, and his vision of harmony amidst a diversity he profoundly honoured. His stance may have been controversial, and it was often misunderstood, but it was no contradiction. Its unambiguous source was, as they say in Jamaica, "One Love."

Today, those of us who share that love need to ask how his thinking on these matters applies to our current dilemmas. Given all the changes that have taken place since his death in 1991, do his views on Quebec and Canada still hold truth and relevance, or have they become mere grist for the historian's mill?

My own search for answers on all this posed a major personal challenge. Gathering together the threads from Dad's many writings on the subject and combining them with other people's recollections and comments was already a formidable task. But I also had to face my own ambivalence about Quebec, deal with my own conflicting affinities. I had to work through Dad's arguments on questions that I had never really discussed with him. I had to try to define which aspects most needed highlighting in today's context, and which, if any, I considered problematic. I engaged in long and sometimes anguished discussions with sovereignist friends, other Quebeckers, non-Quebec francophones, and my sons, both Quebec residents.

In the process, I found that a great deal of my father's thinking on this subject remains remarkably applicable. Many of his critiques and exhortations could be republished now in their entirety, with only a few footnotes to make them current. Some of his specific ideas are dated, but much validity remains.

It would be foolish for me to try to present a mere summary as if it could substitute for the enormous body of detailed analysis of these issues that Dad left behind. The sheer volume of material makes that impossible. Moreover, the situation itself continues to shift, at times clarified, at times clouded by ongoing developments. What I can offer, though, is my evolving understanding of the work he did on Quebec and national unity, and my own assessment of its relevance for Canada now and in the future.

"Canadians are challenged to attempt the impossible," the young Eugene Forsey told his fellow McGill graduates in 1925. "That is the thrill of

One Love

Eugene and Harriet in their Sherbrooke Street apartment, Montreal, New Year's, 1938.

Canadian citizenship. Canada is such a geographical absurdity that her only chance of survival lies in idealism."[2]

His idealism about this country stayed with him throughout his life. Canada for him represented a great experiment in nation-building, formally begun in the mid-1800s by imaginative democratic reformers of both French and British origin. Confederation itself was a creative political venture, marked by mutual respect among its originators and their imperfect but genuine commitment to fairness and the common good. That experiment continued in the years that followed with the evolution of a society of growing tolerance, compassion, and cooperation — an ongoing process in which my parents and their socialist contemporaries played a key role through the 1930s, 1940s, and 1950s.

As the 1960s began, Canada's future as a united and progressive nation looked very promising. This was particularly true in Quebec, where the people had managed to shake off the yoke of a repressive and insular order to embrace a wider world. My father welcomed Quebec's "Quiet Revolution," and saw in it great hope for the province and country he loved.

But soon he began to see those hopes menaced by the spectre of a narrow ethnic nationalism rising from the past. Living in Montreal in the 1930s, he had watched Quebec's elites flirt with fascism under Premier Maurice Duplessis, and he was all too familiar with the implications. Far from being a progressive force, the nationalism of Duplessis and his Union Nationale party had been dangerously reactionary, blending elements of authoritarianism, mob psychology, prejudice, xenophobia, and the repression of basic rights and freedoms.

Initially, the post-war years brought Quebeckers little relief, but progressive young French-Canadians like Pierre Elliott Trudeau and his colleagues at *Cité Libre* were sowing the seeds of change. In the 1950s, Dad began working with them and others in the labour movement and the Institut canadien des affaires publiques, challenging Duplessis and addressing some of the great economic and social issues facing the province and the country. In 1959, with the old tyrant's death, the way opened for those efforts to bear fruit.[3]

The broad-based initiatives of the early 1960s, however, were soon being accompanied by the resurgence of separatist and quasi-separatist forces. This nationalist revival threw into question the vision of an inclusive

Canadian society based on equality, caring, and respect — a society that would welcome diversity as an asset, not spurn it as a liability.

To those who cherished that broad and hopeful vision, the idea of trading it in for a restricted focus on Quebec sovereignty seemed petty and wrong-headed. Of course, federalists in Quebec and beyond were well aware that the ideal of Canada that inspired them was not yet the reality. My father, of all people, acknowledged the multitude of economic, linguistic, and cultural injustices that were still rampant across the country. He was particularly sensitive to the difficult and delicate dilemmas faced by French-speaking Canadians, who constituted a minority everywhere in North America except in Quebec. But he believed fiercely that Canada's history and Constitution provided the best possible framework for righting existing wrongs and creating something immeasurably greater than what a narrow nationalism would permit. Why destroy what was already being built? Why abandon a venture that showed such promise?

He also recognized that Quebec and French-speaking Canadians were far from being the only players in the national unity arena. From Newfoundland to British Columbia, other regions had their own problems with Confederation — rivalries and resentments rooted in geography, history, economics, and local culture. Although public attention had not yet focused on the systemic racial and cultural injustices affecting Aboriginal peoples and visible minorities, there was wide recognition of inequality and exploitation in the economic and social spheres. As early as 1941, Dad was pointing out that "national unity can be broken vertically as well as horizontally," and warning that persistent class-based inequalities and anti-labour government policies could ultimately "shatter national unity to fragments."[4]

By the early 1960s, though, quite a lot had changed. Some of those earlier battles appeared to have been won, at least for the time being. The labour movement had achieved large gains in power and respectability, and the Canadian welfare state was more or less in place. As post-war prosperity continued and provincial economies grew, many regional grievances had also become diffused, while the struggles of First Nations and visible minorities still had not really shown up on the popular radar. Of the various potential threats to national unity occupying the public agenda, only Quebec and the French-English question remained prominent. Dad became increasingly concerned about what was at stake on that front. Writing in 1964, he noted:

Less than two decades ago, the nations of Western Europe were at each other's throats. Today they are in the process of forming a European Economic Community ... In Canada, French and English have not fought each other for more than two centuries, and ninety-seven years ago they had already created their [economic and political] Communities. To kill or cripple these would be a tragic retreat from modern interdependence towards "old, unhappy, far-off things, and battles long ago." It would be tragic not only for Canadians; for if these two peoples, with their common Western Christian tradition, their long common history, their extensive experience of working together, cannot operate their federation, the hope for federations of more diverse peoples is slim indeed.[5]

If this kind of idealistic thinking sounds a bit out of place in today's world, perhaps the time has come to reclaim it. In any event, my father's idealism seldom strayed very far from the level of actual practice.

It was at that practical level where he saw Quebec nationalism posing the greatest threats. He believed that many of the schemes being proposed for resolving the French/English, Quebec/Canada dilemmas, if implemented, would threaten our future as a democratic and humane society. In one proposal after another, he identified grave risks to democracy, human rights, and the ability of the governments involved to meet the needs of their people.

He was convinced the dangers were very real. As a citizen, he feared that the misguided proposals could make a mockery of fairness and equality for Canadians across the country. As a political scientist, he predicted that they could lead to political deadlock, paralyzing many of the essential functions of government. As a civil libertarian, he felt that the rights of linguistic minorities and other vulnerable groups, both in Quebec and beyond, could be at risk.

All this and more was at stake for Dad as he waded into the national unity debate in the 1960s. He simply could not leave unchallenged ideas he considered so foolish, often unprincipled, and dangerous to the country he loved. Moreover, he despised the historical revisionism, the abandonment of dignity and respect, and the airy disregard for facts, logic, and practical consequences that he witnessed again and again, in both languages and on

One Love

Eugene skiing at Ste-Adèle, 1940.

both sides, as the debate went back and forth.

Nor did he lack the background and expertise to give weight to his views. He had years of experience and connections in Quebec, he was fluently bilingual, and he had made a vocation of analyzing constitutional and historical questions. Given all this, he felt a special responsibility to speak out at a time when few others were able or perhaps willing to formulate and express such views with the clarity and authority he could command.

Behind his involvement in these issues was his conviction — right or wrong — that unless the national unity conundrum was resolved, none of the other problems we faced as Canadians could hope to find lasting solutions. In his maiden speech in the Senate in October of 1970 he called national unity "the overmastering issue in this country."

"If we cannot keep the country together, what is the use of talking about magnificent social measures, aid for this or for that? ... What is the use, if we have nothing but the ghost or the empty shell of Canada, a crippled Canada to do these things? We have to maintain the integrity of this country or we shall simply not be able to do any of [them]."[6]

The unity question, like globalization, draws together a host of related matters, economic and social as well as political. Although it is periodically eclipsed in the public mind by other pressing issues, it keeps coming back. Dad understood that national unity would continue to occupy a controversial and powerful place in our political landscape, and that he could not ignore it. For him it reflected — and would eventually determine — who we were as a society and how we dealt with our collective problems.

Nonetheless, he didn't always relish his commitment. In 1964, after a particularly frustrating conference on Quebec's place in Canada, he wrote to his old socialist friend and colleague Graham Spry: "I have pretty well arrived at the conclusion that all further effort from me on this business is utterly vain. One is banging one's head against a moving wall ... I suppose my bad temper will lead me to express my views on this subject in spite of sensible resolves to the contrary. But I am certainly most disinclined to exert myself beyond a few squibs at most ..."[7]

His "few squibs" continued for more than a quarter-century.

The Quiet Revolution of the 1960s transformed Quebec society and spawned a resurgence of nationalistic fervour there. In response to the increasing unrest, Canadians of diverse heritages and differing political stripes sought ways to resolve the underlying problems. My father was among the many people who saw it as a moral and political responsibility, particularly for anglophones like himself, to make that effort. "A satisfied majority," he declared, "just because it *is* a satisfied majority, has a special obligation to try to understand the situation of a dissatisfied minority."[8]

But as he examined the range of proposed "solutions" being advanced in various quarters, he found most of them sorely wanting. Today, as the public discourse continues, he would be finding the same thing. For although the specifics have undergone some permutations and combinations over recent decades, the basic proposals that Quebeckers and other Canadians are periodically urged to consider are still essentially the same.

These perennial options fall into four main categories: the outright separation of Quebec; economic association or "sovereignty-association" with the rest of Canada; various forms of "special status" for the province; and massive overall decentralization of the Canadian nation. Dad's views on the practicality and desirability of each of these supposed alternatives are as pointedly relevant now as they were when he first offered them.

Outright Separation

Complete independence for Quebec was — and still is — the preferred "solution" of hard-line sovereignists. They have their counterparts in the rest of Canada as well, including a certain number of anti-French bigots whose attitude to Quebec seems to be "Go — and good riddance!"

My father rejected such thinking, whatever part of the country it came from. The separation option, he said, would be "bad for Quebec and bad for the rest of us; a heartbreak for many Canadians of both languages; [and] for the world, the end of what long looked to be at least a hopeful experiment in co-existence."[9]

But separation remained a possibility, and he did not shy away from addressing it. As usual, he focused largely on the practical. For one thing, he said, an independent Quebec would face "staggering" economic problems. "Canada as a whole is dependent enough on foreign capital, hard enough put to it to achieve and maintain full employment. An independent Quebec would be very much more so. Canada as a whole has a bad enough balance-of-payments problem; an independent Quebec would have a worse [one]."[10]

Dad believed Quebec separation would impose innumerable other problems of politics, economics, and geography on both countries, and none of them would be resolved quickly or easily. Among his concerns with a hypothetical post-separation situation were the rights of linguistic and other minorities both inside and outside Quebec, and the fate of the Atlantic provinces if they were geographically severed from the rest of Canada. Some sort of connecting corridor would have to be negotiated. "I don't see how you could possibly have a sort of East Pakistan and West Pakistan arrangement in Canada," he said.[11] (In 1947, with independence from Britain, the Indian sub-continent was divided between India and Pakistan — with the latter nation divided into present-day Pakistan in the west, and, more than a thousand kilometres away, East Pakistan, now Bangladesh.)

My father was very clear, however, about people's ultimate right to self-determination, and the need to ensure a peaceful and orderly constitutional process for putting it into practice. "If Quebec really wants independence," he said, "we have neither the right nor the means to stop her. All we can do is sit down and do some very hard bargaining on the terms."[12]

That is also essentially what the Supreme Court of Canada said in its 1998 decision on the Quebec secession reference.[13] The same position was reflected in the Clarity Act of 2000: if a genuine majority of Quebeckers affirmed a true desire to separate, then it would have to be brought about peacefully through a clear democratic process.

There are those who try to portray this position as somehow reactionary. In fact, it is quite the opposite. My father's insistence on legality and due process was the direct expression of his commitment to peaceful and democratic political evolution. He completely rejected the idea of using physical force if Quebec chose to secede.

"I would deplore from the bottom of my heart such an initiative [for separation] on the part of Quebec," he said. "I would oppose it with all the energy of which I am capable. But I would rely on argument, on persuasion. In Canada in the twentieth century, violence — whether for the purpose of gaining independence for Quebec or for repressing it — is unacceptable."[14]

If Quebeckers did end up voting clearly for separation, the next stage would have to be hard bargaining between Quebec and the rest of the country — a process that was bound to be both complicated and prolonged. "The separatists are sometimes under a delusion," an aging but still feisty Eugene Forsey told Victoria's Union Club in 1990, "that if they go out for separation it will be 'roses, roses all the way.' It won't. There would have to be some very tough negotiations."[15]

Negotiations on what exactly? One major item would be the question of boundaries, or the "territorial integrity" of Quebec. For starters, the new country would certainly want to keep Nunavik, "*le grand Nord.*" Formerly known as Ungava, and homeland to the Cree, Inuit, and Innu people, this huge territory is the major source of power — both literally and figuratively — for Hydro-Québec, and in many ways for the provincial government itself. But Dad pointed out that a claim to Ungava by an independent Quebec would not go undisputed: "Ungava was … bought by Canada, with Canadian money, from the Hudson's Bay Company, and given to Quebec in 1912 to administer as part of *a province of Canada*. If Quebec becomes a foreign country, it doesn't follow that they can take that territory out."[16]

Even if Quebec were to retain Nunavik, the question might not end there. "The aborigines in that territory might say, 'You want to secede from Canada? Well, we want to secede from Quebec.' And on what grounds could the most fervent Quebec nationalist deny them the right to self-determination, [after] preaching self-determination for Quebec, world without end?[17]

This scenario might well be played out in non-Aboriginal communities too. "You might also have [other] parts of Quebec that would say, 'Well, if Quebec leaves Canada, we leave Quebec!'"[18] Partition is a very thorny question in many newly independent countries. Quebec, with its First Nations and its anglophone enclaves like Montreal's West Island, would surely be no exception.[19]

Nor would those be the only territorial issues to be resolved. Dad warned that an independent Quebec might want to try to annex Labrador, and perhaps those neighbouring parts of Ontario and New Brunswick that have a French-speaking majority. The 1971 draft constitution of the Parti Québécois actually mentioned those possibilities. But getting the populations of those areas to agree to annexation might, he suggested, be "somewhat problematical." And if Quebec had designs on Labrador, "every Newfoundlander in the world would rise to the defence of that boundary, and all the dead ones would rise from their graves and join us!"[20]

The need for a corridor to link the Atlantic provinces to the rest of the country would have to be on the agenda. Dad objected strenuously to the assumption by some public figures that if Quebec separated, the Atlantic provinces would simply be cut off. "As a Newfoundlander and part Nova Scotian, I say, 'Wait a minute! Who says so? Are you going to give up without even an attempt to preserve the connection?'"[21] As for the arrangements for the St. Lawrence Seaway, he said, the involvement of American interests would introduce "complications beyond anything I ever imagined."[22]

A multitude of other important and complex matters would have to be worked out: how to divide up the national debt and national assets; the transition from Canadian social security to a separate Quebec system; the possible transfer of segments of the population who wished to move; and the termination of Quebeckers' jobs in the federal civil service.[23] Overall, Quebec residents would have to decide whether they were Quebeckers or Canadians.

"If they decided they were Quebeckers, they would automatically become foreigners. Dual citizenship I think is completely impossible; I don't think the rest of the country would put up with it. If they want to be foreigners, all right; but they will then be foreigners with all the rights, duties, obligations, and disadvantages of foreigners, not just the advantages."[24]

Clearly it would all be far from easy for either side. Nonetheless, my father believed that as long as the interests of the rest of Canada were strongly represented in the negotiations, we could survive the split. Without Quebec, he said, we would be left with "a Canada tragically weakened and impoverished, economically and spiritually."[25] But he insisted that we must be prepared to contemplate the possibility of separation and think it through. If we dismissed it as unthinkable, he warned, we might allow ourselves to be manoeuvred into accepting alternative "solutions" that would only delay the inevitable or turn out to be worse than the original problem.

Economic Association: "Sovereignty-Association" or "Associate States"

One of the supposed alternatives to outright separation, conjured up in various forms and vigorously promoted ever since the 1960s, has been "economic association" between "two nations" — an independent Quebec and the rest of Canada. This was the so-called "soft" option that Lucien Bouchard and Jacques Parizeau put to Quebeckers in the 1995 Referendum, and for many people it remains a tempting vision of Quebec's future. It is also the logical sequel to the "two nations" theory of Canada that Dad opposed so vigorously, and that forced his split with the NDP in 1961.[26]

The term "sovereignty-association" was coined by René Lévesque, while others have referred to a concept of two "associate states." But both mean essentially the same thing: a "sovereign" Quebec and a reconfigured remainder of Canada, each running its own affairs in most respects but governing jointly in a few specific areas.

"This notion of independence with economic association with Canada has been one of M. Lévesque's trump cards," my father told CBC Radio in 1977. "He has been playing it in Quebec and out of Quebec, the idea being that you can have independence without any economic cost at all. Everything will be beautifully arranged; there will be a common tariff, perhaps a common monetary policy; absolutely nothing to worry about on the economic side ... This is, of course, exceedingly dangerous."[27]

Why? Because it could lead many Quebeckers to vote for independence on the basis of a completely unrealistic belief that "economic association" would resolve all the problems. To those of us who were biting our nails throughout the 1995 referendum campaign, that scenario sounds all too familiar. Sadly, Eugene Forsey's voice was absent from that debate.

Not so back in 1964, when the Saint-Jean-Baptiste Society of Montreal published a memorandum setting out their version of economic association between an autonomous Quebec and the rest of Canada. It outlined the "principles" they were promoting, but no specifics. Dad went through every line of the document, and proceeded to expose it as vague, ambiguous, and utterly unworkable. He called it "[a] *Through The Looking-Glass* concoction, [a] recipe for total paralysis in everything related to [our] 'common interests.'" He concluded: "It is difficult to believe that the other provinces will ever agree to buy such a very large pig in such a very thick black poke. If they did, they would almost certainly find, when they opened the poke, that the pig was paralyzed."[28]

Over the next several years, my father had plenty of opportunities to elaborate on his prognosis of political paralysis. The Saint-Jean-Baptiste memorandum was followed by a whole series of slightly more specific proposals involving "central authorities," joint boards, and "bi-national" second chambers of Parliament — all variations on the theme of 50/50 decision-making on key economic issues like tariffs and monetary policy. Dad predicted that under a setup of that sort, "Quebec would say, 'Up,' Canada would say, 'Down,' and each would have a veto on something the other considered essential."

"The Parti Québécois laughs that off," he went on, "by saying that Ontario would insist on the 'association.' What this overlooks is that Ontario would be in no position to insist on anything. As long as both Ontario and Quebec are in Canada, Central Canada has a majority in the House of Commons. Take Quebec out, and that majority disappears."[29]

Indeed, in a Canada without Quebec, the Atlantic and western provinces together would have the population-based political power needed to make decisions for the country as a whole. Dad predicted that since the economic interests of the Atlantic and western provinces are often quite different from those of the central regions, Quebec and the new remainder of Canada would soon be at loggerheads. Ultimately, he said, "either Canada has the last word, in which case an independent Quebec would certainly say 'No!'; or nobody has the last word, in which case, it seems to me, neither Quebec nor Canada would touch the thing with a barge pole."[30]

"So sovereignty-association is no option at all. It is a horse that won't even start, let alone run — and this not because of the nastiness or narrow-mindedness of the nine provinces or their leaders, but because of sheer economic fact. To talk of negotiating sovereignty-association is to talk of negotiating the squaring of the circle."[31]

In another speech he drove the point home with a little-known bit of history. "Here in the central provinces," he told his Ontario audience, "people tried to form a two-nation state under the Act of Union, 1840-1867. It broke down, hopelessly. History presents many oddities, but surely nothing more astonishing than the spectacle of people who style themselves

One Love

Eugene on holiday, 1938. His caption for this in their photo album was "Pirate at St-Étienne-de-Bolton."

'progressives,' trying to rally supporters in 1966 with what amounts to the slogan, 'Back to 1860!'"[32]

Some have accused my father of exactly that sort of anachronistic thinking, citing his continuing defence of the century-old British North America Act. But the accusation just doesn't stick. As noted in the previous chapter, one of the major reasons he had such respect for that original Constitution was precisely its flexibility, the "enormous amount of room [it allows] for manoeuvre, for adaptation, for arrangements — written or otherwise — between the central authority and the provinces to cope with new situations."[33]

Sovereignty-association, though, fell far outside the limits of that flexibility, in both political and practical terms. His conclusion: "Either you have a Canada recognizably like the present Canada, with whatever changes in the Constitution we finally decide may be necessary, or you have two completely independent states. That's the only choice you have."[34]

"Special Status"

Of course, not everyone would agree that those are the only two options. In the ongoing search for other ways to meet Quebec nationalist aspirations, the idea of "special status" has carried considerable weight. One of its last incarnations during my father's lifetime was in the Meech Lake Accord, where various elements of special status were combined with provisions for an overall decentralization of powers to the provinces.[35]

Unlike "sovereignty-association," special status per se did not strike Dad as impossible, or even necessarily a bad idea. In fact, he went to some pains to point out that in certain contexts it could be completely appropriate, even necessary. The Canadian Constitution, he noted, already entrenches special status in one form or another not only for Quebec, but for each of the Prairie provinces, Ontario, New Brunswick, and (for some years) Newfoundland.[36]

Once again, he drew attention to the flexibility of existing special status mechanisms, which did not require constitutional change: administrative or legislative delegation, federal-provincial agreements, or concurrent legislation with one or more provinces. Again, he pointed out that if such an arrangement did not work well, it could be relatively easily changed, whereas "if special constitutional status does not work well, the only way to change it is by constitutional amendment, which may take years, and … could be blocked."[37]

On the other hand, he felt that some essentials definitely did require formally entrenched special status. He gave the example of Quebec's Civil Law, which has been part of the Constitution since Confederation. "That is the sort of thing," he said, "that *should* be very hard to change. Indeed, I should say that an absolute Quebec veto on any such change is inescapable."[38]

Because of the scope and importance of the differences between Quebec and the other provinces, Dad considered Quebec's special status to be, quite appropriately, "much more special than the others."[39] He was also open to the possibility of an expanded special status for Quebec that could work within the Canadian reality. "I see no objection," he stated, "to Quebec enjoying a broader special status than it currently possesses, always on condition that the desired arrangement does not harm the Canadian political or economic community."[40]

As usual, the devil was in the details.

"Everything really depends on how 'special,'" he said, "'special' in what ways. It is only when we get down to something concrete that we know what is really being asked or refused."[41]

Obviously, the more special Quebec's status became, the less voice Quebeckers could legitimately have in Canada's affairs. "People who choose to make themselves into half, or three-quarters, foreigners, cannot expect to have the same rights, powers and influence as full citizens. Massive 'special status' for Quebec inevitably would make Quebeckers less than full citizens of Canada."[42]

However, the advocates of many such schemes seemed to think it would be possible to have their Canadian cake and eat it too. Most of the special status trial balloons that were floated in the 1960s and 70s fell into this category. Like their more recent versions, they were supposed to hold the key to keeping Quebec within Canada, and some proponents insisted that this kind of arrangement was the "minimum" that the rest of Canada must accept. They described separation as the "knife at the throat" that would force "English" Canada to make the concessions Quebec nationalists were demanding.[43]

These more extravagant versions of special status had much in common with "sovereignty-association." They involved handing over to the Quebec government any and all of the powers it might want: power to control banking, monetary and fiscal matters; complete jurisdiction over social programs (including old age security and unemployment insurance), health, immigration, housing, agriculture, fisheries, job training, communications, cultural and linguistic matters, parts of the criminal law, and aspects of external affairs; greatly increased jurisdiction over labour and the environment; and a veto over constitutional amendments. When an advisor to the Quebec government proposed this kind of list of jurisdictional transfers after the demise of the Meech Lake Accord, Dad commented: "He could have said it all in fewer words by specifying what would be left for Canada ... Canada would for most purposes be completely *out* of Quebec's affairs, but Quebec would be totally *in* ours ... This would put the nine provinces in a neo-colonial position, with Quebec as the imperial power."[44]

His term for this type of proposal was "in-and-out-ism": "It essentially involves stripping the Dominion of most of its powers in the territory of Quebec, and transferring them to the Province — a process which, in the Newspeak beloved of some members of the Quebec Cabinet, is called 'repatriation' or 'recovery' of powers which Quebec never had — yet leaving Quebec Ministers, MPs and Senators at Ottawa with as big a voice as ever in decisions which would affect only the other nine provinces."[45]

Such a situation, he predicted, could never last.

"It would not be long before the people of the nine provinces would demand full self-government. By the same token, it would not be long before the people of Quebec would weary of sending Members to a Parliament whose powers over Quebec were minimal, and where they would have very little to do except interfere in the affairs of the nine provinces. Either way, special status would be only a chilly, transitory half-way house on the road to two sovereign states."[46]

These disturbing consequences for national unity and for democracy itself somehow remained invisible to many Canadians, who in supporting special status seemed unwilling to follow the thinking through to its logical conclusion. Dad urged a reality check. "[Some people], who call themselves moderates, and who I think genuinely believe that they want to preserve a single Canadian economic and political community, are nevertheless asking for Quebec powers that are impossible within any such community," he wrote. "[They] want things which can be got only by separation. [They] are, to adapt a delightful phrase of the late Maurice Duplessis, 'separatists without knowing it.'"[47]

His conclusion: "The 'knife at our throats' is therefore a knife without a cutting edge. If Quebec threatens to insist on total independence unless Canada accepts neo-colonialism, we must insist on total independence for Canada."[48]

Decentralization

Given all the problems with these three "solutions" to the sovereignist aspirations of Quebec, the promise of a supposedly painless fourth alternative was bound to draw a crowd of adherents.

"Faced with this situation," my father told a Toronto audience in 1977, "many people come forward with a single word which they appear to think possesses all the magic of what the old lady called 'that blessed word Mesopotamia in the Scripture,' from which she had derived such help, strength and comfort. And the blessed word is 'decentralization.' I want to put people on their guard against the magic of that word."[49]

To advocate ever greater powers for the provinces in order to try to deal with Quebec's grievances was, in his view, a foolish and dangerous idea. The reasons for his opposition to increased decentralization had to do with the very fundamentals of Canada's existence as a nation. As he told the Queen's University convocation in 1979: "The Canadian federation has now become, de facto, the most decentralized, or very nearly the most decentralized, in the world. If we go much farther down this slippery path, we shall be colonies again, but this time American colonies; no longer a nation … The poor, tattered remnant of the country that had been could have a new and distinctive coat of arms: ten jackasses eating the leaves off a single maple tree."[50]

One of the high-profile entities recommending massive decentralization of powers to the provinces was the Pépin-Robarts Task Force on National Unity. In a 1979 article in the *Canadian Bar Review*, Dad slammed the recommendations.

The Task Force would give the provinces greatly enhanced powers, and in fields where they manifestly could act contrary to the national interest, on a majestic scale. So the need for some central power to stop them would seem shatteringly obvious. But no; instead … [they propose to] take away the power of the central government to prevent the provinces from injuring the whole country, [and] give the provincial governments the power to hinder the central Parliament from benefiting the whole country …

[This] is an "option" only for those who would replace the Canadian nation with a "boneless wonder," little more than a highly decentralized common market … [We must] harden our hearts against this siren song if we want to preserve a real Canada, a real country, capable of doing real things for real people … something more than a mere geographical expression, a splash on the map with a six-letter label.[51]

"You will perhaps say that all this is negative," Eugene Forsey told the Task Force hearings in 1978, after delivering a critique of special status and decentralization. "But God told Jeremiah 'to root out, and to pull down, and to destroy, and to throw down,' and *then* 'to build and to plant.'"[52]

As to what forms that "building and planting" might take, he had plenty of guidance to offer. "To ensure there will be a real Canada, not just a cobweb," he said, "we [must not] simply sit tight and keep saying, 'Thus far and no farther.'" We must work on "a positive and practicable alternative," starting from a basis of true understanding and mutual respect.[53]

"Canada is not, never was and never will be a country of one language and one culture," he reminded the 1965 Couchiching Conference. "French Canadians are not just one among many ethnic groups, or even just the largest among many minorities … Quebec is not just one province like the others. It always has had and always will have a special position, a special status. It is the citadel of French Canada. That is written into the BNA Act plainly, unequivocally."[54]

FRENCH AND ENGLISH IN CANADA[55]
(From a 1964 article)

Most French-Canadians, except the separatists and very-near-separatists, want some effort by English-Canadians to understand what it feels like to be a tiny island of French-speaking people in a North American ocean of English-speaking. [They want] some attempt to imagine how [we] would feel if the situation were reversed.

Secondly, [they want] to feel "at home" outside Quebec. They resent the tendency of many English-Canadians to call French a "foreign" language in Canada, and to consider French-Canadians just one "minority" or "ethnic group" among many, Quebec just "a province like the others."

They [also] want their fair share in running the whole of Canada, politically and economically. And they want to be "masters in their own house," their citadel, Quebec.

There is no reason why English-Canadians should object to any of these in principle.... The desire for a fair share in running the whole country is not only reasonable and proper, but welcome ... The desire to be "masters in their own house" is also right and reasonable.

But what. Precisely, does it involve? ... Quebec is already to a very large extent, and increasingly, "master in its own house," as its take-over of the private power companies, its projected pension plan and the changes it has made and is making in its education system amply prove. If it really needs wider jurisdiction or more revenue, it should not be impossible to devise arrangements without destroying the economic and political communities created in 1867 ...

The French- and English-speaking communities of Canada [need] to continue to do what they have been doing with fair success for 200 years, namely compose their differences and live together in harmony.

In order to translate that understanding into practice, he called for action in three main areas. The first was to advance linguistic and cultural equality in the country as a whole. "[French Canadians] seem more and more to feel that Dominion power is really pretty much a synonym for English-Canadian power, [that] the government of Canada ... is 'them,' not 'us.' I think the larger the share French Canadians have in running the whole country, the less of the central power they will try to have transferred to Quebec."[56]

In this reading of the public mind in Quebec, my father may or may not have been mistaken. Certainly it was an analysis shared by many at the time, including Pierre Trudeau and his *Cité Libre* colleagues. But the events of recent decades have changed the context in which those views were formed, and the assessment might be different today. What definitely does remain relevant is Dad's commitment to listening to Quebeckers and working with them to define and bring about needed changes.

"The only way we can get French Canadians to feel that the whole country is their show as well as ours," he said, "is to make it so."[57] The most important and effective mechanism he saw for doing this was the expansion of bilingualism from what was then still quite a limited base. Like Trudeau, Dad wanted to see bilingualism encouraged and implemented at many levels and in many contexts, most notably in federal and some provincial public services, in broadcasting, in private industry, and in the appropriate legislatures and courts. He wanted to see French-language education offered wherever feasible across the country, and the removal of obstacles to full francophone participation in every sphere of activity.[58]

In his enthusiastic promotion of bilingualism, though, he sounded one cautionary note: "I think the English-speaking people of Canada can be sold a policy of 'bilingualism — within the limits of the practicable — or bust,'" he said. "I am perfectly sure they cannot be sold a policy of 'bilingualism *and* bust.' The nearer Quebec takes us to 'bust,' the less bilingualism we shall have, and the smaller will be the share of French Canadians in running the whole country."[59]

The second element of his prescription for promoting unity was the ongoing need for openness, empathy, and dialogue. He called for a fair, sensible, workable, and above-board process based on mutual respect and a willingness to confront the complexities of our national reality. "We English Canadians," he said, "must be willing to sit down with our French-speaking fellow-citizens and discuss any specific changes; to look at any grievance whatever, and discuss it, and try to find some means of meeting it."[60] In other words, we must embrace the classic Canadian method of doing things through discussion and guided evolution.

And he insisted we keep at it for as long as it takes. Over the years, as one proposal after another bit the dust, people asked, "What shall we do?" Dad's answer was always: "Go on talking." Addressing a committee of the New Brunswick Legislature on the Meech Lake Accord in the late 1980s, he recalled the long history of trial and error that had preceded the repatriation of the Constitution. "Quebec rejected the Fulton-Favreau formula [in the 1960s]," he reminded them. "Quebec rejected the [1971] Victoria Charter. The governments tried again. Bill C-60 of 1978 collapsed. Mr. Trudeau tried again." The Constitution was finally repatriated and amended in 1982, and the lesson was obvious. "If this Accord fails," Dad asked the committee, "what is to prevent us from trying again?"[61]

Which is, of course, exactly what has happened.

"When we are presented with crisis-laden inevitabilities," wrote John Ralston Saul, "that is the moment when the citizen draws back and says, 'No, we are in no rush. We'd rather have the crisis, thank you very much.'"[62] Dad and his fellow Meech Lake opponents played this role in regard to that Accord, and today, long after its demise, Canadians keep on "trying again."

This continuing dialogue leads logically to the third key element of my father's advocacy: some modified form of our current federal system, taking advantage of and reinforcing the flexibility and sophistication that system embodies. Along with or instead of potential constitutional changes, he recommended considering other types of arrangements, such as the kind of federal-provincial agreements or delegation mentioned above in the discussion of special status, and in Chapter 12.

In my father's best-case scenario, Canadians would actively strengthen support for the "French Fact," both in Quebec and in the rest of the country, without weakening Canada as an economic and political entity. As already noted, he had no problem acknowledging Quebec's distinctiveness, and he was open to the possibility of further special treatment of some sort. Unlike the nine premiers who endorsed the 1997 "Calgary Declaration," which implied identical powers for every province, Dad understood that "equal" does not necessarily have to mean "the same." In his view, provincial equality could — and sometimes should — embrace specific differences, though there were limits on how far that could go in practice.

I have an old CBC tape recording — the clip is unidentified but it is probably from the 1965 Couchiching Conference — that clearly shows where he stood in this regard. "I would not be scared off any specific change," he said, "by the cry that it would give Quebec a special status, a right, a power, a privilege that no other province would have. There may be perfectly good reasons for giving any one province something further the others have not got, and do not even want.... There are, of course, things no province can have as long as it remains part of Canada. If it insists on having them, it'll have to get out. But any specific proposals short of that should be examined on their merits, not just damned on the ground that no province has a right to anything unless every other province gets it too."

These, then, were the fundamentals of Eugene Forsey's prescription for national unity: greater linguistic and cultural equality for French and English in Canada as a whole; an ongoing process of honest dialogue; and some modest adjustments of powers for Quebec. He believed that these measures, taken together, would provide the best chance for long-term survival, not only for Canada as a nation, but for her French-speaking citizens and their language and culture, both inside and outside Quebec.

Was he dreaming in colour? How realistic was this response to the pressures of Quebec nationalism, and how useful is it to us today?

In the linguistic and cultural domain, the past thirty years have seen tremendous progress. Bilingualism in many spheres is now something many of us take for granted — just a normal part of the Canadian reality. While much remains to be done, our impressive achievements in this regard have become commonplace to the point where they are practically invisible, especially to younger people who never experienced the earlier inequities. This transformation came about largely thanks to the efforts of Pierre Trudeau and his fellow Quebec federalists, who, like my Dad, believed passionately in a bilingual Canada with a national government reflecting both cultures.

These days it may sound like a quaint anachronism to suggest that French-Canadian discontents could be satisfied by making the country more fully bilingual. Over the past generation or so, more and more francophone Quebeckers have come to identify their linguistic and cultural interests explicitly with Quebec, and to view the broader Canadian reality as increasingly marginal to their concerns. But that shift has not happened all by itself; it has been actively encouraged by partisan opponents of the federalist vision. In any case, as Dad was quick to point out, sovereignists are not the only ones with a right to speak on behalf of Quebec or of French Canada.[63]

Many Quebeckers today remain federalists. Who knows how many may have stayed in the federalist camp precisely because of the effectiveness of Trudeau's policies of bilingualism and biculturalism? The continuing ambivalence of many Quebec francophones today towards separation, the reluctance of a majority to actually vote "Yes" in a referendum, may be due at least in part to the many improvements that came about through the bilingual federalist policies of the Trudeau era. To dismiss those improvements as irrelevant would be at best premature.

The need for continuing dialogue of course persists. To be sure, there has been a fair amount of discussion and debate over the years, but the kind of rigorously honest, respectful, and, above all, informed discussion that my father favoured — and practised — is still not common enough. Too often the field is left to the ill-informed, the misguided, the cynics and opportunists.

As a result, we get the kind of foolish and opportunistic "feel-good" gestures exemplified by the Harper government's November 2006 declaration of Quebec as "a nation within Canada." A mere two years later, that same government was aggressively stirring up anti-Quebec sentiment across the country in order to attack the opposition's proposed coalition under Stéphane Dion, and retain its own hold on power. There could hardly be more devastating proof that such gestures leave people's underlying prejudices and misunderstandings intact, ready to be called into play the moment political expediency appears to require it.

In regard to the actual transfer of more powers to Quebec, the kind of modest adjustment and fine-tuning of the federalist system that Dad recommended has been largely supplanted. As noted elsewhere, the past few decades have seen more and more federal powers handed over to the provinces in response to the escalating demands of Quebec nationalists and other "provincial war-lords."

Has there been a lessening of nationalistic fervour in Quebec as a result of this expansion of provincial powers and the corresponding weakening of the federal role? Even for those who feel this is the case, it would be a stretch to assume cause and effect. Besides, whatever calm may exist is fragile. We have seen repeatedly how easily it can be broken, how quickly a new wave of sovereignist sentiment can rise in response to real or perceived affronts.

It has been argued that Quebec's nationalist aspirations persist because we did not go far enough, that in saying "No" to the Meech Lake and Charlottetown accords, citizens signed Canada's death warrant. Dad would disagree. He believed there are more ways than one to destroy a country, and perhaps as many ways to save it. He preferred an honest fight with a chance for survival to a slow and certain death by a thousand cuts. Those choices are still before us.

He recognized that even after all the efforts had been made, all the dialogue pursued, all the reasonable compromises explored and implemented, we still might fail. "We might find ourselves so far apart that there would be no alternative to separation," he wrote. "But even if we reached that melancholy conclusion, we should at least know better why, and march forward into that grim future with our eyes wide open, instead of stumbling into a minefield in a rosy haze."[64]

In summary, then, the several elements of my father's approach to Quebec and national unity have yet to fully play themselves out in our history. Progressive linguistic and cultural policies, honest dialogue,

Breakfast by the lake at the rented cottage at Inglis Island, Eastern Townships, 1939.

specific adjustments to the system — clearly these are all still necessary for resolving "our present discontents." Whether they can hope to be sufficient is another question. On that, the jury is still out.

Just as significant as the facts and analysis that my father brought to the national unity debate is the spirit that lay behind his involvement. His energy for that decades-long crusade came from the love with which he embraced Quebec and all of Canada. One may disagree with his arguments, but there is no doubting that "One Love."

His correspondence from the 1960s gives a taste not only of his commitment, but also of the warm response it evoked, even from his political opponents. One of them was Jacques-Yvan Morin, the University of Montreal law professor who later became minister of education in the Parti Québécois government. After several exchanges in the pages of the *Canadian Forum* and at the 1964 Banff Conference on Canadian Unity, Dad wrote Morin to thank him for two articles he had sent.

"*J'espère les lire* ... (I hope to read them very soon, with all the respectful attention they deserve ... although I'm afraid you may reinforce my fears of having to spend the evening of my life in exile ... I hasten to add that your kind messages moved me profoundly, because, despite the abyss that appears to separate us, I should like to count myself among your friends, and to count you among mine ...) *et vous compter parmi les miens.*"

Morin's reply was graciousness itself. "*Je me rappelerai toujours* ... (I will always remember with pleasure our walk at Banff, during which we sketched out this profound debate which divides our country ... Politics are not theology, *Dieu merci*, and if I dared a bad play on words, I would say that what separates us is only what unites us too tightly ... Please Heaven there were more Canadians like yourself ...) *Plût au ciel qu'il existât davantage de Canadiens comme vous.*"[65]

Conservative historian and proud anglophone Donald Creighton said the same thing — in English — in his introduction to Dad's book *Freedom and Order*. Their admiration for Eugene Forsey was probably the only opinion Creighton and Morin ever shared!

When the Fédération des Sociétés Saint-Jean-Baptiste du Québec wrote Dad thanking him for participating in a "colloque" they had sponsored, he wrote back, in French: "What a pleasure the arrival this morning of your too kind and flattering letter. It is another proof of the courtesy of the heart for which French Canadians are renowned ... I also thank the Federation for the largeness of spirit which it showed in inviting me to speak ... despite the indisputable fact that my opinion is not in any respect that of the Federation or its leaders."[66]

Among my parents' friends were a number of francophones, including some notable Quebeckers. The Abbé Gérard Dion, a fearless foe of the repressive Duplessis government, was a champion of Quebec's international labour unions and head of the Department of Industrial Relations at Laval University. Guy Hudon, dean of law at Laval, was on the Board of Broadcast Governors with Dad; they resigned together in 1962 to protest against delays in approving a French-language CBC Television station in Quebec City. Thérèse Casgrain, who was named to the Senate with Dad in 1970, was a civil libertarian, feminist, leader of the Quebec CCF, and a founder of both the Fédération des Femmes du Québec and the Voice of Women's Quebec branch.

Another very personal aspect of my father's commitment to French Canada, mentioned earlier, was his membership in Ottawa's francophone Église Saint-Marc, where he served from the 1960s on as elder, steward, and often substitute preacher. As part of both a linguistic minority within the United Church and a religious minority within French Canada, the tiny French Protestant congregation experienced first-hand the challenges and pressures inherent in such situations. Dad's involvement there was of political and symbolic as well as personal significance.

Given all this, it is easy to see why he felt so at home with French-speaking Canadians, and engaged so readily and sympathetically on the issues they were facing. Nonetheless, I feel that one element may have been missing in his understanding of the separatist movement — something not easily subject to logical analysis, something elusive even on the emotional level.

On the night of the 1976 Quebec election, I watched René Lévesque's victory speech on television. As the great charismatic leader spoke about Quebec's identity and the chance it now had to define itself as something other than just a province of Canada, I was moved to tears. For, in Lévesque's words, I was hearing an echo of my own voice as a woman. At the time, I too was just beginning to aspire to identity and wholeness in my own right, refusing any longer to be limited and defined by a marriage that subordinated my life to that of another and subjected my very existence to his will. The resonance I felt in my heart came out of a lived experience that my father had never had.

This analogy has its imperfections, but when I ran it past Dad's friend the late Professor Michael Oliver, he thought it made sense. "You've put your finger on what I consider a blind spot in Eugene," he said, "and that was his refusal to recognize that unless the French-speaking majority in Quebec had some feeling that it constituted a part of Canada which was distinct, it was going to be almost impossible for it to feel comfortable in Canada." True, Dad did recognize Quebec's "distinctiveness," but there was still a dimension that he may not have grasped.

Yet, on this issue as on others, he could not be slotted into any pigeonhole. People who wanted simple answers to match their prejudices were confused by his obvious empathy for "both sides" and his respect for the complexities involved. Since he would have thought it both cowardly and dishonest to cater to what he considered narrow-mindedness, he was often a target for slings and arrows from the different sides.

> After one speech on the subject [of national unity], I received two anonymous letters. One accused me of being inspired by hatred of Quebec; the other of having sold out to the French Canadians.
>
> I can, and often do, get as furiously exasperated with some English Canadians as I can, and often do, with some French Canadians. And for exactly the same reason: that they appear to me to be talking nonsense, and sometimes pernicious nonsense … Some of the English-speaking Canadians who talk the worst nonsense are not the Colonel Blimps or the antediluvian Orange bigots, but the amiable mugs, usually highly intelligent and highly educated, who lie down on their backs with all four feet in the air, and urge all the rest of us to do likewise and to join them in inviting the wildest Quebec nationalists to dance on our stomachs.[67]

This was what he felt happened at the founding convention of the New Democratic Party in 1961, when a small group of advocates managed to convince the rest of the delegates to expunge the word "national" from the new party's constitution and all its documents. Dad was so disgusted with this decision and the lack of self-respect he felt it indicated, and so perturbed by the very real dangers he was sure it would bring in its wake, that he quit the party — a decision explored in Chapter 15.

My father was always a fierce defender of linguistic minority rights, both French and English. In the mid-70s, he vigorously opposed Quebec's initial Official Languages Act, Bill 22, because it discriminated against the English-speaking minority of that province, notably in the field of education. Later, when Bill 22 was replaced by Bill 101, he fought against that as well, "publicly, energetically, in speech and in writing."[68] But it was always the principles that he was defending, not merely the interests of his own language group.

In 1986, an Ontario "English-rights" organization sent him a letter asking for support. His reply was terse and to the point: "With your aim of making Ontario 'as English as Quebec is French' I have less than no sympathy," he wrote. "That policy would entail a Quebec Bill 101 in reverse ... I bitterly resent the treatment Bill 101 has meted out to the English-speaking citizens of Quebec. The last thing I want is to see Ontario or any other province doing the same sort of thing to its French-speaking citizens ... An Ontario which would be just Bill 101's Quebec upside-down? God forbid!"[69]

He rejoiced that New Brunswick had made itself officially bilingual, and he signed a petition asking Ontario to do likewise. In 1987, when a franco-Albertan MLA was denied the right to speak French in the Alberta Legislature, he defied a worsening heart condition to travel to Edmonton to testify on M. Piquette's behalf.[70] If he had still been alive ten years later when the Ontario government tried to "restructure" Ottawa's Hôpital Montfort out of existence, he would have stood in solidarity with the franco-Ontarian community in their fight — ultimately successful — to keep Montfort as a full-service French-language teaching hospital.

However, he also stood up for his own English-speaking culture when he felt it was getting short shrift. Appreciation and empathy, he felt, "ought to work both ways. We have our grievances too — our rights, our traditions, our history, our feelings, our way of looking at things, our culture — though this is sometimes forgotten. We also are part of the 'bi' in bi-culturalism."[71]

This comment clearly comes from an earlier time, before "multi" replaced the "bi" in the Canadian vision. But as noted earlier, Dad was not entirely oblivious to that aspect of things. His emphasis on the two official languages and their respective cultures was a reflection of the way the public debate was being framed at the time; it did not mean that he was "relegating to second-class citizenship … the Canadians who are neither British nor French."[72]

In any case, Canada's survival was bound to require effort on all parts. "If we really want to keep one country," he insisted, "we must be willing to pay a price for it. If we are not willing to pay the price, then we do not really want one Canada, we only *un*-really want it."[73]

But there was also a price he was unwilling to pay. To accept sovereignty-association, the "in-and-out" variety of special status, or wholesale decentralization of the country, would only be a doomed attempt, at enormous political and social cost, to stave off the separatist threat. Tragic and difficult though actual separation would be, Dad believed that would be "better, far better [than] the hemi-demi-semi separatism" promoted by many Quebec nationalists, which "would only prolong the agony."[74]

> Their scheme[s] would give us all the disadvantages of separatism and a carload of extra, and intolerable, headaches. [They] would leave Canada hardly more than a geographical expression, a political monstrosity unique in history, whose only anthem would have to be something like this:
> O Canada! We don't know what you are.
> Nation, we thought, but that Quebec doth bar.
> And a colony you have ceased to be,
> So we know what you are not;
> And we stand on guard, though it's rather hard,
> When we're not quite sure for what.
> O Canada! Great Undefined!
> O Canada! Can't you make up your mind?
> O Canada! Can't you some status find?[75]

In spite of the loud voices calling for sovereignty in one form or another, Dad knew very well that public opinion among Quebec francophones was not monolithic. His respect for the other voices — the voices of many ordinary people in that province — was reflected in his clarion call to the rest of us, to join in the fight for Canada: "French-Canadians, even Quebec French-Canadians, are not unanimously behind the demands for separation, or Associate States, or hemi-demi-semi separatism ... And the French Canadians who see just what such proposals would mean for the ordinary Quebec worker and farmer and fisherman and miner, and for the French-speaking minorities in the other provinces, are resisting — speaking for Canada, fighting for Canada. They need to have us speak for Canada and fight for Canada too."[76]

In my father's long campaign for peace with justice on the national unity front, there were many times when he felt overwhelmed. "Week after week," he lamented, "salvo after salvo of folly and nonsense, often from very big guns, bursts over us. And after most of these I feel that there is nothing ahead for me when I retire but to walk down the hill to the British High Commission and ask for political asylum."[77]

Of course, he never did do that. Instead, he persisted in speaking for Canada, fighting for the country he believed in. The 1970s — his Senate years — saw momentous developments around Quebec's place in Canada, and a plethora of efforts to cope with them. The October Crisis, the Victoria Charter, the election of René Lévesque and the Parti Québécois, the Pépin-Robarts Task Force on National Unity, the aborted 1978 Constitutional Amendment Bill, the Ryan proposals — Dad observed and commented on them all, in the terms outlined in the foregoing pages. After leaving the Senate in 1979, he carried on, apparently oblivious to what two retirements were supposed to mean. He watched Quebec's first sovereignty referendum go down to defeat in 1980. He welcomed — with reservations — the repatriation of the Canadian Constitution in 1982, with its Charter of Rights and Freedoms and its new amending formulas. And he was there, ready to do battle again, when Brian Mulroney resurrected the whole Quebec-Canada debate with the Meech Lake Accord five years later.

He could almost have been anticipating that Accord when, in a 1979 letter, he denounced the "province-worshippers," whose short-sighted and often self-serving response to Quebec's grievances would, he believed, lead to "the total surrender of Canada."

NAMING THE DANGERS
(From a 1978 presentation to hearings on national unity[78])

Special constitutional status for a particular province or provinces, for particular purposes, is perfectly admissible and practicable. But a massive transfer of power from the Dominion government and Parliament to a provincial legislature is not. Applied to Quebec, it would make the government and Parliament of Canada for many, perhaps most, purposes, simply the government and Parliament of the nine provinces, but with Quebec ministers and Quebec members [in] both Houses.

This would be intolerable. It could not last. To ask for it is to ask for boiling ice, sour sugar, dry water, stationary motion.

[As for] decentralization, ... any substantial reduction in the powers of the central government and Parliament, or any enfeebling of their organs (for example, the Supreme Court), would make Canada hardly more than a splash on the map with a six-letter label.

I am not interested in preserving a Canada which is no more than a splash on the map. I am interested only in preserving a real country, able to do real things for real people, its own people and the people of the world. No splash on the map, no mere label covering ten mini-states, can do that, nor can the ten mini-states. The problems that face us are national, continental, planetary.

The greatest danger this country faces is not the secession of Quebec, infinitely lamentable though that would be. It is the danger of multiple sclerosis resulting from a well-meaning effort to keep Quebec somehow — however tenuously — within the physical boundaries of something — however diaphanous — called "Canada."

Canada without Quebec would be tragically impoverished — materially, intellectually, spiritually. It would be an amputee. But Canada with Quebec — but with a central Parliament whose jurisdiction had been gutted, whose organs had been paralyzed — would be a paraplegic. If I have to choose, which God forbid, I should choose the amputee.

"Macdonald, Cartier, and the other Fathers," he wrote, "founded what they called 'a great nation,' 'a great and powerful nation,' 'to take its place among the nations of the world.' The province-worshippers are out to destroy their work. They can count me out. Indeed, they can count on me to fight to the last against their 'veiled treason.'"[79]

And fight to the last he did. Not only did he play a major role in the three-year struggle against Meech Lake; he continued, in his final months, to engage in skirmishes with Quebec nationalists over their various post-Meech proposals. In early 1991, despite declining health, he took on Quebec's constitutional advisor, Léon Dion, with a scathing critique of the latter's presentation to the Bélanger-Campeau Commission on Quebec's constitutional future.[80] A few weeks later, when the Quebec Liberal Party's constitutional committee issued its "Allaire Report" advocating a fresh version of sovereignty-association, Dad produced his own final "squib." Under the defiant title "No Surrender!" his last essay was published on February 23, 1991, three days after his death.[81]

The old warrior is gone, but his "One Love" has left a living legacy to the people of Quebec and all of Canada. Whether or not this country remains united, Eugene Forsey's clarity and passion can inform, challenge and inspire us as we embrace our future.

CHAPTER FOURTEEN

Strong and Free: Redefining Nationalism

I hope we shall succeed in recreating [and] strengthening the spirit of Canadianism — a devotion transcending all our local loyalties, all our ancestral loyalties, all our linguistic loyalties — a spirit which will enable us to realize, in the lifetime of people now living, the magnificent future that awaits this country if only we will keep our heads, and use our heads, and use our hearts.
— From a speech to the Empire Club, Toronto, 1977[1]

My father described himself as "a Canadian nationalist, by instinct, upbringing and conviction alike — 'nationalist' in quotation marks, not in the offensive sense [of] the word."[2]

What did he mean? If we strip away the offensive aspects so often associated with the term — the "my-country-right-or-wrong" flag-waving that justifies intolerance and abuse, the simplistic competitive patriotism that erodes democracy and common sense, the jingoistic fervour that leads to war — we uncover the kind that Dad embraced. His nationalism meant knowing and loving this country, striving to keep it strong and free, and ensuring its ongoing contribution to a better world.

It was part of a broader vision that transcended the specifics of citizenship but certainly his primary focus was on Canada. This was the country where his ideas were formed and his ideals found expression; its institutions were the vehicles through which he worked. It was Canadian reality that shaped his political philosophy, and Canadian trade unionism that gave him the chance to put it into practice. Canadian history and traditions provided the framework for his lifetime of constitutional and parliamentary work, and an increasingly bilingual, multicultural Canada further inspired his vision as the years passed.

In more subtle ways as well, this country influenced his priorities and approaches. His lifelong love of our rugged northern lands and waters fostered his growing concern for our natural environment and for the planet as a whole. His insistence on reason and persuasion instead of force as a means for solving problems drew on Canada's relatively peaceful past and the "peacemaker" aspect of our identity. A measure of characteristic Canadian caution informed his healthy skepticism about many aspects of modern civilization. And although he often fell short of the genteel politeness Canadians are sometimes tagged with, he set great store by civility and respect.

The principles at the heart of my father's work — democracy, social and economic justice, human rights, and equality — are seldom regarded as aspects of nationalism. Yet I see what he did as a kind of practical nationalism, applying those principles to the unique Canadian context so as to keep the country he loved strong and free.

It would never have occurred to Dad to indulge in the childish "best country in the world" nonsense so popular nowadays with some public figures. His sense of our country's distinctiveness was both more serious and more matter-of-fact than competitive patriotism. He put it very simply to a 1971 conference on nationalism: "Canada has a distinct identity. It is different from any other country in the world, and it's worth preserving."[3]

One of the greatest challenges to preserving that identity was, and is, our giant neighbour to the south. Like many Canadians, my father had a built-in wariness of the United States. Part of it was the natural caution of a mouse sharing space with an elephant, but it also went beyond that. As he confessed to the conference, "I have no special love for the Americans. They drove my ancestors into exile, and I am sometimes inclined to think that the American Revolution was one of the great disasters of history. I don't like American civilization now. It frightens me, even more than other forms of modern civilization."

Obviously he was speaking, not about individual American people, but about American society in general. He used to quote a Congress colleague who was married to a US citizen: "Individually Americans are perfectly charming; collectively they are completely lunatic."

Theirs was not a collectivity he ever wanted to join. As valedictorian at McGill in 1925, my father urged his fellow graduates to resist the siren call of the United States, and warned that "annexation would be a disaster both for Canada and her great neighbour."[4] Four decades later, declining an invitation to be on a panel on economic union with the United States, he explained: "I frankly am not much interested in talking about economic union with the United States. [It] seems to me foolish, and the talk of it merely another manifestation of the lack of will to live."[5]

He repeated the same sentiment in a speech the year before he died. "I do not want to see this country become part of the United States," he said. "I think we have a superior civilization, a superior way of life."[6]

Key elements of that way of life included the bilingual, multicultural nature of Canadian society, and its ongoing political evolution as a parliamentary democracy and constitutional monarchy. He cherished our progressive policies of universality and equalization, our hard-won programs of medicare and social security, our rich and diverse heritage of arts and culture, and our unique national institutions like the CBC and the National Film Board. He was unwilling to see all that sacrificed on the altar of American interests or dubious economic advantage.

Over the years, however, a host of Canadian "opinion leaders" in business and government have shown themselves far too ready to do just that. The American-inspired continentalist agenda, which if successful would ultimately reduce Canada to a colony of the United States, keeps re-emerging throughout our history, each time in a different guise.[7] Dad played his own modest part in the ongoing struggle against it.

Back in 1956, a leading item on that continentalist agenda was a proposal for a TransCanada Pipeline to carry natural gas from Alberta to the central United States, with massive subsidies provided by the Canadian government. It was a pet project of a powerful minister in the Liberal Cabinet, American-born C.D. Howe, who shamelessly touted the pipeline as "all-Canadian."

In an article in the *Canadian Forum*, my father denounced that claim as "a fraud." The pipeline was 83.4 percent American-controlled, and was being built with no guarantee of any benefits to Canada, simply to carry gas across the border for American consumers. However, he noted, "When it came to paying, the thing did indeed come fairly close to being 'all-Canadian.' The Americans were to retain control, but the Canadian taxpayer was kindly invited to come and bring his cheque-book."

Just as outrageous as the Pipeline Bill itself was the way the Liberal government had rammed it through Parliament, making a mockery of Canada's system of responsible government. Appalled by this betrayal of the democratic process, Dad tersely summed up the way the way the decision had been made: "Who makes Canadian law? Parliament. And who, in this case, controlled Parliament? The Government. Who controlled the Government? Mr. Howe. Who controlled Mr. Howe? The American owners of Trans-Canada Pipe Lines."[8]

The TransCanada Pipeline was only one of many instances of American corporate power infringing on Canadian sovereignty after the end of World War II. Historian Desmond Morton describes the post-war period as a time of "rapid economic growth [and] a corresponding Americanization of both ownership and lifestye."[9]

In this economic context, Dad's nationalism reflected both his sense of the practical and his respect for ordinary workers and citizens. He had a long record of opposing policies that put private business interests — whether foreign or domestic — ahead of the rights of the Canadian people. Nonetheless, some of the positions he took on American involvement in our economy were less than radical. As his speech to a 1971 nationalism conference makes clear, he was no purist, and he was always wary of simple wholesale solutions to complex problems.

> Whatever our position may be with regard to American investment, there are inevitably very marked limitations upon our political sovereignty. This is just part of the modern world. I don't think any country now is able to enjoy complete political sovereignty.
>
> Legally and constitutionally, it seems to me, we can have as much independence of the United States and of multi-national corporations as we choose — as much as we really want, that is, and are willing to pay for. The payment may be in some reduction of our standard of living ... in inconvenience, in preferences ...
>
> One factor in this situation is not merely the large corporations, but the international unions [and] the plants that their members are working in ... You are up against the fact that [many] ordinary working people have chosen international unions, and they may take a very dim view of attempts to interfere with these ... Also in many cases they are working in plants which might be seriously dislocated if you went in for a policy of economic nationalism ... It's easier for comfortably-off people to be — shall we say — altruistic, spiritual about these things than it is for the poor, the disadvantaged, the tired, who might have to pay the price in large measure.

Reluctantly, he sounded a similar note in regard to popular culture, notably broadcasting.

> When some government body sets out to try to promote Canadian culture, it runs up against the strong preferences of a great many of our people for something quite different.... Over and over again, the efforts of the authorities to try and promote Canadian culture and improve and expand Canadian content in [radio and TV] programs have been frustrated largely because the people of Canada were not prepared, in fact, to sacrifice their preferences and their convenience in order to promote Canadian culture.

There again the problem is really one of will and willingness. Do we want to promote Canadian culture, and if so are we prepared to pay the price — in convenience and possibly in standard of living and taxes — that it may involve?

This is a question we have to ask ourselves. "What exactly do we want, and how much are we prepared to pay for it?"[10]

Consensus on that pivotal question has evaded us now for decades, during which the controversy over trade "liberalization" has continued. Canadians have had to consider (or ignore) the pros and cons of the Canada-US Free Trade Agreement, NAFTA, the aborted Multilateral Agreement on Investment (MAI) and the various WTO and regional "free" trade agreements that continue be negotiated by successive governments. Although these agreements typically result in enormous advantages for global corporations at the expense of ordinary citizens, they are increasingly being ratified with little or no democratic process or even public discussion.

For reasons discussed elsewhere, my father was not active in the opposition to the initial Free Trade Agreement (FTA) with the US in 1988, which opened the floodgates to the rest. But he was nonetheless highly skeptical about it. In an interview with Tom Earle shortly after the Agreement was signed, he explained that it did not in fact implement the Macdonald Commission's recommendations as the Mulroney government claimed it did. Instead, it included things the commission had said should be explicitly excluded, and left out things the commission had said should definitely be put in. He called it "'free trade' with knobs on and bits out" — and some of those knobs and bits were far from negligible.

Moreover, he said: "A lot of the essential matters are still to be negotiated. What is a 'subsidy'? What is an 'unfair subsidy'? Already, I believe, the Americans have drawn up lists of the things that they say we must get rid of ... It seems to me that the Americans throughout the negotiations have taken and will take the position — and perfectly reasonably from their point of view — 'Look, if you want our markets, you'll do everything our way, is that clear?'"

Dad was acutely aware of how closely the economic and political spheres were intertwined, and he recognized the danger — today an increasing reality — that so-called "trade" agreements could end up dictating Canadian policy on all sorts of matters far beyond the legitimate purview of commerce.

"This [Free Trade Agreement] in the long run may easily destroy our political institutions," he told Earle. "The moment may come when people may say, 'All the real decisions are being made in Washington, and we haven't got any representation there!'"[11]

In that situation, he was afraid people might be tempted to just give up and join the United States — a prospect towards which his opposition never softened. "The Free Trade Agreement may have put us on that path," he told a Victoria audience in 1990. "I devoutly hope not. Perish the thought."[12]

If my father was somewhat cautious in his views on economic nationalism, he was fiercely radical in his defence of our country's political and cultural identity. He bridled at suggestions that Canada was, or should be, pretty much like the United States.

"Our system of government is, in its most important points, the diametric opposite of the American," he said, "and is so because we deliberately chose to make it so. Our history also is, at its most important points, the diametric opposite of American history, and is so because we deliberately chose to make it so. Canada … has repeatedly and firmly declined to be a carbon copy of the United States."[13]

Dad's highlighting of our political distinctiveness caused a miniature international incident during the World University Service seminar in India in 1953, which demonstrated why, despite his many aptitudes, he could never have made a career in the diplomatic service.

> I was giving a lecture on the Canadian and American Constitutions, and I observed, with truth, that the Canadian was much the more modern of the two. To liven what I felt was a somewhat tedious discourse, I was foolish enough to say that the American Constitution was an eighteenth-century sedan chair, which only the political genius of the American people enabled them to manoeuvre through modern traffic.

"THE CARBON COPY THEORY OF CANADA"
(From a 1967 article[14])

The carbon copy theory of Canada assumes that this country really is, and certainly ought to be, a carbon copy of the United States. (Why on earth there should be a second, no one bothers to explain.) But plainly, it is a poor copy. The Fathers of Confederation smudged it. It is high time we got busy with erasers and cleaned it up.

There could not be a wilder misconception of the origin and nature of Canada. The Fathers of Confederation were not "a lot of mixed-up kids" who tried to copy the United States and failed. They tried to make a very different kind of country, and they succeeded.

The Americans deliberately broke with their past. We have repeatedly and deliberately refused to break with ours. The Americans deliberately set out to make theirs a country of one language and one culture. We deliberately chose to preserve two languages and two cultures.

The Americans chose a decentralized federation. We set out to create a highly centralized federation. The Americans provided no central control for the states, except what might be necessary to preserve a republican form of government. We … gave the central government power to wipe any provincial act off the statute book within one year.

The Americans wrote into their Constitution a very explicit and detailed Bill of Rights. We relied on the "well understood" unwritten "principles of the British Constitution." [They] provided for fixed election dates. We provided only for a maximum duration of Parliament, with no "term" at all for the government.

The American Congress and state legislatures are hedged around by constitutional prohibitions. Our Parliament, within the limits of subject and area laid down by the BNA Act, can do anything. So can our provincial legislatures, subject to the Dominion power of disallowance.

No wonder our Constitution does not work like the American! No wonder the "carbon copy" looks smudged!

I had spoken lightly of sacred things. The Americans were deeply hurt. Their chief delegate told me: "We always think of the Canadians as just like us." I felt inclined to say that that was just the trouble. But she was so distressed that I hadn't the heart.[15]

Diplomatic missteps aside, my father viewed with alarm the many forces at work to draw Canada ever further into the American orbit. The political face of this continentalist agenda was what he called "creeping republicanism" — the subtle undermining of Canadian traditions and institutions, whether through ignorance or through deliberate efforts to erase our distinctiveness. One piece of it, already discussed, was the covert but sustained effort by Liberal governments in the 1940s and 50s to eliminate the word "Dominion" as the title of our country. There were various other ways as well in which our status as a constitutional monarchy was chipped away at, from the surreptitious removal of the word "Royal" from the mail delivery trucks[16] to a 1978 suggestion — resurrected, incredibly, in 2010 in talk show chit-chat about the vice-regal office — that we should have a hockey star as governor general.[17]

Dad responded to that suggestion at the time: "If we [were] to have a second republic north of the [forty-ninth] parallel, we'd all struggle to keep our own identity, to keep the one thing which would mark us off from every other people in the world, a hockey-player head of state. Let laws and learning, wealth and commerce die, but leave us still our hockey-hero head!"[18]

My father's determination to maintain Canada's political uniqueness was about far more than tradition; more, too, than just the common sense rule of not fixing what ain't broke. It was grounded in his belief that the differences between our evolutionary approach and the American model of armed revolution were of crucial and continuing importance. He pointed with pride to the generations of nation-builders, from the Fathers of Confederation to Laurier, Meighen, and Trudeau, who have demonstrated the reasons for, and the value of, those differences. Canada's heritage of gradual, non-revolutionary change is embodied today in our ever-evolving Constitution and in the ways in which most Canadians seem to prefer to go about doing things.

Some years ago, on CBC Radio's *Morningside*, Peter Gzowski asked listeners to suggest ways to complete the phrase "as Canadian as …" The hands-down winning entry was "as Canadian as possible under the circumstances." I think Dad would have enjoyed the self-deprecating irony, and he might also have seen in the phrase a recognition of aspects of our national character that influenced his own — the thoughtful practicality, the respect for context and complexity, which have evolved from our geographical and historical realities.

That subtle cultural bias takes its political form as a preference for dialogue, negotiations — what might be termed "transformation by discussion." It need not be namby-pamby or half-hearted. Nor does it in any way deny the role of protest and resistance of the sort that, for example, my father and his socialist contemporaries engaged in during and after the Depression. In fact, the methods of Canadian democratic socialism mesh very well with this penchant for deliberate process that combines action with reflection, commitment with respect. If the proof is in the social pudding, Canadian progressives would seem not to have done too badly in comparison with the "revolutionaries" south of the border.

However, this traditionally Canadian approach to change, which my Dad upheld and practised, has been seriously eroded in recent years. Various governments appear to prefer to use a wrecking ball to get rid of things they don't like. It is no accident that former Conservative premier Mike Harris of Ontario officially labelled his program of social demolition — a massive campaign targetting environmental regulations, social programs and welfare — a "revolution."

Those destructive policies and others like them were, and are, the product of the imported ideology of "small government" — the American notion that the less government there is, the better. It is a comparatively recent arrival in Canada, but like purple loosestrife, zebra mussels, and other invasive species, it has been spreading apace. My father's understanding of the responsibilities and mechanisms of government can be a useful tool for controlling the plague.

Dad also vigorously resisted pressures in other spheres that seemed to be pushing Canada closer to absorption by the United States. His ongoing protest against the Americanization of our English language has already been touched on. The mass media constituted an enormously important vehicle for such influences, and he did his best, on the Board of Broadcast Governors, in the Senate, and as a private citizen, to strengthen the bulwarks of Canadian content and regulation.

In a Senate speech on the mass media, he gave his view of what would happen if those controls were loosened and the private broadcasters given free rein: "In my opinion we would get American tripe dished up to us morning, noon and night over the air ... I do not wish to be regarded as one of those foolish people who condemn everything American. I know perfectly well there are excellent American programs ... But we have here a distinct civilization, quite different from the American, and I believe in preserving it."[19]

Another of his nationalist battlefields was education, where he tried to combat the encroachment of American content and methods into our schools and universities. In a 1957 speech he denounced "the uncritical worship, or lazy copying, of American education."

> A year ago, a friend of mine, a very distinguished political scientist was asked to write a simple book for Ontario schools on how Canada is governed. He agreed, but said it would take him some time. One of the departmental big-wigs pooh-poohed this: "All you need to do is take a simple book on American government and change a few things here and there." ... Just think of ignoramuses like that being in positions of power in the educational system of Canada's largest province! ... If Providence had not intervened, the children of Ontario would have been hit with a text-book almost every word of which they would have had to unlearn before they could act as intelligent Canadian citizens.[20]

In Dad's view, maintaining our distinctiveness from our giant neighbour was hugely important, whether it was a question of politics, education, culture, or language. It was his love for Canada, not a lack of respect for the Americans, that motivated his resistance to mimicking the US — that, and his customary insistence on common sense.

"The worst of it is that we so often seem to take over the silliest things," he said, "just when the Americans have come to realize how silly they are. We pick up their cast-off clothes of ten or twenty years ago, and go strutting around in them under the impression that they are the latest thing from Fifth Avenue. Let us learn from the Americans, and from everyone else, but let us use our heads about it."[21]

Given his broad perspective and his rejection of narrow dogmas, it is not surprising that my father's nationalism defined itself as much in contrast to provincialism — in many senses of the term — as to any outside force. Some of the very practical economic and administrative issues that made him wary of political fragmentation have already been outlined, as have various constitutional aspects of federal and provincial jurisdiction, particularly in relation to Quebec. But he recognized even more facets to this quintessential Canadian question.

"I am horrified by the decline in the spirit of national pride, national belief in our country," Dad told Toronto's Empire Club in 1977, "by the rise of provincialism, regionalism, all over the country. I am convinced that we need a strong Canadian state."

In no way did this position reflect a lack of sympathy on Dad's part for provincial and regional loyalties. On the contrary. "Nobody who is a Newfoundlander," he said, "can for one moment decry the virtue of local tradition." He went on to express his pride in the variegated regional strands of his own heritage. "My pride in all these things is part of my pride in being a Canadian. All these local traditions are subsumed ... in the Canadian tradition."[22]

Nor was this just a pleasing expression of nationalist sentiment. The positions Dad took on policy questions repeatedly showed how seriously he took regional loyalties and priorities. "We must conserve the historical communities that are the provinces," he told a 1964 conference on Canadian goals. "I could not accept, for example, that Newfoundland or the Maritime provinces be depopulated, or nearly so, keeping only enough population to satisfy the needs of the tourists — even if depopulation were to increase both the GDP and the income of every resident of those provinces ... Local patriotism should reinforce, not rival, Canadian patriotism."[23]

His belief that membership in the broader Canadian nation actually strengthens regional identity and survival was firmly based in reality. The small and the local are able to thrive thanks to Canada's tradition of respect for diversity, and are supported by the structures we have developed at the national level. These national structures are largely dependent on a central government with the capacity to implement sharing and equality.

The historical basis for a strong national government in the Canadian federation goes back a long way. Dad pointed out that it was partly a response to the American model, where "states rights" were given pride of place. "The Fathers of Confederation," he said, "gazing with horror at the American Civil War, decided that 'states' rights' were precisely what had caused it, and acted accordingly."[24] This meant they gave most of the power to the Dominion. Later judicial rulings, however, expanded provincial jurisdiction far beyond the original intent, and in the 1960s pressure was growing to further decentralize the country.

My father questioned the wisdom of a trend that, he believed, would end up subordinating the common good of all Canadians to narrower interests. He did not want to see Confederation reduced to little more than a mechanism for co-operation among quasi-sovereign powers. As he told the conference on Canadian goals, "[That] would result in the transformation of our domestic problems into international problems. *À quoi bon* — to what end? We already have enough international problems, which need to be resolved by difficult, slow and costly means. Why add others?"

The phrase "co-operative federalism" was being bandied about at the time. Dad was all for co-operation, but he was dubious about how this particular version might work in practice.

"There are certainly examples," he acknowledged, "of effective and fruitful federal-provincial co-operation. Certainly those could be extended. But on the large questions, given the attitude of many heads of provincial governments, I ask myself, 'Why do so many people have such confidence that these high personages will co-operate with the federal government?' It reminds me of the words of the great English writer Samuel Johnson on the subject of second marriages: 'the triumph of hope over experience.'"[25]

Joking aside, his concerns were very serious. In another speech, noting the globalizing effects of modern technology and various political forces, he asked: "Can we, in a technologically post-post-post-Confederation world, go back, politically, to a very pre-pre-pre-Confederation Constitution? The rest of the world is moving towards internationalism. Can this country move towards [anything] less than Canadian nationalism?"[26]

The nationalism he was talking about was embodied in the kind of flexible, practical, evolving arrangements between the nation and its provinces that have characterized this country from its beginnings. Depending on the specifics, he said, such arrangements could be "admissible and sometimes even desirable … Each proposal must be examined carefully in the light of the facts, keeping always in mind the imperative never to weaken the Canadian economic and political community."[27]

As time went on, more and more proposals came forward purporting to address the problems of national unity, but almost invariably they failed to meet Dad's criteria for keeping Canada itself strong. The report of the Pépin-Robarts Task Force on National Unity in 1979 nearly made him despair, particularly the assumptions on which its specific proposals seemed to be based. He detailed his assessment in the *Canadian Bar Review*.

"What are the assumptions?" he asked. "First, that the provinces are primary, the nation secondary, that the central government and Parliament are really little more than conveniences [for] the provinces … Second, that the central government, shorn of some of its powers and confined in the exercise of others, is itself to be decentralized, made more completely the instrument of the provinces … Third, that loyalty to one's province is primary … The whole tenor is that we all are, or ought to be, provincial nationalists, and that if we are not, we should be encouraged, pushed, prodded into becoming so."[28]

The concept of "provincial nationalism" was of course the very antithesis of the kind my father embraced, and he fought it tooth and nail. "The voice of the province-worshipper is loud in the land," he wrote. "If [they] have their way, there will be no real Canada, just a boneless wonder. The province-worshippers are reactionaries. They would turn the clock back one hundred years or more … They would make us again a group of colonies — American colonies this time — with a life 'poor, nasty, brutish and short.'"[29]

Fortunately, the constitutional package adopted with repatriation in 1982 was not shaped by that task force report. However, some of the assumptions Dad warned against still persist, and now, more than thirty years later, those warnings retain their relevance. The "blessed word 'decentralization'" still seems to hold a magical fascination, particularly among the country's elite. Numerous federal and provincial politicians, business leaders, media pundits, and academics have joined a promotional chorus prescribing decentralization as the cure for what ails us.

Popular grassroots response to the idea of wholesale provincialization, however, has been mostly lukewarm, ranging from sluggish apathy to outright rejection at the ballot box. There are indications that ordinary Canadians remain generally cautious about decentralization — a skepticism that finds substance and support in the analysis my father outlined years ago. As we come to realize more and more what the recent fragmenting trends have brought us, we can once again opt for a stronger Canada, with broad national programs and policies that reflect our traditional shared values of equity and compassion.

In June of 1990, the options for a stronger, united country were on the verge of extinction. The Meech Lake Accord, a package of constitutional amendments based on demands from Quebec and tradeoffs with the other provinces, was in the final stages of its approval process. Under the amendment formulas in the repatriated Constitution, the Accord needed the endorsement of Parliament and all ten provincial legislatures within three years. If it made it through, Canadians would awake to find massive decentralization embedded in constitutional concrete, together with an attendant host of extremely serious problems.

A quarter century earlier, observing some of the responses to the Quebec sovereignist agenda, my father had warned of "the great danger … that in a mood of saccharine amiability, the governments [of Canada and the other nine provinces] will shut their eyes, open their mouths, and swallow, and Canada will die."[30] Now he feared that scenario was about to come true. That it did not was thanks in no small part to the valiant efforts of a small band of unbelievers, Eugene Forsey prominent among them, who waged a relentless three-year battle to prevent the Accord from becoming part of the supreme law of the land.

"SPEAK FOR CANADA!"[31]
(From a 1979 convocation address)

The voice of the provincialist is loud in the land. The air is thick with projects which would transform this country from a nation into a loose common market, a league of semi-sovereign provinces; a territory in which the central government and Parliament would be merely marginal conveniences to do for the glorious and immortal provinces the odd jobs they could not somehow manage to do, after a fashion, for themselves. I see no future for such a Canada, which would be hardly more than a geographical expression, like eighteenth-century Germany; a splash on the map, with a six-letter label. I see a future only for a real country, able to do real things for its own people and to bear its share of the burdens of the world.

These burdens are already heavy. They will be heavier. The problems we face are utterly without precedent, in urgency, in complexity and scope: the growing inflation and growing unemployment; the growing pollution of the environment; the growing scarcity of, and the soaring demand for, energy and raw materials; the doubtful promise, and far from doubtful menace, of nuclear energy; the intractable hunger and poverty of the Third World, and that world's just demand that they should end; the horrendous armaments race.

Against this "swelling tide of woes" even powerful national states seem able to do little enough. Against the waves of that tide that beat on Canada's shores, a league of semi-sovereign Canadian provinces could do no more than put ten fingers in the dike.

In the early days of the last war, when Chamberlain, in the British House of Commons, was stumbling and bumbling through an unworthy speech, Leopold Amery shouted: "Speak for England!" It is time, in this country, for someone to shout above the din of the contending provincial warlords and their apologists, "Speak for Canada!"

When the Meech Lake agreement was first announced on April 30, 1987, it didn't look so bad. Even discounting the initial hype that touted it as a miraculous deliverance from all our constitutional woes, it seemed to represent at least a step in a positive direction. Prime Minister Brian Mulroney and the ten provincial premiers urged us to trust them, that it was all for our own good. It was tempting to hope the Accord might represent a characteristically Canadian compromise that would mollify the "soft" separatists in Quebec and forestall future troubling of the constitutional waters.

At the start, Dad was cautiously hopeful himself, but the initial communiqué left him with some serious unanswered questions. Those questions quickly became full-fledged doubts, and within weeks he had joined his old friend Pierre Trudeau in "a clarion call to think, and think hard, about the Meech Lake Accord." He proceeded to go through the formal text with a fine-toothed comb, and found his fears amply justified. The Accord, he said, was full of "ambiguities and obscurities which, unless they are cleared up, could be very dangerous."[32]

On July 21, he presented a twenty-eight-page brief detailing those concerns to the Special Joint Committee of the House of Commons and Senate studying the matter. "The Accord substantially transforms our Constitution," he told them. For one thing, it would radically decentralize a "formidable list" of areas of national or shared jurisdiction, and would institute a "massive shift of power" from the people's elected parliamentary representatives to the first ministers and the courts.

He examined the practical consequences of these and other provisions, detailing what they would really mean for our system of government as well as in ordinary people's lives. He alerted the committee to the way the wording of the Accord watered down national standards for social programs to a requirement for mere "compatibility" with vague and elusive "national objectives." He questioned the democratic implications as well as the actual feasibility of the proposed provisions for the Senate and the Supreme Court.

Further, he documented the impossibility of implementing the "guarantee" to Quebec (and potentially to other provinces) of a given proportion of immigrants, and the inherent contradiction between that guarantee and the Accord's own promise of mobility rights for those same immigrants. He protested the Accord's neglect of Aboriginal peoples and its effective disenfranchisement of the governments and citizens of the territories. He denounced its potentially very negative effects on the rights of Quebec's English-speaking minority and francophone minorities in the rest of the country.

As a human rights advocate, he challenged the implications of giving the "duality principle" and the "distinct society" clause primacy over the Charter of Rights and Freedoms. He told the committee that, at least in Quebec, and perhaps to some extent elsewhere, those two new interpretive principles represented a potential threat to almost everything in the Charter of Rights and Freedoms. "[They] could put in jeopardy … freedom of speech, thought, opinion, the press, peaceful assembly, association, … the right to vote, to be a candidate; … the right not to be arbitrarily imprisoned, the right to *habeas corpus*, … freedom from discrimination on the ground of race, national or ethnic origin, colour, religion, sex, age, or mental or physical disability …"[33]

My father was especially dismayed by the erosion of democracy that he saw, not only in many of the provisions of the Accord itself, but in the process by which it had come into being.

"The First Ministers are not eleven Moseses," he told the committee "coming down the stairs of the Langevin Block with the Tables of the Law, writ in stone. 'Minister' means servant, not master. The First Ministers are the first servants of the Queen — that is, of the people of Canada."

The Meech Lake Accord, itself the product of a conference of first ministers, would have formally entrenched those conferences in the Constitution. Dad feared this would ultimately subvert parliamentary government by enhancing their perceived legitimacy and authority on matters of vital importance. The public, he said, might come to view those exclusive, closed-door gatherings of first ministers as "a new supreme, sovereign, omniscient, inerrant, infallible power, before which the function of Parliament and the Legislatures would be simply to say, '*Roma locuta est*. The First Ministers have spoken. Let all the earth keep silence before them.'"

He pointed out that these arguments against the Accord were made all the more urgent by its proposed unanimity requirement, which, once in place, would render any future constitutional change practically impossible. This would make the Constitution extremely rigid, impervious to the needs of the citizenry or the shifting realities of a changing world, and he urged the Joint Committee to proceed with caution. "If Parliament and the provincial legislatures make an unwise decision now," he said. "it will be a labour of Sisyphus to undo it."[34]

As the Meech Lake debate continued over the next three years, my aging father kept up a hectic pace as a critic. He presented briefs to various other official committees, spoke to numerous groups and to the media, and wrote an astounding amount of material detailing the problems of both principle and practicality that he saw embedded in the Accord's "seamless web."

For Dad, one of the most dangerous aspects of the Accord was the "quagmire of ambiguities" it presented, leaving vitally important matters in limbo, to be interpreted by the courts.[35] "Constitutions should be as plain and unambiguous as their framers can make them," he said. "A light-hearted, smiling, 'Oh! The courts will settle all that!' is a frivolous abdication of responsibility, a surrender of the very citadel of democratic government, a time-bomb against national survival."[36]

This ambiguity was something the Quebec government actually insisted on preserving. In particular, it demanded that the crucial term identifying Quebec as a "distinct society" be left undefined. Dad pointed out that this calculated vagueness was allowing the Accord to be pushed in Quebec on the promise that it would bring sweeping changes, while being soft-pedalled in the rest of Canada as something that would really amount to very little. In his April 1990 speech in Victoria he described the situation:

> The Prime Minister says [the distinct society clause] doesn't really mean very much; it would have a marginal effect in a few grey areas. Then you turn to what Mr. Bourassa said in the Quebec Legislative Assembly: [that] it opens up an enormous and enticing and delightful vista of hugely enlarged powers. "The greatest victory in two hundred years," said Mr. Bourassa. "It gives us all sorts of new powers. And we cannot limit it, we cannot be precise about it because it would restrict the possibilities."
>
> This is a very grave matter. We are left in a state of hovering uncertainty … If the Supreme Court brings down a decision that [the term distinct society] doesn't really mean much, Quebec will go right through the roof into the stratosphere and won't come down till the twelfth of July. If on the other hand the Court says, "Oh yes, this

opens up a new field for the Quebec legislature," then the rest of us will say we've been had.

Meech Lake is not a cure for the Canadian disease; it is a narcotic. And when the Supreme Court brings us out of the narcotic, when the effect has worn off, we shall have not brotherly love but fratricidal strife.[37]

In addition to all the issues around the Accord itself, my father was appalled by the way this crucial national debate was being conducted. "One of the most astonishing, and frightening, things about the proceedings before the Joint Committee," he told the Alberta NDP's public hearings on the subject, "has been that the defenders of the Accord seem to have made not the faintest attempt to analyze, and answer, the very specific, detailed, adverse criticism of one section after another, by people eminently qualified to speak ... It passes by the Accord's official defenders as the idle wind, which they respect not."[38]

Nonetheless, the anti-Meech forces were making their voices heard, and Canadians were listening. Despite the soothing reassurances from its promoters, public skepticism was building.

Midway through the three-year debate, Clyde Wells became premier of Newfoundland and Labrador, and began questioning that province's endorsement of the Accord. Dad saw hope that Newfoundland might actually "save the country," and offered to help in any way he could. His offer that was gratefully accepted.

"During the whole course of meetings and negotiations and discussions about how to cope with the Meech Lake proposal," Premier Wells told me later, "having your father's knowledge and advice and guidance available was perhaps the best asset that I had. There was nothing could replace what he provided at that time."

As the June 1990 deadline approached, public skepticism grew into widespread opposition, especially outside Quebec. Certain political interests were not above using this incipient divide for their own purposes by painting the opponents of Meech as anti-Quebec. Some pro-Meech federalists hoped this tactic would discredit or silence the critics and ensure approval of the Accord, while some separatists were happy to use the same accusation to justify their rejection of Canada. Dad and other leading Meech opponents made it very clear that they were in no way anti-Quebec. "We must insist that rejection of Meech Lake is NOT a rejection of Quebec," he wrote. "There are a dozen things in the Accord that have nothing at all to do with Quebec's five demands, but everything to do with what [Premier] Wells rightly calls 'dismantling federalism.' That is why the Accord needs changes."[39]

In the end, of course, the Accord was not changed. Instead, it expired, stopped by the groundswell of popular opposition in Newfoundland and Labrador that resulted in the last-minute rejection vote there, and by Elijah Harper, the respected Aboriginal member of the Manitoba legislature, holding an eagle feather and saying "No!"[40]

Throughout the Meech Lake marathon, Dad was upholding the principles of a lifetime. As one of Canada's political elders, he was sharing with the people of his nation the tools they needed to fight the good fight — durable tools of knowledge and reason, integrity and outrage. The year following his death, when another unwanted constitutional road-show was playing across the country, Canadians took up those tools again, and used them to bring the Charlottetown encore to an end.

"Eugene Forsey had a concept of Canada — a pretty progressive concept," recalled veteran activist and journalist Ed Finn, who first knew Dad in the early 1960s. "[It was] based on his understanding of the kind of country the Constitution created and was protecting. He didn't give himself airs, but he saw himself as a guardian of the constitutional and economic and social rights of Canadians, and he was quick to defend and champion them when he felt they were in danger." Coming from another such guardian, that's quite a tribute.

My father's brand of nationalism was all about what he called "a real Canada, able to do real things for its own people and for people beyond its borders."[41] It was the kind Canada and the world need today — "not a dividing, but a uniting nationalism,"[42] based on respect and co-operation, and implemented with honesty and common sense.

Dad's love of country inspired him to a lifetime of work for the common good. He would rejoice if it did the same for others.

Chapter Fifteen

Partisanship and Independence

> My tragedy, if that's not too strong a word, is that I'm too radical to be a good Conservative and too conservative to be a good radical. I am also too academic to be a good trade unionist, and too good a trade unionist to be a good academic man; too partisan to be independent, and too independent to be a good party man.
> — From a 1951 letter to Arthur Meighen[1]

Woven throughout the fabric of my father's life is a theme of stubborn independence, an insistence on thinking for himself, a refusal to toe a party line. The positions he took reflected his own analysis, his own conscience, and they were not always widely shared. Even political friends and allies saw some of his choices as either contradictory or incomprehensible.

For the most part, though, this puzzlement betrayed a lack of understanding of the fundamental values and principles on which Dad based his politics. Previous chapters have explored those fundamentals, and now it is time to take another look at his unusual political career.

Although formal party politics was far from being the central element in Dad's public life, it was nevertheless the stage on which some of his most dramatic moments were played out. A certain amount of drama may have been inevitable, for there was always a degree of creative tension between his principled independence of thought and what he saw as the practical potential of parties for solidarity and action.

He served under three different party banners over the years — Conservative, CCF and Liberal — and finally traded them all in for complete autonomy. Despite his Victorian sensibilities, I think he might chuckle if I described his history of relationships with political parties as a sort of serial monogamy, with three political marriages, three divorces, and an eventual return to single status.

Regardless of this rather varied record, Dad was never a political flirt. When he joined a party, he made a serious commitment, and gave generously of his time and effort. Nonetheless, he steadfastly refused to allow partisanship to overwhelm principle. When he came to believe a party had seriously transgressed his political or moral boundaries, he ended the relationship, though he always tried to remain friends.

His friend R. L. Calder, after a similarly mobile political career, wound up in the CCF. Dad liked to quote him: "I change my party as I change my shirt, and for the same reason."

Still, that hardly constitutes a full explanation of my father's movements on the formal political stage. For that explanation, it's necessary to go deeper, drawing together the personal and political threads of his history with — and without — political parties.

Coming from a solidly Conservative background, with tradition permeating the very air he breathed, the young Eugene Forsey saw himself as a Conservative from an early age. This childhood allegiance was reinforced by his personal admiration for the Tory leader Arthur Meighen, whose intellect, integrity, and parliamentary brilliance impressed him deeply.

When it came, though, his conversion to socialism was heartfelt and thorough. As a young "Tory Democrat," he had already been leaning towards the Left, and at Oxford he encountered moral and intellectual arguments for radical change that fully convinced him. Back in Montreal, in the worsening conditions of the Depression, he was soon intensely involved in Canada's budding socialist movement.

His parting of ways with the political establishment in which he had grown up raised some eyebrows, and exposed him to a variety of pressures. In January of 1932, for example, he received a letter from Alice Massey, wife of the future governor general, whose children he had briefly tutored at the Masseys' country house a few years before. "I wonder what you are thinking of the whole world situation now," Mrs. Massey wrote. "You must have many ideas, as I know how interested and keen you are about things. Would you become an interested and keen member of a reorganized Liberal Party? All sorts of plans are in the offing ..."[2]

But she couldn't tempt him. "I intimated politely that I wouldn't touch any Liberal Party with a pair of tongs" he told his mother.[3]

A few weeks later, in another letter home, he described a visit to the Meighens' home in Toronto.

> Mr. Meighen has put on a little weight, but he looked old and tired, and very Ulsterish ... He was very cordial, but at first I felt a slight strain ... Then we fell to at the Byng question and had a grand time ... Young Gordon Ford was there and drew me out about our new society, Socialism, and Russia. Mr. Meighen chafed noticeably under this, and looked almost hurt when I avowed my change of views. I've had from him since a formal, frigid, rather pompous note thanking me for the Byng pamphlets and acknowledging two notes I'd sent him ... So there's another friendship gone, I suppose. I'm sorry. But I can't suit my views on public questions to my personal friendships. I'm afraid he has a closed mind. His remarks on Russia were very narrow-minded and intolerant ...[4]

It wasn't only Mr. Meighen who had reservations about Dad's "change of views." Family members remained loyal and supportive, but they weren't necessarily happy about the tilt to the left. Even his doting mother had occasional qualms. Shortly after the publication of *Towards the Christian Revolution*, she commented to an old friend: "I think they might have chosen a title less likely to be misconstrued."[5]

The Forsey relatives in Newfoundland, like the family in Ottawa, were lifelong Tories, but they had a different and creative way of dealing with the situation — denial. In 1948, when Dad was running in a by-election against the new federal Conservative leader, George Drew, our cousin Alex Hickman was in Grand Bank where the Forsey aunts still lived. "When I went in to see them one day," Alex told me, "I couldn't resist. I said: 'What's this I hear about Eugene running for the CCF against George Drew?' 'Oh, my son,' one of them said, 'don't you worry about it. He's a great admirer of George Drew's. But he told me that he believes as a matter of principle that no one should ever get elected by acclamation. That's why he's running, no other reason. And there'll be no one happier than Eugene when George Drew gets elected.'"

This makes a good story, and it is certainly possible that Dad had left a good deal unsaid in trying to spare his aunts' feelings. But I'm not convinced that the family in Newfoundland has even to this day truly acknowledged the more unorthodox aspects of my father's politics. When I asked Alex in 1995 if he took Dad's socialism seriously, his answer was emphatic. "No. No! I used to say to him, 'It's only the wealthy can afford to be socialists, or the very poor. You're not very poor, what are you doing being a socialist?' He used to say 'It's a matter of principle.' But I never regarded your father as much of a socialist anyway."

The authorities at McGill University in the 1930s took a rather different view. To those pillars of Montreal society, he appeared as a daring radical intent on flouting the conventional views of his respectable upbringing. One of the plump files in the "Principal and Chancellor's Records" section of the McGill Archives is entitled: "Communism & Socialism — Forsey, Gordon, Scott & the CCF, 1918–1933." It includes a three-page memorandum from McGill's then principal, Sir Arthur Currie, stating that "a professor in a University has no right or license to devote his time and energy in agitating for political changes," and sharing an advisor's opinion that "Mr. Forsey's ... realization of the uncertainty of his position will ultimately result in great benefit to himself."[6]

The details of that "uncertainty," and its eventual result, are partially documented in a later file, entitled "Eugene Forsey Dismissal, 1939–41." This file is noticeably thinner, and most of the key letters are missing from it. Professor Michiel Horn, researching his book on academic freedom, could find no trace of them; nor could I. But there is quite enough in the various other files to show conclusively that what spelled the end of my father's teaching career at McGill was the combination of his independence of thought, his insistence on speaking his mind, and his principled refusal to comply with what he considered outrageous directives on political and academic matters.

Professor Alan Whitehorn admires Dad's repeated decision throughout his time at McGill to take that professional risk. He sees him as "a Left intellectual ... who probably could have lived a comfortable life as an academic, perhaps as a politician representing one of the two older more established parties. He chose not to. He chose to follow his conscience."

That same conscience, though, prevented him from finding any lasting peace, even in the bosom of his chosen political party. Well before the McGill drama had worked itself through to its finish, he was chastising his CCF comrades over what he saw as their failure to push hard enough for disallowance of Duplessis's 1937 Padlock Act in Quebec. In the difficult, even bitter exchanges he had with the CCF's national executive on that issue, his frustration was sometimes more apparent than his tact.

Nor was that the last time my father would find himself seriously at odds with his political comrades. His thesis on the royal power of dissolution of Parliament highlighted what some of his fellow CCFers considered his constitutional conservatism. Moreover, the thesis, and the book that followed, re-established his connection with Arthur Meighen, whom many of them detested. As that remarkable friendship progressed from an initial reserved cordiality to an enduring intellectual and political intimacy, it became one more bone of contention between Dad and others in his own party.

Thus began a twenty-year dance between Eugene Forsey the socialist and Eugene Forsey the apostate Conservative — a dance for which Canadian politics provided the stage, Arthur Meighen the music, and the dancer himself the choreography.

"My dear Eugene," Mr. Meighen wrote in January of 1942, "I do not know when I enjoyed anything more than reading in the *Forum* the contribution which you sent them ["Mr. King, Parliament, the Constitution and Labour Policy"]. The more I see your work, the more I am convinced as to where you ought to be, and I can say further to you with all the earnestness in my power, and as one who believes he knows you thoroughly well, that I also know the Party you should be with."[7]

This fantasy of seeing my father on the Conservative benches in the House of Commons was one the older man never relinquished in all the years of their friendship. Throughout those years, Dad, with equal tenacity and resolve, soldiered on in the CCF. The ups and downs of his commitment to his party, combined with the ongoing tug-of-war with his beloved mentor, tested and refined his understanding of politics and partisanship, loyalty and limits. Above all, the experience strengthened his conviction — which Meighen shared — that wherever partisan interests conflicted with truth and principle, truth and principle must take precedence.

Then, as now, that conviction was far from universally held in political circles.

"A generation brought up under the shadow of Mr. King's political ethics," Dad wrote in a 1951 letter, "simply cannot understand how any leader, faced with a choice between principle and votes, could choose principle. This is the measure of Mr. King's success in debauching our political life. I am thankful to say that I can remember an earlier time when different standards were in vogue, and when the choice of principle, far from being inexplicable, required no explanation."[8]

In his 1943 book on the dissolution of Parliament, my father had done a thorough job of exposing Mackenzie King's "political ethics," and Liberal reactions to the book shone further light on the pitfalls of partisanship. The most notable example was the three-month debate in which Dad slugged it out with *Winnipeg Free Press* editor J.W. Dafoe in the paper's editorial pages.[9] Dafoe, a leading voice in the Liberal Party, launched a furious defence of King, indulging in outright falsehoods as well as what Dad described as "an ingenious selection of quotations, and slippery use of words and dates."

"There was a man," he commented later of Dafoe, "who, 'born for the Universe, narrow'd his mind, and to Party gave up what was meant for mankind.'"[10]

Eugene being interviewed by Ottawa Journal *columnist Jim Robb in 1979 in his Senate office. On the wall behind him, the portrait of his dear friend Arthur Meighen, former prime minister of Canada, had pride of place. (Courtesy City of Ottawa Archives/MG011/J-79-649#1/2 no. 17)*

However, as Dad had already learned to his dismay, such partisanship was by no means the exclusive property of the Liberals. The by-election of 1942 in the Toronto riding of South York had shown that the CCF itself was not immune. Meighen, recently reinstated as Conservative leader, was running for the seat, and the Liberals were quaking in their boots at the prospect of the veteran parliamentarian and master debater returning to the Commons. They decided the best chance of beating Mackenzie King's old nemesis was to rally behind — of all things — the CCF. Dad called the resulting united campaign against the Tory leader "a most shocking and outrageous performance," filled with personal attacks, lies, and innuendo. But it achieved its purpose: Meighen was defeated and the Liberal-backed CCF candidate won the seat.

My father never forgave himself for not leaving his work at Harvard to come back to Canada and take the stump in the older man's defence. "I thought Meighen could look after it," he told Peter Stursberg in 1978, "and naturally I was not very anxious to take part in a campaign against my own party. But I should have done it."[11]

It was, again, a matter of principle. As he explained at the time in an urgent letter to the *Canadian Forum*:

> Mr. Meighen is our political opponent. No one can reasonably object to attacks on him or his policies or actions, nor to the use of vigorous language in such attacks. But even political opponents are entitled to have the case against them stated with fairness and accuracy. No party has suffered more from the contrary practice than the CCF; no party has more to gain by strict adherence to the highest possible standards of public discussion. In any campaign conducted along other lines, our opponents will have all the advantages, if only because they control most of the press.
>
> That, however, is not the most important reason for exercising restraint in this matter. The prime consideration is the interests of democracy itself, which can scarcely fail to suffer if public controversy is carried on without scrupulous regard for the justice which, traditionally, is extended even to the devil.[12]

In its own sad display of partisanship, the *Forum* delayed printing that letter until after the by-election was over.

His party's mistreatment of his friend and mentor seriously dampened my father's enthusiasm for political campaigning. Although the CCF was on a roll in Ontario in 1943, winning voters and seats, Dad described himself as being "on the shelf, politically." Asked if he intended to run as a CCF candidate for Parliament some day, he answered, "No. For one thing, no one would nominate me, and for another, I should have no chance of election if I were nominated." To Meighen he added, "I did not on this occasion say what I have often said before, that after the way you had been treated I had had a sickening of the whole business."[13]

Nonetheless, he continued his involvement in the party to the extent that his heavy workload at the Canadian Congress of Labour would allow, sometimes sharing with Meighen in general terms his assessment of what was happening. In a 1944 letter he mentioned a "closed session at the CCF Convention" where he had found French-Canadian participation "very heartening." In another, from 1948, he expressed his ambivalence about his role: "I had a furious argument with some CCF big-wigs, [in which] I was given to understand that I was just a back number. I was so disgusted that I congratulated myself that circumstances had made it impossible for me to take any part in public affairs. Clearly, if these people were right, the kind of politics I knew something about was gone, forever. For that kind I had both aptitude (I think) and appetite; for this, neither … However, apparently the bulk of the party, and especially the local people, took my view, not the big-wigs', so I feel rather cheered."[14]

Just a few weeks later, much to his own surprise, Dad found himself recruited by the CCF to take on Conservative Leader George Drew in the Carleton by-election. Drew won handily. The morning after the vote, Meighen wrote him: "It is anything but a happiness to me to see you defeated in whatever you try to do, but my thinking is so definitely the opposite of your own in things economic and social that I could not honestly wish that your ideas would triumph."[15]

Dad replied: "Of course you couldn't want me to win. Mr. W. said if you were an elector in Carleton you'd be 'torn.' I said, not at all: you'd be sorry to have to vote against me, but you'd go 'marching up the great, bare staircase of your duty, uncheered and undepressed.'"

In that same election post-mortem, he told Meighen:

> The Progressive Conservative party seems to be trying to kill me with kindness. There is your letter. There is Mr. Jeffers' column. There is a Christmas card from Jim Macdonnell, "hoping" I saw [the] column. There is an *Ottawa Journal* editorial, compounded of ecstatic praise of Mr. Drew, vicious snarls at the CCF generally and Mr. Coldwell in particular, and honeyed words for me and Pat Conroy, as too good for the company we keep … There is, of all things in the world, a Christmas card from the Drew family!

"WHY I AM A CANDIDATE FOR THE CCF"
(From Eugene Forsey's December 1948 campaign literature[16])

I started to work just before the Depression. I saw what it did to farmers, industrial workers and the people generally. I could not help feeling that a system which produces such calamities was basically un-Christian.

What was the answer? I became convinced that only the CCF policies can give us prosperity, security and full freedom. I believe that the policies of Mr. Drew and his party would deny us all three.

I would ask you to insist that both candidates stick to the issues: high prices, poor housing, power shortages, social security, farm problems, and all the other things that matter to you and me. Do not let my opponent — or me, for that matter — run away from these issues by dragging bogeys into the campaign.

We all recognize the communist threat to our democratic institutions. The question is, how do we meet it? I have had some first-hand experience in fighting communist influence in church organizations, trade unions, and other bodies. The only way to defeat communism is to remove the evils it thrives on. Those who promote monopoly control and high profits at the expense of the people, in fact, promote communism, whether they intend to or not.

Between now and December 20, I hope you will consider carefully the real issues of the campaign. I ask you to give both sides a fair hearing and to judge the case on its merits. If you select me, I shall do my best to deserve the honour and to serve you faithfully.

Incidentally, it does not seem to have struck [*Ottawa Journal* editor] Grattan O'Leary that his *ex post facto* compliments to my intelligence hardly chime with his election speech statement that, in accepting nomination, I was "motivated solely by personal political ambitions." Anyone with a tithe of the intelligence he now credits me with would hardly have chosen to gratify his "personal political ambitions" by running as a CCF candidate in

Carleton! I must be either a great deal stupider than he thinks, or not nearly as nasty![17]

Three years after that, Meighen was still urging his young friend to rethink his political affiliation and return to the Conservative fold. Dad, with yet another defeat as a CCF candidate behind him, continued to resist.

You say you have never been able to get me "into a real discussion on CCF fundamental policies." The reason is that I'm quite sure I would make no impression on you (I have no such presumptuous notion of my own powers) and, from what I've read of your arguments on the subject, I don't think you'd make much impression on me. All that would happen is that I'd cause you even more distress than you already feel whenever you think of my economic and social opinions; and what would be the good of that?

Besides, I'm no longer active in the CCF, nor likely to be, and I have neither the strength nor the capacity to be active in any other party, even if my opinions permitted. The Liberal Party is out of the question anyway, and the spectacle of me as a supporter of Mr. Drew ... would not be edifying. I'd be quite useless, and the welkin would ring with the denunciations of my present friends. So even if you could convert me, there would be no appreciable result. I can be of far more use ... where I am; and I can't be of much use except on one or two specific questions ... This will strike you as pusillanimous, but I know myself better than you do![18]

Two situations where Dad's views did coincide with those of the Conservative Party, and where he undoubtedly was of some use, have already been described: his battle to save the term "Dominion" as Canada's official title, and his opposition to the Liberal government's imposition of the TransCanada Pipeline legislation in 1956. During the infamous debate on that issue, my mother took my sister and me up to the House of Commons. I remember sitting in the gallery, trying to understand "which side" Dad was on, whether they were "winning," and why he wasn't down there himself in the thick of things, arguing with all those other people!

Indeed he would have loved to be. As he had previously confided to Meighen, "I remain obstinately convinced that I should be a useful member [of Parliament], especially if no party got a clear majority. I should then be in a position to talk turkey to the CCF on the position it ought to adopt."[19] He could have been a great help to his party on constitutional matters, and contributed directly to its progressive economic and social policies. But he never got to the House.

In describing himself as "no longer active" in the CCF, he was perhaps being overly modest. His level of involvement in the 1950s was nowhere near what it had been some years before, but the change was mainly due to the claims of a young family and an extremely demanding job that severely limited the time and energy he had for anything else. He was, in fact, very present to the CCF during that period, as his personal letters to people like M.J. Coldwell, Tommy Douglas and Angus McInnes make clear.

For instance, in 1955 he wrote to Coldwell to warn him about the dangers of a potential change to election procedures that he believed might be used to prevent CCF candidates from running in areas where the party was weak.[20] Characteristically, he also wrote to his Progressive Conservative friend Davie Fulton in the same vein, though in non-partisan terms; the interests of democracy transcended party lines.

But his real enthusiasm was reserved for the CCF. After the 1957 federal election he wrote to Coldwell: "Dear M.J, Belated but very hearty congratulations on your election, and on the various gains we have made ... The three gains in Northern Ontario are really exciting, and may be the portent of things to come ..."[21]

To Tommy Douglas he wrote: "It is evident that the funeral services some people were ready to conduct over the CCF will now have to be postponed." Ever the principled pragmatist, he added a bit of gentle advice: "I am inclined to think that next time we should do better not to run candidates in a lot of places like this Ottawa area, where the deposits alone have absorbed more than twelve years of my contributions to party funds."[22]

> ## "POVERTY, INSECURITY AND WANT"
> *(Excerpts from a 1948 exchange of letters with Arthur Meighen[23])*
>
> Meighen had written:
>
> ... In your post-election statement, you say that your war against poverty, insecurity and want will go on. Last evening when snow was falling heavily, [we] engaged a man to come this morning and shovel our walks. We have known John for years. He is a strong, healthy man, but he does not like work, and likes liquor somewhat too well. This morning he did not come. The walks were heavy in snow and slush; I had to get out and shovel the snow myself. Now, this man has always had security — as much security as can by any possibility be good for him. What strategy do you propose that will make effective war against his poverty and want?
>
> My father's reply:
>
> ... In trying to answer your letter I am faced with my old trouble: my inability to be polite and frank at the same time. However, I shall try. As an old "continuing Methodist," I should say "John" needed to be "soundly

His public identification with the CCF was unambiguous. Early in 1955, when David Lewis was attacked in the press for a statement he had made on behalf of the CCF's national council, Dad rose to Lewis's defence both publicly and privately.[24] In 1957, when the CCF celebrated its twenty-fifth anniversary with a "birthday party" in Ottawa, Dad spoke to the gathering about the past and future of the party, noting that although progress had been made, the "social revolution ... hasn't gone as far as some of us would like to go."[25] And his sharp criticisms of private broadcasting while on the Board of Broadcast Governors might, he joked later, have been dismissed by some as merely those of "that Socialist, that CCFer, that revolutionary, preaching his revolutionary doctrine."[26]

He was skeptical, however, about any possible future for himself in electoral politics. "If I ever do run anywhere," he wrote to Meighen, "I converted." In secular terms, he's a case for a social case-worker.

I should like to know what made "John" what he is: heredity; environmental factors, [or] both. Unless I had some idea of his background, I couldn't propose any effective "strategy" for dealing with his "poverty and want." I do not subscribe to a lot of the current talk that absolves the individual of moral responsibility; but I don't think individual moral responsibility is the whole story either.

Hard cases make bad law. I doubt if "John" is typical, and I question the validity of general conclusions based on cases like his.

I think a sound political program can do much to get rid of some causes of poverty, insecurity and want; not all. Nothing can get rid of the whole problem, any more than perfect health services could get rid of all pain and illness. But good health services can greatly reduce pain and illness, and good social policy can greatly reduce poverty, insecurity and want.

Some of your own party's policy, e.g. on social security, bears a considerable resemblance to CCF policy. There are important differences; but your party accepts the general principle of social security, at least. I should think your inquiry might be addressed also to Mr. Drew!

P.S. Don't do any more shovelling!

want it to be where I have some kind of fighting chance to poll at least a respectable vote; and I doubt whether any party will ever want to make itself responsible for my curious combination of ideas!"[27]

Meighen's predictable rejoinder was: "Eugene, you belong where I belong. Neither of us can ever find a Party with whose every creed we can fully comply. In matters big and vital, though, we agree."[28]

That my father's idea of what was "big and vital" differed from that of his old friend became crystal clear prior to the 1957 election, when Conservative leader John Diefenbaker offered Dad a nomination. He refused. After the Tory victory, in anticipation of the next election, he was invited to reconsider the offer. Among his papers I found a pencilled, hand-written draft of his response, directed to Derek Bedson, private secretary to Prime Minister Diefenbaker. Whether or not the letter was sent, I do not know for sure. But the draft is a moving statement of personal integrity and loyalty, and is worth quoting at length:

> The Prime Minister, this afternoon, was kind enough to remind me of his pre-election suggestion that I accept a Conservative nomination, and to ask if I was "still uninduceable." I said I was afraid so. He asked what was "wrong" with me. If he really wants to know, … you can show him this.
>
> On some basic issues, I agree with the Government's policy, so far as I know it. On no specific policy that I know of do I strongly differ. (The qualifications may, of course, be important …) Why, then, am I "still uninduceable"?
>
> 1. I have been a dues-paying member of the CCF for 25 years. I helped draft its Regina Manifesto. I have twice sat on its National Council. I have twice headed one of its provincial sections. I have four times been a CCF candidate, twice against the Leader of the Conservative Party. I owe my present position to the CCF … I have lived on terms of intimate friendship with the CCF leaders. I have fought by their side. I have described both the old parties as "political company unions." I have repeatedly, and strongly, spoken and written in favour of Labour's backing the CCF. In such circumstances, I do not see how anything less than a *crise de conscience* could justify my deserting my friends and comrades. No such reason exists.
>
> 2. I have been for 15 years a member and servant of the trade union movement. That movement welcomed an outsider unreservedly and has treated him generously; indeed, that is a gross understatement. I think I am trusted by the membership. I have not the smallest doubt that if I accepted a Conservative nomination without the most compelling reasons of conscience, the membership would feel betrayed. There are no such compelling reasons.

3. Such standing and reputation as I have, I owe entirely to a) my position in the Labour movement (apart from that, I'd just be an obscure minor crank), and b) (I think) people's belief that I'm honest. If I left my party on some great issue, and paid a price by losing my job, people could understand and respect that. If I left simply to further my own interests or ambitions, everyone could understand it, but who could respect it? That is inevitably what it would look like, ... and my usefulness to anyone, or to any of the things I believe in, would be utterly gone.

4. I think it goes even beyond that. I think if I did such a thing, it would really shock people, and would contribute to a growth of political cynicism which is already very dangerous ... I am sure that if I "ratted" (as CCF people and trade unionists would rightly consider it, unless there was obvious and compelling reason of principle) it would be a long time before the trade unions could trust any other middle class importation ...

5. This is all rather negative. Let me put it positively. I believe in most of the things the CCF and the unions advocate. (There are a few items I am dubious about, but not many.) It has yet to be proved (to put it mildly) that the Conservative Party can be a reliable instrument for getting those things done ... [or] that it does not contain powerful elements which don't want those things done, and will try to do very different things. It certainly contains people who have what seems to me a doctrinaire devotion to "free enterprise," a devotion with which I have no sympathy whatever.

The CCF, on the other hand, contains only people who want to do the things I think need doing. It contains some cranks, but a diminishing number, with diminishing influence. It shows less and less doctrinaire devotion to what used to be called "socialism," more and more willingness to use any honourable and effective method of attaining its basic objectives.

To sum up, there is less than no respectable reason why I should leave my own party; I should do only harm by leaving. Incidentally, I should certainly be worse than useless to the Conservative Party. That's what's "wrong" with me, and that's why I am "still uninduceable," and indeed, more so than ever.[29]

Dad's admission that he had reservations about a few aspects of trade union and CCF policy speaks more to his unwillingness to sacrifice critical thinking for political conformity than to any particular problems with the Congress or the party. The same goes for his rather odd reference to "what used to be called 'socialism.'" Both his own understanding of socialism and that of the CCF as a whole had been tempered and refined through experience, and his phrasing reflected, not a dampening of his fundamental political beliefs, but his rejection of "doctrinaire devotion" to blanket ideology of whatever sort.

Much more significant, in retrospect, is his repeated reference to some hypothetical "*crise de conscience*" over "some great issue," some "obvious and compelling reason of principle" that alone would justify his leaving his party. Sadly, his allusion turned out to be uncannily prophetic.

Several years earlier, Dad had seen one of his former comrades from the League for Social Reconstruction, Harry Cassidy, leave the CCF for the Liberals. In a letter to a fellow CCFer, Dad wrote: "Harry's attempt to get the provincial Liberal leadership hurt some of our [trade union] people very much. I thought, and still think, that attempt was a mistake. But I think I can understand why Harry made it. What would be not merely foolish but wrong for me, may be perfectly all right for other people with different tastes, capacities, opinions and associations. The older I get, the more inclined I am to follow the scriptural injunction, 'Judge not, that ye be not judged.'"[30]

When his time came, though, he too was judged.

Reflecting on the metamorphosis of the CCF into the NDP, historian Alan Whitehorn told me: "Your dad was a logical person to have carried on into the

New Party. Certainly he was an excellent contact for the linkage of the party and the labour movement, and introducing individuals within those various groups." For years, indeed, Dad had been urging trade unionists to support the CCF. So, in the late 1950s, when the long slow courtship between the two movements began to build towards a marriage, he was naturally involved.

Not as deeply involved as some might have expected, however. This was largely because of the heavy time demands of his research job at the Canadian Labour Congress and his work with the Board of Broadcast Governors. But other factors probably played a part as well.

I spoke at length with the late Michael Oliver, who chaired the committee charged with designing the proposed platform for the New Party (the interim name used during the negotiations between the CCF and the Labour Congress). "I'm not sure that Eugene didn't have some kind of worry that the New Party was going to be more closely related to some aspects of organized labour than he would really feel comfortable with," Professor Oliver mused. "[Perhaps] he looked back to a party which had constituency organizations, people from the universities and the churches and so on taking moral stands on issues, and wondered whether this new party wasn't going to be too opportunistic, too power-oriented ... Now that is pure speculation."

Be that as it may, Dad did share in the work of preparing for the transition. He helped draft the parts of the New Party Program dealing with labour legislation and with the CBC. He also provided detailed comments and suggestions on a series of preliminary documents, notably a discussion paper on the program early in 1960, and a revised draft program in March 1961.[31]

While some of his comments were relatively minor, many were substantive, like his criticism of the committee's proposed "Guaranteed Employment Act." Despite his best efforts to stop this wildly impracticable proposal at an earlier stage, it reached the floor of the NDP's 1961 Founding Convention intact. In the CBC's radio archives there is a lively clip of convention delegate Eugene Forsey saying what he thought of the idea, and trying to have the motion sent back to the drafting committee, presumably to die an unmemorable death.[32]

I don't think he ever actually carried out his threat to put to the convention a parallel motion for a "Guaranteed Perfect Health Act," but I found the draft thirty-seven years later among his papers. It reads:

THE GUARANTEED EMPLOYMENT ACT[33]
(Ottawa, July 21, 1961)

Hon. T.C. Douglas, MLA,
Prime Minister, Legislative Building,
Regina, Saskatchewan

Dear Tommy,
Just a brief note to beg you to use your influence in the New Party to get rid of one proposal in the Draft Program which will be a millstone round your neck when you take office: the Guaranteed Employment Act. I need not say that this proposal is utterly unworkable in a free society. Even a totalitarian Government could not produce results instantly.

Even if all the things we propose are put in train the day you take office, even if you proceed at full speed with all of them, even if they produce all the results we expect, and there are no hitches: even then, providing the necessary number of jobs will take many months. But this simple demagogic nonsense doesn't allow for a moment's delay: every citizen can pop into the National Employment Service office the morning after you're sworn in, and

I move that the section "National Health Plan" be referred back to the drafting committee with instructions to add a fourth paragraph, as follows: "To meet the temporary situation which will exist until the National Health Plan comes into full operation, the New Party will enact a Guaranteed Perfect Health Act. This Act will enable every sick Canadian to claim perfect health as a social right by applying at the office of the local Health Officer. The government will stand ready to supply perfect health for all age levels at fair prices."[34]

Foolish as the Guaranteed Employment Act proposal was, it took much more than that to get my father to leave the New Party. The "great demand a job... I doubt if the proposal is even smart politically. The public may be mugs, but not such mugs as to believe this rubbish, especially after the other parties and the press have finished making game of it.

How any grown-up person could have proposed such a thing is beyond me. How any committee could have been imprudent enough to approve [it] without asking the opinion of a single professional economist is one of the mysteries which are quite insoluble. I have long regarded myself as one of the most imprudent, incautious, rash, indiscreet people in the world; but behaviour like this would never even have entered my imagination in my wildest moments ...

No need to answer. I shall see you, if only from the audience, at the Convention. Best wishes.

Yours ever,

Eugene Forsey

Douglas did reply. "Like yourself," he wrote, "I am appalled when [people] concoct proposals which insult one's intelligence ... I have already suggested the elimination of the Guaranteed Employment Act ... Looking forward to seeing you at the Convention..."

issue" that pushed him to take that drastic action was no mere one-time foolishness. Rather, he felt it represented a fundamental political and philosophical shift that called into question the country's very existence. His "compelling reason of principle" was the NDP founding convention's deliberate denial that Canada was, in the words of the Fathers of Confederation, *"une seule et grand nation,"* "one nation," "a great nation," *"une puissante nation, une nation prospère."*

There are, of course, different views on what happened at that convention. Professor Oliver outlined the background to me. "We'd done all sorts of work on the Program Committee trying to find language which described a relationship of Quebec to the rest of Canada which would be acceptable. We recognized that French Canadians thought of themselves as a nation, and that they did so legitimately, but also that Canadians as a whole thought of themselves as a nation, and by implication this was a perfectly legitimate use of the term too. For better or worse, in both English and French, the word 'nation' is totally ambiguous, in some cases it's a synonym for 'state' and in other cases a synonym for something else."

On the linguistic ambiguity Dad agreed. What he had trouble with was the deliberate attempt to take advantage of that ambiguity for political purposes. As already explained, he objected to the sleight-of-hand by which one use of the word "nation" could be magically substituted for the other, and "French Canada" quietly exchanged for "Quebec," in order to hoodwink the unwary into supporting a thinly disguised separatist agenda.

Professor Whitehorn, who has written extensively about the CCF and the NDP and was the researcher for David Lewis's book *The Good Fight*, told me that at the time of the transition, the New Party "embraced very strongly the notion of two nations. A key plank in the formation of the NDP was to win over the progressive forces in Quebec, and the perception was that the young nationalists might be part of that progressive wave … The NDP was frankly embracing the new nationalism of the Quebecois in an uncritical way."

"Your father was much more skeptical of the new nationalism," Whitehorn said. "I think he was more an internationalist at heart, and very distrusting of the force of nationalism in terms of its proclivity to erode the rights of individuals and minorities. [He] could see perhaps the excessive optimism of many in the CCF who thought Quebec nationalism could be won over to social democracy and achieve a breakthrough for the New Party."

As well, there were almost certainly differing interpretations and intentions among the "two nations" proponents themselves. According to Oliver, the architects of the New Party "never really did talk about an English-Canadian nation and a French-Canadian nation. That has been claimed; but the notion of two nations, one English-speaking and one French-speaking, was something the NDP never jumped onto. The two nations we were talking about were Canada — a political nation, if you like — and the sociological kind of nation which French-speaking Quebeckers felt they were a part of." (I can almost hear Dad's comments on that!)

However, Oliver continued, "once the convention got under way, there was no controlling it, whatsoever. All this careful work, recognizing French Canada but asserting the notion of Canada as a whole, went down the drain when you had this unholy alliance between Michel Chartrand and Hazen Argue, who proceeded to get a resolution denying the validity of the adjective 'national' to anything to do with the federal government. The convention, in a great wave of '*bon entente*' enthusiasm, passed this absolutely ridiculous motion to substitute the adjective 'federal' for the adjective 'national' in all documents of the party, which I thought was a silly, silly thing. But I didn't feel that it was quite the matter of absolute principle that Eugene thought it was."

One of Dad's files in the national archives contains three pages of scrap paper with his hastily scribbled notes, obviously written during the convention. Phrases like "shameful and degrading," "not actual grievances," "strait-jackets flapping," "the revolt against reason," and "no room for me," give the flavour of his fury and frustration with what he saw as a craven capitulation to a fraudulent doctrine.[35] He rose on the convention floor and argued against the motion with all the reason and passion at his command. He went to Tommy Douglas personally and told him, "You cannot build a party on a lie." But his protestations had no visible effect. He resigned from the new party shortly afterwards.

During his campaign to keep the word "Dominion" some years earlier, Dad had anticipated how the CCF would react to his protests on that subject. "It's no use, I fear, saying anything to the leaders of my own party," he wrote to Mr. Meighen. "They will simply laugh, and consider it an eccentricity."[36] That was apparently what happened at the convention on the "two nations" issue.

Desmond Morton, professor emeritus and founding director of the McGill Institute for the Study of Canada, was a young NDPer at the time of the 1961 convention. "Back in those days," he told me, "I certainly didn't understand the arguments particularly. I did want the new party to succeed where the old party had failed, and the old party had failed at the Ottawa River. The CCF in Quebec, like the NDP now, was really a tiny rump of devoted people ... That was something I wanted to change." Dad of course shared that goal, but rejected the notion that the way to achieve it was to perform what he called "the ceremonial kowtow to the Quebec nationalists."

I asked Morton how my father was seen in the NDP after he quit. "Well, I suppose when you're in a cause, you don't like defectors," he said. "Ramsay Cook, who left for rather similar reasons a year later, was also seen with great indignation by people who had accepted the compromises, who couldn't understand what it was all about. Here were two people who kept saying how important it was to get support from Quebec; who had led the party in this province; all of a sudden here seems to be a serious chance to get into the province ... I don't think we were very sympathetic to [Eugene's] reasons for going. I understand them a lot better now than I did then."

"He understood the issue of 'two nations,' *'deux nations*,'" Morton explained, "[and] its full implications in the eyes of Quebeckers. He thought it was nonsense, and he said so. People like me were willing to say, 'Well, if that's what they believe, in a free and democratic society, there should be different views on how the country operates.' The problem is that when those ideas operate at a very considerable level of influence and importance, and are not reflected across the country, there is the greatest possibility of misunderstanding. That misunderstanding has come to pass, and may threaten the future of this country."

Alan Whitehorn shared with me his own retrospective view. "Ultimately, I think your father was right to be more skeptical. In the 1960s, it was easy to assume that nationalism would be a modern, progressive force for Quebec, but I think increasingly those of us in the Left now appreciate that nationalism can cut both ways: it can be a force of liberation but it can also be a force of repression."

"In all the many discussions that I had with David Lewis working on the memoirs," Whitehorn told me, "he only had positive things to say about your dad. Clearly he was disappointed that Eugene did not stay with the NDP, but I think he very much respected Eugene's independence and sharp analytical mind. Later in life, I think David may have appreciated a bit more that the new wave of Quebec nationalism was not the panacea for the NDP that he might have hoped for and worked for in 1961."

In August 1965, Dad addressed the Couchiching Conference on the national unity issue.[37] Afterwards, the research director for the United Steelworkers, Harry Waisglass, wrote to congratulate him. "I wish there were many more voices like yours speaking out persuasively for a strengthened Canadian federalism," Waisglass wrote. "Unfortunately, the NDP Founding Convention was in no mood to listen to such voices. Now, as then, you have my full sympathy and support."[38]

Deeply moved, Dad replied: "It is quite beyond me to say how pleased I was to get your letter, the more so as I know that you are far from uncritical. I am particularly interested and pleased to find that you thought I took the right line in 1961 on this matter. I am afraid subsequent events have made me feel like Cassandra."[39]

So ended my father's long-time membership in Canada's party of social democracy. It was not an end he welcomed. On the contrary, despite his differences with the CCF over the years, such an end was something he had made every effort to avoid. But it finally came down to choosing between his principles and his party. For Dad, there really wasn't any choice.

"Without Dr. Eugene Forsey," commented a newspaper editorial at the time, "the NDP will be duller than it might have been. And it will have less hope of keeping its feet on the ground without his honed logic to puncture utopian balloons. Dr. Forsey's capacity for articulate indignation, which rose to noble heights during the Pipe Line Debate and the imposition of closure in the Commons, is too valuable to be considered the property of any one party … It will do Canada no harm to have Dr. Forsey without political ties, free to be a thorn in the side of all parties."[40]

That was in fact the role my father played throughout the last thirty years of his life, his stint with the Liberals notwithstanding. It had long been the role he was most comfortable in. "I should be a very uneasy member of any caucus," he once confided to a friend, "which makes it fortunate that I have had such an extremely unsuccessful political career."

So, however unwillingly it had been entered upon, Dad's new-found independence from party affiliation fitted him like a glove. After his electoral defeat in 1949, he had told Mr. Meighen: "I am really glad I am out of politics. It leaves me much freer to call nonsense by its right name."[41] Truly unfettered at last, he took advantage of his many opportunities to do just that.

Through most of the 1960s, whenever he could spare time from his labour history work, he happily wandered the political landscape, pricking here and prodding there. He wrote speeches and articles on national unity and various constitutional questions, and in a stream of letters to the press, addressed not only those issues, but also matters as diverse as incorrect

English, exorbitant consultants' fees, the rights of non-smokers, and the risks of joining the Organization of American States. He denounced and dismantled whatever he saw as "nonsense," regardless of its source — and that included any or all of the political parties.

At the same time, he managed to maintain strong ties with people he liked and respected, whatever their party. And the feelings were mutual. At a Conservative-sponsored conference in 1964, Tory Senator Jacques Flynn introduced him with these words: "I will now call on none other than Monsieur Eugène Forsey. It may explain the personality of Mr. Forsey to know that he was born in Newfoundland, that he is now research director of the Canadian Labour Congress, but never misses a Conservative meeting."[42] The crowd — and my Dad — roared with laughter.

It was in those same years that Dad met World War II veteran John Matheson, newly elected as a Liberal MP and soon to become parliamentary secretary to Prime Minister Lester Pearson. Despite his own strong party affiliation, Matheson always truly appreciated Dad's lack of partisanship. "Most people in a political party fit into categories," he told me, "and have to be loyal to the party to some degree. Well, here was Eugene Forsey without any burden of responsibility in that sense, willing to do what he saw was right at the time … That was not only a liability but also his great asset."

On the liability side, Matheson admitted that he "wouldn't have wanted [Eugene] as commander of a regiment, or put too much store in him as a strategist for the Liberal Party … He was truly a maverick, in the sense of a person who was his own man. Nobody could entirely predict what he might do."

Dad's friend John Hastings put it a little differently. "I always thought your father was enormously consistent in his approach to things," he said. "But you had to know these various principles, the underlying values that had shaped his thinking." Exactly.

Proof of this supposed unpredictability — and of its paradoxical consistency — came in 1968, when Pearson was retiring and the Liberal Party was preparing to choose a new leader. One of the candidates was Pierre Elliott Trudeau, Dad's friend from the Institut canadien des affaires publiques, who had already distinguished himself as a progressive minister of justice in Pearson's cabinet. Dad believed that Trudeau's powerful stand on national unity was not only "profoundly right" but in fact essential for the future of the country. He publicly supported Trudeau's leadership bid, and was delighted when Trudeau won.

Even so, he maintained his non-partisan status as a "rank outsider" to the Liberal Party. He made clear his continuing endorsement of the new prime minister's policies on Quebec and Canada, but he did so without joining up. Nor did he accept Trudeau's two offers of patronage appointments, one as Indian claims commissioner and the other as — of all things — ambassador to the Vatican! In the original manuscript of his memoirs, his accout of these offers was part of a section headed: "Jobs I had Sense Enough to Refuse."

In 1970, however, when Trudeau invited him to sit in the Senate, Dad accepted. What's more, he chose to sit as a member of the government's caucus.

On the graph of my father's political life, his Liberal period appears as a large blip in the middle of three decades of non-partisan independence. Given his life story, it was indeed extraordinary to see him wearing the label of the party he had hitherto so vigorously and steadfastly condemned.

Our Newfoundland cousin Alex Hickman's reaction was typical. Alex had himself once been provincial attorney general in Joey Smallwood's Liberal cabinet, but had subsequently crossed the floor to sit as a Tory. When Dad arrived in St. John's for a visit not long after his appointment to the Senate, Alex went to pick him up. "I congratulated him on his appointment, and I said, 'What party are you with?' And he said, 'Liberal.' I said, 'You're not! You're pulling my leg. You hate Liberals! You despise them. You told me how wise I was to get away from them. What are you doing with the Liberals?'"

Sixteen years later, the CBC's Ian Alexander asked Dad the same question, only more gently. "For someone who had so little use for 'Grits,'" he said, "someone who felt the way you did about Mackenzie King, becoming a card-carrying Liberal must have been a little difficult for you, surely, no?"

"Yes," my father replied, "but it was completely outweighed by the importance of the issue."[43]

His reasons for this assertion should be clear from the previous chapter's discussion of the national unity question. But I would situate his incarnation as a Liberal in an even broader context: the historical anomaly of the 1970s. During those years, the spirit and practice of the Liberal Party were far more closely aligned with my father's cherished beliefs than they have been at any time before or since.

Although the memory of it is sadly fading, that decade, especially early on, was an era of relative openness and generosity in Canada — an ambience actively fostered by the federal Liberal government. Trudeau's dream of a "just society" was still fresh and widely shared. Women's rights and Aboriginal rights were beginning to be recognized; the country's multicultural reality was increasingly being acknowledged; international co-operation was receiving funding and attention. The public institutions Canadians cherish — medicare, the CBC, unemployment insurance, the Canada Council, the National Film Board, as well as numerous programs for youth and local communities — were being strengthened and expanded, not attacked and diminished. "Government" had not yet become a dirty word.

There were people of principle in Trudeau's cabinet — people like Warren Allmand, Charles Caccia, Monique Bégin, and Eugene Whelan — individuals who, like my father, believed in a vision of the public good and stood up for those beliefs regardless of consequences to themselves. Not surprisingly, some of Trudeau's Senate appointments were similarly progressive — besides my Dad, Thérèse Casgrain, Carl Goldenberg, and Florence Bird all spring to mind.

So if my father was ever to do the unheard-of and take on a Liberal identity, the 1970s was the time to do it. Moreover, the Senate was the place. As already noted, the relative non-partisanship of the Red Chamber back then was something he appreciated from the day he made his maiden speech. "I do not feel that there is an obligation on every … supporter of the Government to be a rubber stamp, to sign on the dotted line," he told his fellow senators. "If I feel strongly enough on [a] subject, I shall be prepared to stand up and be counted."[44] And that is precisely what he did throughout his nine years there.

He took every opportunity to publicly extol the freedom senators had to discuss each issue on its merits rather than being pushed to divide along party lines. For him, this freedom meant that he was able to sit on the Liberal benches and do what he felt needed doing, without having to change either his ideas or the independence with which he expressed and practised them. Of course, as he recounts in *A Life on the Fringe*, this penchant for autonomy did not always sit well with the party establishment, who initially were reluctant even to give him credentials for a Liberal conference![45]

In retrospect, Dad often said that he should have sat in the Senate as an independent, especially since he always spoke and voted as if he were. Such a choice might also have been easier for many of his critics on the Left to accept. After all, as an independent senator he could still have supported the many Trudeau policies he agreed with, without actually adopting the party label. At the time, however, he felt that joining the Liberal caucus was the most powerful way for him to show his support for Trudeau's position on national unity, and having made that decision, he gave it his best effort.

While doing the research for this book, I came across a speech he gave to a Liberal gathering in 1976, just after Trudeau had introduced anti-inflation controls on prices and wages. The phrasing, shaped for his partisan audience, sounds odd to my ears, not my father's usual style. Yet the speech is actually a good example of both his integrity and his political astuteness. He began with a pitch that linked the concept of liberalism — "at its best" — to his own basic values.

"Liberalism," he said, "has always recognized the necessity of some limits to, some controls upon, individual and corporate freedom ... Liberalism at its best has never stood for the right of individuals or groups of individuals to grab, grind, oppress, cheat, swindle, pollute, poison or destroy ..."

He went on to address the specific issue of the controls.

"No Liberal ever wants controls for their own sake. Very few other people do either. Controls are a headache to controller and controlled alike ... Our Liberal Government, with proper Liberal reluctance to impose controls, tried hard to get business and the unions to adopt the policies which would make government intervention superfluous ..."[46]

And so on — selecting and appealing to the best of the ideals the Liberals claimed as their own; begging the question of the party's actual record on those ideals; and staking out the moral high ground in such a way that his audience was pretty well obliged to join him there.

Reading this determinedly Liberal exhortation from — of all people — my father, I also had to chuckle at how he managed to incorporate into it not only an opening quotation from his old CCF colleague Frank Underhill, but also a second one, from "a great Canadian nearly forty years ago" — his Tory friend and mentor, Arthur Meighen![47]

This ability to subtly undermine people's narrow partisan attitudes was something he used to good effect with other parties as well. One example was his 1980 *Maclean's* article on neo-conservatism, in which he cited a reported statement by a policy advisor to Mulroney.

"'A traditional conservative,' we were told, 'believes that no government is the best government, in the most narrow of all senses.' What that last phrase may mean, I have no idea. But the rest of it made me sit up. By that definition a traditional conservative is simply an anarchist. This would have surprised every British Conservative leader since 1834."[48]

As early as the 1950s, Dad had been lamenting the demise of what he saw as the true Conservative tradition in Canada. He had become more and more disillusioned with the Tories, particularly after 1967 when they too adopted a "two nations" policy. In the Senate, of course, he had friends on both sides of the Chamber, and the largely non-partisan atmosphere there helped him maintain those friendships. But by the time Brian Mulroney had been in power for a few years, my father's opinion of the Tory party had sunk to a permanent low. Indeed, he now spoke of the Mulroney Conservatives in the kind of terms he had formerly reserved for Mackenzie King's Liberals: "pirates," "knaves," "skunks," "swindlers."[49]

"I can see no resemblance whatever," he told Tom Earle in 1989, "between the present Progressive Conservative party and the Conservative party in which I was brought up. None. This crowd are all American free enterprisers. This is not traditional Canadian Conservatism."

In the same interview, he described what had led him to leave the Liberal Party after twelve years in its ranks. "I was disgusted by the attitude the Government took up on the inquiry into the 'dirty tricks' practices of the RCMP, [and] by the cuts in Via Rail. They'd cut various services, particularly in the Maritime provinces ... I was incensed by this fresh attack upon the interests of the Atlantic provinces, so I got out of the Party; I formally resigned."[50]

As on previous occasions, however, he stayed on cordial terms with his friends in the party he had left. Pierre Trudeau responded to his resignation by saying, "We were lucky to have you for as long as we did." Dad called it "a very gracious and generous reply." The graciousness and generosity were hardly surprising. After all, as John Matheson told me, Pierre Trudeau and Eugene Forsey "were rather alike. They were both free spirits."

In 1983, my father received a letter from the NDP's federal secretary, Gerry Caplan, inviting him to Regina for the party's "anniversary convention," celebrating fifty years since the Regina Manifesto and the founding of the CCF. Dad was to be honoured as one of the movement's pioneers. "We would love you to be there," Caplan wrote, "sitting at the head table, getting the tribute you deserve."[51]

Dad replied: "I am most grateful for your kind letter … But I don't think I should go. I think my presence would, to say the least, not be welcomed by many, perhaps most, of the delegates." He then proceeded to outline in a few paragraphs the story of his changing political affiliations — the same story recounted in this chapter. "In the light of all this," he concluded, "I think my presence in Regina would be inappropriate, and would be widely resented by members of the Party … So, though I should greatly like to be present, I am convinced I ought not to be. I am, again, most grateful for the invitation; but it just wouldn't do."[52]

Reading his words a quarter century later, I can feel my father's pain. I don't recall him even mentioning the matter to me at the time. But now I wish I could have been there for him, to offer perhaps some small comfort, some bit of understanding, as once again he went "marching up the great, bare staircase of his duty" — alone.

CHAPTER SIXTEEN

Canada and the World: A Progressive Legacy

This generation faces the worst problems any generation has ever faced. You, and your like across the world, confront problems which might daunt the brightest and the bravest. You have a right to expect us older people to give what help we can. I hope also that you will be willing to draw upon those deep spiritual resources which our generation has too often rejected or neglected.
— From a 1976 convocation address at Carleton University[1]

One of my favourite pictures of my father appeared in the *Ottawa Citizen* on a September day in 1974. It showed him picketing in front of the Chilean Embassy on the first anniversary of the bloody military coup that overthrew that country's democratically elected socialist government and launched the brutal Pinochet regime. He was carrying a sign that read: RESTORE CIVIL LIBERTIES IN CHILE.

Eugene demonstrating in solidarity with the Chilean people against the brutal Pinochet regime, 1974. (Courtesy Ottawa Citizen*)*

A year earlier, the day after the coup itself, he had risen in the Senate to declare:

> This was a tragedy, not only for Chile and for South America, but for the world. Here was a case where there seemed to be some hope that revolutionary developments — which

I think were highly necessary in that country — would be carried through by democratic and constitutional means.

It now appears that this hope has been destroyed, and I cannot help feeling that this will provide sad ammunition for subversive elements throughout the world, who will be in a position to say ... "Learn the lesson. The thing is hopeless. It cannot be done except by violence." To my mind this is a great tragedy.[2]

That picture and the excerpt from the Senate Hansard sum up for me a great deal of what my father was about. It's all there: his enduring commitment both to "revolutionary developments" and to peaceful, constitutional means for achieving them; his concern for civil liberties, here and elsewhere in the world; his own unassuming personal participation in grassroots protest.

In Dad's later years, public coverage of his ideas and activities focused mainly on the constitutional and national unity aspects of his work. As a result, it was not always obvious how broad and progressive his perspective was. Yet that perspective was never absent. As the world changed and new challenges emerged, he continued to dedicate his energies to the common good.

To some, the Canadian Senate might seem an odd place for a progressive elder statesman like Eugene Forsey to find his niche. Long-time NDP MP Svend Robinson first knew Dad in the early 1970s. He told me he had been "a little bit perplexed" by the fact that this man whom he had "admired from afar" was now sitting in Parliament's upper house. "He was feisty, he was a fighter," Robinson said. "What the hell was he doing in the Senate, right? But ultimately, I think he saw that as a platform from which to advocate."

Exactly. As my father told Peter Gzowski in a 1990 interview, "I thought I could be of some use there."[3]

In his memoirs, Dad outlined some of his efforts to be of use during his nine years as a senator. Among them, of course, were his speeches and committee work on constitutional matters, and the frustrating and time-consuming work of the Statutory Instruments Committee, which he co-chaired. He certainly provided a lively counterbalance to the all-too-common idea of "senators as lazy old busters who sit twiddling their thumbs and don't earn their keep."[4]

DEFENDING CHILEAN DEMONSTRATORS
(From a letter to Solicitor-General Warren Allmand, September 1973[5])

Dear Warren,
Yesterday as I came out from lunch, there was a group of Chilean students marching around in front of the [Parliament] Building. They carried placards denouncing the coup in Chile, and asking for help for the victims ... [As] I was conversing with two or three, an RCMP officer came up and informed them they must disperse.

I at once protested, strongly, pointing out that there had been scores of such demonstrations on the Hill over the past three years, and that I had even taken part in one or two of them myself. The officers kept insisting it was forbidden ... They then showed me a copy of the National Capital Commission Traffic and Property Regulation. [It] prohibits displaying signs or flags or distributing leaflets.

I entered a strong protest against what appeared to me to be rank discrimination, [and] sent in a note to [External Affairs Minister] Sharp, which he showed to the Prime Minister.

If this is NCC property, and the Regulation applies, I have not the slightest objection to its being enforced, provided it is enforced against everybody. I object strongly to its being not enforced against Ukrainians, railway workers, *les gars de Lapalme*, the Communist Party, etc., all of whom have paraded up here with apparent impunity, and [its] then being suddenly enforced against this particular group.

I need hardly point out that this could blow up into a very considerable *cause célèbre*. Indeed, if proper action is not taken, I shall consider it my duty to see that public attention is drawn, very pointedly, to what appears to be going on. And where I might chastise with whips, the NDP and even the Conservatives might chastise with scorpions. There may be some perfectly satisfactory explanation ... But the matter certainly needs to be cleared up ...

From a follow-up memo:
The Solicitor-General has cleared the whole thing up ... Parliament Hill does not come under [those] Regulations. The ... officers were under [a] misapprehension. I venture to think there may have been some relation between my protests and the clarification which ensued. Perhaps I may have earned my keep for one day, anyhow!

I'm ashamed to say that even after I got back to Canada in 1974, I never went up to the Senate Gallery to hear him speak, though my sons and I enjoyed visits to his office and lunches in the Parliamentary Restaurant. But he quite often sent me issues of *Hansard* with his speeches, which offer ample evidence of the "feistiness" that Robinson referred to. They also show the wide range of his concerns, and demonstrate the progressive views he held on all sorts of issues.

From his seat in the Red Chamber, he spoke and voted in favour of Aboriginal rights and limits on the powers of bureaucrats.[6] He supported affirmative action measures for women and native people in the public service, and pressed for the protection of linguistic minorities.[7] He questioned the government's prohibition on political advocacy by charitable organizations, urging that such groups be allowed to "engage in petitions or peaceful demonstrations on behalf of ... people who they feel are being oppressed," without risking the loss of their charitable status.[8]

Never forgetting his labour background, he spoke and voted against back-to-work legislation in a strike by air traffic controllers, arguing that the bill made free collective bargaining an illusion, and insisting that a better way had to be found.[9] He urged an inquiry into the wage practices of Canadian companies in South Africa and Namibia, citing information that he found "disquieting to even a moderately sensitive Canadian conscience."[10] In a vigorous 1976 speech opposing a national lottery, he called it a form of regressive taxation and, in the words of a former Labour Congress colleague, "a method for skinning the poor."[11]

Allying himself with his NDP friends in "the other place," he argued (unsuccessfully) for important amendments to the Liberals' 1978 unemployment insurance legislation.[12] He also echoed the NDP's opposition to the proposal to entrench property rights in the Constitution, a proposal which fortunately was not enacted in the 1982 repatriation package.[13] That persistent American idea is nonetheless still being recycled in various forms by the right wing in this country, who must see the huge advantages such a guarantee would give to the biggest owners of property — the global corporations — at the expense of ordinary citizens and the environment.

My father's senatorial status also gave him a public profile beyond Parliament Hill, which he used to full advantage for promoting the public good. And his concerns were not circumscribed by lines on a map.

"Senator Rails Canadians to Help Third World" ran the headline on an *Ottawa Citizen* article in November 1976. "The wealth of Canadians is scandalous in contrast to the horrifying poverty of most the world's people, Senator Eugene Forsey said Sunday. In a vigorous speech, the 72-year-old senator told Carleton University's 64th convocation that egotism and indifference must end if Canada is to respond properly to the needs of the Third World ..."[14]

Dad had always been an internationalist by inclination. His travels as a young man in Europe and the Soviet Union, his facility with different languages, his study of constitutional issues in Commonwealth countries, and his international connections with other democratic socialists and labour people had all broadened his horizons far beyond Canada's borders.

His trip to India in 1953 for the World University Service Seminar, and the friendships that resulted from it, strengthened his international perspective and deepened his awareness of the so-called "developing" world. On his return, he reflected on what had been, for him, a hugely significant experience: "Across half the world, across differences of creed and colour and political belief, we built bridges which I think will last."[15]

And last they did. Not long before his death he wrote: "My six weeks on the sub-continent left me with an abiding interest in, and affection for, its peoples, but also with a strong consciousness of the enormous, and intractable, problems they faced. That India has survived is evidence of the strength of its civilization, and the genius of its people. India, and my generous, warm-hearted Indian friends, will always have a special place in my heart."[16]

Latin America was another part of the world where my father had strong personal connections. He had, after all, been conceived in Mexico, and he was pleased when I spent two summers there on a student exchange in the 1960s. By the early 1970s, I had been working for several years in international co-operation, and he had a son-in-law and two grandsons of Ecuadorian heritage.

During Dad's first few years in the Senate, my family and I were overseas with CUSO, first in West Africa and then back in South America. There was a *coup d'état* in Ghana during our time there, and shortly after we arrived in Ecuador that country too underwent a bloodless "*golpe militar.*" As we planned our return to Canada in 1974, Dad joked: "I'd better warn Pierre you're coming!"

INDIA AND CANADA: A SENSE OF PROPORTION[17]
(From a report on the 1953 World University Service seminar in Mysore, India)

The biggest thing the Seminar did for me was to give me a better sense of proportion. We in Canada think we have problems, and we have. But they are simplicity itself beside India's. India's population is [twenty-five times that of Canada] and increasing [rapidly]; India's per capita national income is 4 percent of ours. We have two [official] languages; India has fourteen. Over 80% of [her] people are illiterate; expectation of life is about 32 years ...

One could go on, almost indefinitely: problem after problem, each one staggering in size, baffling in complexity; poverty, hunger, disease, ignorance, unemployment and underemployment on a gigantic scale, infinite personal tragedy; and everything that looks like a remedy for the situation blocked by a variety of formidable obstacles.

India is making a stupendous effort to solve her problems by democratic means. If it succeeds, it will be a triumph unparalleled in history. But if it fails — and the odds against it are appalling — it will be a disaster, not only for India but for us ... [Given] our common membership in the Commonwealth and our common humanity, we must help, must bear our share in a common task.

We are helping now, yes: 25 million dollars a year: between one-tenth and one-fifth of one percent of our national income. Not too impressive for the second richest country in the world, especially one which has just cut taxes by 250 million and some of whose political leaders are proposing to cut them [even more]. We ought to be doing much more ...

It's bound to be a long pull, even if it's a pull all together. But the first essential, for us, is to waken up to the need, and to be ready to take our share in meeting it; to rouse ourselves from indifference and lethargy and the patronizing attitude that [it] is a matter of "hand-outs." Canada can make a big contribution, the bigger because no one can accuse her of "imperialistic" ambitions. We should start now.

That bit of levity, however, belied the very serious apprehensions he felt about the state of the world. He had always had a far-reaching concern for people and the earth, but in his later years he was deeply troubled by the overwhelming scope and urgency of planetary problems.

His message to Carleton's 1976 graduating class was not a soothing one. In it he challenged the graduates to address the "new and inescapable realities" facing Canadians and the world — the growing scarcity of energy, raw materials, and food; the growing power and rising expectations of the people producing those things; the exponential growth of world population; and, last but not least, the massive threat of pollution.

Still, his speech was neither a guilt trip nor a dirge of despair; it was a call to action. The future, he said, would demand: "much plainer living, much harder thinking, much more intense feeling for the disadvantaged and the disinherited, in our own country and across the world. We, the non-poor, are going to have to adjust ourselves to a new scale of priorities … to accept a considerable, even a massive, redistribution of wealth and resources."

That adjustment would mean we would have to change not only our economic expectations but also much of our dependence on modern conveniences and technology. Dad emphasized that this would be far from easy.

"Getting large masses of people to change their minds on those subjects which directly, and deeply, affect their own incomes and their own convenience is a huge and daunting job," he said. "The changes that will have to be made will run into fierce, and understandable, resistance … 'What! Clear the private automobile out of the city centres, stop poisoning the atmosphere and stop gargantuan waste of an irreplaceable source of energy?'"

Then, risking the wrath of purists on the left, he ventured further. "That resistance will come not only from the rich, the tycoons, the multinational corporations, but also from the unions in the prosperous industries which flourish on squandering resources, on polluting air and water and devastating countrysides … The welkin will ring with the outraged cries of big business and little, of unions and their members, of municipal, provincial and national electors."

His blunt realism was also constructive. He stressed the need for the kind of approach the labour movement has called "a just transition" for affected sectors and communities.

Devising the means to cushion the blows, to provide alternative employment and income for people displaced by the changes, will tax the ingenuity of statesmen and economists. Persuading the democratic electorate to accept the changes, even with workable plans to look after the displaced, will tax the resources of educators, elected politicians, and elected labour leaders.

Government and labour politicians can get only so far ahead of those whose support they must seek. They need all the help their constituents — which means us — can give them. Democracy, in its true sense, means not simply a system of government. It means us.[18]

My father had always taken very seriously the "us" in democracy, and that did not cease when he retired from the Senate in 1979. His ongoing work on many fronts earned him the epithet of "the most un-retired of retired senators," and it continued as long as he drew breath.

One of the "odd jobs" on his plate following that second retirement was to complete the remaining work on the mammoth labour history book, *Trade Unions in Canada: 1812–1902*, which was finally published in 1982.[19] He was also asked to write the authoritative popular handbook on our system of government. *How Canadians Govern Themselves* first came out in 1980, and has graced the desks of MPs in their constituency offices and the shelves of school libraries across the country ever since. The Library of Parliament recently published the latest edition, in French and English, both in book form and on the Internet.[20]

When a group of prominent Canadians came together in the early 1980s to push for solutions to the urgent global questions of nuclear disarmament, human rights and a fairer international economic order, Dad was honoured to join. His fellow members included his old friends and socialist colleagues King Gordon and Frank Scott, as well as Margaret Atwood, Tommy Douglas, Thérèse Casgrain, the Reverend Lois Wilson, Jacques Hébert, Marion Dewar, and Ursula Franklin. Today the Group of 78 is still in existence, focussing on issues of peace and security, economic equity, global governance and environmental quality.

Eugene speaking to the Rotary Club in Belleville, Ontario, 1978.

In 1985, the Special Committee on Parliamentary Reform commissioned Dad and Graham Eglington to research and write a comprehensive paper on the question of "confidence" in our parliamentary system. Together with *Freedom and Order*, his 1974 book of constitutional essays, *The Question of Confidence in Responsible Government* probably represents the closest Dad came to fulfilling his longstanding intention of completing the work on cabinet government that he had begun with the Guggenheim Fellowship in 1941. Although the 324-page treatise was never published, it sits on the shelves of the Library of Parliament where it continues to serve as a reference.[21]

Some of the things my father did during his "retirement" years I know of only vaguely. I recall him mentioning at one point some involvement in the process of drafting a new bill of rights for post-apartheid South Africa. I suspect he assisted with many other worthy causes of which I remain oblivious. Dad was not one to boast. Of course, I knew about his three-year fight against the Meech Lake Accord and about his work on his memoirs, but beyond that I had no clear idea of his various projects. It was only in 1990, when he presented me with a pristine copy of *Evatt and Forsey on the Reserve Powers*, that I realized he had laboured for half a decade to research and write the hundred-page introductory update to this third edition of his magnum opus.[22]

The summer of 1990 was labelled Canada's "Indian summer." When Mohawk men and women took a stand in defence of their ancestral lands at Oka near Montreal, troops invaded their communities and turned them into militarized zones. The seventy-seven-day stand-off rocked the country, filling the TV screens and launching a sea change in public awareness about Aboriginal peoples.

That was also Dad's last summer, and his physical feebleness was becoming increasingly evident. But in the fall, when the government refused to hold a full parliamentary inquiry into "the Oka affair," he summoned up his erstwhile vigour and wrote to the *Globe and Mail* about this "staggering piece of news."

"What, precisely, did the army find to warrant the horrendous, the blood-curdling tales we were treated to, day after day, week after week? What did all the 'sound and fury' signify? The helicopters turned their searchlight on the Mohawks. Is Parliament not to be allowed to turn its searchlight on the actions of the governments, the police and the army? ... If there is nothing to hide, why should it be hidden from the people's representatives?"[23]

That role of watchdog in the public sphere was one my father never resigned. To do so would have been to abandon the habits and principles of a lifetime. Given his prodigious abilities, his "bad-tempered" penchant for argument, and his belief in a God of justice and love, that role really seemed to be what he was called to do.

True, that calling meant he was constantly drawn into battle, and perennially found himself in a minority position of one sort or another. But he knew that battles can be worthwhile, even when they are not won, and he knew that minorities can offer leadership and inspiration for necessary change. Moreover, as he told the young people at the temperance conference, for the most part he had "a whale of a time" in the process.[24]

Twenty years after his death, I see that same spirit reflected in the work of citizens in Canada and around the world who carry on the multi-facetted struggle for the common good. Despite setbacks and discouragement, they continue trying to curb the illegitimate use of government and corporate power, protesting abuses and hypocrisy wherever they occur, and practising solidarity and compassion. In all those struggles — and in the love and laughter that are part of them — my father's progressive legacy lives on.

Epilogue

My father had a story from his days with the Labour Congress about being introduced as a speaker by the then premier of Prince Edward Island. The introduction was brief. "This is Mr. Forsey," the premier said. "I don't know much about him, but here he is."

During Dad's speech, the premier sat glowering, for he was not a man known for his socialist sympathies. Then he rose to give the formal vote of thanks. "When I introduced Mr. Forsey, I said I didn't know much about him," he growled. "I know plenty now!"

The reader may now be able to say the same, though I hope in a different tone. But more important than simply knowing about my father is to understand what he stood for and why, so as to continue his legacy by working for the common good of our country and the planet.

That is why I chose to write, not a biography, but a different kind of book — a portable package of his gifts, a kit filled with the tools that he left us. If more Canadians now find themselves quoting my Dad, reflecting on what he said and did about the perennial issues that face our country and the world, following his example of integrity and participatory citizenship, they will be paying him the best tribute his spirit could wish.

I have caught glimpses along the way of how this has in fact been happening. While this manuscript was still in its early stages, I got a call from a woman in Toronto whom I had never met. "I've been reading your father's book," said the stranger, and before I could ask which one she launched into an excited explanation. She was part of a citizens' group fighting the good fight against some retrograde governmental scheme, and the book she was talking about was — of all things — *The Royal Power of Dissolution of Parliament in the British Commonwealth*. It had opened up a whole new range of strategic possibilities for their political battle, she said. His Ph.D. thesis was hardly the aspect of his work that I would have expected to come to the fore in the 1990s, but there it was. I could hear Dad chuckling in the background.

It is characteristic of my father's "life on the fringe" that his work is still out there in so many places, making mischief in obscure or more obvious ways. Maude Barlow of the Council of Canadians and Bruce Campbell of the Canadian Centre for Policy Alternatives chose a quotation from Dad to open their book on the abandonment of the "Just Society."[1] Peter Gzowski's *Morningside* finale on CBC Radio in May 1997 featured the gently satirical "national anthem" for a decentralized Canada that Dad had composed thirty years before.[2] A 1999 meeting of union and environmental activists fighting the privatization of Canadian water drew encouragement from a participant's copy of Dad's 1980 *Maclean's* column on privatization and "neo-conservatism."[3] And when Prime Minister Stephen Harper evaded an imminent non-confidence vote by having Parliament suspended in December 2008, outraged citizens drew on Dad's authority to denounce this as a subversion of our Constitution.

My own role in keeping my father's voice "out there" in the public arena brings with it its own dilemmas. I doubt if anyone would question the legitimacy of my quoting him in the occasional letter to the editor in response to yet another "constitutional fairy tale," or citing his support for public funding of the CBC in a presentation to the Canadian Radio-television and Telecommunications Commission. But sometimes the question is more complex.

In 1998, when I publicly supported David Orchard in the federal Progressive Conservative leadership race, I was taken to task for using Dad's name in that context. I had stated that the Saskatchewan farmer-activist shared many of my father's qualities and ideas. I had cited Orchard's emphasis on the relevance of history, his advocacy of a strong central government, and his insistence on the progressive nationalism that the Tory party of the past had at least sometimes espoused. There was more, too: Orchard's stubborn preference for principle over partisanship, his concern for democracy, and his willingness to fight unpopular battles all reminded me strongly of my Dad. Yet to say that publicly during the campaign struck some as inappropriate, especially since no one else involved could claim the same privileged basis to respond from.

But the alternative, as far as I could see, was to keep silent when the parallels were crying out to be drawn. It seemed wrong to refrain, for reasons of protocol, from making vital political arguments in the strongest way I could — a way I knew to be entirely legitimate in terms of my father's own thinking. I had to choose, and I chose to use his name, recognizing that the onus was on me to explain as fully as possible why I was doing so.

Such choices are not always crystal clear, but nor do we always have the luxury of time to agonize over them. This country and the world face urgent problems. My Dad had something to say on them and so have I. Once our views are out there, people can judge for themselves.

There are many, particularly of a younger generation, who, if they know the name Eugene Forsey at all, know of him only as a former senator, an ardent monarchist and federalist, and a fastidious critic on obscure points of the Constitution. To them, my portrait of him as a committed progressive may come as a surprise. But in fact, he was all of those things. His was a multiplicity acknowledged and appreciated by those who knew him, and reflected in the assessments I gathered from so many different people.

The late "Red Tory" Senator emeritus Heath Macquarrie praised my father's "mental acuity, independence of mind, strong academic discipline, and, to use an old-fashioned word, downright patriotism." The NDP's Svend Robinson recalled his "tremendous integrity, his irreverent wit, and his ability to so eloquently voice what a lot of people felt about the institutions of government." John Matheson, too, spoke of his "shining integrity," as well as his "dedicated scholarship, sensitivity to situations, and genuine concern for people."

My sister, Margaret, highlighted his persistence in "being true to his own principles, saying exactly what was true in his own heart and mind." Desmond Morton echoed that, calling Dad's legacy one of "passionate honesty and compassionate honesty" from someone who understood the issues. A friend who never met my father personally summed up what he knew of him by saying that he seemed to have been "remarkably engaged in the issues of the day," someone who "participated with incredible zeal."

That participation never slackened. "I keep forgetting how old he was," the late Dawn Dobson told me, as she finished another anecdote about her old friend. "I keep having to remind myself that he was born in 1904! He would say, 'Oh, I just missed the bus,' and I'd say, 'It's not one of the buses you ran for, is it?' Because he was running for buses until he was eighty years old! I guess it was just instinct. You know, the bus was there, he was in a hurry, so he just ran."

Dad was like that. Injustice was there, so he "just" worked to overcome it. Mistakes and "fairy tales" were there, so he just corrected them. Friends and family were there, so he helped them out, shared love and laughter, worry and wisdom. There was always something "there" that needed doing, something he thought he could do. So whatever it was, he "just ran."

When I went up to Temagami in northern Ontario in 1989 to join the blockade against corporate logging on native land, he told me, "If I were twenty years younger, I'd be going with you."

I wish he could come with me now, for I long to walk with him again the path of love and struggle, to share again the stimulation of that vigorous mind, the delights of that sparkling sense of fun, the warmth of that gentle and sometimes downcast heart. I wish he could come with us all, as we join together to restore and advance the kind of vision he fought for — the vision of a better country, the hope for a better world.

Yet, in many ways he *is* with us, very much so. That has been the joy of writing this book — gathering and sharing what I could, not only of his wisdom and insights on specific matters, but of his personal example. That example — his integrity, his intellectual rigour and political courage, his respect for history and complexity, his passion for justice and his love of life — that is Eugene Forsey's continuing legacy to us all.

APPENDIX

Eugene Forsey – A Brief Chronology

1904 — Newfoundland
Eugene Alfred Forsey is born in Grand Bank, Newfoundland.
Father dies in Mexico; mother and son return to Ottawa.

1904–22 — Ottawa
Grows up in Ottawa, familiar with Parliament Hill.
Attends Normal School and Ottawa Collegiate Institute.

1922–26 — Montreal
Studies economics and political science at McGill University in Montreal.
1924: Tutors sons of Vincent and Alice Massey.
1925: Receives first-class honours bachelor of arts in economics, political science, and English; receives graduate fellowship.

1926: Publishes *Economic and Social Aspects of the Nova Scotia Coal Industry*; receives master of arts from McGill.

1926–29 — Oxford
Studies at Balliol College, Oxford, on Rhodes Scholarship.
1928: Receives bachelor of arts from Oxford, first-class in philosophy, politics, and economics.

1929–41 — Montreal
Teaches economics and political science at McGill University.
1931: Founding member of League for Social Reconstruction (LSR).
1932: Receives master of arts from Oxford University; travels to the Soviet Union with King Gordon; joins fledgling Co-operative Commonwealth Federation (CCF).
1932–33: Member of United Church Committee on Social and Economic Research.
1933: Attends Regina Convention of the CCF.
1934: Founding member of Fellowship for a Christian Social Order (FCSO).
1934–35: Contributor and editor for *Social Planning for Canada* (LSR).
1935: Meets Harriet Roberts of Saint John, New Brunswick, at Student Christian Movement (SCM) camp; they marry.
1936: Contributes to *Towards the Christian Revolution* (FCSO).
1937: Co-founds Civil Liberties Union; fights Quebec Padlock Act.
1940: Runs for Montreal City Council as CCF candidate and is defeated; begins Ph.D. thesis on royal power of dissolution of parliament; renews friendship with Arthur Meighen.
1941: Completes Ph.D. thesis and receives doctorate from McGill; fired from McGill.

1941–42 — Cambridge, Massachusetts
Takes up Guggenheim Fellowship at Harvard University.
Works on book about cabinet government.

1942–69 — Ottawa
1942: Begins as director of research for Canadian Congress of Labour (CCL); first daughter, Margaret, is born.

A Brief Chronology

1943: Publishes *The Royal Power of Dissolution of Parliament in the British Commonwealth*.
1945: CCF candidate for Ontario Legislature but is defeated; second daughter, Helen, is born.
1948: CCF by-election candidate for House of Commons but is defeated.
1949: CCF candidate for House of Commons in general election but is defeated.
1953: Attends World University Service (WUS) Seminar in Mysore, India.
1955: Attends Vienna meeting of International Confederation of Free Trade Unions (ICFTU).
1956: CCL merges with Trades and Labour Congress (TLC), forming Canadian Labour Congress (CLC); begins as director of research for CLC; intervenes in debate over TransCanada Pipeline.
1957: Refuses offer of Progressive Conservative Party nomination.
1958: Appointed to Board of Broadcast Governors (BBG).
1960: Mourns death of Arthur Meighen.
1961: Leaves newly formed New Democratic Party (NDP) over national unity.
1962: Resigns from BBG to protest rejection of CBC French-language station.
1962–63: Takes up Skelton-Clark Fellowship at Queen's University in Kingston.
1963–69: Director, Special Project (Labour History) for CLC.
1964–70: Teaches political science at Carleton University.
1967: Named Fellow of the Royal Society of Canada.
1968: Named Officer of the Order of Canada; publicly supports Pierre Trudeau for the Liberal Party leadership; mourns death of mother, Florence Forsey, at age ninety-one.

1969–70 — Ottawa and Waterloo
Teaches political science and history at the University of Waterloo.

1970–91 — Ottawa
1970: Appointed to the Senate by Pierre Trudeau and sits as Liberal; wife Harriet is diagnosed with Parkinson's disease; first grandson, Rodrigo Fernando Contreras, is born.
1971: Named co-chair of Statutory Instruments Committee; Second grandson, Eugene Benjamin Contreras, is born.
1973–77: Chancellor of Trent University.

1973: Visits daughter Helen and family in Ecuador.
1974: Publishes *Freedom and Order: Collected Essays*.
1979: Retires from Senate at age seventy-five.
1980: Publishes first edition of *How Canadians Govern Themselves*.
1982: Publishes *Trade Unions in Canada: 1812–1902*; resigns from Liberal Party.
1985: Named Privy Councillor; authors *The Question of Confidence in Responsible Government* with Graham Eglington.
1987–90: Embroiled in Meech Lake controversy.
1988: Undergoes triple-bypass heart surgery; wife, Harriet, dies after long illness.
1989: Made Companion of the Order of Canada.
1990: Publishes *A Life on the Fringe: The Memoirs of Eugene Forsey*; publishes *Evatt and Forsey on the Reserve Powers*; Newfoundland government establishes Eugene Forsey Scholarship.
1991: Dies in Victoria, British Columbia, at the home of friends.

Note on Sources

Personal letters to me from my father, and personal communications from people I interviewed, are not referenced in these notes. Those letters, as well as tape recordings and notes from phone conversations, are in my personal files, with the corresponding dates and other details. All this material will eventually, I hope, be added to the Eugene Forsey collection at Library and Archives Canada (MG 30 A 25).

Where there is no author name given, the author is my father. For noted material where no repository information is given, the material is from my personal files. Where other information is not given, such as the page number of an article, it is unavailable. Unavailable authors, dates and places are indicated by "n.a.," "n.d.," and "n.p." respectively.

For sources that are frequently referred to, the following short forms are used:

- CBC — Canadian Broadcasting Corporation.
- Earle 1989 — Transcript of a series of interviews of EF by Tom Earle of the Parliamentary Library, May 24 and 29, and June 2 and 5, 1989, 1985–0238, Audio-visual Section, Library and Archives Canada.
- EFP — Eugene Forsey Papers, MG 30 A 25, Library and Archives Canada.
- Forsey-Coyne correspondence — Collection kindly given to the author by Deborah Coyne. Also in EFP Vol. 63.
- *Fringe* — Eugene Forsey, *A Life on the Fringe: The Memoirs of Eugene Forsey* (Toronto: Oxford University Press, 1990).
- *F&O* — Eugene Forsey, *Freedom and Order, Collected Essays* (Toronto: McClelland & Stewart, 1974).
- *Forum* — *Canadian Forum* magazine
- *HCGT* — *How Canadians Govern Themselves*, seventh ed. (Ottawa: Library of Parliament, 2010), www.parl.gc.ca/publications.
- LAC — Library and Archives Canada, Ottawa.
- Millar — Audio tapes of series of interviews of EF by David Millar, June 25, July 3, and July 9, 1970, Audio-Visual Section, Library and Archives Canada.
- *One Voice* — *The Sound of One Voice: Eugene Forsey and his Letters to the Press,* E. Hodgetts, ed. (Toronto: University of Toronto Press, 2000).
- *Senate Debates* — Canada. Senate, *Debates.*
- *SPC* — League for Social Reconstruction, *Social Planning for Canada* (Toronto: Thomas Nelson & Sons, 1935; republished, Toronto: University of Toronto Press, 1975).
- *TCR* — R.B.Y. Scott and Gregory Vlastos, *Towards the Christian Revolution* (New York and Chicago: Willett Clark & Company, 1936; republished, Kingston, ON: Ronald P. Frye & Company, 1989).

Notes

Chapter One
1. "The First Ten Years of Eugene A. Forsey," unpublished paper.
2. Millar.
3. Letters to Florence Forsey, October 29 and November 19, 1922. EFP Vol. 45.
4. Millar.
5. Letters to Florence Forsey, September 2, 4, 5, 9, 11, 14, 21, 1924. EFP Vol. 45.
6. "Quebec on the Road to Fascism," *Forum* 17 (December 1937), 298–300.
7. Seminar, Brandon University (Brandon, MB), February 1969, EFP Vol. 15.
8. "Why a 'Rank Outsider' Chooses Pierre Trudeau," *Trudeau Today*, April 1968, EFP Vol. 38.
9. *Ibid.*

10. *Senate Debates*, October 27, 1970, 55–61.
11. *Fringe*, 187–201.
12. Interview by Ian Alexander, *Music in My Life* (Arts National), CBC Radio, February 14, 1986.
13. Christmas letter to friends, December 1989.
14. Interview by Peter Gzowski, *Morningside*, CBC Radio, October 4, 1990, audio tape 901004–04/00, CBC Radio Archives, Toronto.
15. Christmas letter.

Chapter Two
1. Letter to Harriet Forsey, Winter 1962–63, EFP Vol. 47.
2. Millar.
3. *Ibid.*
4. "The Canadian Trade Union Movement," unpublished article, May 30, 1949, EFP Vol. 47.
5. *TCR*, 98.
6. "The Church and Labour," unpublished article, circa 1957.
7. *Ibid.*
8. *TCR*, 102.
9. *Ibid.*, 102–03.
10. Jerry Mander, *In the Absence of the Sacred: The Future of Technology and the Survival of the Indian Nations* (San Francisco: Sierra Club Books, 1991), 120–37.
11. "Clerical Fascism," *Forum* 17 (June 1937), 90–92.
12. "Land of Padlock's Pride," *Forum* 19 (July 1939), 109–11.
13. "Post-War Problems of Canadian Labour, with Special Reference to the Responsibilities of the Church," n.d. (circa 1945), EFP Vol. 48.
14. "Newfoundland's Labour Legislation," *United Church Observer*, May 1959, 11, 37.
15. N.a., "Stop Loans to S.A., Forsey Tells Royal," *Ottawa Citizen*, January 12, 1979; N.a., "Forsey Slams Bank's Policy on S. Africa," *Ottawa Citizen*, January 16, 1979; Jim Webb, "Bank People Reject Church Questions on Loans," *Catholic New Times*, January 28, 1979.
16. Presentation, Annual General Meeting, Royal Bank of Canada (n.p.), January 11, 1979.
17. "Our Present Discontents," *F&O*, 324.

18. Sermon, Église Saint-Marc (Ottawa), August 12, 1984.
19. Letter from Arthur Meighen, December 28, 1952, EFP Vol. 4.
20. "Valedictory, McGill, Arts," McGill University, 1925, EFP Vol. 8.
21. N.a., "Labour Expert Describes Church as Powerhouse," *Hamilton Spectator* (circa 1963), EFP Vol. 8.
22. Ecumenical address, n.d. (circa mid-1960s).
23. "A Passage to India," unpublished segment from *Fringe*, 1989.
24. "Interview — Labour's Eugene Forsey on Social Drinking and Minorities," interview by Kenneth Bagnell, *United Church Observer*, June 15, 1962, 25.
25. "Guest Editorial," *Concerns* (Don Mills, ON), February 1974, 2.
26. "Interview," Bagnell, 25.
27. "Ghost-Writing Is Simply Dishonest," *My Biggest Beef* column, *Toronto Star*, November 21, 1962, EFP Vol. 8.
28. Millar.
29. Letter to the Editor, *Forum* 26 (February 1946), 262.
30. Letter to Dr. Richards, May 13, 1986.
31. Letter to the Editor, *Ottawa Citizen*, February 24, 1983.

Chapter Three
1. *Senate Debates*, October 27, 1970, 61.
2. *Fringe*, 103.
3. *The Royal Power of Dissolution of Parliament in the British Commonwealth* (Toronto: Oxford University Press, 1943), 259; see also "The Crown and the Constitution," *F&O*, 34–49.
4. Millar.
5. Frank H. Underhill, "Socialists and the Monarchy," *Forum* 16 (January 1937), 8–10; Forsey, "More Socialists on the Monarchy," *Forum* 16 (February 1937), 17.
6. "Position of the Governor General If No Party Gets a Clear Majority in the Election," unpublished paper, August 15, 1984.
7. Speech, Union Club (Victoria, BC), April 17, 1990, private tape; see also EFP Vol. 63.
8. Excerpted from "Mr. Abbott and the Flag," written in response to *Montreal Star* item March 14, 1952, and enclosed in Meighen correspondence, EFP Vol. 4.

9. "Pipeline and Parliament," *Forum* 37 (July 1956), 73 and 96.
10. *Ibid.*
11. *Fringe*, 190.
12. *Ibid.*, 189–98. For more on disallowance see "Canada and Alberta: The Revival of Dominion Control over the Provinces," *F&O*, 177–205.
13. Letter to Arthur Meighen, July 5, 1949, EFP Vol. 4.
14. *Fringe*, 170–86.
15. See, for example, his exchanges with Donald Smiley in the *Globe and Mail* in January 1975, *One Voice*, 169–71, and with Denis Smith, *Forum* 55 (October 1975), 3, and *Forum* 55 (December 1975/January 1976), 22.
16. *Senate Debates*, October 27, 1970, 56.
17. For an examination of Scott's position on the War Measures Act, see Sandra Djwa, *The Politics of the Imagination: A Life of F.R. Scott* (Toronto: McClelland & Stewart, 1987), 404–18.
18. The preceding argument and quotations are all from *Senate Debates*, October 27, 1970, 59–61.
19. "Why We Need a Charter of Rights," interview by Courtney Tower, *Reader's Digest*, December 1980, 96–100.
20. From reply to questions on Speech, Union Club (private tape).
21. "The New Constitutional Package," media release, November 25, 1981.
22. Interview by Ian Alexander, *Music in My Life* (Arts National), CBC Radio, February 14, 1986.
23. "The Crown, the Constitution, and the CCF," *Forum* 24 (June 1943), 54–56.
24. Letter to the Editor, *Ottawa Journal*, May 31, 1956; see also *Fringe*, 135–36.
25. Introductory Note for "The British North America Act and Biculturalism," *F&O*, xvi.
26. N.a., *Globe and Mail*, February 2, 1982, and EF's unpublished response.
27. N.a., "When Forsey Writes Letters He Can Cause a Lot of Rows," *Ottawa Journal*, January 2, 1974.
28. John Ralston Saul, "The Good Citizen," *Forum* 77 (December 1997), 13–17.

Chapter Four
1. "Democracy," radio address, February 1939, EFP Vol. 8.
2. Letter to Florence Forsey, February 2, 1932, EFP Vol. 45.
3. *Ibid.*, January 19, 1932, EFP Vol. 45.
4. *Ibid.*, February 2, 1932, EFP Vol. 45.
5. Michiel Horn, *The League for Social Reconstruction: Intellectual Origins of the Democratic Left in Canada* (Toronto: University of Toronto Press, 1980).
6. See, for example, Alan Whitehorn, *Canadian Socialism: Essays on the CCF-NDP* (Toronto: Oxford University Press, 1992); Irving Abella, *Nationalism, Communism and Canadian Labour: The CIO, the Communist Party, and the Canadian Congress of Labour, 1935–1956* (Toronto: University of Toronto Press, 1973); Peter S. McInnis, *Harnessing Labour Confrontation: Shaping the Postwar Settlement in Canada, 1943–1950* (Toronto: University of Toronto Press, 2002).
7. *SPC*, vii.
8. See, for example, Committee on Social and Economic Research, *Information Bulletin* 1: 4 (February 1933), EFP Vol. 8.
9. "Equality of Sacrifice: Dividends, Salaries and Wages in Canada in the Great Depression," *Forum* 14 (November 1933), 47–51.
10. "Recovery — For Whom?" *Forum* 17 (August 1937), 156–59.
11. *Ibid*; "More Unemployment, Less Relief," *Forum* 18 (February 1939), 331–32; "The Budget," *Forum* 19 (June 1939), 76–77.
12. "Facts, Figures and Finance," *Forum* 17 (February 1937), 22.
13. "The Taxpayers' Money — The Cost of Government," *Forum* 19 (July 1939), 106–07.
14. *Ibid.*
15. "Bedtime Stories for Workingmen," *Forum* 16 (December 1936), 24–26.
16. "From the Seats of the Mighty," *Forum* 17 (May 1937), 54; "Some Questions for Mr. Macdonnell," *Forum* 23 (September 1943), 133–34.
17. *TCR*, 134–36.
18. *Ibid.*, 135.
19. Letter to Florence Forsey, June 28, 1932, EFP Vol. 48.
20. *Ibid.*, July 8, 1932, EFP Vol. 48.
21. *TCR*, 143–44.
22. Joanna Smith, "Canadian Security Forces Spied on Constitutional Expert Eugene Forsey: Declassified Documents," *Toronto Star*, January 27, 2012.

23. "Planning from the Bottom — Can It Be Done? (Part II)," *Forum* 25 (April 1945), 20–23.
24. *SPC*, see particularly 234–40. EF further elaborated these ideas in "Planning from the Bottom — Can It Be Done?" *Forum* 24 (March 1945), 277–79, and *Forum* 25 (April 1945), 20–23.
25. Letters to Florence Forsey, November 19 and 28, 1939, EFP Vol. 45.
26. "Democracy."
27. "Planned Economy," Papers and Proceedings: Canadian Political Science Association, Fourth Annual Meeting, May 1932, 179.
28. *TCR*, 116.
29. *Ibid.*, 139–40.
30. See Chapter 11.
31. "Labour and National Development," Speech to Canadian Federation of University Students National Seminar (University of British Columbia, Vancouver, BC), August 3, 1960, untitled and wrongly identified in EFP Vol. 8.
32. "Letterman," interview by Charlotte Gray, *Saturday Night*, October 1986, 52–53.
33. N.a., "When Forsey Writes Letters He Can Cause a Lot of Rows," *Ottawa Journal*, January 2, 1974.
34. Note typed on back of schedule for Labour Relations seminar, Princeton University, June 1948, EFP Vol. 47.
35. Letter to Florence Forsey, February 25, 1934, EFP Vol. 45.
36. Michiel Horn, *The League for Social Reconstruction*, 55.
37. "Planned Economy," 177, 179.
38. *Ibid.*
39. N.a., *Montreal Star*, October 18, 1933, and n.a., *Quebec Chronicle-Telegraph*, October 19, 1933, McGill University Archives, RG2, Record of the Principal and Chancellor's Office, Container 42, File 00301.
40. Letter from Premier Taschereau to Sir Arthur Currie, October 20, 1933, McGill University Archives, RG2, Record of the Principal and Chancellor's Office, Container 42, File 00301.
41. Michiel Horn, *Academic Freedom in Canada* (Toronto: University of Toronto Press, 1999), 128–44; see also Chapter 9.
42. Letter to Edgar Ritchie, August 1, 1937, cited in Michiel Horn, *The League for Social Reconstruction*, 134–35.

43. "Planned Economy," 179.
44. *Senate Debates*, March 23, 1972, 222.
45. Letter to Arthur Meighen, October 9, 1948.
46. "Planning from the Bottom: Part I," *Forum* 24 (March 1945), 277–79, and "Planning from the Bottom: Part II" *Forum* 25 (April 1945), 20–23; "Post-War Problems of Canadian Labour," *The Canadian Unionist*, January 1945, 7–8, 10, 16.
47. Millar.

Chapter Five

1. *Economic and Social Aspects of the Nova Scotia Coal Industry* (Toronto: Macmillan, 1926).
2. *Fringe*, 76.
3. See, for example, Letter to the Editor, *McGill Daily* (Montreal), March 5, 1934, EFP Vol. 45.
4. Letter from Norman Dowd, April 29, 1942; letter to Norman Dowd, April 30, 1942. EFP Vol. 5.
5. *Ibid.*
6. "The Canadian Trade Union Movement," typewritten speech, May 30, 1949, EFP Vol. 47.
7. *Labour Research*, various issues, 1948–56.
8. Millar.
9. Letter to Canon A.R. Kelley, May 11, 1944, EFP Vol. 48.
10. See *Fringe*, 89–93.
11. Irving Abella, *Nationalism, Communism, and Canadian Labour*; Desmond Morton with Terry Copp, *Working People: An Illustrated History of Canadian Labour*, (Ottawa: Deneau & Greenberg, 1980); Peter S. McInnis, *Harnessing Labour Confrontation*.
12. Abella.
13. Millar.
14. Letter to Arthur Meighen, January 11, 1946, EFP Vol. 4.
15. Millar.
16. Letters to Reverend J.R. Mutchmor, May 17 and June 6, 1945, EFP Vol. 48.
17. Draft of letter to Derek Bedson, September 11, 1957, EFP Vol. 5; see also Chapter 15.

18. Itinerary, 1962, EFP Vol. 47.
19. "The Canadian Trade Union Movement."
20. "Democracy," radio address, February 1939, EFP Vol. 8.
21. "Mr. King, Parliament, the Constitution and Labour Policy," *Forum* 21 (January 1942), 296–98.
22. "Mr. King and the Government's Labour Policy," *Forum* 21 (November 1941), 231–32.
23. Millar.
24. Letter to J. R. Mutchmor, May 17, 1945.
25. "The New British Columbia Acts," *Labour Research*, June–July 1954, 3–5.
26. "Newfoundland Labour Legislation," *Forum* 39 (July 1959), 35–37.
27. Seminar, Brandon University, 1969, EFP Vol. 15.
28. *Trade Unions in Canada: 1812–1902* (Toronto: University of Toronto Press, 1982).
29. Letter to the editor, *Globe and Mail*, January 19, 1976.

Chapter Six
1. Letter to Arthur Meighen, October 9, 1948, EFP Vol. 4.
2. "Arthur Meighen," *Forum* 40 (September 1960), 121–22.
3. Letter to Deborah Coyne, February 19, 1989, Forsey-Coyne correspondence.
4. *Senate Debates*, January 28, 1971, 442.
5. Letter to David Alexander, December 14, 1978, EFP Vol. 52.
6. *Senate Debates*, March 28, 1972, 268.
7. Convocation Address, Memorial University of Newfoundland (St. John's, NL), May 1966.
8. Letter to Mose Morgan, June 14, 1966, Memorial University Archives.
9. *Senate Debates*, June 14, 1972, 483.
10. Speech, Union Club (Victoria, BC) April 17, 1990, EFP, Vol. 63.

Chapter Seven
1. Letter to Arthur Meighen, July 5, 1949, EFP Vol. 4.
2. Letter to Florence Forsey, March 21, 1941, EFP Vol. 45.
3. Letter to George Drew, November 23, 1949, *One Voice*, 37–38.
4. Charles Gordon, *Ottawa Citizen*, Febuary 21, 1991; "A Pen Like a Wand," *Globe and Mail*, February 22, 1991; Geoffrey Stevens, *Montreal Gazette*, February 24, 1991.

5. Letter from C. Bowman, July 21, 1949, and EF's reply, July 26, 1949, enclosed to Meighen, EFP Vol. 4.
6. Letter to Arthur Meighen, July 5, 1949, EFP Vol. 4.
7. The quotations that follow are from the correspondence in the "FCSO" file, EFP Vol. 15.
8. See *Fringe*, 59–60.
9. Letter to Mrs. Wasserman, May 6, 1964, EFP Vol. 45.
10. Letter to Harriet Forsey, Winter 1962–63, EFP Vol. 47.
11. *Fringe*, 25, 56.
12. Harriet Forsey, "Will Women Win the Peace?" *Forum* 24 (August 1944), 106–08.
13. "Constitutional Monarchy and the Provinces," *F&O*, 25.
14. "A Crisis in Canadian Education?" Typewritten speech to a conference on education (n.p), n.d., 1957. A version of this speech, "Canadian Schools' Greatest Need — Money or Brains?" was published in *Saturday Night*, March 29, 1958, 10–11, EFP. Vol. 8.
15. "Jobs I Had Sense Enough to Refuse," unpublished segment of *Fringe*, 1989.
16. Letter to Donald Fleming, December 10, 1957, EFP Vol. 5.
17. Letter to Mr. Sutherland, Ottawa Board of Education, February 14, 1984.
18. Dave Mullington, "Forsey Lectures OBE on 'Proper English,'" *Ottawa Citizen*, February 28, 1984.
19. *Fringe*, iii.
20. See Notes by Harriet and Eugene Forsey on Religion in the Modern World, EFP Vol. 47, File 21; and The Royal Power of Dissolution of Parliament, xv.
21. Letter to Arthur Meighen, October 9, 1948, EFP Vol. 4 (The article "Parliament Is Endangered by Mr. King's Principle" appeared in *Saturday Night* in October 1948, and can be found in EFP Vol. 38.)
22. *Ibid.*
23. Letter to Arthur Meighen, December 26, 1951, EFP Vol. 4.
24. *Fringe*, 74–75.
25. Letter to Arthur Meighen, December 26, 1951, EFP Vol. 4.
26. See Chapter 14 for more on Meech Lake.
27. Note to Clyde Wells, June 8, 1990, Forsey-Coyne correspondence.

28. Letters to Deborah Coyne, August 22 and September 14, 1990, Forsey-Coyne correspondence.

Chapter Eight
1. Interview by Ian Alexander, *Music in My Life* (Arts National), CBC Radio, February 14, 1986.
2. Convocation Address, McGill University, May 30, 1966.
3. "Planned Economy," Papers and Proceedings: 4th Annual Meeting, Canadian Political Science Association, May 1932, 180.
4. *Encyclopaedia Britannica*, editions of 1911 and 1958.
5. Millar.
6. *Ottawa Journal*, December 11, 1952; see also letter to Arthur Meighen, December 10, 1952, EFP Vol. 4.
7. Speech, Union Club (Victoria, BC), April 17, 1990, EFP Vol. 63.
8. "The Canadian Tradition," Encaenial Address, University of New Brunswick (Fredericton, NB), May 17, 1962.
9. "National Unity and the Loyalist Contribution," Speech to the United Empire Loyalists' Association (London, ON), May 6, 1978, EFP Vol. 39.
10. *Trade Unions in Canada — 1812–1902*, 5.
11. *F&O*, xvi.
12. Convocation Address, McMaster University (Hamilton, ON), May 26, 1984.
13. *Ibid.*
14. "Our Present Discontents," *F&O*, 318.
15. John Ralston Saul, *Reflections of a Siamese Twin: Canada at the End of the Twentieth Century* (Toronto: Viking Canada, 1997), 11, 27.
16. Submission to the New Brunswick Legislature Select Committee on the 1987 Constitutional Accord, 1988, 51, EFP Vol. 63.
17. "Constitutional Monarchy and the Provinces," *F&O*, 26.
18. Saul, *Reflections of a Siamese Twin*, 124.
19. "Trying to Stop the Theft of Canada's History," unpublished chapter of *Fringe*; see also Chapter 10.
20. Letter to Arthur Meighen, February 12, 1952; letters from Meighen, February 19, 1952 and December 28, 1951, EFP Vol. 4.
21. Letter to Arthur Meighen, Dec, 26, 1951, EFP Vol. 4.
22. Submission on behalf of the Royal Commonwealth Society,

National Council in Canada, to the Senate Committee on Legal and Constitutional Affairs, October, 1982.
23. David Orchard, *The Fight for Canada: Four Centuries of Resistance to American Expansionism* (Toronto: Stoddart, 1993), 93–96.
24. Earle 1989, 79.
25. "Canadian Sovereignty," memorandum to Cabinet, 1985, quoted in Orchard, 137.
26. *One Voice*, 241–42.
27. Convocation Address, McGill.
28. *Ibid.*
29. "Ghost-Writing Is Simply Dishonest," *Toronto Star*, November 21, 1962, EFP Vol. 8.
30. "The British Share in the Canadian Identity," Queen's University, 1978, EFP Vol. 38.
31. *Fringe*, 200.
32. "Canada's National Symbols — An Appeal to Mr. Pearson," *Forum* 44 (June 1964), 54.
33. "The British Share," citing from "Mr. Abbott and the Flag," written in response to *Montreal Star* item March 14, 1952, and enclosed in Meighen correspondence, EFP Vol. 4.
34. "The Canadian Tradition."
35. "The British Share."
36. "Mr. McGregor's Garden — Keep Out!" *Public Affairs* XV: 2 (Winter 1953); see also *Fringe*, 170–201.
37. "The British Share."
38. John Ralston Saul, *A Fair Country: Telling Truths About Canada* (Toronto: Penguin, 2008), 3.
39. "The Canadian Tradition."
40. "The British Share."
41. Convocation Address, Queen's University, October 27, 1979.
42. *Peterborough Examiner*, May 13, 1971.
43. "The British Share."
44. "Trying to Stop the Theft."

Chapter Nine
1. Convocation Address, McGill University, May 30, 1966.

2. Speech, Union Club (Victoria, BC), April 17, 1990, EFP Vol. 63.
3. Letter to Florence Forsey, November 19, 1922, EFP Vol 45.
4. "A Crisis in Canadian Education?" n.d. 1957, EFP Vol. 8.
5. "Memorandum on Promotion," June 19, 1939, EFP Vol. 45.
6. Michiel Horn, *Academic Freedom in Canada* (Toronto: University of Toronto Press, 1999), 144.
7. Letters to Florence Forsey, February 6, 1941 and March 26, 1941, EFP Vol. 45.
8. "Concepts of Federalism: Some Canadian Aspects," Speech to the 34th Annual Couchiching Conference (Lake Couchiching, ON), August 2, 1965, audio tape 650802-3, CBC Radio Archives, Toronto; see also EFP Vol. 38.
9. "Maritime Rights," Letter to the Editor, *McGill Daily* (Montreal), December 1, 1925, EFP Vol. 46.
10. "Planned Economy," Papers and Proceedings: 4th Annual Meeting, Canadian Political Science Association, 1932, 177.
11. "Remembering Regina," *Saturday Night*, July 1983, 24–26.
12. Convocation Address, McMaster University (Hamilton, ON), May 26, 1984.
13. "Government Defeats in the Canadian House of Commons, 1867–73," *F&O*, 123.
14. *Senate Debates*, March 23, 1972, 224.
15. Letter to Tommy Douglas, July 21, 1961; see also Chapter 15.
16. For more on these matters see Chapter 13.
17. "Senate Reform," Speech to section of the Canadian Bar Association (n.p.), August 19, 1985.
18. Submission to the Alberta NDP's public hearings on the Meech Lake Accord (Calgary) September 22, 1987.
19. "Our Present Discontents," *F&O*, 328.
20. *Ibid.*, 326.
21. "The British Share in the Canadian Identity," Queen's University, 1978, EFP Vol. 38.
22. "Labour and National Development," speech to the Canadian Federation of University Students National Seminar (University of British Columbia, Vancouver, BC) August 3, 1960, EFP Vol. 8.
23. "Democracy," radio address, February 1939, EFP Vol. 8.

24. "Labour and National Development."
25. "A Crisis in Canadian Education?"
26. *Ibid.*
27. *Ibid.*
28. *Ibid.*
29. Letter to Hilda Neatby, December 9, 1955.
30. "A Crisis in Canadian Education?"
31. *Forum 17* (September 1936), 15–16.
32. "A Crisis in Canadian Education?"
33. *Ibid.*
34. Letter to Florence Forsey, February 6, 1941, EFP Vol. 45.
35. Convocation Address, McGill University.
36. "Take That! And That! And That!" Letter to the Editor, *Ottawa Citizen*, circa November 1954, EFP Vol. 5.
37. "A Crisis in Canadian Education?"
38. "Labour and National Development."
39. "Post-War Problems of Canadian Labour, with Special Reference to the Responsibility of the Church," n.d., ca 1945, EFP Vol. 48.
40. Review of Hilda Neatby's *So Little for the Mind*, 1954. EFP Vol. 5.
41. "A Crisis in Canadian Education?"
42. *Senate Debates*, March 24, 1977, 570.
43. Millar.
44. Letter to Arthur Meighen, July 5, 1949, EFP Vol. 4.
45. *Fringe*, 152–53.
46. "Our Present Discontents," *F&O*, 332; see also Chapter 13.
47. Convocation Address, McMaster University.
48. *Fringe*, viii.
49. See "Eugene Forsey: Reluctant Intellectual," by Helen Forsey, an essay-review of "Eugene A. Forsey: An Intellectual Biography," *Journal of Canadian Studies* 41:1 (Winter 2007), 218–25.
50. "A Crisis in Canadian Education?"
51. Convocation Address, York University (Toronto), October 21, 1972.
52. Convocation Address, McMaster University.
53. Convocation Address, Mount Allison University (Sackville, NB), May 8, 1973.
54. Convocation Address, Memorial University of Newfoundland (St.

John's, NL), May 1966.
55. *Ibid.*
56. Convocation Address, York University.
57. Convocation Address, McMaster University.
58. Convocation Address, McGill University.

Chapter Ten
1. "Trying to Stop the Theft of Canada's History," unpublished chapter of *Fringe*, 1989.
2. Diana Paterson, "Profile: Eugene Forsey," *Glebe Report* (Ottawa), June 15, 1984.
3. "The Ottawa Collegiate Institute, Sixty Years On," unpublished paper, circa 1982.
4. Letter to Florence Forsey, November 22, 1927, EFP Vol. 45.
5. "Canada: Two Nations or One?" *F&O*, 248.
6. Charles Taylor, *Radical Tories: The Conservative Tradition in Canada* (Toronto: Anansi, 1982), 120.
7. Jacques Yvan Morin, Letter to Eugene Forsey, February 9, 1965, EFP Vol. 8.
8. Taylor, 103, 98; Sandra Gwyn, "Forsey and Spry: the Grand Old Gents of Ottawa," *Saturday Night*, November 1976, 13–15; Paterson, "Profile: Eugene Forsey."
9. "What's in a Name?" *Forum* 18 (September 1938), 180.
10. From "Humorous Verse" file, EFP Vol. 47.
11. "The Literary Consequences of Section 98," *Forum* 12 (January 1932), 131–32.
12. *TCR*, 99.
13. Among many such authors, see Dale Spender, *Man Made Language* (London, ON: Pandora Press, 1980), and Susan Brownmiller, *Against Our Will: Men, Women and Rape* (Harmondsworth, U.K.: Penguin, 1977).
14. Millar.
15. "A Rose by Any Other Name," published anonymously, *Forum* 17 (September 1937), 201.
16. "Mr. King, Parliament, the Constitution and Labour Policy," *Forum* 21 (January 1942), 296–98; "Some Questions for Mr. MacDonnell," *Forum* 23 (September 1943), 133–34; "The Case for Price Controls,"

Forum 31 (June 1951), 54–55; "Pipeline and Parliament," *Forum* 36 (July 1956), 308–10.
17. "Our Present Discontents," *F&O*, 326.
18. Dag Hammarskjöld, *Markings* (London: Faber & Faber, 1964), 101.
19. "Trying to Stop the Theft."
20. Submission to the Senate Legal and Constitutional Affairs Committee examining Bill C-201, on behalf of the Royal Commonwealth Society, National Council in Canada, October 1982.
21. "Trying to Stop the Theft."
22. *Ibid.*
23. *Ibid.*
24. *Ibid.*
25. John Ralston Saul, *A Fair Country: Telling Truths About Canada* (Toronto: Viking Canada, 2008), 250–59.
26. "Trying to Stop the Theft." Interestingly, the *Year Book* restored "House of Commons" and "Parliament" to their rightful place in later editions, though it retained "federal" as its adjective of choice.
27. "The Third Option," *Canadian Bar Review* LVII (1979), 478.
28. *Senate Debates*, June 14, 1972, 481.
29. "Canada: Two Nations or One?" *F&O*, 252.
30. "Canada, 1967," *F&O*, 293–94; see also *Fringe*, 213–14.
31. See broader discussion in Chapter 13.
32. "The British Share in the Canadian Identity," Queen's University, 1978, EFP Vol. 38.
33. "The Fussifiers," hand-pencilled notes, EFP Vol. 58.
34. Many of these complaints appeared in letters to the editor; see *One Voice*, 71–79.
35. Convocation Address, Memorial University of Newfoundland (St. John's, NL), May, 1966.
36. *Canada Year Book*, 1997 edition (Ottawa: Statistics Canada, 1997).
37. "A Crisis in Canadian Education?" n.d., 1957, EFP Vol. 8.
38. Letter to Mr. Davidson, University of Toronto Press, September 9, 1979.
39. Letter to Mr. Fleming, December 3, 1987, EFP Vol. 58.
40. Letter to J. March, December 4, 1986, EFP Vol. 60.
41. Letter to Miss Thorne, November 23, 1987, EFP Vol. 58.

42. Letter to Mr. Davidson.
43. Jeffrey Simpson, "Eugene Forsey Was a Fine Man with a Sharp Mind, and a Sharp Pen to Boot," *Globe and Mail*, February 21, 1991.
44. Charles Lynch, "Forsey Remembered: A Long, Turbulent and Quotable Life," *Ottawa Sun*, February 24, 1991.

Chapter Eleven
1. *HCGT*, 1.
2. *TCR*, 99, and "Planning from the Bottom: Can It Be Done?" *Forum* 24 (March 1945), 277–79, and *Forum* 25 (April 1945), 20–23.
3. *HCGT*, 1.
4. *SPC*, see especially Chapter VI and all of Part II.
5. See, for example, "Employment and Income," *The Canadian Unionist*, August 1945, 190–93, 195–96; "Old Age Security," *Labour Research*, April–May 1950, pagination unavailable; "Housing — Unfinished Business," *Labour Research*, May 1949, 1–4; "Housing — A National Emergency," *Labour Research*, January–February 1950, 1–8; "Unemployment Again," *Labour Research*, February–March 1952, 1–6.
6. "The Outlook for Freedom in the Garrison State," Couchiching Conference (Lake Couchiching, ON), August 14, 1952, audio tape 520814–1, CBC Radio Archives, Toronto.
7. "Labour and National Development," speech to Canadian Federation of University Students National Seminar (University of British Columbia, Vancouver, BC), August 3, 1960, EFP Vol.8.
8. "Labour and National Health," *Canadian Labour*, June 1957, 42–47.
9. *SPC*, 144.
10. *Canada Year Book 2009* (Ottawa: Industry Canada, 2009), 191.
11. *SPC*, 144–45.
12. *Senate Debates*, January 28, 1971, 438.
13. "Convocation Address," Carleton University (Ottawa), November 14, 1976.
14. "Liberalism and Controls," February 1976, EFP Vol. 38.
15. Letter to Mr. Elzinga, July 21, 1983.
16. *Senate Debates*, October 4, 1974, 57.
17. "National Unity and the Loyalist Contribution," EFP Vol. 39; see also *Fringe*, 170–86.

18. For examples, see Shiv Chopra, *Corrupt to the Core: Memoirs of a Health Canada Scientist* (Caledon, ON: KOS Publishing, 2008).
19. Media release, MiningWatch Canada (Ottawa), July 10, 2008.
20. John Ralston Saul, "The Good Citizen," *Forum* 77 (December 1997), 13–17.
21. "Liberalism and Controls."
22. *Senate Debates*, December 2, 1971, 1,550.
23. "A Slick Way to Skin the Public," *Maclean's*, February 11, 1980, 6.
24. *Ibid.*
25. *SPC*, 173–74.
26. *Senate Debates*, December, 2, 1971, 1549.
27. *Ibid.*, 1550.
28. Convocation Address, York University (Toronto), October 21, 1972.
29. *Senate Debates*, January 28, 1971, 441.
30. *Ibid.*, 440–41; see also *Fringe*, 138–50.
31. *Senate Debates*, June 17, 1976, 2,218.
32. "Oral History Interview of Senator Eugene Forsey by Tom Earle" (Parliamentary Library), audio tape, 1985–0248, audiovisual section, LAC.
33. "A Slick Way to Skin the Public."
34. Letter to John S. Scott, Victoria, April 30, 1979, EFP Vol. 58.
35. National Conference on Canadian Goals, September 12, 1964, audio tape 1990–0386, audiovisual section, LAC.
36. Ontario Conference on Economic and Cultural Nationalism, June 1971, EFP Vol. 38.
37. *Ibid.*
38. "The Third Option," *Canadian Bar Review* LVII (September 1979), 480.
39. Convocation Address, Queen's University, October 27, 1979.
40. Earle 1989, 76.

Chapter Twelve
1. "Our Present Discontents," *F&O*, 319.
2. *Ibid.*, 324. For a similar analysis, see feminist author Jo Freeman, "The Tyranny of Structurelessness."
3. "Mr. King and Parliamentary Government," *F&O*, 109.

4. "Our Present Discontents," *F&O*, 319, 326.
5. *Ibid.,* 318; see also Chapters 8 and 9.
6. "Constitutional Aspects of the Canadian Pipe Line Debate," *F&O*, 132.
7. "Our Present Discontents," *F&O*, 319.
8. *HCGT*, 33.
9. "Constitutional Monarchy and the Provinces," *F&O*, 30.
10. "Constitutional Aspects of the Canadian Pipe Line Debate," 132.
11. See *Fringe*, 151–69.
12. Submission on behalf of the Royal Commonwealth Society, National Council in Canada, to the Senate Committee on Legal and Constitutional Affairs, October 1982.
13. "Don't Take Our Bulwark, No Matter How Frail," *The Financial Post*, February 23, 1974.
14. *HCGT*, 27.
15. "Constitutional Monarchy and the Provinces," 30.
16. *HCGT*, 26–27.
17. "Mr. King and Parliamentary Government," 87–109.
18. "The Problem of Minority Government in Canada," *F&O*, 116.
19. *Ibid.*, 113.
20. *Ibid.*, 122.
21. *Ibid.*, 109–23.
22. "Constitutional Monarchy and the Provinces," 30.
23. "More Socialists on the Monarchy," *Forum* 16 (February 1937), 17, commenting on Frank H. Underhill, "Socialists and the Monarchy," *Forum* 16 (January 1937), 8–10.
24. See Amir Attaran and Gar Pardy, "Colvin Is Just Doing His Job," *Ottawa Citizen*, December 2, 2009.
25. "Crown and Commonwealth," August 1973, EFP Vol. 38.
26. "Mr. King, Parliament, the Constitution and Labour Policy," *Forum* 12 (January 1932), 296–98.
27. "Position of the Governor General If No Party Gets a Clear Majority in the Election," unpublished paper, August 1984.
28. "Constitutional Monarchy and the Provinces," 30.
29. *Ibid.*
30. See, for example, Thomas Walkom, "Forsey Outraged at Schreyer's Career Musings," *Globe and Mail*, April 30, 1984.

31. "Constitutional Monarchy and the Provinces," 30–31.
32. *HCGT*, 30.
33. "Mr. McGregor's Garden — Keep Out!" *Public Affairs* XV: 2 (Winter 1953), 20–29.
34. *HCGT*, 8.
35. "Canada: Two Nations or One?" *F&O*, 253–55.
36. *Ibid.*, 253.
37. "Our Present Discontents," 311.
38. *Senate Debates*, March 28, 1972, 267; and Saul, *A Fair Country: Telling Truths About Canada* (Toronto: Viking Canada, 2008), 111–16.
39. *HCGT*, 20–22.
40. "Canada: Two Nations or One?" 255.
41. See *Senate Debates*, March 28, 1972, 268; "Disallowance: A Contrast," *Forum* 18 (June 1938), 73–74; and "Canada and Alberta: The Revival of Dominion Control over the Provinces," *F&O*, 177–205.
42. "The Third Option," *Canadian Bar Review* LVII (September 1979), 491.
43. "On the Manifesto of the Committee for a New Constitution," manuscript for broadcast, April 23, 1977, EFP Vol. 38.
44. "In Defence of Macdonald's Constitution," *Dalhousie Law Journal* 3: 2 (October 1976), 539, 533.
45. HCGT, 10–11.
46. "The British Share in the Canadian Identity," Queen's University, 1978, EFP Vol. 38.
47. Draft submission, Task Force on National Unity, March 1978, EFP Vol. 39.
48. "The Third Option," 491.
49. Draft submission, Task Force.
50. "The Third Option," 491.
51. "Our Present Discontents," 309, and "The Third Option," 492.
52. "Our Present Discontents," 318.
53. "Canada: Two Nations or One?" 268.
54. Convocation address, York University (Toronto) October 21, 1972.
55. "Our Present Discontents," 318.
56. *Sunday Magazine*, CBC Radio, transcript of interview, September 25, 1977, EFP Vol. 38.
57. "Senate Reform," speech to Canadian Bar Association section, August

19, 1985.
58. "A Forsey to Be Reckoned With," interview by Victoria Lees, *McGill News* (Montreal), 2: 2 (Winter 1978), 4–5.
59. *Senate Debates*, March 28, 1972, 270; see also *HCGT*, 12.
60. Speech, Rotary Club (Ottawa), August 15, 1977, EFP Vol. 38.
61. Draft submission, Task Force.
62. John Ralston Saul, *Reflections of a Siamese Twin: Canada at the End of the Twentieth Century* (Toronto: Viking Canada, 1997), 247–64.
63. "Of Referenda and Plebiscites," *Ottawa Citizen*, August 30, 1977.
64. Earle 1989, 79; Speech, Union Club (Victoria, BC) April 17, 1990, EFP Vol. 63.
65. Earle 1989, 79–80.
66. "The Third Option," 472.
67. *Senate Debates*, March 28, 1972, 267.
68. "On Referenda and Plebiscites."
69. Earle 1989, 79.
70. "On Referenda and Plebiscites."
71. "Senate Reform."
72. "Constitutional Aspects of the Canadian Pipe Line Debate," 128–48.
73. Earle 1989, 67.
74. Unpublished Letter to the Editor, 1990, *One Voice*, 146–47.
75. Interview by Ian Alexander, *Music in My Life* (Arts National), CBC Radio, February 14, 1986.
76. "A Forsey to Be Reckoned With."
77. "Views on Giving Back-Bench MPs More Clout Heard," *Evening Times-Globe* (Saint John, NB), January 31, 1985; Minutes of Proceedings and Evidence of the Special Committee on the Reform of the House of Commons, Issue No. 5, January 1985.
78. Submission to Joint Committee on the Constitutional Accord, 1987, Parliament of Canada, July 21, 1987, 24; see also Chapter 14.
79. Letter to Arthur Meighen, December 6, 1951, EFP Vol. 4.

Chapter Thirteen
1. Speech, Union Club (Victoria, BC) April 17, 1990, EFP Vol. 63.
2. "Valedictory, McGill Arts," McGill University, 1925, EFP Vol. 8.
3. "Present Problems of Confederation: An English Canadian View,"

F&O, 272–75.
4. "Mr. King and the Government's Labour Policy," *Forum* 21 (November 1941), 231–32.
5. "French and English in Canada: A Crisis of Confederation?" *The Round Table: Quarterly Review of British Commonwealth Affairs*, No. 214, March 1964, 161.
6. *Senate Debates*, October 27, 1970, 57.
7. Letter to Graham Spry, July 2, 1964, EFP Vol. 5.
8. "Our Present Discontents," *F&O*, 321.
9. "Eugene Forsey Urges a Flight into Reason," shortened version of address to the 1965 Couchiching Conference, *Ottawa Journal*, August 9, 1965, EFP Vol. 8.
10. "French and English in Canada," 157.
11. Speech, Rotary Club (Ottawa), August 15, 1977, EFP Vol. 38.
12. "Present Problems of Confederation," *F&O*, 279.
13. Supreme Court of Canada, Reference re Secession of Quebec, (1998) 2 S.C.R.217.
14. National Conference on Canadian Goals, September 12, 1964, audio tape, audiovisual audiovisual section, LAC.
15. Speech, Union Club.
16. "Canada, Quebec and the Constitution," speech to the Empire Club (Toronto), April 28, 1977.
17. Speech, Union Club.
18. Speech, Rotary Club.
19. See William Shaw and Lionel Albert, *Partition: The Price of Quebec's Independence* (Montreal: Thornhill Publishing, 1980); and Scott Reid, *Canada Remapped: How the Partition of Quebec Will Reshape the Nation* (Vancouver: Arsenal Pulp Press, 1992).
20. "Canada, Quebec and the Constitution."
21. Speech, Union Club.
22. Speech, Rotary Club.
23. *Ibid.*; see also Speech, Union Club.
24. Speech, Union Club.
25. "On the Manifesto of the Committee for a New Constitution," April 23, 1977, EFP Vol. 38.
26. See Chapters 10 and 15.

27. *Sunday Magazine*, CBC Radio, transcript of interview, September 25, 1977, EFP Vol. 38.
28. "Memorandum on the Associate States," *F&O*, 284–88.
29. "The Third Option," *Canadian Bar Review*, LVII (September 1979), 473.
30. Speech, Rotary Club.
31. "The Third Option," 474.
32. "Canada, 1967," *F&O*, 301.
33. "Canada, Quebec and the Constitution."
34. *Sunday Magazine*.
35. For more on Meech Lake, see Chapter 14.
36. "Canada, 1967," 291.
37. Draft Submission, Task Force on National Unity, March, 1978, EFP Vol. 39.
38. *Ibid.*
39. "The Third Option," 474.
40. National Conference on Canadian Goals.
41. "Present Problems of Confederation," 282.
42. "French Canada in our Second Century," *Saskatchewan Law Review* 32 (Fall 1967), 234.
43. "No Surrender," *Ottawa Citizen*, February 23, 1991.
44. "Professor Dion and Quebec's Constitutional Future," undated typescript, circa January 1991. (This may be the draft of the letter to the *Vancouver Sun* cited in Note 80.)
45. "Present Problems of Confederation," 276.
46. "The Third Option," 476.
47. "Eugene Forsey Urges." (An error that appeared in this shortened newspaper version of the Couchiching speech is corrected here.)
48. "Professor Dion and Quebec's Constitutional Future."
49. "Canada, Quebec and the Constitution."
50. Convocation Address, Queen's University, October 27, 1979.
51. "The Third Option," 486–87, 490–91.
52. Draft Submission, Task Force.
53. "Canada, 1967," 301.
54. "Eugene Forsey Urges."
55. "French and English in Canada." 160–61.
56. "Present Problems of Confederation," 280–81.

57. *Ibid.*, 281.
58. "Canada, 1967," 302.
59. "French Canada in our Second Century," 234.
60. "Eugene Forsey Urges."
61. Submission to New Brunswick Legislature Select Committee on the 1987 Constitutional Accord, 1988, 49, EFP Vol. 63.
62. John Ralston Saul, "The Good Citizen," *Forum* 77 (December 1997), 13–17.
63. "Our Present Discontents," 325.
64. "Present Problems of Confederation," 280.
65. Letters exchanged with Jacques-Yvan Morin, February 5 and 9, 1965, EFP Vol 8.
66. Letter to Léo Gagné, Fédération des Sociétés Saint-Jean-Baptiste du Québec, May 28, 1965, EFP Vol. 8.
67. "Canada, 1967," 290.
68. See *Fringe*, 197–98.
69. Letter to "APEC Canada," September 11, 1986, EFP Vol. 60.
70. *Fringe*, 199–200.
71. "Eugene Forsey Urges."
72. "Present Problems of Confederation," 283.
73. "Concepts of Federalism: Some Canadian Aspects," Speech to the 34th Annual Couchiching Conference, August 2, 1965, audio tape 650802-3, CBC Radio Archives, Toronto; see also EFP Vol. 38.
74. "Our Present Discontents," 332.
75. "Canada, 1967," 299.
76. "Our Present Discontents," 325.
77. "Concepts of Federalism."
78. Draft Submission, Task Force.
79. Letter to John S. Scott, April 30, 1979, EFP Vol. 58.
80. "Sovereignty Association Won't Work," Letter to the Editor, *Vancouver Sun*, January 25, 1991, cited in *One Voice*, 66.
81. "No Surrender," *Ottawa Citizen*, February 23, 1991.

Chapter Fourteen

1. "Canada, Quebec and the Constitution," speech to the Empire Club (Toronto), April 28, 1977.

2. Speech, Ontario Conference on Economic and Cultural Nationalism, June 1971, EFP Vol. 38.
3. *Ibid.*
4. "Valedictory, McGill, Arts," McGill University, 1925, EFP Vol. 8.
5. Letter to Howard Simmons, June 30, 1964, EFP Vol. 8.
6. Speech, Union Club (Victoria, BC), April 17, 1990, EFP Vol. 63.
7. See David Orchard, *The Fight for Canada: Four Centuries of Resistance to American Expansionism* (Toronto: Stoddart, 1993); and Maude Barlow, *Too Close for Comfort: Canada's Future Within Fortress North America* (Toronto: McClelland & Stewart, 2005).
8. "Pipeline and Parliament," *Forum* 36 (July 1956), 73, 96.
9. Desmond Morton, *Working People: An Illustrated History of the Canadian Labour Movement* (Montreal and Kingston: McGill-Queen's University Press, 2007), 213.
10. Speech, Ontario Conference on Nationalism.
11. Earle 1989, 24–25.
12. Speech, Union Club.
13. "A Crisis in Canadian Education?" n.d., 1957, EFP Vol. 8.
14. "Constitutional Monarchy and the Provinces," *F&O*, 26–28.
15. "A Passage to India," unpublished segment of *Fringe*, 1989.
16. See "Trying to Stop the Theft of Canada's History," unpublished chapter of *Fringe*, 1989.
17. See Helen Forsey, "The Governor General Is the Guardian of Our Constitution," *CCPA Monitor*, May 2010.
18. Letter to Jean Chevrier, September 16, 1978, re: Gordon Peckover, "The Decline and Fall of the Canadian Monarchy," *Opinion* 7: 4 (September 1978).
19. *Senate Debates*, January 28, 1971, 441.
20. "A Crisis in Canadian Education?"
21. *Ibid.*
22. "Canada, Quebec and the Constitution."
23. National Conference on Canadian Goals, September 12, 1964, audio tape, audiovisual section, LAC.
24. *HCGT*, 28.
25. National Conference on Canadian Goals.
26. "Canada: Two Nations or One?" *F&O*, 261.

27. National Conference on Canadian Goals.
28. "The Third Option," *Canadian Bar Review*, XVII (September 1979), 477–80.
29. "... But If We Pick the Wrong Party?" letter to unidentified newspaper, probably *Montreal Gazette*, circa May 1979.
30. "Memorandum on the Associate States," *F&O*, 288.
31. Convocation Address, Queen's University, October 27, 1979.
32. Letter to the Editor, *Globe and Mail*, sent June 1, 1987.
33. Submission, Special Joint Committee on the 1987 Constitutional Accord, Parliament of Canada, July 21, 1987.
34. *Ibid*.
35. Speech, Union Club.
36. Submission, Alberta NDP public hearings on the Meech Lake Accord (Calgary), September 22, 1987.
37. Speech, Union Club.
38. Submission, Alberta NDP public hearings on the Meech Lake Accord.
39. Letter to Deborah Coyne, October 7, 1989, and Letter to the Editor, *Globe and Mail*, February 25, 1990, Forsey-Coyne Correspondence.
40. The difficult personal role my father played in the final weeks of the drama is touched on in Chapter 7.
41. "National Unity and the Loyalist Contribution." speech to the United Empire Loyalists' Association (London, ON), May 6, 1978, EFP Vol. 39.
42. "Canada: Two Nations or One?" 268.

Chapter Fifteen
1. Letter to Arthur Meighen, November 20, 1951, EFP Vol. 4.
2. Letter from Alice Massey, December 31, 1931, EFP Vol. 45.
3. Letter to Florence Forsey, January 19, 1932, EFP Vol. 45.
4. *Ibid.*, February 2, 1932, EFP Vol. 45.
5. Letter from Florence Forsey to Tom Tweedie, May 12, 1937, Mount Allison University Archives, "Tweedie Correspondence" file.
6. Memorandum from Sir Arthur Currie, October 26, 1933, McGill University Archives, RG2, Record of the Principal and Chancellor's Office, Container 42, File 00301.
7. Letter from Arthur Meighen, January 9, 1942, EFP Vol. 4.
8. Letter to the Editor, *Chatelaine*, enclosed in letter to Meighen, October

23, 1951, EFP Vol. 4.
9. See Chapter 3; also *Fringe*, 106–08.
10. Millar.
11. Interview by Peter Stursberg, September 5, 1978, audio tape CA 1978–135/1&2, audiovisual section, LAC; see also *Fringe*, 112–13.
12. Letter to the Editor, *Forum* 22 (March 1942), 370–71.
13. Letter to Arthur Meighen, July 11, 1943, EFP Vol. 4.
14. Letters to Arthur Meighen, December 18, 1944, and October 9, 1948, EFP Vol. 4.
15. Letter from Arthur Meighen, December 21, 1948, EFP Vol. 4.
16. Candidate's letter, Carleton CCF Campaign Headquarters (Ottawa), December 1948.
17. Letter to Arthur Meighen, December 28, 1948, EFP Vol. 4.
18. *Ibid.*, December 26, 1951, EFP Vol. 4.
19. *Ibid.*, April 13, 1953, EFP Vol. 4.
20. Letter to M.J. Coldwell, March 14, 1955, EFP Vol. 5.
21. *Ibid.*, July 5, 1957, EFP Vol. 5.
22. Letter to T.C. Douglas, July 5, 1957, EFP Vol. 5.
23. Letter from Arthur Meighen, December 21, 1948; letter to Meighen, December 28, 1948, EFP Vol. 4.
24. Letter to W.C. Good, February 8, 1955, EFP Vol. 5.
25. "CCF Birthday Party," *StarPhoenix* (Saskatoon), December 11, 1957, EFP Vol. 8.
26. *Senate Debates*, January 28, 1971, 440.
27. Letter to Arthur Meighen, February 12, 1952, EFP Vol. 4.
28. Letter from Arthur Meighen, February 14, 1952, EFP Vol. 4.
29. Pencilled draft of letter to Derek Bedson, September 11, 1957, EFP Vol. 5.
30. Letter to Lorne T. Morgan, April 2, 1953, EFP Vol. 5.
31. Letter to Carl Hamilton, February 17, 1960; "Notes on the New Draft Program for the New Party," March 24, 1961, EFP Vol. 18.
32. Address to NDP Founding Convention, August 1, 1961, audio tape 610801–3, CBC Radio Archives, Toronto.
33. Letter to T.C. Douglas, July 21, 1961; letter from Douglas, July 26, 1961, EFP Vol. 18.
34. Guaranteed Perfect Health Act, draft motion enclosed with letter to T.C. Douglas, July 21, 1961, EFP Vol. 18.

35. Handwritten notes from NDP founding convention, August 1961, EFP Vol. 58.
36. Letter to Arthur Meighen, December 26, 1951, EFP Vol. 4.
37. See "Eugene Forsey Urges a Flight into Reason," *Ottawa Journal*, August 9, 1965, EFP Vol. 8.
38. Letter from Harry Waisglass, September 30, 1965, EFP Vol. 8.
39. Letter to Harry Waisglass, October 6, 1965, EFP Vol. 8.
40. "Dr. Forsey Dissents," newspaper editorial, n.d., 1961 EFP Vol. 46.
41. Letter to Arthur Meighen, November 20, 1951, EFP Vol. 4.
42. National Conference on Canadian Goals, September 12, 1964, audio tape, audiovisual section, LAC.
43. Interview by Ian Alexander, *Music in My Life* (Arts National), CBC Radio, February 14, 1986.
44. *Senate Debates*, October 27, 1970, 58.
45. *Fringe*, 152.
46. "Liberalism and Controls," February 1976, EFP Vol. 38.
47. *Ibid.*
48. "A Slick Way to Skin the Public," *Maclean's*, February 11, 1980.
49. Letters to Deborah Coyne, August 22 and September 14, 1990, Forsey-Coyne correspondence.
50. Earle 1989, 90–91.
51. Letter from Gerry Caplan, May 31, 1983, EFP Vol. 52.
52. Letter to Gerry Caplan, June 8, 1983, EFP Vol. 52.

Chapter Sixteen
1. Convocation Address, Carleton University (Ottawa), November 14, 1976.
2. *Senate Debates*, September 12, 1973.
3. Interview by Peter Gzowski, *Morningside*, CBC Radio, October 4, 1990, audio tape 901004–04/00, CBC Radio Archives, Toronto.
4. "A Forsey to Be Reckoned With," interview by Victoria Lees, *McGill News* (Montreal), 2: 2 (Winter 1978), 4–5.
5. Letter to Solicitor-General Warren Allmand, September 21, 1973.
6. *Fringe*, 159–60.
7. *Senate Debates*, June 14, 1972, 482, and October 8, 1974, 54–58.
8. *Senate Debates*, June 8, 1976, 2183–2184.

9. *Senate Debates*, August 9, 1977, 1303–1304.
10. *Senate Debates*, November 20, 1973, 1176–1180.
11. *Senate Debates*, May 26, 1976, 2162.
12. *Fringe*, 163.
13. *Senate Debates*, March 28, 1972, 270–71.
14. *Ottawa Citizen*, November 15, 1976.
15. Report on India to the Canadian Congress of Labour, 1953, EFP Vol. 5.
16. "A Passage to India," unpublished segment of *Fringe*, circa 1990.
17. Report on India.
18. Convocation Address, Carleton University.
19. *Trade Unions in Canada: 1812–1902* (Toronto: University of Toronto Press, 1982).
20. *HCGT*.
21. Eugene A. Forsey and G.C. Eglington, *The Question of Confidence in Responsible Government* (Ottawa: Library of Parliament, 1985).
22. *Evatt and Forsey on the Reserve Powers* (Sydney, Australia: Legal Books, 1990).
23. Letter to the Editor, *Globe and Mail*, October 30, 1990.
24. "Labour's Eugene Forsey on Social Drinking and Minorities," interview by Kenneth Bagnell, *United Church Observer*, June 15, 1962, 25.

Epilogue
1. Maude Barlow and Bruce Campbell, *Straight Through the Heart: How the Liberals Abandoned the Just Society* (Toronto: HarperCollins, 1995).
2. See "Canada, 1967," *F&O*, 299, cited in Chapter 13.
3. "A Slick Way to Skin the Public," *Maclean's*, February 11, 1980.

SELECTED BIBLIOGRAPHY

Works by Eugene Forsey

Economic and Social Aspects of the Nova Scotia Coal Industry. Toronto: Macmillan, 1926.
Freedom and Order: Collected Essays. Toronto: McClelland & Stewart, 1974.
How Canadians Govern Themselves, 7th ed. Ottawa: Library of Parliament, 2010. Accessed at *www.parl.gc.ca/publications*.
A Life on the Fringe: The Memoirs of Eugene Forsey. Toronto: Oxford University Press, 1990.
The Royal Power of Dissolution of Parliament in the British Commonwealth. Toronto: Oxford University Press, 1943.
Trade Unions in Canada: 1812–1902. Toronto: University of Toronto Press, 1982.

Works by Eugene Forsey with Others

Evatt and Forsey on the Reserve Powers. Sydney, Australia: Legal Books, 1990.
The Question of Confidence in Responsible Government. Eugene Forsey and G.C. Eglington. Ottawa: Library of Parliament, 1985.
Social Planning for Canada. League for Social Reconstruction. Toronto: Thomas Nelson & Sons, 1935; republished, Toronto: University of Toronto Press, 1975.
The Sound of One Voice: Eugene Forsey and His Letters to the Press. E. Hodgetts, ed. Toronto: University of Toronto Press, 2000.
Towards the Christian Revolution. R.B.Y. Scott and Gregory Vlastos. New York and Chicago: Willett Clark & Company, 1936; republished, Kingston, ON: Ronald P. Frye & Company, 1989.

Other Authors

Abella, Irving. *Nationalism, Communism, and Canadian Labour: The CIO, the Communist Party, and the Canadian Congress of Labour, 1935–1956.* Toronto: University of Toronto Press, 1973.
Barlow, Maude, and Bruce Campbell. *Straight Through the Heart: How the Liberals Abandoned the Just Society.* Toronto: HarperCollins, 1995.
Coyne, Deborah. *Roll of the Dice: Working with Clyde Wells During the Meech Lake Negotiations.* Toronto: James Lorimer, 1992.
Horn, Michiel. *The League for Social Reconstruction: Intellectual Origins of the Democratic Left in Canada.* Toronto: University of Toronto Press, 1980.
____. *Academic Freedom in Canada.* Toronto: University of Toronto Press, 1999.
Ingle, Lorne, ed. *Meech Lake Reconsidered.* Hull, QC: Voyageur Publishing, 1989.
Lynch, Charles. *A Funny Way to Run a Country: Further Memoirs of a Political Voyeur.* Edmonton: Hurtig Publishers, 1986.
Morton, Desmond, with Terry Copp. *Working People: An Illustrated History of Canadian Labour.* Ottawa: Deneau & Greenberg, 1980.
Neatby, Hilda. *So Little for the Mind.* Toronto: Clark, Irwin, 1953.
Orchard, David. *The Fight for Canada: Four Centuries of Resistance to American Expansionism.* Toronto: Stoddart, 1993.

Saul, John Ralston. *A Fair Country: Telling Truths About Canada*. Toronto: Penguin, 2008.

———. *Reflections of a Siamese Twin: Canada at the End of the Twentieth Century*. Toronto: Viking, 1997.

Shaw, William F., and Lionel Albert. *Partition: The Price of Quebec's Independence*. Montreal: Thornhill Publishing, 1980.

Taylor, Charles. *Radical Tories: The Conservative Tradition in Canada*. Toronto: Anansi, 1982.

Whitehorn, Alan. *Canadian Socialism: Essays on the CCF-NDP*. Toronto: Oxford University Press, 1992.

INDEX

Page numbers in italics refer to photographs and their captions.

Abella, Irving, 133, 147
Aboriginal people, 73, 91, 192,
    212, 232, 236, 310, 327, 339,
    345, 385, 389, 430
    Cree, 217, 345
    First Nations, 234–36, 339, 345
    Haudenosaunee (Six Nations),
        232
    Innu, 345
    Inuit, 217, 234, 236, 345
    Métis, 232, 234, 236
    Mohawk, 430
Aboriginal rights, 203, 235, 416,
    424

academic freedom, 37, 116,
    181, 196, 240, 394
affirmative action, 192, 424
Alberta, 90, 303, 364, 372, 388
Algonquin Park, *35*, 165
Allaire Report, 368
Allende, Salvador, 75–76
Allmand, Warren, 416, 423
American Federation of Labour
    (AFL), 128, 132, 137
Americanization, 372, 378
animals, 38, 152, 159–60
Annapolis Valley, 23, 24

Balliol College (Oxford), 31
Barlow, Maude, 433
Barrett, Silby, 39, 69, 131–32, 138, 141, 171, 245
Bedson, Derek, 403
Bégin, Monique, 416
Bélanger-Campeau Commission, 368
Bell, Russell, 271–72
bilingualism, 43, 244, 355–56, 358–59
Bills 22 and 101 (Quebec), 87, 293, 294, 364
Bird, Florence, 416
Blake, Edward, 232
Board of Broadcast Governors (BBG), 40–41, 292, 298, 362, 379, 402, 407
Book of Common Prayer, 149, 267
Borden, Sir Robert, 161, 218, 243, 296, 315
Bouchard, Lucien, 347
Bourassa, Robert, 387
Bowles, Hazel, 26, 155–56, 177, 188–89
Bowles, Jeffrey "Jeff," 28, 29, 181
Bowles, Letitia Shaw, *25*, 26
Bowles, William Cochrane "Goppa," *25*, 26, *27*, 28, 91, *219*, 265
British Columbia, 48, 65, 142, 299, 339
British North America (BNA) Act, 223, 231, 276, 278, 322–24, 350, 354, 376
Byng, Lord (*see also* King-Byng affair), 78–79, 274–75, 317

cabinet (*see also* Constitution of Canada, cabinet; Forsey, Eugene A., cabinet government), 96, 142, 161, 164, 294, 320, 372, 415–16
Caccia, Charles, 164, 178, 272, 416
Calder, R.L., 391
Calgary Declaration (1997), 357
Campbell, Bruce, 433
Canada Year Book, 129, 279, 291
Canadian Broadcasting Corporation (CBC), 41, 91, 114, 130, 152, 182, 203, 211, 296–98, 347, 357, 362, 371, 378, 407, 415–16, 433
Canadian Centre for Policy Alternatives, 102, 433
Canadian Chamber of Commerce, 105, 130, 270, 274
Canadian Congress of Labour (CCL), 38, 40, 119, 125–26, 128, 131–34, 136–38, 143, 245, 250, 398
Canadian Forum, 31, 36, 69, 92, 103, 112, 129, 142, 162, 192, 204, 251, 269, 272, 274, 361, 372, 397
Canadian Labour Congress (CLC), 40, 42–44, 137–38, 139, 143, 144, 146, 164, 201, 256, 432
Canadian Political Science Association, 42, 110, 114, 130, 242, 266
Canadian Radio-television and Telecommunications

Commission (CRTC), 40–41, 433
capitalism, 51, 54, 105, 106, 113, 115, 242, 251
Caplan, Gerry, 419
Cartier, George-Étienne, 218, 220, 368
Casgrain, Thérèse, 89, 362, 416, 428
Cassidy, Harry, 406
CCF News, 129
Charlottetown Accord (1992), 360, 389
Charter of Rights and Freedoms, 90–91, 366, 386
Chile, 75–76, 78, 420, *421*, 423
Chisholm, Brock, 69
Christianity, 43, 52, 54, 58, 61–64, 108, 140
Churchill, Sir Winston, 84, 236
civil disobedience, 321
Civil Liberties Union (CLU), 36, 86, 89, 110, 116, 125
Congress of Industrial Organizations (CIO), 128, 132, 136–37
Coldwell, M.J., 398, 401
communism, 33, 108, 134–36, 393, 399
Confederation, 43, 166, 223–24, 278, 299, 301, 322, 338–39, 351, 381
confidence (*see* Constitution of Canada)
Conroy, Pat, 39, 126, 129, 131, 133, 137, 398
Conservative Party (*see also* Progressive Conservative Party),
30–31, 51, 78, 94, 162–63, 313, 332, 390, 391, 394–96, 400, 400
Constitution of Canada:
amendment, 89, 91, 311, 324–27, 329, 351–52, 366, 383, 424
cabinet, 223, 231–32, 309, 312–13, 318–20, 333–34, 352
confidence, 312–14, 381, 429, 433
conventions, 81, 308, 323–24, 331, 334
Crown, 79, 80, 92, 96, 206, 214, 232, 297, 299, 305, 309, 316–19
"fairy tales," 45, 87, 222, 226, 235, 322, 326, 435
governor general, 30, 78–80, 86, 317–19, 334, 377, 392
"notwithstanding clause," 90–91
repatriation, 47, 90, 352, 357, 366, 383, 424
responsible government, 85–86, 231, 278, 295, 305, 314, 316–19, 327, 332, 372, 429
Contreras, Eugene, *71*, 72
Contreras, Roddy, 67, *71*, 72, 172, *173*, 174–75, 194, 202, 215
Co-operative Commonwealth Federation (CCF) (*see also* New Democratic Party), 18, 32–34, 36, 38–42, 53, 77, 81, 87, 92, 101, 109, 112, 114, 116–20,

122, 125, 129, 133, 134, 143, 160, 182, 186, 192, 198, 242, 243, 245, 255, 256, 270, 289, 303, 362, 391, 393–407, 410, 411, 413, 418, 419
Coote, J.A., 102
corporations, 55, 64, 96, 199, 235, 290, 294–95, 297, 302, 305, 373–74, 424, 427
Council of Canadians, 102, 433
Coyne, Deborah, 164, 209
Creighton, Donald, 361
Currie, Sir Arthur, 393

Dafoe, J.W., 80, 395
decentralization, 303, 343, 350, 353–54, 365, 367, 383
Diefenbaker, John, 40, 142, 169, 201, 403
Dion, Gérard, 362
disallowance and reservation of provincial acts, 86–87, 169, 376, 394
dissolution of Parliament, 37, 79–80, 87, 181, 274–75, 313, 317, 318, 333, 395
Dobson, Dawn, 40, 138–40, 144, 147, 164, 176–78, 191, 251, 283, 435
Dominion Institute, 235
Douglas, Thomas Clement "Tommy," 401, 408–09, 411, 428
Dowd, Norman, 125–26
Drew, George, 120, 182, 393, 398
Dunbar, George, 135

Duplessis, Maurice, 36–37, 40, 55, 64, 87, 94, 116, 125, 181, 184, 338, 353, 362, 394

Eardley, Allworth, 30, 51
Earle, Tom, 374
Ecuador, 44, 46, 75, 172, *173*, 425
ecumenical movement, 64, 102
education:
    crisis in education, 41, 245–46, 248, 251, 253–54, 256, 258–59, 260, 262
    national education and rights, 45, 86, 110, 112, 140
    political/popular education, 92, 95, 112, 113, 116, 126–27, 129–31, 190, 197, 273, 290–91, 300–01, 322
efficiency, 102, 294–95
Eglington, Graham, 46, 164, 178, 429
Église Unie Saint-Marc, 43, 57, 62, 160, 266, 362
elections:
    constitutional aspects, 81–82, 85, 94
    Eugene Forsey as candidate in, 119–20, 182, 185, 396–97, 399–401, 404
    proportional representation, 315, 321, 330
Elizabeth II, Queen, 214
Empire Club (Toronto), 57, 369, 380

Employment (Unemployment) Insurance, 127, 289, 301, 305, 325, 352, 416, 424
England (*see also* Great Britain, United Kingdom), 31, 43, 113, 115, 157, 158, 165, 269, 272, 309, 384

fascism, 36, 55, 110, 134, 338
Fathers of Confederation, 223–24, 231, 277–78, 321, 326, 376–77, 381, 409
federalism, 95, 232, 321–22, 331, 335, 381, 412
Fellowship for a Christian Social Order (FCSO), 116–17, 185–88, 207
feminism and feminists, 190, 192–93, 273, 362
Finn, Ed, 139, 389
first ministers' conferences, 90, 208, *209*, 333, 386
Fisheries Act, 294
Fleming, Donald, 201
Flynn, Jacques, 414
Forsey, Blanche, 168, 192
Forsey, Eugene Alfred:
  advocacy of reserve powers of Crown, 18, 80, 92, 174, 317–20
  alcohol, 66, 108, 246
  birth, 24–25
  books:
    Evatt and Forsey on the Reserve Powers, 430
    Freedom and Order:

Collected Essays, 46, 221, 267, 308, 361, 429
How Canadians Govern Themselves, 287, 288, 313, *325*, 428
A Life on the Fringe: The Memoirs of Eugene Forsey, 48, 65, 81, 88, 101–02, 146, 162, 207, 257, 286, 417
The Question of Confidence in Responsible Government, 429
The Royal Power of Dissolution of Parliament in the British Commonwealth, 79, 207, 433
Social Planning for Canada, 36, 101, 109, 121, 290–92
The Sound of One Voice: Eugene Forsey and His Letters to the Press, 183
Towards the Christian Revolution, 36, 53–54, 106, 273, 393
Trade Unions in Canada: 1812–1902, 145, 146, 221, 428
cabinet government, 37, 42, 125, 157, 309, 312–16, 318, 429
cats, 36, 152, *159*
civil liberties, 36–37, 40, 45,

78, 81, 88–90, 99, 102–03, 110, 113, 116–17, 125, 134, 325, 327, 420, *421*, 422
death, 18–19, 67, 95, 180, 183, 195, *285*, 286, 336, 368, 431
dogs, 27–28, *29*, 152, *159*, 160
drugs, 66
editing, 28, 283–84, *285*
environment and environmentalism, 19, 55, 57, 78, 164, 262, 288, 293, 302, 304, 312, 320, 327, 352, 370, 378, 384, 424, 428, 433
experts, views on, 41, 70, 246, 248, 253–54
flag, maple leaf, 229–30
gays and lesbians, 194
ghost-writing, 68
human rights, 78, 86, 90, 109, 110
letters to the press, 21, 92, 113, 129, 196, 227, 413–14
minorities (ethnic, linguistic, religious, social), 43, 57, 81, 87, 235, 327, 330, 339, 340, 344, 354–55, 362, 364, 366, 385–86, 410, 424, 431
non-experts, views on, 200
opposition to "two nations" theory, 18, 41, 181, 196, 207, 280–81, 347, 410–12, 418

Order of Canada, 48
senator, 119, 146, 164–65, 169–70, 176, 225, 243–44, 251, 255–56, 277, 292, 296–99, 306, 311, 327, 330, 332–33, 342, 362, 366, 379, 385, 396, 415–18, 421
social justice, 77–78, 99, 109, 116, 122–23, 130–31, 212–13, 307, 320
student days, 19, 29–31, 79, 215
teachers and teaching, 31, 33–33, 42, 92, 239–41, 247–50, 258–63, 394
theses:
　"Economic and Social Aspects of the Nova Scotia Coal Industry," 31, 52, 125, 134
　"The Royal Power of Dissolution of Parliament in the British Commonwealth," 37, 79, 92, 174, 204, 313, 317, 394, 433
tobacco, 246
university degrees:
　B.A., 31, 250
　honourary, 42, 46, 169, 251
　LL.D., 251, 262, *263*
　M.A., 31, 52, 154
　Ph.D., 33, 37, 65, 79, 92,

117, 126, 154, 174, 252, 257, *263*, 313, 317
women, attitude towards, 56, 91, 150, 190–95, 282, 424
workers, 39, 55–56, 69, 99, 103, 105–06, 108, 125–27, 129–32, 134–37, 139, 141–43, 147, 168, 187–88, 190, 251, 271, 289, 327, 366, 372, 399, 423
Forsey, Florence Elvira Bowles, *24*, 25, *33*, *219*
Forsey, Harriet Roberts, 34, *35*, 36–38, *39*, 46, *47*, 48, 59, *118*, 126, *155*, 159, 169, *177*, 205, *214*, *337*
Forsey, Mab, 168, 192
Forsey, Margaret, 38, *39*, 84, 131, 147, *153*, *155*, 157–58, 174, 178, 191, 435
Forsey, Maria, 191–92
Forsey Sr., Eugene, 24, *25*, 26, *27*, 28
Franco, Francisco, 36
free enterprise, 111, 146, 163, 290, 293, 295, 296, 300, 305, 405, 418
Free Trade Agreement (Canada-US), 198, 200, 226, 330, 374–75
Freire, Paolo, 273
Fulton-Favreau Formula (1964–65), 357

Gaspé, 23, 24, 35

Gilbert and Sullivan, 176, 267, 298, 332
globalization, 89, 102, 312, 342
Globe and Mail, 96, 146, 183, 286, 430
Goldenberg, Carl, 416
Gordon, King, 35, 52
governor general (*see* Constitution of Canada)
Grand Bank (Newfoundland), 24–26, 28, 166, *167*, 168–69, *170*, 171, 192, *228*, 250, 393
Great Britain (*see also* England, United Kingdom), 292
Great Depression, 31, 55, 86, 98, 100, 102–03, 106, 108, 116, 120–21, 125, 273, 378, 399
Gupta, Taanta, 165
Gzowski, Peter, 378, 422, 433

"HACCP" self-regulation, 293, 294
Hammarskjöld, Dag, 276, 281
Harper, Elijah, 389
Harper, Stephen, 94, 281, 309, 313, 319, 433
Hastings, John, 161, 179, 183–84, 224, 414, 433
Hemmeon, J.C., 30–31, 51, 125
Hickman, Jonathan, 23
Hickman, T. Alex, 82, 156, 169, 171–72, 255, 393, 415
Hitler, Adolf, 142
Hodgetts, J.E. "Ted," 183, 227
Horn, Michiel, 101, 240, 394
Howe, C.D., 84, 296, 372
Hudon, Guy, 362

immigration (*see* multiculturalism)
India, 40, 66, 160–63, 192, 344, 375, 425–26
Institut canadien des affaires publiques, 40, 338, 414
International Confederation of Free Trade Unions (ICFTU), 40

Johnson, Daniel, 280
Johnson, Samuel, 314, 381
Joncas, Pierre, 70, 121, 182, 191, 193, 243
Judicial Committee of the Privy Council, 322
"just transition," 427

Kealey, Greg, 133
Kierans, Eric, 223
King, William Lyon Mackenzie, 37, 67, 69, 78–81, 94, 129, 141, 183–84, 204, 216, 225–26, 274–76, 296, 313, 317, 395–96, 415, 418
King-Byng affair (*see also* Byng, Lord), 37, 78–80, 184, 392
Kingston, 42, 59, 60, 92, 157, 187, 189
Knowles, Stanley, 256, 270

Labour Research, 127, 142, 289
Laurier, Sir Wilfrid, 26, 218, 377
Leacock, Stephen, 30–31
League for Social Reconstruction (LSR), 32–33, 35–36, 53, 101, 109–10, 114, 116–17, 121,

125, 160, 204, 240, 289–90, 296, 406
Levellers (England), 213, 231
Lévesque, René, 347, 362, 366
Lewis, David, 125, 133, 402, 410, 412
Liberal Party (Canada), 37, 47, 299, 392, 395, 400, 414–16, 418
Liberal Party (Quebec), 19, 368
Lisgar Collegiate (Ottawa), 28
Lynch, Charles, 286

MacDonald, Donald, 131
Macdonald, Sir John A., 216, 267
Macdonnell, Jim, 105, 398
MacInnis, Angus, 255
MacInnis, Grace, *118*
Maclean's, 112, 129, 418, 433
Macmurray, John, 31, 35, 204
MacPhail, Agnes, 192
Macquarrie, Heath, 156, 434
Mander, Jerry, 55
Manitoba, 389
Massey, Alice, 392
Massey, Vincent, 392
Matheson, John, 73, 81–82, 88, 92, 307, 414, 419, 435
McLachlan, J.B., 135
Meech Lake Accord, 18, 19, 47, 48, 164, 174, 178, 181, 196, 199, 208, *209*, 223, 244, 326, 333, 350, 352, 357, 360, 366, 368, 383–89. 430
Meighen, Arthur, 18, 26, 28, 30, 37, 41, 61, 77–79, 81, 87, 119, 132, 134, 150, 152,

160–63, 179, 180, 184, 204, 206–08, 224–25, 255, 267, 296, 334, 377, 390–92, 394–95, *396*, 397–98, 400–03, 411, 413, 418
Mexico, 25, 26, 156, 192, 215, 265, 425
Millar, David, 26, 52, 67, 141, 147, 215
Millard, Charlie, 131
Milliken, Peter, 309
minority government, 78, 85, 94, 313–15, 333
monarchy (*see also* Constitution of Canada, Crown), 80, 220, 231, 316, 319, 320, 371, 377
Montreal, 18, 29, 30, 31, 34–36, 40, 53, 65, 86, 87, 89, 100, 101, 110, 113, 116, 119, 125, 134, 165, 174, 184, 204, 213, *214*, 249, 335, *337*, 338, 345, 347, 361, 392, 393, 430
Montreal Star, 115
Morgentaler, Henry, 194
Morin, Jacques-Yvan, 266, 361
Morton, Desmond, 125, 127, 131, 137, 140, 144, 146, 170, 182–83, 241, 372, 411–12, 435
Mosher, A.R., 39, 128, 133, 137
Mulroney, Brian, 47, 190, 199, 208–09, 226, 366, 374, 384, 418
multiculturalism, 234, 370–71, 416, 229, 365
Mussolini, Benito, 36
Mutchmor, J.R., 136

National Film Board (NFB), 371, 416
national standards, 302, 304, 385
nationalism, Canadian, 319, 370, 372–73, 375, 380, 382, 389
Neatby, Hilda, 246–49, 252–54
neo-conservatism, 300, 418
New Brunswick, 34–35, 345, 350, 357, 364
New Democratic Party (NDP) (*see also* Co-operative Commonwealth Federation), 41, 42, 44, 88, 125, 143, 144, 181, 207, 243, 295, 347, 364, 388, 406–07, 409–13, 419, 422–24, 434
Newfoundland and Labrador, 23–24, 26, 34–35, 39, 52, 56, 142, 345–46, 388–89, 407
Nova Scotia, 23–24, 30–31, 52, 58, 125, 134, 302, 346
Nunavik, 345

October Crisis (1970), 88, 366
Oka Crisis (1990), 174, 200
O'Leary, Grattan, 89, 399
Oliver, Michael, 137, 241, 363, 407
Ontario, 28, 30, 36, 39, 40, 43, 67, 70, 81, 119, 135, 139, 216, 257, 259, 272, 296, 345, 348, 350, 364, 378–79, 397, 401, *429*, 435
Ontario Advisory Committee on Confederation, 43
Ontario Medical Association, 70
Orchard, David, 226, 434

Ottawa, 26, *27*, 28, *29*, 31, 38, *39*, 41, 43, 45, *47*, 48, 57, 65, 71, *118*, 119, 125, 126, 136, 139, 143, 144, 150, *151*, *155*, 157, 159, 160, 162, 165, 168, *177*, 178, 179, 181, 195, 202, 208, 214–16, 238, 265, 323, *325*, 352, 362, 364, 393, 401, 402, 408

Ottawa Board of Education, 202

Ottawa Citizen, 203, 252, 420, 425

Ottawa Journal, 94, 396, 398, 399

Ottawa River, 215, 411

Padlock Act (Quebec, 1937), 36, 86, 90, 110, 134, 269, 397

Parizeau, Jacques, 347

Parliament of Canada:
closure rule, 331
Committee on Regulations and Other Statutory Instruments, 45, 88, 164, 181, 292, 295, 321
confidence, votes of, 85–86, 94, 312–14, 433
dissolution, 37, 79–80, 87, 181, 207, 274–75, 313, 317–18
House of Commons, 26, 45, 78–79, 85, 91, 94, 114, 279, 281, 309–10, 312–14, 318, 330–33, 348, 384–85, 395
prorogation, 78, 94, 318
Queen, 214, 267, 317, 319, 386

Senate, 44–46, 48, 75, *93*, 119, 146, 163–65, 169–70, 176, 222, 225, 227, 243–44, 251, 255–56, 277, 292, 295–96, 298–99, 306, 309–11, 327, 330–33, 342, 362, 366, 379, 385, *396*, 415–18, 421

Parti Québécois, 345, 348, 361, 366

parties and partisanship, 82, 226, 333, 391, 395–97, 414, 416

Pearson, Lester B. "Mike," 81, 229, 414, 415

Pépin-Robarts Task Force, 326, 353, 366, 382

Pipeline Debate (1956), 40, 85, 94, 181, 196

planning, economic, 109, 289, 432

pollution, 95, 284, 288, 293, 320

Prince Edward Island, 87, 130, 156, 432

privatization, 293, 297, 299–300, 305

Privy Council, 48, 96, 322

Progressive Conservative Party (*see also* Conservative Party), 40, 80, 82, 120, 182, 201, 292–93, 299, 300, 361, 378, 393, 398, 401, 403–06, 414, 418, 423, 434

proportional representation (*see* elections)

prorogation (*see* Parliament of Canada)

provincial powers, 359

public ownership, 111, 296

Quebec, 47, 53, 195, 217, 223, 238, 243, 328–29, 338, 342–48, 350–54, 357–60, 365–66, 368
Quebec City, 26, 41, 89, 139, 362

railways, 163, 215, 235, 295
referenda and plebiscites, 328–29
Regina Convention (1933), 33, 35, *112*, 192
Regina Manifesto (1933), 109, 121, 242, 404, 419
Regina (Saskatchewan), *34*, 408, 419
responsible government (*see* Constitution of Canada)
Roberts, Winton, 249
Robinson, Svend, 88, 295, 434
Rowe, Frederick, 170
rule of law, 76, 181–82, 220, 232, 292, 309, 320–21, 327
Russia (*see also* Union of Soviet Socialist Republics), 99, 106, 108, 134, 392

Saint-Jean-Baptiste Society, 347
Saskatchewan, 246, 289, 408, 434
Saturday Night, 113
Saul, John Ralston, 97, 223–24, 278, 281, 295, 328, 357
Scott, F.R. "Frank," 52, 87, 89, 100, 101, 278, 393, 428
Shaw, George Bernard, 258
Shaw, Joseph, 24
Simpson, Jeffrey, 286
Sivasankar "Singh" Manoranjna, 163
Smallwood, Joseph R. "Joey," 56, 82–84, 142, 166, 168
socialism, 52, 98–101, 106, 108, 111–12, 115, 117, 121–23, 140, 163, 335, 378, 391–92
South Africa, 57
Sparkes, Grace, 166, 169
St. Laurent, Louis, 40, 84
Student Christian Movement (SCM), 31, 34–36, 53, 116
Supreme Court of Canada, 82, 344
Symes, "Granfer," 24

taxation, 99, 104, 109, 111, 127, 300
Temagami (Ontario), 435
Toronto, 57, 67, 100, 101, 114, 130, 139, 161, 162, 241, 353, 369, 380, 392, 396, 433
Toronto Star, 68
Trades and Labour Congress (TLC), 132, 137, 143
transportation, 109, 176, 292, 295, 299, 324
Trudeau, Pierre Elliott, 40, 44–45, 48, 77, 81, 88, 164, 198, 225, 256, 299, 332–33, 338, 356–59, 385, 414–19

Underhill, F.H. "Frank," 100–01, 316, 418
unemployment, 45, 99, 102, 104–05, 125, 127, 227, 274, 289, 301, 305, 325, 352, 384, 416, 424, 426
Ungava, 217, 345

Union Club (Victoria), 335, 345
Union of Soviet Socialist Republics (Soviet Union, U.S.S.R.; *see also* Russia), 32, 35, *107*, 108, 110, 114, 425
United Kingdom (*see also* England, Great Britain), 31
United States (US), 132, 141, 218, 226, 256, 278, 281, 288, 296–97, 313, 328, 371–73, 375–76, 378
universities:
    Acadia, 58, 222, 256, 306
    Brandon, 144
    Carleton, 241, 293, 398, 400, 420, 425, 427
    Harvard, 37, 42, 396
    McGill University, 29, 30–31, 33–38, 42, 51, 79, 98–99, 114–17, 125, 174, 181–82, 187, 196, 215, 237–42, 249, 252, 258, 262, *263*, 336, 371, 393–94, 411
    McMaster, 221, 256, 262–63, 336, 371, 393–94, 411
    Memorial of Newfoundland, 166, 169, 171, 190, 281
    Mount Allison, 25–26, 259
    New Brunswick, 42, 233
    Oxford, 31, *32*, 79, 113, 165, 168, 238, *239*, 392
    Queen's, 42, 143–44, 230, 317, 319, 353
    Trent, 46, 259
    Waterloo, 44–45, 241

Western Ontario, 280
York, 258, 260

Vancouver, 139
VIA Rail, 299, 418
Victoria, Queen, 267
Victoria (British Columbia), 48, 335, 345, 375, 387
Victoria Charter (1971), 357, 366
Vlastos, Gregory, 52, 187–88

wage and price controls, 96, 127, 146
Waisglass, Harry, 412
War Measures Act (1970), 18, 45, 88–90
Wells, Clyde, 183, 208–09, 216, 276, 281, 388–89
Whelan, Eugene, 416
Whitehorn, Alan, 92, 121, 143, 303, 394, 406, 410, 412
Winnipeg, 139
Winnipeg Free Press, 80, 395
Winnipeg General Strike (1919), 89, 272
Wodehouse, P.G., 268
World University Service (WUS), 425–426
World Trade Organization (WTO), 302, 312, 374